First World War

and Army of Occupation

War Diary

France, Belgium and Germany

28 DIVISION
83 Infantry Brigade
York and Lancaster Regiment
1st Battalion
15 January 1915 - 31 October 1915

WO95/2275/2

The Naval & Military Press Ltd
www.nmarchive.com
Published in association with The National Archives

Published by

The Naval & Military Press Ltd

Unit 10 Ridgewood Industrial Park,

Uckfield, East Sussex,

TN22 5QE England

Tel: +44 (0) 1825 749494

www.naval-military-press.com

www.nmarchive.com

This diary has been reprinted in facsimile from the original. Any imperfections are inevitably reproduced and the quality may fall short of modern type and cartographic standards.

Contents

Document type	Place/Title	Date From	Date To
Heading	WO95/2275-2		
War Diary	1st Bn York & Lanc Asst Regt Jan-Oct 1915		
Heading	War Diary Disembarked Havre from U.K. 17.1.15 1st York & Lancs 15th to 31st January 1915		
Heading	On His Majesty's Service.		
War Diary	Winchester	15/01/1915	15/01/1915
War Diary	Havre	17/01/1915	17/01/1915
War Diary	Hazebrouck	18/01/1915	18/01/1915
War Diary	Meteren	19/01/1915	28/01/1915
War Diary	Near Ypres	29/01/1915	30/01/1915
War Diary	Meteren	31/01/1915	31/01/1915
Miscellaneous	Appendix No. 1 By Capt E.S. Bamford		
Heading	War Diary 1st York & Lancasters. February 1915		
Heading	On His Majesty's Service.		
War Diary	Meteren	01/02/1915	01/02/1915
War Diary	Vlamertinghe	01/02/1915	01/02/1915
War Diary	Ypres	01/02/1915	01/02/1915
War Diary	St Eloi	02/02/1915	03/02/1915
War Diary	Ypres	04/02/1915	04/02/1915
War Diary	La Ferme St Maurice	05/02/1915	05/02/1915
War Diary	Chateau Rosental	05/02/1915	05/02/1915
War Diary	Ferme St Maurice	05/02/1915	06/02/1915
War Diary	Ypres	07/02/1915	07/02/1915
War Diary	Ouderdom	10/02/1915	11/02/1915
War Diary	Ypres	11/02/1915	13/02/1915
War Diary	Verbrandenmolen	13/02/1915	14/02/1915
War Diary	Ypres	13/02/1915	13/02/1915
War Diary	Verbranden Molen	14/02/1915	16/02/1915
War Diary	Ypres	16/02/1915	17/02/1915
War Diary	Tuilerie	17/02/1915	17/02/1915
War Diary	Ypres	17/02/1915	17/02/1915
War Diary	Blauwe Port Farm	17/02/1915	17/02/1915
War Diary	Verbranden Molen	18/02/1915	20/02/1915
War Diary	Ypres	20/02/1915	21/02/1915
War Diary	Near Vlamertinghe	22/02/1915	26/02/1915
War Diary	Vlamertinghe	26/02/1915	26/02/1915
War Diary	Ypres	26/02/1915	26/02/1915
War Diary	Verbrandemolen	26/02/1915	28/02/1915
Miscellaneous	List Of Appendices To Volume 2	28/02/1915	28/02/1915
Diagram etc	Appendix No. II By Captain E.S. Bamford		
Diagram etc			
Diagram etc	Appendix No III By Captain E.S. Bamford		
Miscellaneous	Appendix No 4 By Captain E.S. Bamford		
Diagram etc	Appendix No 5 By Captain L.E.H. Judkins		
Diagram etc	Appendix No VI By L.B.C. Lousada		
Miscellaneous	Appendix No VII By Capt. E.S. Bamford	28/02/1915	28/02/1915
Diagram etc	Appendix No VIII By Capt. E.S. Bamford		
Operation(al) Order(s)	Operation Order No. 8 By Brigadier General R.C. Boyle Commanding 83rd Infantry Brigade	10/02/1915	10/02/1915

Operation(al) Order(s)	Operation Order No. 9 By Brigadier General R.C. Boyle Commanding 83rd Infantry Brigade Appendix No. X	12/02/1915	12/02/1915
Operation(al) Order(s)	Operation Order No. 10 By Brigadier General R.C. Boyle Commanding 83rd Infantry Brigade Appendix No. XI	15/02/1915	15/02/1915
Operation(al) Order(s)	Operation Order No. 11 By Brigadier General R.C. Boyle Commanding 83rd Infantry Brigade Appendix No. XII	19/02/1915	19/02/1915
Operation(al) Order(s)	Operation Order No. 12 By Brigadier General R.C. Boyle Commanding 83rd Infantry Brigade Appendix No. XIII	20/02/1915	20/02/1915
Miscellaneous			
Heading	Bde. temporarily attached to 5th Division 3rd March till 6th April 1915		
Heading	On His Majesty's Service.		
War Diary	Verbrandemolen-Ypres	01/03/1915	01/03/1915
War Diary	Huts	03/03/1915	03/03/1915
War Diary	Bailleul	06/03/1915	13/03/1915
War Diary	Bus Farm	13/03/1915	14/03/1915
War Diary	Bailleul	14/03/1915	15/03/1915
War Diary	Bus Farm	15/03/1915	15/03/1915
War Diary	Elbow Farm	17/03/1915	17/03/1915
War Diary	R.E. Farm	17/03/1915	22/03/1915
War Diary	Pack Horse Farm	22/03/1915	22/03/1915
War Diary	R.E. Farm	23/03/1915	23/03/1915
War Diary	Bailleul	14/03/1915	14/03/1915
War Diary	Neuve Eglise	25/03/1915	29/03/1915
War Diary	R.E. Farm	30/03/1915	31/03/1915
Miscellaneous	List Of Appendices To Vol III		
Miscellaneous			
Operation(al) Order(s)	Operation Order No. 16 By Brig. General R.C. Boyle C.B., Commanding 83 Infantry Brigade.	01/03/1915	01/03/1915
Map			
Map	Appendix No 2		
Operation(al) Order(s)	Operation Order No. 17 By Brigade General R.C., Boyle C.B. Commanding 83rd Infantry Brigade.	02/03/1915	02/03/1915
Miscellaneous			
Operation(al) Order(s)	Operation Order No. 18 By Brigadier General R.C. Boyle Commanding 83rd Infantry Brigade. Appendix No 4	06/03/1915	06/03/1915
Map	Appendix No. 5		
Diagram etc	Appendix No. 6		
Miscellaneous			
Operation(al) Order(s)	Operation Order No. 19 By Brig. Gen R.C. Boyle C.B. Comdg 83rd Inf. Bde.	10/03/1915	10/03/1915
Operation(al) Order(s)	Operation Order No. 20 By Brig. Gen R.C. Boyle C.B. Commanding 83rd Infantry Brigade Appendix No. 8	11/03/1915	11/03/1915
Operation(al) Order(s)	Operation Order No. 21 By Brigadier. General R.C. Boyle C.B. Commanding 83rd Infantry Brigade Appendix No. 9	16/03/1915	16/03/1915
Miscellaneous			
Operation(al) Order(s)	Operation Order No. 3 By Lieut Colonel A.G. Burt Commanding 1st Infy Lancaster Rgt. Appendix No. 10	17/03/1915	17/03/1915
Miscellaneous			
Miscellaneous	Appendix No. 11	19/03/1915	19/03/1915

Operation(al) Order(s)	Operation Order No. 22 By Brigadier General R.C. Boyle C.B. Commanding 83rd Infantry Brigade. Appendix No. 12	22/03/1915	22/03/1915
Miscellaneous			
Operation(al) Order(s)	Operation Order No. 23 By Brigadier General B.C. Boyle C.B. Commanding 83rd Infantry Brigade. Appendix 13	22/03/1915	22/03/1915
Miscellaneous			
Miscellaneous	1st Bn York & Lancaster Regt. Appendix 14		
Operation(al) Order(s)	Operation Order No. 24 By Brigadier General R.C. Boyle C.B. Commanding 83rd Brigade Appendix No. 15	28/03/1915	28/03/1915
Operation(al) Order(s)	Operation Order No. 4 By Lieut Colonel A.G. Burt Commanding 1st Battn Yorks & Lancaster Rgt Appendix No 16	29/03/1915	29/03/1915
Miscellaneous			
Heading	1 Yorks & Lancs April 1915		
Miscellaneous			
War Diary	R.E. Farm	01/04/1915	01/04/1915
War Diary	Bailleul	02/04/1915	03/04/1915
War Diary	Westoutre	04/04/1915	04/04/1915
War Diary	Ypres	06/04/1915	06/04/1915
War Diary	Westoutre	07/04/1915	07/04/1915
War Diary	Westoutre Ypres	08/04/1915	08/04/1915
War Diary	Ypres	08/04/1915	08/04/1915
War Diary	Trenches near Zonnebeke	09/04/1915	09/04/1915
War Diary	Trenches near Zonnebeke	09/04/1915	13/04/1915
War Diary	Zonnebeke	13/04/1915	13/04/1915
War Diary	Ypres	15/04/1915	16/04/1915
War Diary	Zonnebeke	17/04/1915	21/04/1915
War Diary	Huts nr Ypres	22/04/1915	23/04/1915
War Diary	St Jean	23/04/1915	23/04/1915
War Diary	Near St Jean	23/04/1915	26/04/1915
War Diary	Potijze	27/04/1915	27/04/1915
War Diary	Nr Wieltje	28/04/1915	28/04/1915
War Diary	Nr St Jean	28/04/1915	28/04/1915
War Diary	Nr Ypres	29/04/1915	29/04/1915
War Diary	Ypres	30/04/1915	30/04/1915
Map	Appendix 251		
Map			
Heading			
Operation(al) Order(s)	Operation Order No. 25 By Brigadier General R.C. Boyle C.B. Commanding 83rd Infantry Brigade. Appendix No. 2	01/04/1915	01/04/1915
Miscellaneous	83rd Infantry Brigade		
Operation(al) Order(s)	Operation Order No. 5 By Lt. Colonel A.G. Burt Commanding 1st Battn Yorks & Lancaster Rgt. Appendix No. 3	01/04/1915	01/04/1915
Miscellaneous	Table Of Relief 1st April 1915 Issued With Operation Order No. 4		
Operation(al) Order(s)	Operation Order No. 5 By Lt. Col. A.G. Burt Commanding 1 York & Lancaster Rgt. Appendix No 4	03/04/1915	03/04/1915
Operation(al) Order(s)	Operation Order No. 6 By Lt Colonel A.G. Burt Commanding 1st Battn Infy Lancaster Rgt. Appendix No. 6		

Operation(al) Order(s)	Operation Order No. 26 By Brigade General R.C. Boyle C.B., Commanding 83rd Infantry Brigade. Appendix No. 5	01/04/1915	01/04/1915
Miscellaneous	83rd Infantry Brigade March Table 8th April Issued With Operation Order No. 26		
Operation(al) Order(s)	Operation Order No. 29 By Brigadier General R.C. Boyle C.B., Commanding 83rd Infantry Brigade Appendix No. 9	11/04/1915	11/04/1915
Operation(al) Order(s)	Operation Order By Lieut. Colonel A.G. Burt Commanding 1st York & Lancaster Regt, Appendix No. 10	12/04/1915	12/04/1915
Operation(al) Order(s)	Operation Order No. 7 By Lt. Col. A.G. Burt Commanding 1 Yorks & Lancaster Regt. Appendix No. 11	10/04/1915	10/04/1915
Miscellaneous	Appendix No. 12	09/04/1915	09/04/1915
Miscellaneous	Appendix 13		
Operation(al) Order(s)	Operation Order No. 9 By Lt Col A.G. Burt Commanding 1st Yorks Rgt Appendix 14	16/04/1915	16/04/1915
Miscellaneous	Issued with Operation Order March to 8.4.15		
Operation(al) Order(s)	Operation Order No. 11 By Lt. Colonel A.G. Burt Commanding 1st Battn. Yorks & Lancaster Rgt. Appendix 15	22/04/1915	22/04/1915
Miscellaneous	A Form. Messages And Signals. Appendix 16	23/04/1915	23/04/1915
Miscellaneous	A Form. Messages And Signals. Appendix 17	23/04/1915	23/04/1915
Miscellaneous	A Form. Messages And Signals. Appendix 18		
Diagram etc	Appendix 19		
Miscellaneous	A Form. Messages And Signals. Appendix 21	28/04/1915	28/04/1915
Miscellaneous	Special Order Of The Day Appendix 22		
Miscellaneous	A Form Messages And Signals.	26/04/1915	26/04/1915
Heading	1st York & Lancs May 1915		
War Diary	Autments Ypres	01/05/1915	02/05/1915
War Diary	Btn H.Q. Dugout.	03/05/1915	07/05/1915
War Diary	In Huts At Ypres	08/05/1915	12/05/1915
War Diary	Poperinghe	13/05/1915	14/05/1915
War Diary	Vlamertinghe	15/05/1915	16/05/1915
War Diary	Farm Vlamertinghe	17/05/1915	19/05/1915
War Diary	H.Q. Farm Winnezeele	20/05/1915	21/05/1915
War Diary	Poperinghe	22/05/1915	22/05/1915
War Diary	H.Q. Dugout Sanetuary Wood	23/05/1915	26/05/1915
War Diary	H.Q. Dugout Behind Trenches	27/05/1915	01/06/1915
Miscellaneous	Appendix 1		
Miscellaneous	Appendix 2		
Miscellaneous	A Form. Messages And Signals. Appendix 3		
Miscellaneous	A Form. Messages And Signals. Appendix 4		
Miscellaneous	A Form. Messages And Signals. Appendix 5	04/05/1915	04/05/1915
Miscellaneous	A Form. Messages And Signals. Appendix 6	04/05/1915	04/05/1915
Miscellaneous	28th Division. App VII	28/05/1915	28/05/1915
Map			
Map	Appendix No. 7		
Miscellaneous	Issued With 2nd Army Routine Order No. 94 dated 22nd May 1915 App VIII		
Miscellaneous			
Miscellaneous	A Form. Messages And Signals.	24/05/1915	24/05/1915
Miscellaneous	Report on the action near Zourve Wood on 24th May 1915	27/06/1915	27/06/1915
Map			

Miscellaneous	A Form. Messages And Signals.	24/05/1915	24/05/1915
Miscellaneous	App XII		
Miscellaneous	A Form. Messages And Signals.	26/05/1915	26/05/1915
Miscellaneous	Extract From Report By Lieut-General E.A.H. Alderson C.B. On Operations Embraced In The Period 22nd April to 4th May Both Dates Inclusive		
Heading	1st York & Lancs. June 1915		
War Diary	Sanctuary Wood	02/06/1915	03/06/1915
War Diary	In The Huts		
War Diary	H.Q. Farm Winnezeele	04/06/1915	14/06/1915
War Diary	H.Q. Farm Rentirrer	15/06/1915	15/06/1915
War Diary	H.Q. Farm near Locre	16/06/1915	16/06/1915
War Diary	Nr Locre	17/06/1915	19/06/1915
War Diary	Howitzer Farm	20/06/1915	23/06/1915
War Diary	Farm at Scherfenberg	24/06/1915	29/06/1915
War Diary	H.Q. at York House Kemmel	30/06/1915	30/06/1915
Operation(al) Order(s)	Operation Order No. by Brigadier General H.S.L. Ravenshaw C.M.G. Commanding 83rd Infantry Brigade. App I	02/06/1915	02/06/1915
Miscellaneous	A Form. Messages And Signals. App II	02/06/1915	02/06/1915
Miscellaneous	A Form. Messages And Signals. App III	02/06/1915	02/06/1915
Operation(al) Order(s)	Operation Order No. 33 by Brigadier General H.S.L. Ravenshaw C.M.G. Commanding 83rd Infantry Brigade. App IV	03/06/1915	03/06/1915
Miscellaneous	March Table		
Miscellaneous	83rd Infantry Brigade. Training When At "Rest" App V	04/06/1915	04/06/1915
Operation(al) Order(s)	Operation Order No. 34 by Brigadier General H.S.L. Ravenshaw C.M.G., Commanding 83rd Infantry Brigade.	14/06/1915	14/06/1915
Miscellaneous	March Table		
Miscellaneous	Operation Order By Major G.E. Bayley D.S.O. Comdg. 1st York & Lancaster Regt. App VII		
Operation(al) Order(s)	Operation Order No. 35 By Brigadier General H.S.L. Ravenshaw C.M.G., Commanding 83rd Infantry Brigade. App VIII	19/06/1915	19/06/1915
Operation(al) Order(s)	Operation Order By Lt. Col. G.E. Bayley D.S.O. Comdg. 1st Bn. York. & Lancaster Regt. App IX	19/06/1915	19/06/1915
Miscellaneous	Notes by Brigadier General H.S.L. Ravenshaw C.M.G. Commanding 83rd Infantry Brigade. App X		
Diagram etc			
Diagram etc	App XI		
Operation(al) Order(s)	Operation Order No. 37 By Brigadier General H.S.L. Ravenshaw C.M.G. Commanding 83rd Infantry Brigade. App XII	23/06/1915	23/06/1915
Operation(al) Order(s)	Operation Order By Lieut Colonel G.E. Bayley D.S.O. Comdg. 1st Bn York & Lancaster Regiment. App XIII	23/06/1915	23/06/1915
Miscellaneous	Officer Commanding. 1st York & Lancaster Regt. App XIV	23/06/1915	23/06/1915
Operation(al) Order(s)	Operation Order No. 38 By Brigadier General H.S.L. Ravenshaw C.M.G. Commanding 83rd Infantry Brigade	24/06/1915	24/06/1915
Operation(al) Order(s)	Operation Order No. 39 By Brigadier General H.S.L. Ravenshaw C.M.G. Commanding 83rd Infantry Brigade	26/06/1915	26/06/1915

Operation(al) Order(s)	Operation Order No. 40 By Brigadier H.S.L. Ravenshaw C.M.G. Commanding 83rd Infantry Brigade App XVII	28/06/1915	28/06/1915
Operation(al) Order(s)	Operation Orders By Lieut. Col. G.E. Bayley D.S.O. Comdg 1st Bn York & Lancaster Regiment.	29/06/1915	29/06/1915
Heading	1st York & Lancs. July 1915		
War Diary	York House Kemmel	01/07/1915	01/07/1915
War Diary	York House	02/07/1915	05/07/1915
War Diary	Scherpenberg	06/07/1915	10/07/1915
War Diary	York House	11/07/1915	15/07/1915
War Diary	Rossignol Estaminet	16/07/1915	17/07/1915
War Diary	Scherpenberg	18/07/1915	23/07/1915
War Diary	Rossignol Estaminet	24/07/1915	27/07/1915
War Diary	H.Q. at Locre	28/07/1915	29/07/1915
War Diary	Farm at Scherpenberg	30/07/1915	31/07/1915
Miscellaneous	A Form. Messages And Signals.	02/07/1915	02/07/1915
Miscellaneous	Lt. C.E. Wales 1st Yorks & Lanc Rgt App II		
Miscellaneous	A Form. Messages And Signals. App III	03/07/1915	03/07/1915
Operation(al) Order(s)	Operation Order No. 41 By Brigadier General H.S.L. Ravenshaw C.M.G. Commanding 83rd Infantry Brigade.	03/07/1915	03/07/1915
Operation(al) Order(s)	Operation Order No. 42 By Brigadier General H.S.L. Ravenshaw C.M.G. Commanding 83rd Infantry Brigade.	04/07/1915	04/07/1915
Miscellaneous	Artillery Support. Appx VI	28/06/1915	28/06/1915
Operation(al) Order(s)	Operation Order No. 43 by Brigadier General H.S.L. Ravenshaw C.M.G. Commanding 83rd Infantry Brigade App VII	10/07/1915	10/07/1915
Operation(al) Order(s)	Operation Orders By Lieut, Colonel G.E. Bayley D.S.O. Commanding 1st Bn York & Lancaster Regt.	05/07/1915	05/07/1915
Operation(al) Order(s)	Operation Orders By Lieut. Colonel G.E. Bayley D.S.O. Commanding 1st Bn York & Lancaster Regt. App VIII	11/07/1915	11/07/1915
Operation(al) Order(s)	Operation Order No. 44 by Brigadier General H.S.L. Ravenshaw C.M.G. Commanding 83rd Infantry Brigade	12/07/1915	12/07/1915
Miscellaneous	1/Yorkshire & Lancaster Regt.		
Operation(al) Order(s)	Operation Orders By Lieut Colonel G.E. Bayley D.S.O. Commanding 1st York & Lancaster Regiment. App X	12/07/1915	12/07/1915
Map			
Operation(al) Order(s)	Operation Order No. 45 By Brigadier General H.S.L. Ravenshaw C.M.G. Commanding 83rd Infantry Brigade.	15/07/1915	15/07/1915
Operation(al) Order(s)	Operation Orders By Lieut Colonel G.E. Bayley D.S.O. Commanding 1st Bn York & Lancaster Regiment. App XII	15/07/1915	15/07/1915
Operation(al) Order(s)	Operation Order No. 46 by Brigadier General H.S.L. Ravenshaw C.M.G. Commanding 83rd Infantry Brigade.	16/07/1915	16/07/1915
Operation(al) Order(s)	Operation Orders By Lieut. Col. G.E. Bayley D.S.O. Comdg. 1st Bn. York & Lancaster Regt. App XIV	17/07/1915	17/07/1915
Operation(al) Order(s)	Operation Order No. 47 by Brigadier General H.S.L. Ravenshaw C.M.G. Commanding 83rd Infantry Brigade	17/07/1915	17/07/1915

Operation(al) Order(s)	Operation Order No. 48 by Brigadier General H.S.L. Ravenshaw C.M.G. Commanding 83rd Infantry Brigade App XVI	17/07/1915	17/07/1915
Operation(al) Order(s)	Operation Order No. 41a by Brigadier General H.S.L. Ravenshaw C.M.G. Commanding 83rd Infantry Brigade App XVII	17/07/1915	17/07/1915
Miscellaneous		16/07/1915	16/07/1915
Operation(al) Order(s)	Operation Orders By Lieut. Colonel G.E. Bayley D.S.O. Commanding 1st Bn York & Lancaster Regt App XVIII	17/07/1915	17/07/1915
Operation(al) Order(s)	Operation Order No. 49 by Brigadier General H.S.L. Ravenshaw C.M.G. Commanding 83rd Infantry Brigade. App XIX	20/07/1915	20/07/1915
Operation(al) Order(s)	Operation Order No. 50 by Brigadier General H.S.L. Ravenshaw C.M.G. Commanding 83rd Infantry Brigade. App XX	20/07/1915	20/07/1915
Miscellaneous			
Operation(al) Order(s)	Operation Order No. 51 by Brigadier General H.S.L. Ravenshaw C.M.G. Commanding 83rd Infantry Brigade. App XXI	22/07/1915	22/07/1915
Miscellaneous	Trenches Etc		
Operation(al) Order(s)	Operation Orders No. 11 By Lieut Colonel G.E. Bayley D.S.O. Commanding 1st York & Lancaster Regiment. App XXII	23/07/1915	23/07/1915
Miscellaneous			
Miscellaneous	A Form Messages And Signals. App XXIII	24/07/1915	24/07/1915
Operation(al) Order(s)	Operation Order No. 52 by Brigadier General H.S.L. Ravenshaw C.M.G. Commanding 83rd Infantry Brigade.	27/07/1915	27/07/1915
Operation(al) Order(s)	Operation Order No. 12 By Lieut Col G.E. Bayley D.S.O. Comdg. 1st Bn York and Lancaster Regt. App XXV	27/07/1915	27/07/1915
Miscellaneous	10th (Service) Battalion. West Yorkshire Regt. App XXVI		
Operation(al) Order(s)	Operation Order No. 53 by Brigadier General H.S.L. Ravenshaw C.M.G. Commanding 83rd Infantry Brigade.	28/07/1915	28/07/1915
Operation(al) Order(s)	Operation Order By Lt. Col. G.E. Bayley D.S.O. Comdg. 1st Bn York & Lancaster Rgt.	29/07/1915	29/07/1915
Operation(al) Order(s)	Operation Order No. 54 by Brigadier General H.S.L. Ravenshaw C.M.G. Commanding 83rd Infy Brigade.	29/07/1915	29/07/1915
Operation(al) Order(s)	Operation Order No. 55 by Brigadier General H.S.L. Ravenshaw C.M.G. Commanding 83rd Infy Brigade.	31/07/1915	31/07/1915
Operation(al) Order(s)	Operation Order No. 14-A By Major E.C. Robertson Commanding 1st York & Lancaster Regt. App XXII	31/07/1915	31/07/1915
Heading	1st York & Lancs August 1915		
Heading	On His Majesty's Service.		
War Diary	Farm at Scherpenberg	01/08/1915	03/08/1915
War Diary	Rossignol Estaminet	04/08/1915	09/08/1915
War Diary	Rossignol H.Q.	09/08/1915	11/08/1915
War Diary	Sherpenberg	12/08/1915	17/08/1915
War Diary	Rossignol H.Q.	13/08/1915	23/08/1915
War Diary	Scherpenberg	24/08/1915	29/08/1915
War Diary	Rossignol H.Q.	29/08/1915	31/08/1915

Operation(al) Order(s)	Operation Order No. 56 by Brigadier General H.S.L. Ravenshaw C.M.G. Commanding 83rd Infantry Brigade	02/08/1915	02/08/1915
Miscellaneous	Amendment To Operation Order No 56	02/08/1915	02/08/1915
Miscellaneous	Distribution Of Troops In Trenches		
Operation(al) Order(s)	Operation Order No. 14 By Major E.C. Robertson Commanding 1st Bn York & Lancaster Regt.	03/08/1915	03/08/1915
Miscellaneous	Schedule Of Reliefs		
Miscellaneous	A Form. Messages And Signals.	04/08/1915	04/08/1915
Operation(al) Order(s)	Operation Order No. 58 By Brigadier General H.S.L. Ravenshaw C.M.G. Commanding 83rd Infantry Brigade.	09/08/1915	09/08/1915
Operation(al) Order(s)	Operation Order No. 59 By Brigadier General H.S.L. Ravenshaw C.M.G. Commanding 83rd Infantry Brigade.	10/08/1915	10/08/1915
Operation(al) Order(s)	Operation Order No. 60 By Brigadier General H.S.L. Ravenshaw C.M.G. Commanding 83rd Infantry Brigade.	11/08/1915	11/08/1915
Operation(al) Order(s)	Operation Order No. 15 by Lt. Col. G.E. Bayley D.S.O. Comdg. 1st York & Lancaster Regt.	11/08/1915	11/08/1915
Miscellaneous	A Form. Messages And Signals.	11/08/1915	11/08/1915
Operation(al) Order(s)	Operation Order No. 62 by Brigadier General H.S.L. Ravenshaw C.M.G. Commanding 83rd Infantry Brigade	16/08/1915	16/08/1915
Operation(al) Order(s)	Operation Order No. 17 by Lt. Col. G.E. Bayley D.S.O. Comdg. 1st York & Lancaster Regt.	17/08/1915	17/08/1915
Miscellaneous			
Miscellaneous	A Form. Messages And Signals.	18/08/1915	18/08/1915
Miscellaneous	1st Bn York & Lancaster Regt App XI		
Operation(al) Order(s)	Operation Order No. 65 by Brigadier General H.S.L. Ravenshaw C.M.G. Commanding 83rd Infantry Brigade.	22/08/1915	22/08/1915
Operation(al) Order(s)	Operation Order No. 18 By Lt. Col. G.E. Bayley D.S.O. Comdg. 1st Bn York & Lancaster Regt.	23/08/1915	23/08/1915
Miscellaneous	Report on observations by 1st Bn York & Lancaster Regt. App XIV	23/08/1915	23/08/1915
Operation(al) Order(s)	Operation Order No. 66 by Brigadier General H.S.L. Ravenshaw C.M.G. Commanding 83rd Infantry Brigade.	27/08/1915	27/08/1915
Operation(al) Order(s)	1st Bn York & Lancaster Regiment Appx XVI	28/08/1915	28/08/1915
Operation(al) Order(s)	Operation Order No. 19 By Lieut. Colonel G.E. Bayley D.S.O. Commanding 1st Bn York & Lancaster Regiment.	29/08/1915	29/08/1915
Miscellaneous			
Miscellaneous	A Form Messages And Signals. App XVIII	30/08/1915	30/08/1915
Heading	1st York & Lancs September 1915		
Heading			
War Diary	Rossignol H.Q	01/09/1915	04/09/1915
War Diary	Sur Bruedus on Ousters Locre	05/09/1915	09/09/1915
War Diary	Locre	10/09/1915	10/09/1915
War Diary	Rossignol H.Q.	11/09/1915	12/09/1915
War Diary	Rossignol Estaminet	13/09/1915	17/09/1915
War Diary	Locre	18/09/1915	23/09/1915
War Diary	near Meteren	24/09/1915	24/09/1915
War Diary	near Outersteen	25/09/1915	26/09/1915
War Diary	Robecq	26/09/1915	27/09/1915

War Diary	Noyelle	28/09/1915	28/09/1915
War Diary	Vermelles	28/09/1915	29/09/1915
War Diary	Nr Trenches Opposite Hohenzollen Re Doubt	29/09/1915	30/09/1915
Operation(al) Order(s)	Operation Order No. 67 by Brigadier General H.S.L. Ravenshaw C.M.G., Commanding 83rd Infantry Brigade. Appendix I	02/09/1915	02/09/1915
Miscellaneous	Garrisons	02/09/1915	02/09/1915
Miscellaneous	Machine Guns		
Operation(al) Order(s)	Operation Order No. 20 By Lieut. Col. G.E. Bayley D.S.O. Comdg. 1st Bn York & Lancaster Regt. Appendix II	03/09/1915	03/09/1915
Operation(al) Order(s)	Operation Order No. 68 by Brigadier General H.S.L. Ravenshaw C.M.G., Commanding 83rd Infantry Brigade. Appendix III	04/09/1915	04/09/1915
Operation(al) Order(s)	Operation Order No. 21 By Lieut, Col. G.E. Bayley D.S.O. Comdg. 1st York & Lancaster Regiment. App IV	04/09/1915	04/09/1915
Miscellaneous	1st Bn York & Lancaster Regt. Appendix V	07/09/1915	07/09/1915
Operation(al) Order(s)	Operation Order No. 70 by Brigadier General H.S.L. Ravenshaw C.M.G. Commanding 83rd Infantry Brigade.	09/09/1915	09/09/1915
Operation(al) Order(s)	Operations Orders No 22 By Lieut. Colonel G.E. Bayley D.S.O. Cmdg. 1st York. & Lancaster Regt. Appendix 7		
Miscellaneous	A Form. Messages And Signals. Appendix 8	11/09/1915	11/09/1915
Miscellaneous	A Form. Messages And Signals.		
Miscellaneous	1st Bn York & Lancaster Regt. Appx 9	14/09/1915	14/09/1915
Operation(al) Order(s)	Operation Order No. 71 by Brigadier General H.S.L. Ravenshaw C.M.G. Commanding 83rd Infantry Brigade.	14/09/1915	14/09/1915
Operation(al) Order(s)	Operation Orders No. 23 By Lieut. Colonel G.E. Bayley D.S.O. Cmdg. 1st York. & Lancaster Regiment.	16/09/1915	16/09/1915
Operation(al) Order(s)	Operations Order No. 72 by Brigadier General H.S.L. Ravenshaw C.M.G. Commanding 83rd Infantry Brigade. App 12	19/09/1915	19/09/1915
Operation(al) Order(s)	Operation Order No. 73 by Brigadier General H.S.L. Ravenshaw C.M.G. Commanding 83rd Infantry Brigade.	20/09/1915	20/09/1915
Operation(al) Order(s)	Operation Order No. 74 by Brigadier General H.S.L. Ravenshaw C.M.G. Commanding 83rd Infantry Brigade. App 14	21/09/1915	21/09/1915
Operation(al) Order(s)	Operation Order No. By Lieut. Colonel G.E. Bayley D.S.O. Commanding 1st Bn York & Lancaster Regt. Appx 15	22/09/1915	22/09/1915
Operation(al) Order(s)	Operation Order No. 74 by Brigadier General H.S.L. Ravenshaw C.M.G. Commanding 83rd Infantry Brigade. App 16	26/09/1915	26/09/1915
Miscellaneous	Starting Point Outtersteene Cross Roads.		
Operation(al) Order(s)	Operation Order No. 27 By Lieut. Colonel G.E. Bayley D.S.O., Commanding 1st Bn York & Lancaster Regt. App 17	26/09/1915	26/09/1915
Operation(al) Order(s)	Operation Order No. 74 by Brigadier General H.S.L. Ravenshaw C.M.G., Commanding 83rd Infantry Brigade. App 18	26/09/1915	26/09/1915

Operation(al) Order(s)	Operation Order No. 75 by Brigadier General H.S.L. Ravenshaw C.M.G. Commanding 83rd Infantry Brigade. App 19	26/09/1915	26/09/1915
Operation(al) Order(s)	Operation Order No. 28 By Lieut. Col. G.E. Bayley D.S.O. Commanding 1st York & Lancaster Regt. App 20	26/09/1915	26/09/1915
Operation(al) Order(s)	Operation Order No. 76 by Brigadier General H.S.L. Ravenshaw C.M.G. Commanding 83rd Infantry Brigade. App 21	27/09/1915	27/09/1915
Operation(al) Order(s)	Operation Order No. 29 By Lieut. Colonel G.E. Bayley D.S.O. Commanding 1st Bn York & Lancaster Regt. App 22	27/09/1915	27/09/1915
Heading	War Diary Division left for Salonika November 1915 1st York & Lancs October 1915		
Heading	On His Majesty's Service.		
War Diary	Vermelles	01/10/1915	01/10/1915
War Diary	Annequin	02/10/1915	03/10/1915
War Diary	H.Q. Bn Reserve Trench	04/10/1915	05/10/1915
War Diary	Annequin	06/10/1915	06/10/1915
War Diary	Gonnehem	07/10/1915	15/10/1915
War Diary	Beuvry	16/10/1915	18/10/1915
War Diary	Harley St.	19/10/1915	21/10/1915
War Diary	Gonnehem	22/10/1915	23/10/1915
War Diary	Train	24/10/1915	25/10/1915
War Diary	S.S. Bornu	26/10/1915	31/10/1915
Operation(al) Order(s)	Operation Order No. 30 By Lieut. Col. G.E. Bayley D.S.O. Commanding 1st Bn York & Lancaster Regt. Appendix 17	03/10/1915	03/10/1915
Miscellaneous	Messages And Signals.	04/10/1915	04/10/1915
Miscellaneous	A Form. Messages And Signals.	04/10/1915	04/10/1915
Miscellaneous	Messages And Signals.	04/10/1915	04/10/1915
Miscellaneous	App 3	05/09/1915	05/09/1915
Miscellaneous	Table Of Reliefs	05/09/1915	05/09/1915
Operation(al) Order(s)	Operation Order No. 31 App 4		
Operation(al) Order(s)	Operation Order No. 77 by Brigadier General H.S.L. Ravenshaw C.M.G. Commanding 83rd Infantry Brigade. App 5	06/10/1915	06/10/1915
Operation(al) Order(s)	Operation Order No. 31 By Lieut. Colonel G.C. Bayley D.S.O. Commanding 1st Bn York & Lancaster Regt. App 6	06/10/1915	06/10/1915
Operation(al) Order(s)	Operation Order No. 73 by Brigadier General H.S.L. Ravenshaw C.M.G. Commanding 83rd Infantry Brigade.	13/10/1915	13/10/1915
Miscellaneous	B.A.C.D.		
Operation(al) Order(s)	Operation Order No. 79 by Brigadier General H.S.L. Ravenshaw C.M.G. Commanding 83rd Infantry Brigade. Appendix 8	16/10/1915	16/10/1915
Operation(al) Order(s)	Operation Order No. 31 By Lieut. Colonel G.E. Bayley D.S.O. Commanding. 1st Bn. York & Lancaster Regt.	16/10/1915	16/10/1915
Operation(al) Order(s)	83rd Brigade Operation Order No. 80	20/10/1915	20/10/1915
Miscellaneous			
Miscellaneous	Machine Guns Will Be Relieved As Follows.		
Miscellaneous	After Operation Order No. 80 83rd Brigade.	20/10/1915	20/10/1915
Operation(al) Order(s)	Operation Order No. 92 By Lieut. Colonel G.E. Bayley D.S.O. Commanding 1st Bn York & Lancaster Regt. App 11	20/10/1915	20/10/1915

Miscellaneous	Schedule Of Reliefs		
Operation(al) Order(s)	83rd Brigade Operation Order No. 81 App 12	21/10/1915	21/10/1915
Operation(al) Order(s)	Operation Order No. 39 by Lieut Colonel G.E. Bayley D.S.O., Commanding 1st Bn York & Lancaster Regt. App 13	22/10/1915	22/10/1915
Miscellaneous	1st Bn York & Lancaster Regt.	23/10/1915	23/10/1915

28TH DIVISION
83RD INFY BDE

1ST BN YORK & LANCASTER REGT

JAN - OCT 1915

TO SALONIKA

83rd Bde.

28th Div.

WAR
DIARY

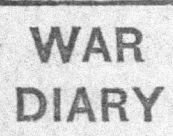

Disembarked Havre from U.K. 17.1.15.

1st YORK & LANCS.

15th to 31st JANUARY.

1 9 1 5

OA 15

On His Majesty's Service.

Vol I

Vol I page I

Instructions regarding War Diaries and Intelligence Summaries are contained in F. S. Regs., Part II. and the Staff Manual respectively. Title pages will be prepared in manuscript.

WAR DIARY or ~~INTELLIGENCE SUMMARY~~ of 1st Battalion The York & Lancaster Regt.

Army Form C. 2118.

(Erase heading not required.)

Hour, Date, Place	Summary of Events and Information	Remarks and references to Appendices
8am 15th Jan 1915 WINCHESTER	The Battalion left WINCHESTER marched to SOUTHAMPTON and embarked on the S.S. LAKE MICHIGAN.—	The Battalion formed part of 83rd Brigade of 28th Division.—
	The following message was received from His Majesty the King a copy of which was given to every man in the battalion.—	For strength of Battalion on departure & Roll of officers see appendix No I
	"Buckingham Palace. Message from the King to 28th Division.— I was very glad to have been able to inspect the 28th Division & I wish to express my entire satisfaction with the general appearance of the troops.— In spite of the bad weather and of the difficulties attending concentration & training, it is evident to me that no time has been lost in establishing that Esprit de Corps which counts for so much on the field of battle.— I have been unable to inspect you in the field, but from all I saw to day I have carried away the impression that a resolute spirit pervades all ranks to join their comrades at the front in ~~maintaining~~ maintaining the glorious traditions of my Army.— ~~Farewell~~ Farewell my soldiers. May God bless you and protect you.— 12th January 1915"	

Vol I Page 2

Instructions regarding War Diaries and Intelligence Summaries are contained in F. S. Regs., Part II. and the Staff Manual respectively. Title pages will be prepared in manuscript.

WAR DIARY of 1st Battn York & Lancaster Regt

~~INTELLIGENCE SUMMARY~~

(Erase heading not required.)

Army Form C. 2118.

Hour, Date, Place	Summary of Events and Information	Remarks and references to Appendices
10 am, 17th Jan 1915 HAVRE	The Battalion disembarked at HAVRE at 10 am, left there at 4 pm	
9 pm 18th Jan 1915 HAZEBROUCK	by troop train to HAZEBROUCK. – The Battalion arrived at HAZEBROUCK at 9 pm on 18th. – The Battalion detrained & marched	
6 am 19th Jan 1915 METEREN.	to METEREN. a distance of about 9 miles arriving there at 6 am on the morning of 19th. – The Battalion went into Billets at METEREN – On the march from HAZEBROUCK to METEREN, one man* died from heart failure. –	* 203671 Pte. J. Hill 'A' Company
P.H.B. Capt		
19th Jan 1915 to 1st February 1915 METEREN	The Battalion remained in billets at METEREN from 19th January 1915 till 1st February 1915, being daily exercised in Route Marching Entrenching, & in practising relieving trenches at night. –	
P.H.B. Capt		
24th January 1915	Captains G. H. Wedgwood & S. E. Palmer were sent to the trenches for one night, the former with the Northumberland Fusiliers the latter with the King's Royal Rifle Corps. –	
P.H.B. Capt		
26th January 1915	Captain P.H.C. Collins was sent to the trenches of the Royal Irish Fusiliers for one night. –	
P.H.B. Capt		

1247 W.3299 200,000 (E) 8/14 J.B.C. & A. Forms/C. 2118/11.

Instructions regarding War Diaries and Intelligence Summaries are contained in F. S. Regs., Part II. and the Staff Manual respectively. Title pages will be prepared in manuscript.

Army Form C. 2118.

VOL I
PAGE III

WAR DIARY OF 1st BATTN YORK & LANCASTER RGT

~~or~~ ~~INTELLIGENCE SUMMARY~~

(Erase heading not required.)

Hour, Date, Place	Summary of Events and Information	Remarks and references to Appendices
28th January 1915 METEREN	Captain H J. East & Lieut. L. E. H. Jackkins, were sent to the trenches for one night. the former with Royal Irish Fusiliers, the latter with the Kings Royal Rifle Corps.— the Brigade was inspected by the Commanding-in-Chief of the British army in the field.—	
CEB Capt		
29th January 1915 near YPRES	Captain E. S. Bamford, sent to see the trenches to be taken over by the Battalion.—	
CEB Capt		
30th January 1915 near YPRES	Lieuts H. G. Gauntlett, H. F. Litchfield, R. B. Lethbridge, J. R. Mather & Qr Mr H M C Howard with four Company Sergt-Majors sent to see the trenches to be taken over by the Battalion.—	
CEB Capt		
7.45 pm 31st January 1915 METEREN	The transport of the Battalion with 140 N.C.O's and men under the Command of Lieut. L. E. H. Jackkins left METEREN for VLAMERTINGHE.—	
5 pm. 31st January 1915 METEREN	The Battalion Received orders to leave METEREN by Motor Busses for VLAMERTINGHE on 1st February 1915	

APPENDIX. No I By CAPT E. S. BAMFORD.

Nominal Roll of Officers of 1st Battn York & Lancaster Regt

on leaving WINCHESTER 15th January 1915

Lieut. Colonel A. J. BURT (In Command)
Major H. K. COLSTON
Captain G. H. WEDGWOOD (D Company)
" A. E. PALMER (A Company)
" H. J. EAST (B Company)
" P. H. C. COLLINS (C Company)
" E. S. BAMFORD (Adjutant)
Lieutenant L. E. H. JUDKINS
" K. P. WALKER (Transport Officer)
" H. G. GAUNTLETT
" B. C. LOUSADA (Machine Guns)
" J. K. MATHER.
" H. F. LITCHFIELD
" N. B. LETHBRIDGE
" A. G. LYNCH.
" A. L. KENT-LEMON
" C. K. CHAMIER
2nd " H. C. M. HOWARD
" " E. H. TAYLER.
" " E. E. BATTLE
" " D. CONNORS
" " H. H. MOORSE.
" " E. R. FOLKER (3rd BATTN)
" " C. E. WALES (3rd Battn)
" " F. BISCOE (3rd BATTN).
Lieut & QM. W. T. GILLIARD
Lieut W. YEO. ROYAL ARMY MEDICAL CORPS.

Strength 985 other Ranks

"

[illegible]

83rd Bde.
28th Div.

WAR
DIARY

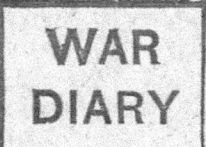

1st YORK & LANCASTERS.

F E B R U A R Y

1 9 1 5

On His Majesty's Service.

Vol II page 1

WAR DIARY ~~or~~ of 1st Batt. York & Lancaster Regt.—

~~INTELLIGENCE~~ SUMMARY

Army Form C. 2118.

Instructions regarding War Diaries and Intelligence Summaries are contained in F. S. Regs., Part II. and the Staff Manual respectively. Title pages will be prepared in manuscript.

(Erase heading not required.)

Hour, Date, Place	Summary of Events and Information	Remarks and references to Appendices
2.30 pm 1.2.15 METEREN	The Battalion left METEREN in 38 Motor Busses and arrived	Lieut C.K. CHAMIER & 2nd Lt. E.H. TAYLER were left in Hospital at METEREN.—
7.30 pm 1.2.15 VLAMERTINGHE	at VLAMERTINGHE at 7.30 pm.— At 7.45 pm orders were Received that the KINGS OWN YORKSHIRE LIGHT INFANTRY and 1st YORK & LANCASTER REGT would Relieve the "French" 62nd Infantry Brigade, from the trenches to night.— The Battn left VLAMERTINGHE at 9.30 pm and Marched to YPRES.—	
10.30 pm 1.2.15 YPRES	The Battn arrived at the PONT DE LILLE, YPRES at 10.30 pm.— the Rifle Ammunition tools and trench stores were drawn.— the Battn Marched off by Companies to take over from the French, Stores being provided by the French.— Nothing of Importance took place during the Relief which was completed by 2.30 am.—	See APPENDIX No I for position of Companies Etc.—
C.H.B. Capt		
2.30 am 2.2.15 St ELOI	Discription of trenches 1. The position of our trenches was on the Reverse slope of a hill Rising E[?]ward from St ELOI village on the Right, to the Canal on the left.— 2. On the whole the state of the trenches was bad, those of B. C & D Companies being the best, those occupied by 'A' Company were bad, the parapet being very low & Not Bullet proof at	See Appendix No I

1247 W 3299 200,000 (E) 8/14 J.B.C. & A. Forms/C. 2118/11.

VOL II

Instructions regarding War Diaries and Intelligence Summaries are contained in F. S. Regs., Part II. and the Staff Manual respectively. Title pages will be prepared in manuscript.

Page 2.

WAR DIARY ~~or~~ INTELLIGENCE SUMMARY

of 1st Battn Yorks & Lancaster Regt 65th

(Erase heading not required.)

Army Form C. 2118.

Hour, Date, Place	Summary of Events and Information	Remarks and references to Appendices
	Up. – In the trench held by "A" Company there was a good deal of water. –	
	The Germans had made a sap up towards our Right trench	See APPENDIX No I R
	The trenches were for the most part not connected and consequently communication was very difficult by night owing to the country not being known, & impossible by day. – Two telephones only were available, with one communication was established with "A" Company, but none of the others could be found, altho' it was known from the French that B. C & D Companies had taken over from them. –	
	The remainder of the night & day passed quietly. – It commenced to rain at daybreak on 2nd, this made the trenches very uncomfortable especially those occupied by A Company. During the night, about 40 large & small fascines were brought up to A Company, by the Battalion in Reserve, these were used for the men to stand on. –	Casualties from taking over to 8AM 2nd fcb were Nil. –
	During the night, communication was established with "B" Company by telephone & with the remainder by orderly. –	

1247 W 3299 200,000 (E) 8/14 J.B.C. & A. Forms/C. 2118/11.

Vol II page 3.

Instructions regarding War Diaries and Intelligence Summaries are contained in F. S. Regs., Part II. and the Staff Manual respectively. Title pages will be prepared in manuscript.

WAR DIARY
or
~~INTELLIGENCE SUMMARY~~ OF 1st BATTN. THE YORK & LANCASTER REGT.

(Erase heading not required.)

Army Form C. 2118.

6th

Hour, Date, Place	Summary of Events and Information	Remarks and references to Appendices
	This was not at all satisfactory because it meant that any message took a long time to reach C or D Companies in the night & during the day communication owing to the enemy's fire was impossible. [The fact that telephones & wire are very valuable is amply brought out.—] During the night one machine gun was moved from its position in B Company to A Company in order to meet any movement on the part of the enemy from the sap they had made.—	See appendix I K + K D
ELB Capt		
8 am 3.2.15 St Eloi	The casualties of the Battn from 8 am 2nd to 8 am 3rd Feb were Killed 1. Wounded 2.—	
10 am to 1 pm 3.2.15 St Eloi	During the day of 3rd Feb between 10 am & 1 pm the enemy shelled the right trench of the Battn without doing much damage a few shells were also directed at Battn Hd Qrs, but no damage was done.—	
9.30 pm to 11.30 pm 3.2.15 St Eloi	The Battalion was relieved from duty in the trenches, the two Right Companies (A & B) by the Princess Patricia's Canadian Light Infantry the two left Companies (C & D) by the King's Own (Royal Lancaster) Regt.—	
ELB Capt		
2 am 4.2.15 Ypres	The Battalion went into Billets in the Infantry Barracks Ypres.— The casualties of the Battalion from 8 AM 3rd Feb to 8 am 4th Feb were Killed Nil Wounded 6 men.—	

1247 W 3299 200,000 (E) 8/11 J.B.C. & A. Forms/C. 2118/11.

Instructions regarding War Diaries and Intelligence Summaries are contained in F. S. Regs., Part II. and the Staff Manual respectively. Title pages will be prepared in manuscript.

Vol II
Page 4

WAR DIARY
or
INTELLIGENCE SUMMARY
(Erase heading not required.)

OF 1st BATTN THE YORK & LANCASTER REGT.

Army Form C. 2118.

6th

Hour, Date, Place	Summary of Events and Information	Remarks and references to Appendices
2am to 3pm 4.2.15 YPRES	The Battn Rested till 3pm when orders were Received that the Battn would hold itself in readiness to leave the Infantry Barracks at 5 pm and take up a position in the Reserve trenches, Running from FERME LA CHAPELLE to the CHATEAU LANKHOF.—	for position of Reserve trenches see APPENDIX No II
	At 4.15 pm orders were Received to move the Battn immediately to Brigade Head Quarters, & on arrival there instructions would be Received.— The Battn did not leave YPRES till 4.50 pm, the issue of Rations causing a certain amount of delay.—	
	On arrival at Brigade Head Quarters, orders were Received to occupy the Reserve trenches Running from LA FERME ST MAURICE to CHATEAU LANKHOF with 3 Companies & to send one Company to the Headqrs of the East Yorkshire Regt at LA FERME ST MAURICE. D Company under Captain Wedgwood was sent to the East Yorkshire Regt. A.B & C Companies holding the Reserve trenches.—	for disposition of Companies see APPENDIX No II
	It was ascertained on arrival at the Head Qrs, East Yorkshire Regt. that the Germans had captured the portion of a trench and two machine guns from the East Yorkshires.—	
C.L.B. Capt		

Instructions regarding War Diaries and Intelligence Summaries are contained in F. S. Regs., Part II. and the Staff Manual respectively. Title pages will be prepared in manuscript.

Vol II

page 5

WAR DIARY
or
~~INTELLIGENCE SUMMARY~~
(Erase heading not required.)

OF 1st Battn The York & Lancaster Regt

Army Form C. 2118.

6th

Hour, Date, Place	Summary of Events and Information	Remarks and references to Appendices
4.30 am 5.2.15 La Ferme St Maurice	A.B & C Companies received orders to move to the Chateau Rosental, D Company staying with the East Yorkshire Regt. —	See Appendix No II
5.30 am Chateau Rosental 5.2.15	The Battn arrived at the Chateau Rosental at 5.30 am. & found there was not sufficient room for the men, so the Battalion was ~~[illegible]~~ distributed in Chateau Rosental and Lankhof and some dug outs on the Ypres – Messines Road. —	See Appendix No II A. B & C
8. am 5.2.16	The casualties during the 24 hours 8 am 4th Feb to 8 am 5th Feb were: Killed 1 N.C.O. Wounded 1 man. — Owing to men continually moving about they were seen by a German Aeroplane with the result that the Chateau Rosental was shelled, a lesson which should not require learning again, tho' the actual damage done was small. —	

1247 W 3299 200,000 (E) 8/14 J.B.C. & A. Forms/C. 2118/11.

Vol II   Page 6.

Instructions regarding War Diaries and Intelligence Summaries are contained in F. S. Regs., Part II. and the Staff Manual respectively. Title pages will be prepared in manuscript.

WAR DIARY
or
~~INTELLIGENCE SUMMARY~~ OF 1st BATTN THE YORK & LANCASTER REGT.

(Erase heading not required.)

Army Form C. 2118.

Hour, Date, Place	Summary of Events and Information	Remarks and references to Appendices
5 pm CHATEAU ROSENTAL 5.2.15	The Battn Received orders to move to LA FERME ST MAURICE immediately & attack the trenches which had been captured.–	
7 pm 5.2.15 FERME ST MAURICE	The Battalion arrived at LA FERME ST MAURICE at 7pm & was placed in Reserve, an attacking column having been formed of the K.O. Yorkshire Light Infantry, some of the East Yorkshire Regt. & D Company 1st York & Lancaster Regt.– The trench which it was intended to attack could	
C.B. Capt	not be found & the Battalion Relieved the East Yorkshire Regt from	See APPENDIX No III for position of Companies.—
9.30 am 6.2.15 FERME ST MAURICE	the trenches.—	
8 am 5.2.15 to 8 am 6.2.15	The Casualties of the Battalion during the previous 24 hours were Killed 4 2 C.O's & men wounded Captain G H WEDGWOOD (Slightly in the head) and 6 men.— The difficulties of this part of the Country are worthy of note the trenches were very badly made & very wet, those occupied by D Company had practically no parapit & the water was in most places up to the mens knees, those of the other Companies were not so bad in this Respect.– The woods in Rear held a few Snipers who were troublesome, also passage thro' the woods except on Roads was very difficult because Artillery fire had knocked down so many Branches of trees that the whole place	

1247 W 3299 200,000 (E) 8/14 J.B.C. & A. Forms/C. 2118/11.

Vol II

Instructions regarding War Diaries and Intelligence Summaries are contained in F. S. Regs., Part II. and the Staff Manual respectively. Title pages will be prepared in manuscript.

page 6, 7

WAR DIARY ~~or~~ ~~INTELLIGENCE SUMMARY~~

(Erase heading not required.)

Army Form C. 2118.

OF 1st BATTN THE YORK + LANCASTER REGT.

Hour, Date, Place	Summary of Events and Information	Remarks and references to Appendices
	was turned into a most effective abbatis. — It was very hard to get men to act as reliable guides, because the country was difficult, & could not be seen in daylight. —	
	Communication was established between all companies by orderly + communication by telephone. — The lack of telephone with Brigade Headquarters was again felt. —	
	The enemy shelled the trenches of A Company very heavily during the day causing a good deal of damage to the parapet, in some cases men had to be dug out of the trench where the parapet had been knocked down on them. —	See APPENDIX No III
	Owing to enfilade fire being brought on him the O.C. B Company (Captain East) was compelled to withdraw his men to the left of his trench, but re-occupied the right again as soon as it became dark. —	
	The Battn was relieved from the trenches by the Buffs between 1.30 am and 4.30 am. — The Battalion returned by companies to the Infantry Barracks YPRES. —	
Returned 4 AM + 6.30 AM. 7.2.15 YPRES —	The casualties of the Battn during the previous 24 hours were Killed 1 man wounded 15 N.C.O's & men. —	
8 AM 6.2.15 to 8 AM 7.2.15	The wastage from sick during the previous 7 days was 46 N.C.O's & men sent to hospital. —	

[signature] Capt.

1247 W 3299 200,000 (E) 8/14 J.B.C. & A. Forms/C. 2118/11.

VOL II

Page 8

WAR DIARY or ~~INTELLIGENCE SUMMARY~~

(Erase heading not required.)

OF 1st BATTN. THE YORK & LANCASTER REGT.

Army Form C. 2118.

Instructions regarding War Diaries and Intelligence Summaries are contained in F. S. Regs., Part II. and the Staff Manual respectively. Title pages will be prepared in manuscript.

Hour, Date, Place	Summary of Events and Information	Remarks and references to Appendices
2.45 to 3.25. 7.2.15 YPRES.	The Battalion left YPRES by Companies at intervals of 10 minutes & went into Billets in the neighbourhood of OUDERDOM. —	
	The Battalion remained in OUDERDOM from 7.2.15 till 11.2.15 (CHB Capt.)	
10.2.15 OUDERDOM	Orders were received from 83rd Brigade to form two Platoons of picked men into a "Grenadier Company". — 20 men per Company, under the command of Captain L. E. H. JUDKINS were selected for this. — (CHB. Capt.)	
4 pm 11.2.15 OUDERDOM 6.15 pm 11.2.15 YPRES.	The Battalion, having been warned for duty in the trenches left OUDERDOM at 4 pm and arrived at YPRES at 6.15 pm. — "B" & "C" Companies & the Machine guns, under the command of Major H. K. COLSTON, went to BLAUWEPOORT FARM, in support of the KING'S OWN YORKSHIRE LIGHT INFANTRY. — "A" & "D" Companies, under the Commanding Officer, went into the Infantry Barracks at YPRES. — It rained a lot in the night which made the roads difficult for transport, but the day was fine, tho' cold & raw. — (CHB Capt.)	See APPENDIX No V
12.15 pm 12.2.15 YPRES. —	The following message was received from 83rd Bde by telephone — "Left of Eighty fifth Brigade being heavily attacked, please hold your Battalion in readiness and stand by. I have informed Coys at TUILERIE and BLAUWEPOORT ~~HALLAERT~~ FARM". — The Battalion stood by till 3.30 pm, when orders were received that the Battalion need	
6.20 pm 12.2.15 YPRES	not stand by any longer. — Rations & water were sent up to the two Companies in support at 6.30 pm — the day was wet and cold. — (CHB Capt.)	

1247 W 3299 200,000 (E) 8/14 J.B.C. & A. Forms/C. 2118/11.

VOL II page 89

Instructions regarding War Diaries and Intelligence Summaries are contained in F. S. Regs., Part II. and the Staff Manual respectively. Title pages will be prepared in manuscript.

WAR DIARY
or
~~INTELLIGENCE SUMMARY~~
(Erase heading not required.)

Army Form C. 2118.

OF 1st BATTN. YORK & LANCASTER REGT.

Hour, Date, Place	Summary of Events and Information	Remarks and references to Appendices
6.45 pm 13/2/15 YPRES	The Battalion (i.e.) C and D Company and the Grenadier Company left the Infantry Barracks at YPRES at 6.45 pm to take over trenches from the Kings Own Yorkshire Light Infantry.— The following is the detail of line of trenches which were taken over.— P1, P2, Q, R1 and R2 by 3 Companies and the Grenadier Company. One Company to be placed under orders of the Officer Commanding the Kings Own Regiment, and occupied S2 trench.—	See APPENDIX No V
9.45 pm 13/2/15 VERBRANDENMOLEN	Head Quarters and D Company arrived at VERBRANDENMOLEN at about 9.45 pm and proceeded to take over the trenches.— The Grenadier Company, B and C Companies and the Machine Guns arrived from BLAUWEPORT FARM at	SEE APPENDIX No V
10.20 pm 13/2/15 VERBRANDENMOLEN	10.20 pm. (The Grenadier Company had been carrying Rations up for the Kings Own Yorkshire Light Infantry)—	
2 am 14/2/15 VERBRANDENMOLEN	The Relief was Reported Complete by 2 AM.—	
8 pm 13/2/15 YPRES	A Company left YPRES with the Kings Own Regt at 8 pm on 13.2.15	
	DESCRIPTION OF LINE TAKEN OVER AND DETAIL	
	P1 and P2 "C" Company "Q" B Company and one platoon Grenadier Company — R1 D Company R2 1 platoon Grenadier Company.—	
	Machine Guns were placed in P1, Q and R1.—	
	The trenches are fairly good but Require constant attention. Part of R2 and Q are very wet.— Practically no obstacles in front at present	

1247 W 3299 200,000 (E) 8/14 J.B.C. & A. Forms/C. 2118/11.

Vol II page 10 65a

Instructions regarding War Diaries and Intelligence Summaries are contained in F. S. Regs., Part II. and the Staff Manual respectively. Title pages will be prepared in manuscript.

WAR DIARY
or
~~INTELLIGENCE SUMMARY~~

(Erase heading not required.)

Army Form C. 2118.

1st Battalion York & Lancaster Regt

Hour, Date, Place	Summary of Events and Information	Remarks and references to Appendices
	of a really permanent nature, tho' there were remains of old barbed wire entanglements & lengths of loose barbed wire had been thrown out in front. —	
	Special points. Railway cutting on the left of P2 and centre of P where the enemy are very close, it is estimated that they are only about 25 x away ~~[illegible]~~. — Ravine on the right between P1 and P2, this re-entrant badly wants strong of all barbed wire. —	See Appendix No V
	P1 is directly in touch with the trenches held of 85th Brigade. — In places along the trenches the parapet is low, the present loopholes are well known by German marksmen, and men of the K.O.Y.L.I. using them were wounded. —	
	Communication by telephone is established both P1 and P2 trenches. —	
	During the night it rained at intervals but nothing unusual occurred. —	
8 AM 14/2/15 VERBRANDENMOLEN	Casualties for the previous 24 hours were five N.C.O's and men wounded. — Capt L.E.H. JUDKINS was brought in sick from the trenches and sent to hospital. —	See Appendix No IV
5 pm 14/2/15 VERBRANDENMOLEN	The day of 14th passed quietly. At 5 pm an artillery observation officer came and warned us that the Germans were expected to attack to-night. Companies were so informed. —	
	All Company Commanders reported that a great many sandbags and much	

(signature) Capt

Vol II page 11.

Instructions regarding War Diaries and Intelligence Summaries are contained in F. S. Regs., Part II. and the Staff Manual respectively. Title pages will be prepared in manuscript.

WAR DIARY of 1st Battn. York and Lancaster Regt.
or
~~INTELLIGENCE SUMMARY~~
(Erase heading not required.)

Army Form C. 2118.

65th

Hour, Date, Place	Summary of Events and Information	Remarks and references to Appendices
	Resulting Materials are Required.—	
1 pm. 14/2/15 VERBRANDENMOLEN	The Brigade informed us that Alsatian deserters Reported that a General attack was arranged for 15th or 16th February.— The night passed quietly except for heavy firing on our Right at intervals.—	
9.15 pm " "	Fatigue parties of the King's Own Yorkshire Light Infantry arrived with trench stores, and took them up to the trenches.—	
Night of 14th 15th	The night of 14th 15th was very wet.—	
8 am 15/2/15 " C.H.B. Capt	Casualties during the last 24 hours to 8am were Killed one man Wounded twelve.—	See appendix 204
8.30 am "	Orders were Received that the Battalion would be Relieved from duty in the trenches at 9 pm – 2 Companies to go to Infantry Barracks YPRES and 2 Companies to BLAUWERPORT FARM in support.— A, B and the Grenadier Company were ordered to Return to YPRES, C D Companies and the Machine Guns were ordered to go to BLAUWERPORT after Relief.—	
11 am " "	During day of 15th it was very wet.— G.O.C. asked what possibilities are there for listening patrols	

1247 W 3299 200,000 (E) 8/14 J.B.C. & A. Forms/C. 2118/11.

VOL II

Instructions regarding War Diaries and Intelligence Summaries are contained in F. S. Regs., Part II. and the Staff Manual respectively. Title pages will be prepared in manuscript.

Page 12

WAR DIARY or ~~INTELLIGENCE SUMMARY~~ OF 1st BATTN. YORK AND LANCASTER REGT.

(Erase heading not required.)

Army Form C. 2118.

Hour, Date, Place	Summary of Events and Information	Remarks and references to Appendices
	in front of our trenches, especially P1 and P2?—	
	the O.C. P1 and P2 considered that the best place for this, in fact the only place is the Ravine between P1 and P2.	See Appendix No V
6 pm 13/2/15	the O.C. "C" Company reported that the rain had damaged the parapet of trenches P1 and P2 considerably. the other Companies sent in similar ~~reports~~ information.—	61
9 pm to 9.15 pm 13/2/15	very heavy fire was opened by our artillery for a period of ¼ hour.—	
9.10 pm "	the Machine Guns of K.O.Y.L.I. arrived and proceeded to take over their trenches.—	
9.45 pm to 11 pm 13/2/15	Companies of the Kings Own Yorkshire Light Infantry arrived to take over & proceeded at once on arrival to take over our trenches.—	
12.45 am 14/2/15	the Relief of the Battalion by the K.O.Y.L.I. was completed, B Company and the Grenadier Company marched to YPRES. C and D Companies to BLAUWERPORT FARM.—	
2 am 14/2/15 YPRES	A Company arrived in YPRES at 2 AM for the[illegible]	

1217 W 3299 200,000 (E) 8/14 J.B.C. & A. Forms/C. 2118/11.

Vol II

Page 13

Instructions regarding War Diaries and Intelligence Summaries are contained in F. S. Regs., Part II. and the Staff Manual respectively. Title pages will be prepared in manuscript.

WAR DIARY or INTELLIGENCE SUMMARY of 1st Battn. York & Lancaster Regt.

(Erase heading not required.)

Army Form C. 2118.

Hour, Date, Place	Summary of Events and Information	Remarks and references to Appendices
	Section. —	See Appendix V
8 am 16/2/15. YPRES	The Casualties Reported during the previous 24 hours were — W. I.	See Appendix IV
9 pm 16/2/15. YPRES.	Information was received that the left of 84th Brigade was being	
CWB	heavily attacked, & that the Battalion was to stand to. —	
	The orders to stand to were cancelled. —	SEE APPENDIX
3.15 pm 17.2.15 YPRES	The orders were received to march immediately to the TUILERIE, the Battn	
10.0 am 17.2.15 YPRES	(H A & B Coys & Grenadier Coy) fell in, left YPRES and arrived at TUILERIE at	
11.45 am 17.2.15 TUILERIE	11.45 am, here it was found that trench occupied by the East Yorkshires had been blown up by the	
	enemy, who had occupied it, & that 2 Companies of the Kings Own Regt. in	
	support at TUILERIE had been ordered to re-take it. —	
	At 12.45 pm news was received that the Kings Own Regt had re-taken	
	the trench in question. —	
3 pm 17.2.15 TUILERIE	B Coy & Grenadier Coy ~~Battalion~~ Returned to YPRES arriving there at 4 pm. —	
6 pm 17.2.15 YPRES	B Coy and Grenadier Coy ~~Battalion~~ left YPRES BARRACKS at 6 pm and arrived at Brigade Hdqrs	
	at 7 pm and moved up by Companies to VERBRANDENMOLEN to take over	
CWB Capt	trenches from the Kings' Own Yorkshire Light Infantry. — arriving	
	there between 9 pm and 10 pm by Companies. —	
10 am 17.2.15 BLAUWE POORT FARM	Major COLSTON in command of the ½ Battn at BLAUWEPOORT. FARM. was ordered	
	to send up 3 Platoons to support the K.O.Y.L.I. — Capt Collins with 3 platoons	
	C Company was sent — 2 platoons under Lt GAUNTLETT going to R1 trench the other platoon to some dugouts in Rear of P1. —	

1247 W 3299 200,000 (E) 8/14 J.B.C. & A. Forms/C. 2118/11.

Vol. II page ~~13~~ 14

Instructions regarding War Diaries and Intelligence Summaries are contained in F. S. Regs., Part II. and the Staff Manual respectively. Title pages will be prepared in manuscript.

WAR DIARY
or
~~INTELLIGENCE SUMMARY~~
(Erase heading not required.)

of 1st Battn. York & Lancaster Regt.

Army Form C. 2118.

Hour, Date, Place	Summary of Events and Information	Remarks and references to Appendices
12.10 AM 18.2.15 VERBRANDENMOLEN	Relief of trenches occupied by K.O.Y.L.I. completed by the Battalion.—	
12.30 AM 18.2.15 VERBRANDENMOLEN	The following is a copy of a telegram received from G.O.C. 27th Division Begins to O.C. KOYLI & Y&L. Congratulations on excellent work Result as I always expected from BULFIN Ends.— The following is a copy of a telegram received from Commander 5th Corps to G.O.C. 83rd Brigade. Begins very glad to hear your message BM262. I am sure you and your brigade have done very well to day Ends.—	
	A Company K.O.Y.L.I. had been placed in support in some dug outs behind P1 trench, but owing to heavy rain, it was found that many of them were so full of water that they could not be occupied & that there was only room for ½ a Company.— The other half Coy was sent back to YPRES.—	See appendix V
2 am 18.2.15 "	The following report was sent to 83rd Brigade. "Nothing to report all is quiet.—"	
5.30 am 18.2.15 "	The following report was sent to 83rd Brigade "Nothing to report all is quiet.—"	
9 am 18.2.15 "	All was reported quiet to Brigade Hdqrs.—	
11.20 am 18.2.15	The O.C. "D" Company in R1 reported as follows "About 8 or 9 common shell burst over R1, they appeared to be coming from guns rather close in front".— This was repeated to Brigade Hd Qrs.—	See appendix V

Vol II page ~~14~~ 15

Instructions regarding War Diaries and Intelligence Summaries are contained in F. S. Regs., Part II. and the Staff Manual respectively. Title pages will be prepared in manuscript.

WAR DIARY ~~or~~ OF ~~INTELLIGENCE SUMMARY~~

Army Form C. 2118.

(Erase heading not required.) 1st Battn The York and Lancaster Regt.

Hour, Date, Place	Summary of Events and Information	Remarks and references to Appendices
11.30 am 18.2.15 VERBRANDENMOLEN	Lieutenant N B LETHBRIDGE was reported slightly wounded in the face. —	
11.45 am 18.2.15 "	2/Lieut BATTLE reported from R.1 trench that as nearly as it was possible to tell the position of the Enemy's guns shelling R.1 was at angle of 137° & at a distance of from 800x to 1500x, this was reported to Brigade Head Quarters. —	
1 pm 18.2.15 "	2/Lt BATTLE reported that the first three shells fired by our guns seem to be very close to the spot where the Enemy's guns were firing from. —	
2 pm 18.2.15 "	All was reported quiet to Brigade Hdqrs. —	
2.15 pm 18.2.15 "	As there were only 3 machine guns with the Battn the Commanding Officer ordered one to be brought up from the support at BLAUWPORT FARM, at dusk. —	see appendix V
3.35 pm 18.2.15 "	The O.C. B Company commanding Q trench reported that they were being shelled, and also that they were having ~~and~~ mortars used against them, and that an attack seemed probable	
3.50 pm 18.2.15 "	One company of the K.O.Y.L.I. in support (at BLAUWPORT FARM) was ordered to move to Battn Head Quarters at once, this action was reported to Brigade Head Quarters	
4.30 pm 18.2.15 "	Lieut H. F. LITCHFIELD was wounded by a shell in Q trench in the arm. —	
4.55 pm 18.2.15 "	Lieut J. K. MATHER was killed in S.1 trench, the report was received from the O.C. King's Own Regt to whom A Company was attached. —	

1 officer K, 1 " W

1247 W 3299 200,000 (E) 8/14 J.B.C. & A. Forms/C. 2118/11.

Vol II

Instructions regarding War Diaries and Intelligence Summaries are contained in F. S. Regs., Part II. and the Staff Manual respectively. Title pages will be prepared in manuscript.

Page 3/16

Army Form C. 2118.

WAR DIARY
or
INTELLIGENCE SUMMARY
of 1st Battn York and Lancaster Regt

(Erase heading not required.)

Hour, Date, Place	Summary of Events and Information	Remarks and references to Appendices
Trenches [illegible] 18.2.15 VERBRANDEN [illegible]	Company Sgt Major Lavers with [illegible] difficulty went down y trench, and got within 20x of a house in which some Germans were signalling from, & an [illegible] to get a sniper who had been [illegible] shooting at men in y trench, when he got up to the house, he discovered a man signalling who he shot	See appendix V for Reference Map
	The [illegible] & considerable [illegible] level of fire —	
2 pm 18.2.15	About 15 to 20x of a trench was blown down [illegible] of German further, as soon as this was done, a party of 30 to 40 of the enemy rushed out of their trench unarmed (as far as could be [illegible]) "C" Company in the trench under Lieut GAUNTLETT at once opened rapid fire on them, from what could be seen only 2 men escaped — The order to the O.C. [illegible] to send one Company to Battn Headquarters	
4 pm 18.2.15	was cancelled —	
4.40 pm 18.2.15	The O.C. B Company reported that everything was alright but wished to have some Royal Engineers to help repair the breaches that had been made —	
5 pm 18.2.15	All was reported quiet to Brigade Head Quarters —	
8.30 pm 18.2.15	Fatigue parties belonging to the K.O.Y.L.I. arrived at Battalion Headquarters [illegible] hurdles were [illegible], very lights [illegible] etc these were sent up to the Companies —	
9.30 pm 18.2.15	All was reported quiet to Brigade Headquarters —	

Vol. II page 17

Army Form C. 2113.

Instructions regarding War Diaries and Intelligence Summaries are contained in F. S. Regs., Part II. and the Staff Manual respectively. Title pages will be prepared in manuscript.

WAR DIARY ~~or~~ OF. ~~INTELLIGENCE SUMMARY~~

(Erase heading not required.) 1st BATTN. YORK AND LANCASTER REGT.

Hour, Date, Place	Summary of Events and Information	Remarks and references to Appendices
11.35 PM 18.2.15 VERBRANDEMOLEN	All was Reported Quiet to Brigade Head Quarters.—	
12 Mid Night 18.2.15 / 19.2.15 "	Company Commanders Reported that during the previous 24 hours the following work had been done, Improving parapets, Communication trenches and drainage.—	
2 am 19.2.15 "	All was Reported Quiet to Brigade Headquarters.—	
8 am 19.2.15 "	Casualties of the Battalion, Exclusive of A Company during the previous 24 hours were, Officers, Killed 1 [Lt G.K. MATHER] Wounded 2 [Lieuts H.F. LITCHFIELD and N.B. LETHBRIDGE] other Ranks Killed 1 Wounded 11. Missing None —	See appendix No 4
10.5 am 19.2.15 "	The following message Regarding work done was Reported to Brigade HQrs P1 & P2 trenches Parapet all Repaired with sandbags, Communication trench drained.— Q trench Repair of parapet and putting up wire Entanglement. R1 & R2 Repair to parapet and improvement of drains.—	
9 am 19.2.15 "	Nothing to Report to Brigade Head Quarters all Quiet—	
11.30 am 19.2.15 "	Nothing to Report to Brigade Head Quarters all Quiet—	
2.30 pm 19.2.15 "	Orders were Received to the Effect that the Battalion would Remain in the trenches for another day.—	
5.30 pm 19.2.15 "	Nothing to Report to Brigade Head Quarters. all Quiet.—	
	Between daybreak and sunset the trenches were shelled at intervals.—	
	During the afternoon the parapet of Q trench was again knocked down	

CHB.

Vol II page ~~17~~ 18

Instructions regarding War Diaries and Intelligence Summaries are contained in F. S. Regs., Part II. and the Staff Manual respectively. Title pages will be prepared in manuscript.

WAR DIARY
~~or~~ OF. 1st BATTN

~~INTELLIGENCE SUMMARY~~

(Erase heading not required.) YORK. & LANCASTER REGT.

Army Form C. 2118.

Hour, Date, Place	Summary of Events and Information	Remarks and references to Appendices
	by the Enemy's Mortars. During the night it was Repaired, with the assistance of Lieut MILLER R.E. and 12 men. — During the night ~~[illegible]~~ a trench Mortar was sent up to Q trench.—	
11.15 pm 19.2.15 VERBRANDENMOLEN	The following Message was sent to the O.C B Coy, (Q trench) "The artillery are going to try to demolish the house where the observation Officer says he thinks he has located the Enemy's Mortar aaa At 8.45 tomorrow morning you will clear the Right End of Q trench for 50 to 60 yards keeping the men to the left, the artillery will open fire at 9 am" — The same message was sent to the O.C "C" Company, telling him to clear the men in P2 trench to the Right.—	
11 pm 19.2.15 "	The following Report was Received from the O.C. A Company, who was with the left section.— "2nd Lieut FOLKER killed, he crept down an old sap near S1 and was poisoned by foul air.—	[illegible]
EAB		
2 am 20.2.15 "	Nothing to Report to Brigade Head Quarters all quiet	
5 am 20.2.15 "	Nothing to Report to Brigade Head Quarters all quiet —	
8 am 20.2.15 "	Statement of Casualties incurred by the Battalion during the previous 24 hours was. Officer killed [2nd Lieut F.R. FAULKER] other	

1247 W 3299 200,000 (E) 8/14 J.B.C. & A. Forms/C. 2118/II.

Instructions regarding War Diaries and Intelligence Summaries are contained in F. S. Regs., Part II. and the Staff Manual respectively. Title pages will be prepared in manuscript.

Vol II page ~~18~~ 19

Army Form C. 2118.

WAR DIARY or ~~INTELLIGENCE~~ SUMMARY

OF. 1st Battn. York and Lancaster Regt.

(Erase heading not required.)

Hour, Date, Place	Summary of Events and Information	Remarks and references to Appendices
	Ranks Excluding A Company. Killed 2 Wounded 13, Missing Nine.—	See appendix No 4.
At 9.55 am. 20.2.15 VERBRANDEMOLEN	Report of work done in trenches to Brigade Headquarters was as follows.— P1 and P2 traverses made, & all Front line Re-sandbagged, Communication trench was almost dry.— Improved Parapet. Repaired Breach. Communication trenches dug at back of houses.— R1 and R2, Traverses made, Telephone dugout, made more secure, drainage and parapet improved.—	for positions of trenches and Companies occupying them see Appendix No V
10 am 20.2.15 "	The following Report was Received from the O.C. P1 (Capt COLLINS) "Received a Report that Germans have broken through Wood on Right I am taking ½ Company of Kings Own Regt in support to try and Clear the wood, will Report progress.—	
	The following is an Extract taken from a Report sent by Capt P H C. COLLINS on arrival at OUDERDOM.—	
	At 9 am it was Reported to me by Lieut LOUSADA that the Germans had broken through our line Wood on Right, in some trenches held by the Welsh Regt.— I called for a dozen Volunteers to Come with Lieut LOUSADA and myself to drive them Back — I ordered the ½ Company Kings Own Regt in support to stand to & advanced through the wood.— I met the Officer Commanding the Welsh Regt in the	See appendix No VI for Reference Map.

VOL II
page ~~19~~ 20

Instructions regarding War Diaries and Intelligence Summaries are contained in F. S. Regs., Part II. and the Staff Manual respectively. Title pages will be prepared in manuscript.

WAR DIARY
or
~~INTELLIGENCE~~ SUMMARY OF

(Erase heading not required.) 1st Battn York & Lancaster Regt.

Army Form C. 2118.

Hour, Date, Place	Summary of Events and Information	Remarks and references to Appendices
	wood and asked him what was going to be done as the Right was exposed & that until the Germans were driven out, my position was seriously threatened.— At 11 am I received an order from Colonel Burt to send out an officers patrol to clear up the situation. I sent 2nd Lieutenant H. C. M. HOWARD who returned at about 12.30 pm and reported as follows.— He had been to within 20x of the left of Y trench where he had seen a German sentry, he was also told by a Sergeant of the Welsh Regt who was in the observation post, that he had counted 50 Germans going into Y trench.— He then went across to Z trench reported and returned thro' the wood to me. This report was forwarded to Battn Head Qrs.— At 4 pm 1½ Coy of the King's Own Regt advanced to attack Y trench, they had just cleared the right rear of P1 trench when a Machine gun in our front opened fire;— Lieutenant LOUSADAS Maxim immediately put it out of action. My Company fired on the trenches opposite but there was practically nothing to fire at.—	See appendix VI for Reference Map
5.18 PM 20.2.15 VERBRANDENMOLEN	Nothing to report ~~[illegible]~~ to Brigade Headquarters all quiet.—	
8.30 PM 20.2.15 "	The Commanding Officer and Company Commanders of the King's Own Scottish	

1247 W 3299 200,000 (E) 8/14 J.B.C. & A. Forms/C. 2118/11.

VOL II

page 21.

Instructions regarding War Diaries and Intelligence Summaries are contained in F. S. Regs., Part II. and the Staff Manual respectively. Title pages will be prepared in manuscript.

WAR DIARY
or
INTELLIGENCE SUMMARY

(Erase heading not required.) OF 1st BATTN. YORK AND LANCASTER REGT.

Army Form C. 2118.

Hour, Date, Place	Summary of Events and Information	Remarks and references to Appendices
8.30 pm 20.2.15 VERBRANDENMOLEN	Borderers arrived to take over the trenches occupied by the Battalion.	
9.30 pm to 10.30 pm 20.2.15 "	The K.O.S.B.s arrived by Companies and proceeded straight to the trenches to take over.	
10.30 pm to 11.30 pm 20.2.15 " YPRES	Companies of the Battalion arrived at Battalion headquarters as relieved and marched to YPRES Town Hall, where a hot meal had been prepared.	
3 am & 3.30 am 21.2.15 EHB Capt	The Battalion left YPRES [by Companies] between 3 am and 3.30 am & marched to some huts [which had been put up] half way between VLAMERTINGHE and OUDERDOM.	
EHB Capt	Report received from the DAAG & QMG 5th Army Corps that 2nd Lieutenant P. H. TAYLER had died in hospital from pneumonia. The casualties of the Battalion from 8am 20th Feb to 8am 21st February were killed 6 wounded 4 missing nil.	
8 pm 22.2.15 near VLAMERTINGHE EHB Capt	A draft consisting of 50 N.C.O's and men under the command of 2nd Lieutenant A.C. BRICKWOOD joined the Battalion.	
21.2.15 to 26.2.15 Huts near VLAMERTINGHE	The Battalion remained in the huts between VLAMERTINGHE and OUDERDOM. Resting.	
4.55 pm 26.2.15 VLAMERTINGHE	The Battalion left the huts for YPRES and arrived there at 6.30 pm.	

VOL II page 122.

Army Form C. 2118.

Instructions regarding War Diaries and Intelligence Summaries are contained in F. S. Regs., Part II. and the Staff Manual respectively. Title pages will be prepared in manuscript.

WAR DIARY
~~or~~ OF 1st BATTN
~~INTELLIGENCE SUMMARY~~
(Erase heading not required.)

York & Lancaster Regt

Hour, Date, Place	Summary of Events and Information	Remarks and references to Appendices
7.15 pm 26.2.15 YPRES	The Battalion left YPRES [by Companies at 7.15 pm at intervals of 10 minutes] for VERBRANDEMOLEN in the following order C Coy B Coy D Coy. —	See appendix no V
	A Company going with the Kings Own Regt to TUILERIE. —	
	The Relief of trenches from P1 to R2 inclusive from the K.O.S.Bs was completed at 10.25 pm. — trenches instead of being given letters ~~now~~ are now numbered from Right to Left the numbers of trenches P1 to R2 were P1 33 P2 34 Q 35 R1 36 R2 37. —	
	The night was clear cold & frosty with a bright moon. —	
11.30 pm 26.2.15 ~~YPRES~~ VERBRANDEMOLEN	All was reported quiet to Brigade head quarters —	
11.35 pm " "	One Company K.O.Y.L.I. under the command of Lieut LAW (KOYLI) reported having taken over support dugouts in rear of 33 and 35 trenches. —	
	Owing to losses in the Battalion from Battle casualties and sickness the line from the Right of trench 33 to the left of trench was very weakly held — the lengths of trench and the number of Rifles holding them was as follows	

No. TRENCH	LENGTH IN YDS	NO OF RIFLES
33	110	61
34	205	50
35	280	135

1247 W 3299 200,000 (E) 8/14 J.B.C. & A. Forms/C. 2118/11.

Vol II

Instructions regarding War Diaries and Intelligence Summaries are contained in F. S. Regs., Part II. and the Staff Manual respectively. Title pages will be prepared in manuscript.

Page ~~22~~ 23

WAR DIARY
~~or~~ OF
~~INTELLIGENCE SUMMARY~~
(Erase heading not required.) 1st Battn. York and Lancaster Regt.

Army Form C. 2118.

Hour, Date, Place	Summary of Events and Information	Remarks and references to Appendices
	Trench / Length in Yds. / No of Rifles	
	36 / 290 / 102	
	37 / 61 / 90	
	33.34.35 / 595 / 246	shown in detail on page 21
	946 / 378	
	K.O.Y.L.I. Company in Support = 107	
	946 / 485	
	In Conjunction with the Royal Artillery the following arrangement for support had been arranged by K.O.S.B.s. — The Code word Short Range would direct the 15th Battery R.F.A. to fire on a German Battery located about 1500 (approx) in front of 36 trench. — The Code word Shell would direct the 15th R.F.A. to fire on a German "Minenwerfer"	
	[signature] Capt.	
5.30 am 27.2.15 VERBRANDENMOLEN	Following message sent to Brigade Headquarters "All quiet nothing to report"	
8 am 2 " "	Casualties during previous 24 hours one man wounded. ——	
11.30 am	Following message sent to Brigade Headquarters "All quiet nothing to Report"	
8.50 pm " "	Owing to the length of the ~~[illegible]~~ connecting trench between 36 & 37	

1247 W 3299 200,000 (E) 8/14 J.B.C. & A. Forms/C. 2118/11.

VOL II

Page ~~23~~ 24

Instructions regarding War Diaries and Intelligence Summaries are contained in F. S. Regs., Part II. and the Staff Manual respectively. Title pages will be prepared in manuscript.

WAR DIARY

~~or~~ OF

~~INTELLIGENCE SUMMARY~~

(Erase heading not required.) 1st BATTN YORK AND LANCASTER REGT

Army Form C. 2118.

Hour, Date, Place	Summary of Events and Information	Remarks and references to Appendices
VERBRANDEN MOLEN	~~on Brest~~ trenches, one Machine Gun was brought up from Supporting Company K.O.Y.L.I, and placed on the left of trench Number 36. —	
5 30am 28.2.15 " EB Capt	following Message sent to Brigade Head Quarters, all quiet nothing to Report. —	
	Almost as soon as the Message had been sent, a very heavy burst of Rapid firing took place on our Right (in which several Machine Guns were firing) this was Reported to Brigade Head Quarters. —	
	the following work and improvements were done to the trenches during the previous 24 hours —	
	33 trench — four Reels of Barbed wire put out in front, two traverses made. Crest of Parapet front and Rear improved. —	
	34 trench Seven Knife Rest Entanglements put out also loose wire. Rear parapet built up, and one traverse made. —	
	35 trench Parapets Repaired with Sandbags and Revetted with fascines. Bottom of trench Repaired with Logs and Brushwood. —	
	36 trench Parapet Revetted one new Machine Gun Emplacement made helped Royal Engineers to improve Connecting trench between 36 and 37 trenches. —	
	37 trench Draining trenches improving parapet and Bottom of trenches. Working parties were also supplied to R.E. —	

VOL II

Instructions regarding War Diaries and Intelligence Summaries are contained in F. S. Regs., Part II. and the Staff Manual respectively. Title pages will be prepared in manuscript.

Page ~~24~~ 25.

WAR DIARY ~~or~~ OF ~~INTELLIGENCE SUMMARY~~

(Erase heading not required.) 1st BATTN. YORK. AND. LANCASTER REGT

Army Form C. 2118.

Hour, Date, Place		Summary of Events and Information	Remarks and references to Appendices
11.15 am	28. 2. 15 VERBRANDENMOLEN	Orders for Relief issued —	see appendix 20 VII
11.30 am	" "	All Reported Quiet to Brigade Head Quarters	
12 noon	" "	Casualties for 24 hours ending 12 noon other Ranks Killed one Wounded three Missing None. —	
5.30 pm	" "	All Reported Quiet to Brigade Head Quarters. —	
8.30 pm to 10.40 pm	" "	Companies of K.O.Y.L.I. arrived at intervals	
11 pm	" "	B and C Companies Reported in dugouts in Rear of 33 and 35 trenches. —	
11.5 pm	" "	Battalion Head Quarters left for BLAUWEPOORT FARM and arrived there at 11.30pm. —	
11.30 pm	" "	Nothing to Report to Brigade Head Quarters. —	
		The Chief points brought out during this Month are. —	
		I In this kind of warfare (ie trenches) the great difficulties in taking stores ammunition rations food Etc up to the trenches owing to the few men available for the duty (a fatigue party of 150 to 200 men has on several occasions had to do at least 3 journeys from Battn or Brigade Head Quarters to the trenches —)	
		II The Danger of making loopholes straight the Enemy in most cases had rifles trained on to loopholes and many of our casualties were ~~[illegible]~~ caused by men standing by them. —	

1247 W 3299 200,000 (E) 8/14 J.B.C. & A. Forms/C. 2118/11.

Vol II

Instructions regarding War Diaries and Intelligence Summaries are contained in F. S. Regs., Part II. and the Staff Manual respectively. Title pages will be prepared in manuscript.

Page 26

WAR DIARY
or
INTELLIGENCE SUMMARY
of
(Erase heading not required.)

1st Battn York & Lancaster Regt

Army Form C. 2118.

Hour, Date, Place	Summary of Events and Information	Remarks and references to Appendices
	Loopholes should be made if possible obliquely & if straight must be blinded – If the trenches had been farther apart probably this difficulty would not have been experienced. –	
	III The necessity for ~~the strictest~~ stringent measures to be taken with regard to sanitation. –	
	(The state of the trenches during bad weather even at the best is very bad, and everything should be done to keep them and their surroundings as clean as possible.)	
	IV Men should be given plenty of work to do this ensures them good and to a certain extent keeps their feet from being frostbitten. –	6th
	V Some kind of a cover for the rifle bolt is absolutely necessary to prevent it becoming clogged with sand & dirt. – We used as far as possible the lace top used in India & an old sock but this is not enough the cover should be waterproof ~~and~~ and at the same time easy to take off in case the rifle is wanted for use	

Vol II page 87.

Instructions regarding War Diaries and Intelligence Summaries are contained in F. S. Regs., Part II. and the Staff Manual respectively. Title pages will be prepared in manuscript.

WAR DIARY or INTELLIGENCE SUMMARY

of 1st York & Lancaster Regt.

(Erase heading not required.)

Army Form C. 2118.

Hour, Date, Place	Summary of Events and Information	Remarks and references to Appendices
	VI Instruction in the use of the Hand Grenade, should form part of peace training.—	
	VII The importance of communication by telephone or other means— The Buzzer of our telephones both Army pattern and private pattern does not seem to stand the rough work.—	
	VIII The great importance of care of the feet — 120 men and 1 officer were admitted to hospital with frozen feet, roughly 15% of the numbers of the Battalion in the trenches. Every effort was made to guard against this by greasing mens feet, giving them clean socks and bathing their feet as much as possible, but it is often very difficult to provide accommodation for this, except when back in billets.—	
	IX A case made of two waterproof sheets has been found unsuitable for keeping & carrying machine guns in when not in use	

1247 W 3299 200,000 (E) 8/14 J.B.C. & A. Forms/C. 2118/11.

LIST OF APPENDICES TO VOLUME 2 -

WAR DIARY 1st BATTN YORK & LANCASTER REGT.

NUMBER	CONTENTS	AUTHOR
1	Rough Sketch of trenches taken up by 1st Bn York & Lancaster Regt. on 2nd & 3rd February 1915.	Capt. Bamford.
2.	Rough Sketch of positions to illustrate 4th February 1915.	Captain Bamford.
3.	Rough Sketch to illustrate 6th & 7th February 1915.	Capt. Bamford
4	List of Casualties of 1st Bn York & Lancaster Regt from 2.2.15 to	Capt. Bamford
5.	Rough Sketch to illustrate 1th February 1915 to	Capt. Sadleir
6	Rough Sketch to illustrate 20th February 1915.	Lieut Lowcaden.
7	Orders for Relief of trenches on 28.2.15. -	Capt. Bamford

NUMBER.	CONTENTS	AUTHOR
8	Map of Country S.E of YPRES to show theatre of operations from 1st February to 1st March 1915	Captain Bamford
9.	Brigade Operation Order No. 8 dated 10.2.15	Issued by 8 3rd Bde Copies by. Capt. Bamford
10.	Brigade operation order No. 9 dated 12.2.15	" "
11	Brigade operation order No. 10 dated dated 15.2.15	" "
12	Brigade operation order No. 11 dated 19.2.15	" "
13.	Brigade operation order No 12 dated 20.2.15	

28.2.15

E.H. Bamford Captain
a/Adjt ?[illegible] Lancaster Re

19

2.

APPENDIX No II By CAPTAIN E.S. BAMFORD

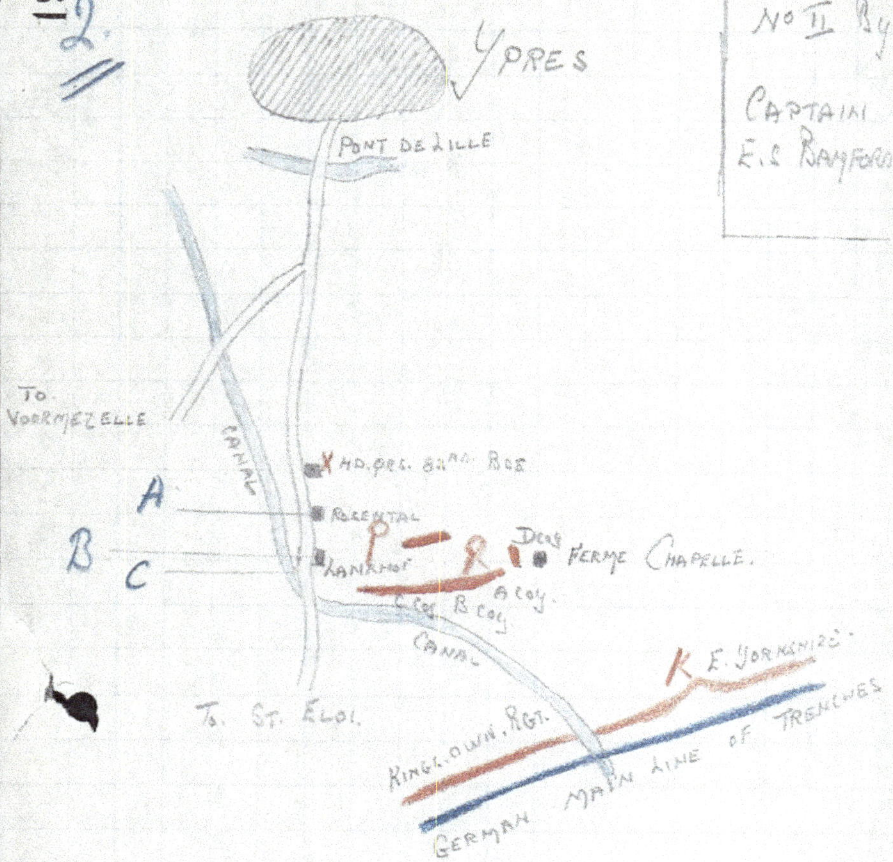

ROUGH SKETCH TO ILLUSTRATE 4TH FEBRUARY 1915

SCALE 1/40 000 abt. –

E S Bamford Capt.

For Lanc ... [illegible]

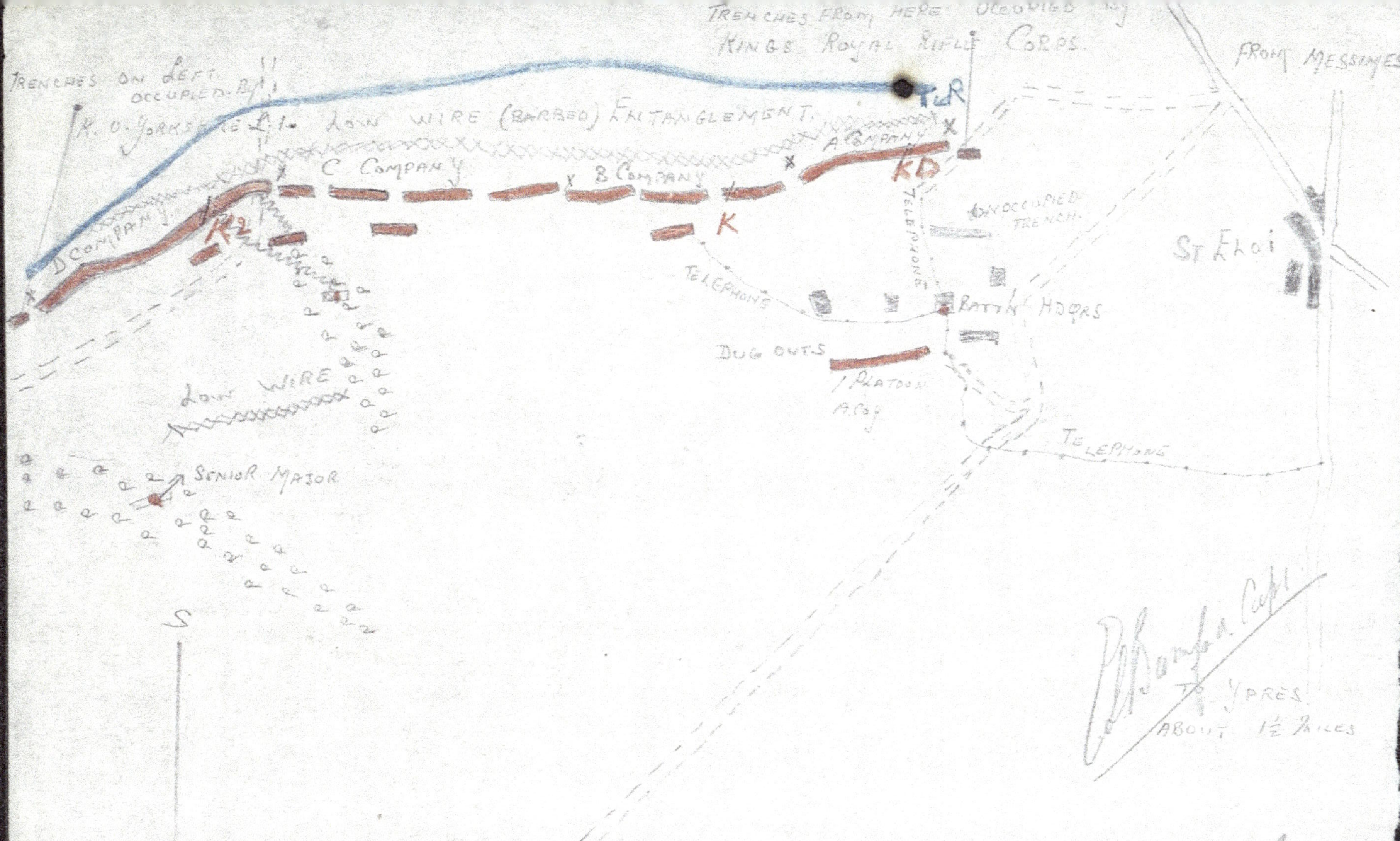

ROUGH SKETCH OF TRENCHES TAKEN UP BY 1st BATTN YORK AND LANCASTER REGT. on 2nd AND 3rd FEBRUARY 1915.

APPENDIX No I BY CAPT. E.S. BAMFORD

— YORK & LANCASTERS
— GERMANS.—
K pt of 2 Machine guns
K1 pt of 2 Machine guns
KD pt of 1 Machine gun
R German Sap head

3

APPENDIX No III By Captain E.S. Bamford

to illustrate 6th & 7th February 1915

Copy from Staff Map.

[illegible] Capt

Adjt. 1st York & Lancaster Rt.

APPENDIX No 4 B4
— CAPT E.S BAMFORD —

List of Casualties in 1st Battn York & Lancaster Regt

8 am 2nd February 1915 to 8 am 3rd February 1915	Killed	No. 12804	Pte	H. HOOLE
	Wounded	" 9711	"	J. STEVENSON.
	"	" 10059	"	J. PARKIN
	"	" 10047	L/Cpl	J. THREADGOLD

8 am. 3.2.15 to 8 am 4.2.15	Killed	Nil		
	Wounded	No 10629	Pte	A. HARBIRD
		" 9245	"	J. OVEREND
		"		SOUTH
		" 8719	"	J. BATSON.
		" 8057	"	J. GALLAGER
		" 3240	"	E. WATKINS

8 am 4.2.15 to 8 am 5.2.15	Killed	No 6883	L/Cpl	B. BLACKHALL
	Wounded	" 9639	Pte	E. CAUSTON.

8 am 5.2.15 to 8 am 6.2.15	Killed	No 10500	Pte	S. UTTLEY.
		" 9036	L/Cpl	W. THOMPKINS
		" 10130	Pte	D. FARMER.
		" 10539	"	W. GOULD
	Wounded	Captain		G. H. WEDGWOOD.
		No 6606	Sgt	E. TOPHAM
		" 4553	Pte	W. KELLY
		" 8362	"	H. BEASLEY.
		" 9828	"	G. CROSS
		" 9581	"	B. BIRD
		" 4521	"	J. WOODHOUSE

8 am 6.2.15 to 8 am 7.2.15.	Killed	No 2635	Pte	W. H. ORRELL
	Wounded	No 3963	L/Cpl	J. LILLEY
		" 10142	Pte	J. SHERWOOD.
		" 9995	"	D. WRIGHT

APPENDIX No 4

page 2.

Date		No.	Rank		Name
8 am 6.2.15 to 8 am 7.2.15	Wounded (Continued)	No 10010	Pte	E	JOHNSON
	"	17642	"	J	CARDLE
	"	9053	"	J	HUTCHINSON
	"	6502	"	T	SMITH
	"	8865	"	W	GOODWIN
	"	10053	"	R	FENTON
	"	9795	"	A	HARRISON
	"	8961	"	C	JOHNSON
	"	8464	L/Cpl	J	SHAW
	"	2953	Pte	W	LEE
	"	3460	"	J	PARKIN
	"	9810	"	J	KENNY

~~[illegible]~~

Date		No.	Rank		Name
14th February	Wounded	No 3201	Pte	J	SMITH
		" 4404	"	R	WALLIS
		" 13346	"	F	WILSON
		" 9798	"	G	HOLLOWAY
		" 8829	"	W	YATES
		" 10489	"	J	WILMOTT
		" 8693	"	J	PADDEN
		" 3611	"	M	LYON
		" 8220	"	T	LOWE
15th February	Killed	" 9669	"	W	McCUTCHEN
		" 9474	"	T	THURKHILL
	Wounded	" 10138	"	R	DAWSON
	"	" 7253	Sergt	F	TURNER
	"	" 8281	L/Cpl	A	AUSTIN

Appendix No 4 page 3

16th February Wounded No 9887 L/Cpl J. TYRELL

17th February Wounded No 9521 Pte G PIPER
" 9439 L/Cpl M PHILLIPS

18th February Killed Lieutenant J. K. MATHER.
" No 9870 C.S.M. D. WALTON.
" " 2173 Pte A. WILSON
Wounded Lieutenant H. F. LITCHFIELD
" N. B. LETHBRIDGE
" No 9010 Sergeant E. SQUIRES
" " 8985 L/Cpl J CAVANAGH.
" " 9883 " J ~~WHITE~~ BURGIN
" " 3134 Pte J. WINTERBOTTOM.
" " 9082 " A ROWARTH
" " 4372 " A VICKERS.
" " 2853 " R. BEVAN.
" " 8643 " J WHITE

19th February Killed 2/Lieutenant E R. FOLKER.
No 7962 Pte F. ALCHIN.
" 2742 " J. CONROY.
Wounded " 9812 " A. SPERIEY.
" 10126 " L PEARSON.
" 8150 " J DIXON
" 8465 " A BULL
" 7254 " W. ROLFE.
" 10115 " F FLOWERS.
" 9656 L/Cpl G WHITELEY.

20th February Killed No 2835 Pte G PERRY
" 10129 " G NEAVE
" 8621 " T BELL
" 8596 " W DANBY.

Appendix No 4 page 4.

20th February Continued

Killed No 9970 Pte T. BIRD

" 9931 " N AULT.

Wounded " 18559 L/Cpl. A PARKER

" " 9925 Pte R BRAND.

" " 2506 " R. LEAMES

" " 9563 " C WALL

Died of Wounds &c

on 16.2.15 No 9056 Sergeant C CROOKES.

on 20.2.15 " 18280 Pte H LODGE.

27. February

Killed 9488 Pte W IRETON

Wounded 9904 " G ELLIS.

28th February Killed No 8521 C/Sgt B. ELVIGE

Wounded " 10143 Pte P WARR.

" " 8954 " J CARREY

" " 9181 " J PYE.

" " 10161 " J ILOTT.

" MORRIS

4570 " CLARKE

to Illustrate 11th to 21st March 1915

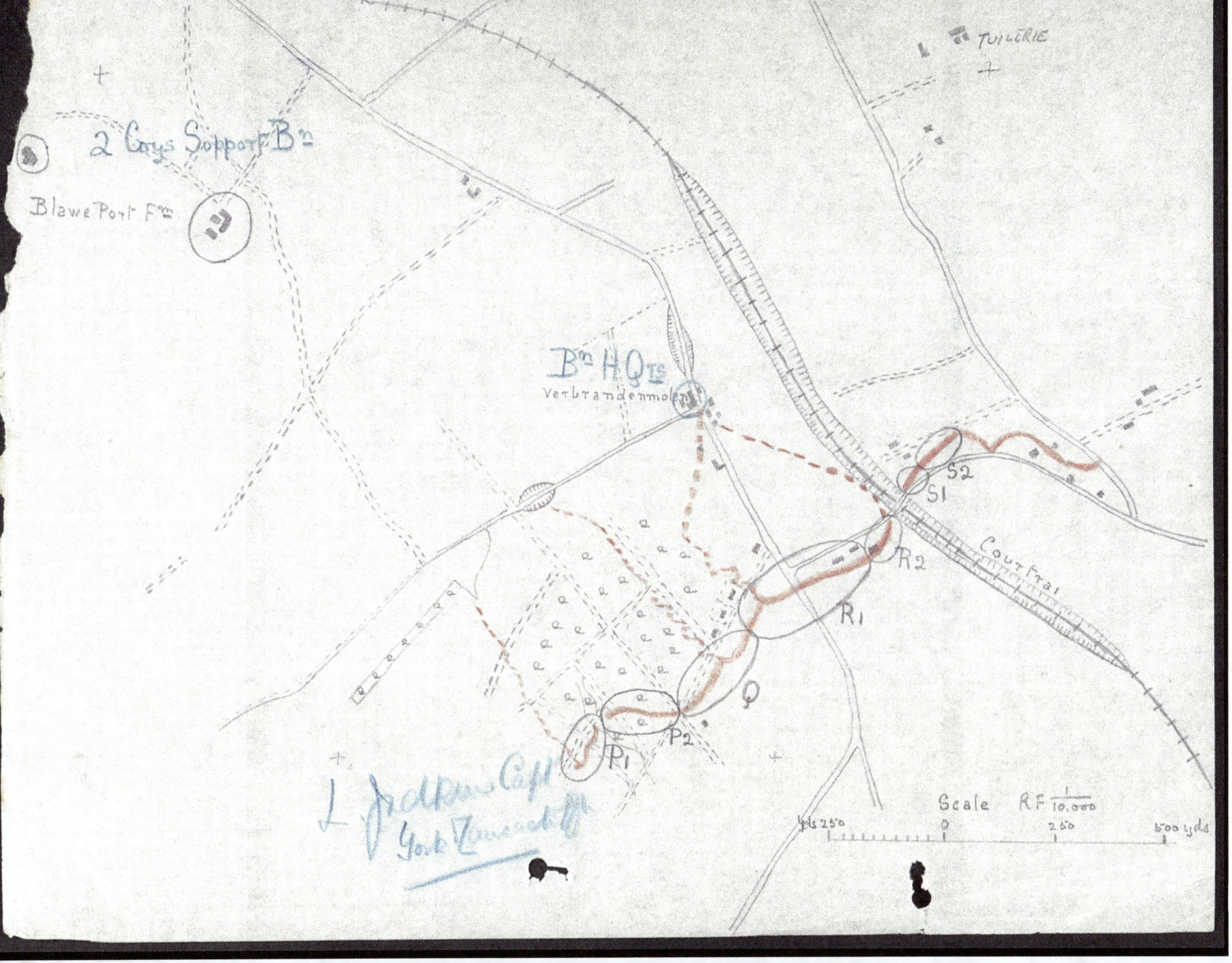

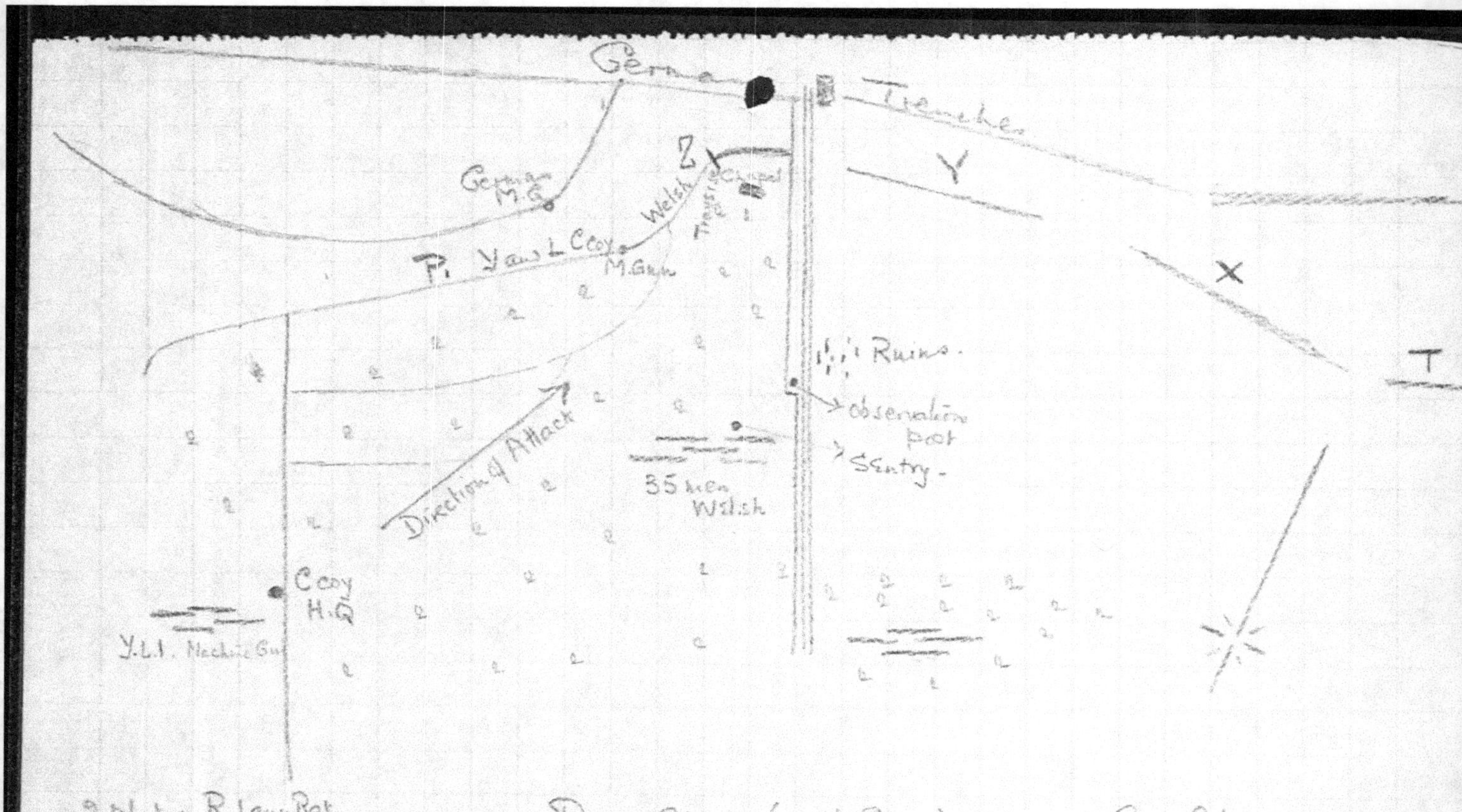

Rough Sketch (not to Scale) Explaining Capt Collins' report

APPENDIX NO VI
By Lt B.C. LOUSADA

APPENDIX NO VII

BY

CAPT. E.S. BAMFORD

Copy of telephone message

TO O.C. B AND C COYS AND MACHINE GUNS

No K38 28.2.15

Relief as follows to night AAA B Company will be Relieved by ~~B~~ K.O.Y.L.I And will Remain in support in dugouts in Rear of thirty five trench, two guides will be sent with Relieving Company AAA "C Company will be Relieved by K.O.Y.L.I. And will Remain in support in dugouts now occupied by K.O.Y.L.I in close support AAA Machine Guns and Grenadier Platoons will remain with Companies they are with now AAA time of Relief will be notified later.—

FROM. YORK LANCASTERS

TIME 11.15 am

E S Bamford Capt.

APPENDIX No VIII By Capt. F.S. Bamford.

Map of Country S.E of Ypres to show theatre of operations from 1st Feb to 1st March

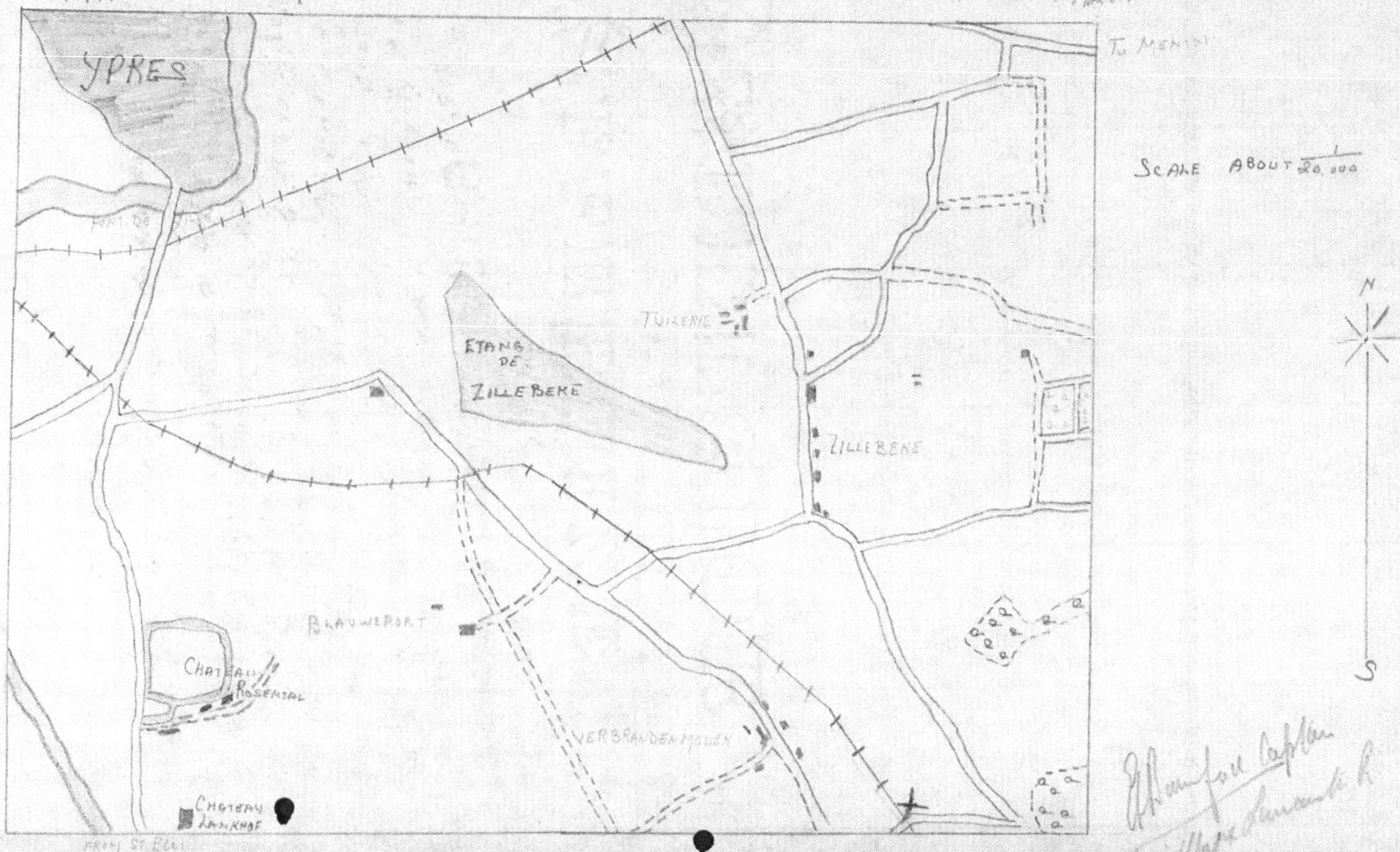

Scale about 1/20,000

N.B.
Except at point marked X the trenches held by us are South of this map. Distances vary from 100x to 500x

F.S. Bamford Captain
[illegible]

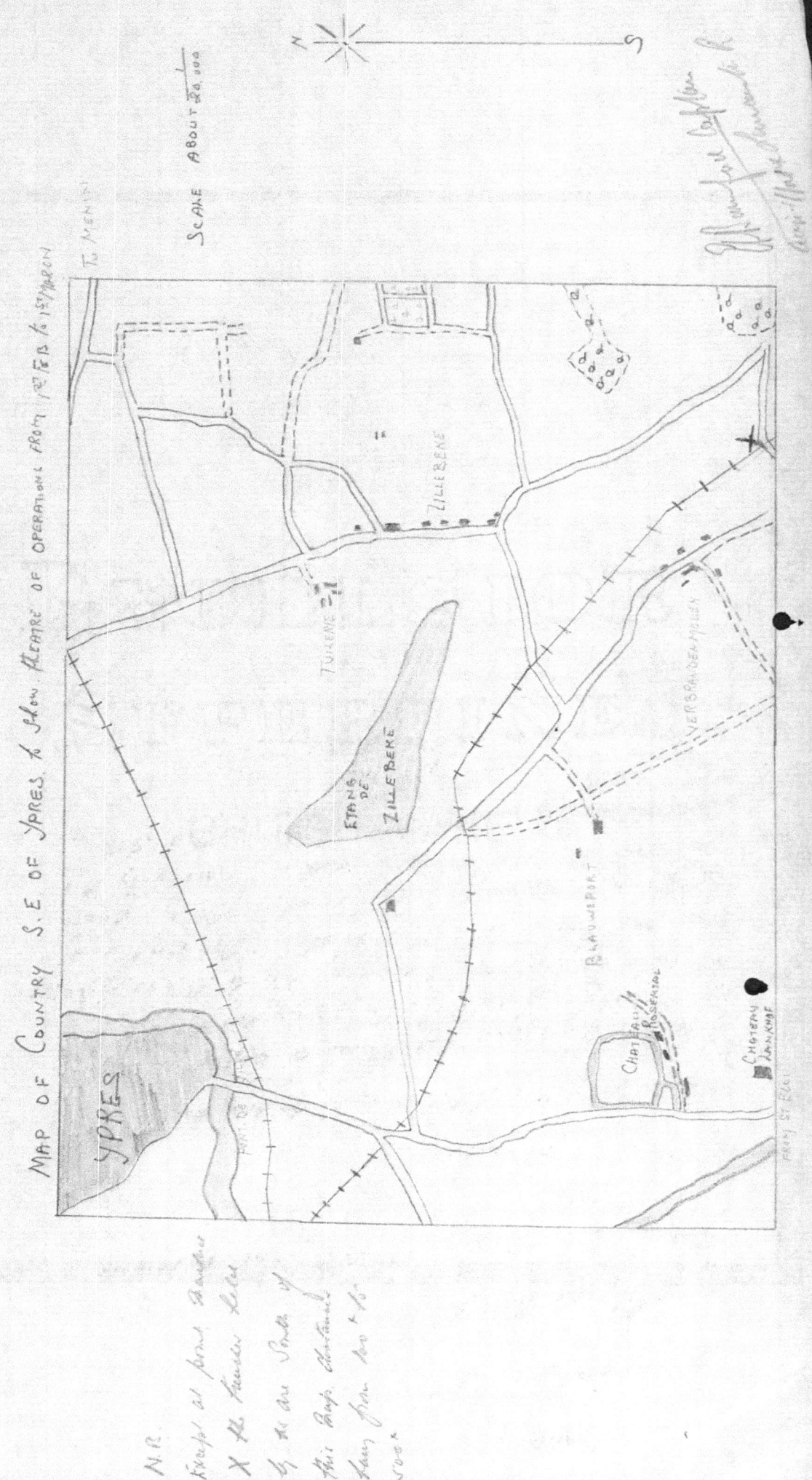

APPENDIX No IX

OPERATION ORDER No 8.

By

Brigadier General R. C. Boyle

Commanding 83rd Infantry Brigade.

10th February 1915

Reference Map - Belgium Sheet 1/40000.

1. The Brigade, with 1 Section of the 1st North Midland Field Coy. R.E will leave the present Billeting Area on the 11th inst. to relieve the 84th Brigade in the trenches.

2. Support Battalions - 2nd The Kings Own Regt and 1st York & Lancaster Regt.

3. Starting Point - H square 14. B 5,8, at 4-30 p.m

Order of march -

2nd Bn The Kings Own Regt.

1st Bn The York & Lancaster Regt.

1 Section 1st North Midland Field Coy. R.E.

Each Battalion will be followed by S.A.A. Carts, Machine Gun wagons water carts, Cooks wagons, Blanket & Baggage wagons.

Battalions will proceed to the Infantry Barracks YPRES.

4. On arrival at YPRES the Section of 1st North Midland Field Coy. R.E. will proceed alone to Brigade Headquarters.

10. Headquarters and 2 Companies of the 2nd Bn The Kings Own Regt will be met by Guide at the Guard Room, Infantry Barracks at 6-45 pm and will proceed via PORTE DE MENIN to TUILERIE. From here 50 men for D.2 and 1 platoon for U will be guided to the Headquarters of the Bns in the trenches and thence to D.2. and U respectively. P.T.O.

5. The Officer Commanding at D.2. and U will report to the O.C. East Yorkshire Regt. at Battalion Headquarters

The Officer Commanding at TUILERIE will be responsible for the forwarding of rations, stores etc. to Headquarters of Bns. in the trenches. The remainder of 2nd Bn The Kings Own Regt. will remain in the Infantry Barracks, YPRES.

6. The O.C York & Lancaster Regt will detail 2 Companies to proceed via PORTE DE LILLE to BLAUWEPOORT FARM. Guides will meet these Companies at the Guard Room, Infantry Barracks at 6-45 pm. The Officer Commanding at BLAUWEPOORTE will be responsible for the forwarding of stores rations etc. to Battalion Headquarters of Right Section, He will find a guard of 1 N.C.O. and 6 men to report to Brigade Headquarters. This guard will mount at 9 p.m. Headquarters and 2 Companies, York & Lancaster Regt will remain at Infantry Barracks, YPRES.

7. The 2 Companies The Kings Own Regt. and 2 Companies The York & Lancaster Regt. will draw one days rations and two sand bags per man. Each man will carry 1 Bandolier Ammunition. Sufficient S.A.A. carts to carry 2 boxes per platoon will go with the Companies to TUILERIE and Brigade Headquarters respectively from which places the boxes will be carried.

Trench Battalions

8. The Right Section now held by the Cheshire Regt. will be relieved by the 1st Bn K.O.Y.L.I. less 1 Company

The Left Section now held by the Northumberland Fusiliers will be relieved by the East Yorkshire Regt. with 1 Company 1st K.O.Y.L.I.

9. Starting Point – H Square 14 B.58 at 5-45 pm

Order of march

7/Bn East Yorkshire Regt.

1st Bn K.O.Y.L.I.

P.T.O.

Each Bn will be followed by S.A.A. carts, machine Guns wagons, water carts & cooks wagons.

Battalions will proceed to YPRES

1 days rations and two sand bags per man will be issued. Each man to have 1 bandolier of ammunition.

Sufficient S.A.A. carts for 2 boxes per platoon will proceed with Battalions as in para. 7

10 The Staff Captain will show the East Yorkshire and 1st K.O.Y.L.I. where to halt at YPRES and arrangements will be made to issue rations and sandbags

11 Guides will be available to guide East Yorkshire with 1 Coy. K.O.Y.L.I. and the 1st K.O.Y.L.I. less 1 Coy. to the Headquarters of the Battalions they are relieving where other guides will be ready to conduct them to the trenches.

12 The Brigade Ammunition Reserve is at the Riding School under Lieut. W.E.F. Davidson 3/E Yorks Regt.

All S.A.A. carts and machine gun wagons will go there direct on arrival at YPRES, except those required by Battalions which will go there as soon as possible.

All other transport will return as soon as possible to FARM H14 C92.

13 After to-morrow Regtl Transport Officers will arrange, before the transport leaves its Billeting Area to have rations for men in the trenches and supports packed in sandbags and oat sacks, eight mens rations per sack.

14. The position of Water carts will be

3 at TUILERIE { 1 of East Yorkshire Regt / 2 of York & Lancaster Regt }

filled at Estaminet just North of TUILERIE

1 at Infantry Barracks, King's Own

2 at Bde Headquarters, K.O.Y.L.I.

P.T.O.

Quartermasters of all Battalions will be at the Infantry Barracks but will proceed as far as TULERIE and Bde Hdqrs each night to see that their rations are correctly handed over.

15. WATER.

Support at BLAUWEPOORTE send back to fill their water bottles at Bde. Hd. Qrs.

Right Section of trenches get water from VERBRANDENMOLEN and a spring in the trenches.

Left Section water is carried up from TUILERIE.

16. FATIGUE.

A detail of men required for fatigue for the following night will be sent daily to O.C. TUILERIE and BLAUWEPOORT.

The Bde. will be assisted by ½ a Coy. of the 12th County of London Regt. in each Section.

Company of East Yorkshire Regt holding C-1. and C.2. trenches will arrange to draw 20 shovels and 5 picks from Staff Captain at YPRES

RESERVE RATIONS

O.C. Supports of each Section will take over 500 rations now at each support position.

They will only be issued on an order from H.Q.

(Sd.) Capt.
for Bde Major,
83rd Infty. Bde.

NOTES ON TRENCHES

1. Trenches B1, B2, B3 are very intricate. They were occupied by 200 men

2. Trenches C.1. C2, C3 are bad trenches. There is a space of 40 yards between C.2 and C3 with no communication

3. Tools are wanted in C1 and C2

4. Railway wants strengthening It is believed that there are trenches on embankment

(Sd) Capt

APPENDIX No X

OPERATION ORDER No: 9

By

Brigadier General R. C. Boyle,

Commanding 83rd Infantry Brigade

Bde Head Quarters,

12th February 1915.

Reference Map - Belgium Sheet 1/40,000

VERBRANDENMOLEN 1/10,000.

1. The Battalions in the trenches will be relieved as follows:—

1st K.O.Y.L.I. less 1 Coy by The York & Lancaster Regt. less 1 Coy.

East Yorkshire Regt with 1 Coy K.O.Y.L.I. by The Kings Own with 1 Coy York & Lancasters

The Coy York & Lancasters will be under the orders of O.C. Kings Own for operations and supplies.

2. Hd Qrs. and 1 Coy York & Lancasters will march at 7 pm. to BLAUWEPOORT FARM via PORTE de LILLE.

Two Cos. Kings Own with 1 Coy York & Lancasters will march at 8-15 pm to TUILERIE & report to O.C. Kings Own.

From TUILERIE and BLAUWEPOORTE FARM the Kings Own with 1 Coy York & Lancasters and the York and Lancasters less 1 Coy. will be guided to Hd Qrs of Battalions where they will be met by guides to guide them to the trenches.

3. The garrison of the Kings Own in U will join its company as it passes.

4. The K.O.Y.L.I will send the following guides:—

(a) Two guides to BLAUWEPOORTE FARM at 8-30 pm to guide York & Lancasters to Bn Hd Qrs.

(b.) Two guides from each of their 3 Companies W. of the Railway to be at Bn Hd qrs at 8-45 pm to conduct 3 Cos York & Lancasters to the trenches.

The East Yorks will send the following guides:—

(a) Two guides to TUILERIE to guide Kings Own and one Coy Y&L to Bn Hdqrs at 9-15. pm

(b) Two guides from each Coy and two guides from K.O.Y.L.I. Company E of Railway to be at Bde Hd. Qrs at 9-30 p.m. to guide Kings Own and 1 Company York & Lancasters to trenches.

(c) Two guides to D.2. to guide this party to it's trenches 9-45 p.m. O.C. Kings Own will inform O.C. East Yorks which trench this party will occupy.

5. The O.C. K.O.Y.L.I. on being relieved will leave two companies at BLAUWEPOORTE FARM

Hd. Qrs. and 1 Coy. will proceed to Infantry Barracks YPRES.

The O.C. East Yorks will leave 1 Platoon at U and 50 men at D.2. Hd. qrs. and 2 Cos. less 1 Platoon and 50 men will proceed to TUILERIE. The two remaining Cos. and 1 Coy K.O.Y.L.I will proceed to Infantry Barracks, YPRES by road point 1.22, d, 9.7. to point 1.28 a 2 8. and thence via Bde Hd. Qrs. and POORTE de LILLE

6. O.C. Kings Own will send two guides to report to O.C. Detachment, Kings Own at Infantry Barracks at 7-45 p.m. to guide two Cos. K.O. and 1 Coy Y.L. to TUILERIE.

The O.C. Y.L. Support Cos. will send two guides to report to O.C. Y.L. at Infantry Barracks at 6-30 p.m. to guide Hd. qrs. and 1 Coy. Y.L. to BLAUWEPOORT FARM.

7. O.C. Kings Own will post 2 men at corner 1.22. d 9.7 to point the way to Bde. Hd Qrs.

8. Cos. in Infantry Barracks will march with 2 days rations on the man.

Cos in support will have 2 days rations sent out to them, which will be carried from the positions where the wagons stop by Companies from the Barracks.

O.C. Supports Left Section will arrange to send up water to U for both relieved and relieving troops. Troops holding D.2 can obtain water 200 yards from the dug out

9. <u>Ammunition</u>

Cos. from Infantry Barracks will draw one bandolier per man and will take with them one S.A.A. cart for each Section of defence. This ammunition will be carried by them from the positions where the wagons stop.

(Sd) R.C. Boyle. Brig. Gen.
for Capt
for Bde Major,
83rd Infantry Brigade.

APPENDIX No XI

OPERATION ORDER No. 10.
By
Brigadier General R. C. Boyle,
Commanding 83rd Infantry Brigade

15th February 1915.

Reference Map. 28 Belgium and VERBRANDENMOLEN.

1. The K.O.Y.L.I. will relieve the York & Lancaster Regt. and the East Yorkshire Regt. the Kings Own Regt. to-night.

Relief to be carried out by Cos. commencing with the right of the York & Lancaster Regt. and finishing with the left of the King's Own Regt.

Guides – 2 per 3 Cos. of Y & L will meet relieving Cos. at I.21.d.10.0. (on the road) commencing at 9. pm.

Two guides per Coy of the Kings Own and 1 Coy. Y & L. will meet relieving Coys at TUILERIE commencing at 10. pm.

2. Battalions will be disposed as follows after being relieved:–

K.O. Trench A.2 2 platoons
 " " 2 "
 " D.2 2 "
 TUILERIE Hd.Qrs. & 2 Cos.
 YPRES (Infantry Barracks) 2 platoons.
Y & L. 2 Cos — BLAUWEPOORT.
 Hd.Qrs. & 2 Cos. – YPRES (Infantry Bcks.)

3. Trench A.2. will now thus be garrisoned by the supporting Battalion and will not be available for the Bn. which garrison the fire trenches.

K.O.Y.L.I to occupy trenches P.1 to S.2 inclusive.

E. Yorks to occupy trenches A.1 to D.1. inclusive

S.1 and 2. will be held by one Coy. K.O.Y.L.I and this Coy. will come under the orders of O.C. E. Yorks.

4. The same procedure will be carried out as regards the carrying of rations and stores as in the last relief with the following exceptions:–

Wagons for right section will go as far as the Railway.

Rations for D & D2 & A2. will be taken up by pack animals.

P.T.O.

The garrisons of these trenches will be prepared to meet these animals about 200 yards N of U trench at 8 pm and carry trench stores into the trenches.

(Sd.) J.E. Munby, Captain,
Brigade Major,
83rd Infantry Brigade

APPENDIX No XII

OPERATION ORDER No. 11
By
Brigadier General R. C. Boyle,
Commanding 83rd Infantry Brigade
19th February 1915.

1. The Brigade will be disposed as under tonight:-

Right Section Commander. Lt Col A. G. Burt
1st York & Lancaster Regt.

Fire Trenches York & Lancaster Regt and
3 Machine Guns.

Support .. (P.3) in rear of P.1. ½ Coy.
K. Own Regt.

Left Section. Commander Lt Col G. R. Ingram-Brooke

Fire Trenches S1 and part of S.2. } 1 Coy. York and Lancaster Regt

Part of S.2. A.1 & B.1 } 2½ Cos. E Yorks and 2 Machine Guns.

B.2. Kings Own (number of men to be detailed by O.C. K.O. Regt

B.3. D.1. 2 Cos. K.O.Y.L.I. and 3 M.G. (one of which to be on right of B.3.)

Support Trenches.

U & A.2 1 Coy. K.O.Y.L.I.

D.2. ½ " E. Yorks.

BLAUWERPOORT FARM. Remainder of Kings Own under O.C. Kings Own.

TUILERIE 1 Coy. K.O.Y.L.I } Under Maj. H.W. Powell,
1 " E. Yorks } E. Yorks Regt.

2. The K.O. Regt. in part of S2 and A.1 and B.1. will send 2 guides per Coy to meet the Detachment, E. Yorkshire Regt at U trench and TUILERIE respectively at 6. pm

The Kings Own Regt. in B 3 and the K.O.Y.L.I now in C.1 - D.1 will send 2 guides per Coy. to meet the 2 relieving Cos. K.O.Y.L.I at ZILLEBEKE at 8. pm

The reliefs concerned must leave the above places at these hours.

(Sd.) J.E. Munby, Captain,
Brigade Major,
83rd Infantry Bde.

APPENDIX No XIV

OPERATION ORDER No 12.

By

Brigadier General R C Boyle,

Commanding 83rd Infantry Brigade

20th February 1915

1. The Brigade will be relieved tonight by the 13th Infantry Brigade and will retire forthwith to Billets near VLAMATINGHE moving thence to BAILLEUL on the 22nd inst

2. All trench stores, ammunition and tools will be handed over to relieving Units with complete inventories.

Very pistols, periscopes and looking glasses will be retained as regimental property by our troops now in the trenches.

3. Commanding Officers & Coy Commanders of relieving Units are expected to arrive at the Hdqrs of both Sections about 6 p.m

Commanders of Sections will send guides to meet these officers at TUILERIE at Bde. Hdqrs

A supply of maps and information is being sent to Commanders of Sections to be handed over to these officers.

4. Table of guides to be furnished is attached. Relieving Companies must be conducted past the Hdqrs. of the section in order to call for their company commanders (see para III)

5. Transport will march with Battalions from YPRES.

(Sd) J.E. Munby Captain,
Brigade Major,
83rd Infantry Bde.

By whom found	To conduct	To report to	At time	Place.
2 per Coy. Right Section	3 Cos. of relief. K.O.S.B.	Sgt. Wiltshire	7. p.m.	Bde. Hd. qrs.
2 from S.1 and 2.	1 Coy. K.O.S.B	Officer K.O.Y.L.I.	7 p.m.	TUILERIE.
2 from E. Yorks. Regt. in A.1. 2 from K.O.Y.L.I. in A.2.	1 Coy West Kent Regt.	— " —	7. p.m.	— " —
2 from E. Yorks Regt. in B.1. 2 from Kings Own Regt in B.2. 2 from K.O.Y.L.I. in B.3.	1 Coy West Kent Regt.	— " —	7. pm.	— " —
2 from K.O.Y.L.I. in C.1.2.3	1 Coy. W. Kent Regt	— " —	7 p.m.	— " —
2 from K.O.Y.L.I. in D.1. 2 from E Yorks Regt in D.2.	1 Coy W. Kent Regt	— " —	7 p.m.	— " —
2 from K.O.Y.L.I. in U	2 platoons W. Kent Regt	— " —	8.45 pm.	— " —
2 from Kings Own in BLAUWERPOORT.	1½ Cos.	Sgt. Wiltshire	6-30 pm.	Bde. Hd. qrs.
2 from Kings Own Regt. in Dug outs behind P.1.	2 platoons	— " —	6.45 pm	— " —

83rd Bde.
28th Div.

WAR DIARY

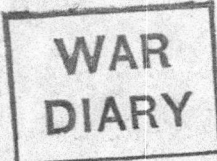

Bde. temporarily attached to 5th Division

3rd March till 6th April 1915.

1st YORK & LANCS.

M A R C H

1 9 1 5

On His Majesty's Service.

Instructions regarding War Diaries and Intelligence Summaries are contained in F. S. Regs., Part II, and the Staff Manual respectively. Title pages will be prepared in manuscript.

WAR DIARY or ~~INTELLIGENCE SUMMARY~~ OF 1st BATTN YORK AND LANCASTER REGT

Army Form C. 2118.

VOL III Page I

(Erase heading not required.)

Hour, Date, Place	Summary of Events and Information	Remarks and references to Appendices
9.30pm to 11.30pm 1.3.15 VERBRANDEMOLEN - YPRES	The Battalion was Relieved by the K.O.S.B's and Marched by Companies to YPRES. — After a short Rest the Battn Marched by Companies to the huts between VLAMERTINGHE and OUDERDOM. —	see appendix No I " " " II
8.15am 3.3.15 HUTS	The Battalion left the huts and marched via REINGHELST & WESTOUTRE CROIX DE POPERINGUE to BAILLEUL where the Battalion was Billeted till 7th March — the Battalion was warned for duty in the trenches on night 6th March. —	
8 pm 6.3.15 BAILLEUL	The Battalion left BAILLEUL at 2.30 pm and marched to NEUVE EGLISE the Battn remained here for two hours and then marched by Companies to WULVERGHEM to take over trenches in sector D. Battn Headquarters arrived at Lease Farm. Sector D and took over trenches ~~as~~ ~~follows~~ in manner of Companies as follows. —	See appendix No III See appendix No IIII
	11 A from Divisional Cyclist Company, 11 A support from the Queen Victoria's Rifles. — 11 B. 12. 12 support 13. 13 support and 14 A from the 1st Suffolk Regt. —	See appendix No 5 " " No 6.
M.S.S.	By 11 am all Companies Reported having taken over, all being quiet. Communication was obtained almost immediately with ~~~~ the 9th Queen Victoria's Rifles on our Right and on the left with the 2nd East Yorkshire Regt. — The trenches on the whole were good being in most cases more of a Breastwork than a trench. —	

1247 W 3299 200,000 (E) 8/14 J.B.C. & A. Forms/C. 2118/11.

Vol III page 8

Instructions regarding War Diaries and Intelligence Summaries are contained in F. S. Regs., Part II. and the Staff Manual respectively. Title pages will be prepared in manuscript.

WAR DIARY
or
INTELLIGENCE SUMMARY
(Erase heading not required.)

Army Form C. 2118.

Of 1st Battn. York and Lancaster Regt.

Hour, Date, Place	Summary of Events and Information	Remarks and references to Appendices
	Communication	
	Battalion Head Quarters have connected with the following by telephone:— with Brigade Head Quarters, with sectors on Right and Left, Dressing Station, R.E. Farm, trenches No 11A, 11B, 12 support & 13	See appendix No 5 & 6
	Support.—	
3 am 8.3.15	The Commanding Officer visited trenches number 13, 13 support and number 14A —	
7 am 8.3.15	Returning to Battn Head Quarters at 5.10 am.—	
	All Reported Quiet.—	
12 noon 8.3.15	Casualties for 24 hours ending 12 noon Eighth (Other Ranks) Killed 1 wounded 2 missing Nil.—	
	Co-operation with Artillery.	
	Should the Enemy attack 11A 11B or 12 trench the following Arrangement being on the fire of 125th Battery RFA on the ground in front of those trenches is "open fire DY"	
	if the Enemy attacked 13 or 14 A trenches "open fire DZ"	
	Should the Enemy attack trenches 11A to 14A "open fire D.S.O.S."	

1247 W 3299 200,000 (E) 8/14 J.B.C. & A. Forms/C. 2118/11.

Vol III

Instructions regarding War Diaries and Intelligence Summaries are contained in F. S. Regs., Part II. and the Staff Manual respectively. Title pages will be prepared in manuscript.

Page 4

WAR DIARY
or
~~INTELLIGENCE SUMMARY~~ of 1st Battn York and Lancaster Regt.

(Erase heading not required.)

Army Form C. 2118.

Hour, Date, Place	Summary of Events and Information	Remarks and references to Appendices
9 pm 8.3.15.	Our Artillery and the Enemy's fired considerably —	See appendix No 5 & 6
	Captain Palmer Commanding Trenches 11A to 12 Reported as follows —	
	"Our guns shelled Enemy's infantry trenches to my half right front; Result nil, also shelled Enemy's Artillery ~~Result nil~~ Result Enemy's guns ceased fire. — Enemy's guns shelled R.E. FARM bad shooting. Trench number 10 shelled three shots and others trench 12 few whizz ditto. —	
	13 to 14A Captain EAST. Reported as follows.	
	Enemy's Artillery has been firing all round my trenches apparently at R.E FARM and WULVERGHEM, but many shrapnel burst about 50 and 100 yards behind 13 S and 14A. —	
	Our Artillery silenced a gun about 250 yards in front of 13 A and were shelling Enemy's trench in front of 14 A successfully. Sale saw a Building catch fire about 1½ miles half right from 13 trench presumably in WYTSCHAETE. — Two Trench Mortars came over 14A but did not explode — There were 20 shrapnel apparently fired at us." —	
4.30pm 8.3.15	Artillery fire died away. —	
8.30pm 8.3.15.	One officer and 9 men (guides) of K.O.Y.L.I. arrived to go round lines they	

1247 W 3299 200,000 (E) 8/14 J.B.C. & A. Forms/C. 2118/11.

Instructions regarding War Diaries and Intelligence Summaries are contained in F. S. Regs., Part II. and the Staff Manual respectively. Title pages will be prepared in manuscript.

Vol. III Page 6.

WAR DIARY or INTELLIGENCE SUMMARY OF 1st YORK AND LANCASTER REGT.

(Erase heading not required.)

Army Form C. 2118.

Hour, Date, Place	Summary of Events and Information	Remarks and references to Appendices
	Left for R.E. FARM at 8.45 pm.—	
11pm 8.3.15	Senior Major visited R.E. FARM and then went to see some dug outs in Rear of 14 trench, which had been improved during the night.—	
	E.H.B. Capt	
3 AM to 4 AM 9.3.15	C.O. visited 12 trench & R.E. FARM Returning at 4 AM.—	
	Work done during the night	
	11A and 11A Support Work on parapet and Communication trench	See appendix Nos 5 & 6
	11B Drainage and Improvement of parapet.—	
	12 and 12 Support Improvement of Connecting Trench & parapet	
	13 Sup worked on and parapet tightened — Connecting trench with 13 Support worked on	
	13 Support & 14A parapet tightened & Connecting trench with 14 Commenced traverse made.—	
	Dugouts near R.E. FARM worked on — The O.C. Number	
1pm	12 Support trench Reported as follows.— "I am being shelled but can not ascertain where from".—	
	A few minutes later O.C. R.E. FARM Reported he was being shelled	

Instructions regarding War Diaries and Intelligence Summaries are contained in F. S. Regs., Part II. and the Staff Manual respectively. Title pages will be prepared in manuscript.

Vol III

page 1

WAR DIARY
or
~~INTELLIGENCE SUMMARY~~

(Erase heading not required.)

Army Form C. 2118.

1st YORK AND LANCASTER REGT.

Hour, Date, Place	Summary of Events and Information	Remarks and references to Appendices
	The 123rd Battery R.F.A were informed and at 2pm it was Reported that shelling had Ceased	
	The O.C. 12 Support trench Reported that the direction from which the shells were coming was eleven degrees S of E, that the time between the Bang of the Gun and the explosion of the shell was 1½ seconds. — The crater made was just under a yard broad and about 2 feet deep pieces of shell have been kept to show R.A observation officer. —	
8.15 pm.	Two platoons Monmouth Regt arrived R.E FARM and went to the trenches with "C" Coy (11 to 12). —	See appendix 20 & 6
	Companies in trenches were relieved by Companies at R.E FARM 20.5 Support and dressing station. —	
	During the night of 9th 10th the following trenches were visited by the C.O or Regtl Staff 11A. 11B 14A 13 Support 20.5 support 12 and 12 Support. —	
6.AM 10.3.15	The numbers in the trenches were as follows. — 11 trench 35, 11A " 30, 11 B 43, 12 74	

CBBl[?] Capt

[illegible signature]

1247 W 3299 200,000 (E) 8/14 J.B.C. & A. Forms/C. 2118/11.

Vol III

Instructions regarding War ~~Diaries~~ and Intelligence Summaries are contained in F. S. Regs., Part II. and the Staff Manual respectively. Title pages will be prepared in manuscript.

Page 8

WAR DIARY
or
INTELLIGENCE SUMMARY
(Erase heading not required.)

of 1st Battn York and Lancaster Regt

Army Form C. 2118.

Hour, Date, Place	Summary of Events and Information	Remarks and references to Appendices
	12 Support 64, 13, 60 13 Support 26	
	14A 44 RE FARM 160 DRESSING STN 90	
	This does not include orderlies, cooks, signallers etc but does include 2 platoons of Monmouth Regt — the work done in the trenches during the previous 24 hours was as follows —	
	11 A. Commencing a sap. —	
	11A & 11B Support improving the Communication trench. —	
	11 B Making up the parapet. —	
	12 Making a parados. —	
	13 Making a sap, improving parapet and Connecting trench between 13 and 12 and 13 and 13 Support. —	See Appendix No 6
	14 Making the parapet higher. —	
	Dugouts near R.E. FARM improved. — A Dugout at Battalion Headquarters was also commenced.	
J.B. Cope		
7.35 to 8.45 am 10.3.15	Vigorous Artillery duel, the fire of our Artillery was reported to be very accurate by O.C. 13 and 14A trenches. —	
1 pm	G.O.C. 83rd Bde visited No 12 trench. —	
9 pm 10.3.15	Orders were Received from 83rd Brigade to show Considerable	

1247 W 3299 200,000 (E) 8/14 J.B.C. & A. Forms/C. 2118/11.

Vol III

Instructions regarding War Diaries and Intelligence Summaries are contained in F. S. Regs., Part II. and the Staff Manual respectively. Title pages will be prepared in manuscript.

Page 9.

WAR DIARY
or
~~INTELLIGENCE SUMMARY~~ of 1st York and Lancaster Regt
(Erase heading not required.)

Army Form C. 2118.

Hour, Date, Place	Summary of Events and Information	Remarks and references to Appendices
	activity during the night.—	
	A patrol from. No 12 trench got to within 30 yards of the Enemy's trenches, and opened Rapid fire on it.— They could hear a good deal of talking and swearing but do not know if anyone was hit.—	
12.30 am. 11.3.15	Bursts of Rapid fire were frequently opened after 12.30 am	
EWB Capt	Work done during previous 24 hours.	
	Connecting trenches Between 11 B, 12, & 13 were further extended, parapets of 14 A Raised and paradoes constructed, all Communication trenches drained and parapets built up,— 11 support channel and much needed general Repairs.— Communication trench in Rear of 11 B started also one from R.E. FARM to 12 S.— Sap from 11 A made good progress now extends 35 yards beyond parapet. work also done on dugouts near R.E. FARM —	See appendix 20 & 26
	The length of the trenches occupied is as follows.—	
	13 trench 70 yards; 12 trench 100 yards	
	13 Support 75 "; 12 Support 75 yards	
	14 55 "; 11 B 35 "	
	11 A 80 yards.—	
	During the night Major Cotton visited trenches 12 and 12 S	

Instructions regarding War Diaries and Intelligence Summaries are contained in F. S. Regs., Part II. and the Staff Manual respectively. Title pages will be prepared in manuscript.

VOL. III

Page 10

WAR DIARY
or
INTELLIGENCE SUMMARY OF 1st Bn. York. and Lancaster Regt.

(Erase heading not required.)

Army Form C. 2118.

Hour, Date, Place	Summary of Events and Information	Remarks and references to Appendices
	During the day at periods, Artillery fire was very heavy. —	
1 pm 11.3.15.	Party at R.E FARM and those from dressing station (1st A & B Coys) Continued work on Dug-outs near R.E. FARM.	
8.25 pm 11.3.15	Head Quarters K.O.Y.L.I. arrived at ELBOW. FARM. — Relief was Completed at 11 pm —	See
	A draft of 135 N.C.Os and Men with 2nd Lieut C.K. CHAMIER & 2nd Lts N.C. PARRY & S. WEBSTER joined the Bn	
4 AM 12.3.15	A & B Coys on work at Dug-outs formed up at R.E FARM at 4 AM and marched to Battn Billets. —	
	The Battalion was Billeted at BUS FARM and neighbouring farms. —	
13.3.15 Bus FARM	The Battalion Remained in Reserve whilst an attack was made on hill 75. —	Appendices
12 pm 14.3.15 Bus FARM	The Battalion left Bus FARM by Companies at intervals Commencing with C Company at 12.15 pm, and marched to BAILLEUL. —	No 7 & 8.
	4 Captain Palmer East Lieut. Romford 2nd Lieuts Lousada & Kent-Lemon went to see the trenches to be taken over by the Battalion near PLOEGSTEERT. —	
1.20 pm 14.3.15 Ploegsteert	Very heavy firing heard in the direction of YPRES. — The Battn was ordered to be Ready to move at a moment's notice. —	

1247 W 3299 200,000 (E) 8/14 J.B.C. & A. Forms/C. 2118/11.

Instructions regarding War Diaries and Intelligence Summaries are contained in F. S. Regs., Part II. and the Staff Manual respectively. Title pages will be prepared in manuscript.

WAR DIARY
or
INTELLIGENCE SUMMARY
(Erase heading not required.)

Army Form C. 2118.

Hour, Date, Place	Summary of Events and Information	Remarks and references to Appendices
	The lengths of the trenches are as follows.—	
	11 A ~~80~~ᵡ · 12 Support 75ᵡ	
	11 A Support 35ᵡ · 13 70ᵡ	
	11 B 55ᵡ · 13 Support 75ᵡ	
	12 100ᵡ · 14 55ᵡ	
	The numbers of men in each trench were as follows.—	
	11 A 35 · 12 S 64	
	11 A Support 30 · 13 60	
	11 B 43 · 13 S 26	
	12 ~~24~~ 50 · 14 A 44	
	Number 5 Support point 55	See appendix No 5 & 6
	RE FARM 160	
	Dressing Station 90.	
	Companys were distributed as follows.—	
	11 A · 14 A Support } A Coy	
	11 B · 12	
	Machine Guns were distributed as follows	
	11 A one · 13 one	
	12 one · 14 A one East Lancashire Regt	
	No 5 Support point one [illegible]	

1247 W 3299 200,000 (E) 8/14 J.B.C. & A. Forms/C. 2118/11.

VOL III Page 11

Instructions regarding War Diaries and Intelligence Summaries are contained in F. S. Regs., Part II. and the Staff Manual respectively. Title pages will be prepared in manuscript.

WAR DIARY ~~or~~ OF ~~INTELLIGENCE SUMMARY~~ 1st Battn. Y York. and Lancaster Regt.

(Erase heading not required.)

Army Form C. 2118.

Hour, Date, Place	Summary of Events and Information	Remarks and references to Appendices
5.30 pm 15.3.15 BAILLEUL	The Battalion was ordered to move at once to BUS FARM.—	see appendix No. 5.
9.25 pm 15.3.15 Bus Farm	The Battalion arrived at BUS FARM at 9.25 pm	
G.H. Pope		
17.3.15 ELBOW FARM	The Battalion having been warned for duty in the trenches, head quarters arrived at ELBOW FARM at 1.45 pm and took over from the 1st K.O.Y.L.I.— The trenches taken over by the Battalion were as follows,—	See appendix No's 5 & 9. and 10
	10 B, 10 B Support, 11 A, 11 Support, 11 B } A COMPANY. 12, 12 Support, 13, 13 Support } B COMPANY.	
	DRESSING STATION "C" Coy. 20 S Support, RE FARM } D Coy	
9.45 pm 17.3.15 R.E FARM	Battalion headquarters moved to R.E FARM.—	
7. am 18.3.15 R.E FARM	The following Report on work done during the night was forwarded to Brigade Hdqrs.— 10 B and Support. Improvement of trench parapet and traverses.— 11 A work being continued on Sap, improvement to 11 A Support being continued.— 12 and 13 Improving parapet.—	

1247 W 3299 200,000 (E) 8/14 J.B.C. & A. Forms/C. 2118/11.

Vol. III Page 12.

Instructions regarding War Diaries and Intelligence Summaries are contained in F. S. Regs., Part II. and the Staff Manual respectively. Title pages will be prepared in manuscript.

WAR DIARY or INTELLIGENCE SUMMARY

(Erase heading not required.)

OF 1st YORK & LANCASTER REGT.

Army Form C. 2118.

Hour, Date, Place	Summary of Events and Information	Remarks and references to Appendices
1	12 Support and 13 Support. Re-Constructing fire trench between these trenches.—	
	Wire was put out during the night by 12, 11A & 10B trenches.—	
	Listening patrols & patrols had nothing to Report.—	
	During both night & day the Enemy were exceptionally quiet.—	
	All trenches were visited by C.O. & night staff during the night.—	
	The number of Rifles in trenches was as follows.—	
	10B 85 — 10B Support 20 — 11A 95	
	11A Support 20 — 11B 95 — 12 56	
	12 Support 38 — 13 75 — 13 Support 31	
	No 5 Support 60 — R.E. FARM 160 — DRESSING STN 210	See appendix No 5.
	Machine Guns were distributed as follows.—	
12 hrs. 18.3.15 R.E. FARM	1 in No 5 Support. 1 in 11A 1 in 12. 1 in R.E. FARM	
	2nd Lieut H. H. MOORSE was killed in number 13 trench.—	
	During the night Reliefs were carried out as follows	
	A Coy in trenches 10B, 10B Support 11A, 11 Support & 11B, were Relieved by "C" Coy.—	
	B Company in trenches Nos 12. 12 Support 13 & 13 Support were Relieved by D Coy.— Reliefs were completed by 12 midnight.—	
	During the day the Machine Gun was hit in the barrel causing a... [illegible] ... rendered useless.—	

W.B. [illegible] Capt.

1247 W 3299 200,000 (E) 8/14 J.B.C. & A. Forms/C. 2118/11.

Vol III Page 13

Instructions regarding War Diaries and Intelligence Summaries are contained in F. S. Regs., Part II. and the Staff Manual respectively. Title pages will be prepared in manuscript.

WAR DIARY or INTELLIGENCE SUMMARY of 1st Battn. York & Lancaster Regt.

(Erase heading not required.)

Army Form C. 2118.

Hour, Date, Place	Summary of Events and Information	Remarks and references to Appendices
7 am 20.3.15 R.E. FARM	Work done during last 24 hours and Report to Brigade.	
	"Patrols Report all quiet. No action or movement of the enemy observed AAA Work done Improvement of sap in front of 11A. AAA. Ten B and 10 B support traverses on right constructed AAA twelve and thirteen parados raised AAA Communication trenches to B & 11 A cleaned & improved, 11 B further 20x completed 12 & 13 support further 25x completed AAA 13 & 13 support, parapet raised on both sides AAA 30x of trench for dugouts near SHELL FARM ~~support~~ dug.—	
12 noon 20.3.15 R.E. FARM	Casualties during last 24 hours Killed one wounded one —	
6 pm 20.3.15 R.E. FARM	following Report sent to 83rd Brigade	
	"No movement of the enemy has been observed no patrols have been sent up during the day AAA Our artillery fire fell short of the enemy's trenches very near our own several shells bursting near 12 support AAA Effect of enemy's artillery fire could not be ascertained AAA A farm about 1000x S of R.E. FARM has been set on fire.—	
7 pm 20.3.15 R.E. FARM	following (is an extract of a) message Received from 83rd Brigade.—	
	"From tomorrow night onwards the line will be held as follows AAA York & Lancaster 14 B & 14 B Support inclusive to 12 & 12 Support inclusive AAA East Yorkshire 11 inclusive to 10 B & 10 B Support inclusive"	
C.H.B. Capt		
7 am 21.3.15 R.E. FARM	The following Report was sent to 83rd Brigade at 7 am.—	

Vol III Page 14

Instructions regarding War Diaries and Intelligence Summaries are contained in F. S. Regs., Part II. and the Staff Manual respectively. Title pages will be prepared in manuscript.

WAR DIARY or INTELLIGENCE SUMMARY

(Erase heading not required.)

Army Form C. 2118.

OF 1st BATTN YORK & LANCASTER REGT.

Hour, Date, Place	Summary of Events and Information	Remarks and references to Appendices
	"Situation Generally Quiet, no Action or Movement of the Enemy observed AAA patrols sent out 11 B & 11 A did not get any information AAA Our Artillery fire appeared ineffective some shells falling short of our own trenches AAA Enemy's Artillery apparently directed on sector on our Right AAA Work done fire trenches Repaired parados Lightened extension of Trenches 12 & 13 about 10 yards Traverses improved on Right 10 B Etc 11 A AAA Communication trenches 11 A to 11A Support is nearly completed, 11 B about 20 yards completed 13 Support to 12 Support about 10 yards completed 13 to 13 Support parapets strengthened flooring improved AAA Dugouts near shell farm about 50 yards of trench and four shelters completed. —	
12 noon 21.3.15 R.E. FARM.	Casualties during last 24 hours other Ranks Killed 1 wounded 6. —	
1 pm to 11.50 pm 21.3.15 R.E. FARM	During the night Reliefs were carried out as follows. — A Company took over trenches 14 A. 14 B & 14 B Support from the East Yorkshire Regt. 13 S from D Company & No 5 Support from B Coy Remainder of Men (55) in R.E FARM. — B Company took over trenches numbers 12 12 Support and 13 from D Company. — C Company were Relieved from trenches numbers 10 B. 10 B Support. 11 A 11 A Support & 11 B by the East Yorkshire Regiment. —	See appendix No 11 " " " 12.

Vol III page 16

Instructions regarding War Diaries and Intelligence Summaries are contained in F. S. Regs., Part II, and the Staff Manual respectively. Title pages will be prepared in manuscript.

WAR DIARY
or
~~INTELLIGENCE SUMMARY~~
(Erase heading not required.)

of 1st Battn York & Lancaster Regt

Army Form C. 2118.

Hour, Date, Place	Summary of Events and Information	Remarks and references to Appendices
	After Relief Companies were distributed as follows:—	See Appendix 2 & 5
	A Company: Trench or Farm — Numbers.	
	14A — 31	
	14B — 21	
	13 Support — 74	
	14B " — 21	
	3 Support Point — 55	
	R.E. Farm — 55	
	B. Company:	
	12 — 48	
	12 Support — 60	
	13 — 76	
	C Coy: R.E. Farm — 110	
	Dugouts T.S.B. — 75	
	D Coy: Tea Farm — 106	
	Pack Horse Farm — 90.	
	The Relief was completed by 12 midnight.—	
6 p.m.	Report to 83rd Brigade — No movement of the Enemy has been	

1247 W 3299 200,000 (E) 8/14 J.B.C.&A. Forms/C. 2118/11.

Vol III page 17

Instructions regarding War Diaries and Intelligence Summaries are contained in F. S. Regs., Part II. and the Staff Manual respectively. Title pages will be prepared in manuscript.

WAR DIARY ~~or~~ ~~INTELLIGENCE SUMMARY~~ OF 1st BATTN YORK AND LANCASTER REGT

(Erase heading not required.)

Army Form C. 2118.

Hour, Date, Place	Summary of Events and Information	Remarks and references to Appendices
	observed during the day AAA No patrols have been sent out during the day by us AAA Enemy fired a few shots at 10 B without result they were coming as far as [illegible] the direction from [illegible] East shells were high explosive AAA Result of our artillery fire not observed.—	
	ESB Capt	
7 am 22.3.15. R.E. FARM	Report to 83rd Brigade	
	No action or movement of the Enemy has been observed AAA Patrols report all quiet AAA Enemy fired a few shells at No 11A trench this evening but did no damage AAA General situation quiet AAA Summary of work done All trenches repairs carried out parados raised parapet 11A Machine Gun Emplacement re-made 2012 re-constructed & made platform Communication trenches 11B finished 12S to R.E FARM nearly dug to FARM Extension of trench 12 - 15 feet 12S 20 sandbags AAA Shelter near SHELL FARM six [illegible] row [illegible] trench dug but not completed.— Completed short [illegible] of [illegible]	
	Casualties during last 24 hours – other Ranks 4 wounded.—	
12 noon 22.3.15 R.E FARM	O.C. 80th Battery R.F.A arrived at R.E.FARM the following	
4 pm 22.3.15 R.E FARM	Arrangement was made with him should the Enemy attack.— If the Enemy attack 12 or 13 trenches the following message to be sent.— Open fire D.Z.	

1247 W 3299 200,000 (E) 8/14 J.B.C. & A. Forms/C. 2118/11.

Vol III page 18.

Instructions regarding War Diaries and Intelligence Summaries are contained in F. S. Regs., Part II. and the Staff Manual respectively. Title pages will be prepared in manuscript.

WAR DIARY of ~~INTELLIGENCE SUMMARY~~ of 1st Battn. York and Lancaster Regt

(Erase heading not required.)

Army Form C. 2118.

Hour, Date, Place	Summary of Events and Information	Remarks and references to Appendices
	If the Enemy attack 14 A or 14 B "Open fire DY"	
	If the Enemy attack the whole line.— "Open fire D. S. O. S.—	
6 pm 22.3.15. R.E. FARM.	"At about 1 pm the Enemy in trench opposite No 13 were shouting to us, but could not be seen AAA. At 4 pm about 6 of Enemy were seen going down Communication trench on N side of German trench opposite to No 13 they had light grey uniform with Round grey caps they were fired on Result unknown AAA Our Artillery put some shells in the Enemy's parapet in front of 13 trench making breach in parapet AAA At 2.50 pm two of our shells fell in Rear of 13 about 10 and 25 yards away Respectively AAA No other action or movement of the Enemy observed.—	
8 pm 22.3.15. PACK HORSE FARM	A Draft of 100 N.C.O's & men for the Battn arrived at PACK HORSE FARM.	
E.H. Blake		
7 am 23.3.15 R.E FARM.	"General situation very quiet patrols have nothing to Report No action or movement of the Enemy observed AAA Work done during 24 hours 12 trench parapet strengthened firing platform boarded & improved 12 Support trenches at South End made stronger & higher firing platform improved Communication trench drainage improved AAA 13 Building new dugouts in Rear of parados firing platform Revised & Boarded 13 Support firing platform improved 14 A firing platform Reconstructed	

1247 W 3299 200,000 (E) 8/14 J.B.C. & A. Forms/C. 2118/11.

Vol III page 19

Instructions regarding War Diaries and Intelligence Summaries are contained in F. S. Regs., Part II. and the Staff Manual respectively. Title pages will be prepared in manuscript.

WAR DIARY
or
INTELLIGENCE SUMMARY
(Erase heading not required.)

Army Form C. 2118.

of 1st Battn York & Lancaster Regt.

Hour, Date, Place	Summary of Events and Information	Remarks and references to Appendices
	14 B parapet made bullet proof trench changed communication trench changed AAA Shelter near R.E. FARM balled on.—	
3.45 pm 23.3.15 R.E. FARM.	The Enemy shelled trenches Numbers 9 & 10 & their fire appeared to be accurate.—	
6 pm. 23.3.15 R.E. FARM	Report to 83rd BRIGADE "No movements or actions of the Enemy have been observed. No patrols have been sent out during the day AAA Enemy have been shelling trenches on our Right so far as Rule be Numbers 9 & 10 trenches fire appeared to be accurate AAA Our Artillery burst two shells in front of 13 doing little damage others could not be observed.—	
8 pm. 23.3.15 R.E. FARM.	The Battalion was Relieved by 1st K.O.Y.L.I. and Returned [less C Company] to the billets at NEUVE EGLISE.—	See Appendix No 13.
~~24.3.15 R.E. FARM~~	~~A draft of 100 N.C.Os and men from England joined the Battn~~	
14.3.15. BAILLEUL	2/Lieut. T. L. Boyd with a draft of 60 N.C.Os and men joined the Battalion.—	
25.3.15 NEUVE EGLISE	Major T.T. GRESSON. D.S.O. joined the Battalion from England.—	
28.3.15 NEUVE EGLISE	Lieut R.B. COWLEY and 1 man joined the Battn from 83rd Battn.—	

1247 W 3299 200,000 (E) 8/14 J.B.C. & A. Forms/C. 2118/11.

VOL III page.

Instructions regarding War Diaries and Intelligence Summaries are contained in F. S. Regs., Part II. and the Staff Manual respectively. Title pages will be prepared in manuscript.

WAR DIARY
or
INTELLIGENCE SUMMARY
(Erase heading not required.)

OF. 1ST BATTN. YORK. & LANCASTER REGT.

Army Form C. 2118.

Hour, Date, Place	Summary of Events and Information	Remarks and references to Appendices
7 pm to 7.30 pm 29.3.15 NEUVE EGLISE	The Battn left NEUVE EGLISE Lettments to take over trenches 11B. 12. 12S 13, 13S 14 & 14S. – (Left Sector of Defence). – By 10.25 pm all trenches reported having taken over. –	See appendices Nos. 15 & 16. also No 5 (map)
EHB Capt.		
7 am 30.3.15 R.E. FARM. –	Report to Brigade Headqrs. Situation generally quiet AAA Patrols report no movement or action of the Enemy except movement of transport in rear of German lines, at 10.30 pm last night & at 12 midnight AAA Work done since taking over 11 B. improving communication trench & extending trench towards 11.A a new Bay 10 x long completed 2 new Bays on Right and left. Commenced AAA 12 Sandbagged trench between 12 & 13 for 30 x Continued dapping for 8 x 12 Support improved & lighting parados AAA 13 traverse made Right end AAA Communication trench 12 Support R.E. FARM improved. —	
6 pm 30.3.15 R.E. FARM.	Report to BRIGADE HDQRS. Situation generally quiet no movement or action of the Enemy has been observed. At 9 am Enemy fired 6 shells which burst behind 13 S 14 & 14 S Shells were common shell & shrapnel direction of guns as near as can be ascertained due East from 14 trench AAA Enemy's heavy Artillery fired about 6 shells into WULVERGHEM extent of damage unknown AAA Enemy fired at one of our Aeroplanes with Anti Air Craft guns. – they did not appear to do any damage AAA our Artillery fire unobserved. –	
EHB Capt.		
12.5 AM 31.3.15. RE FARM	Numbers in trenches as follows. – 11 B. 51 men. 12. 106 men 12S 56 men 13 61 " 14. 46 " 14S 25. RE FARM 168 men. TEA FARM 49 PACKHORSE FARM 219 men	

1247 W 3209 200,000 (E) 8/14 J.B.C. & A. Forms/C. 2118/11.

Instructions regarding War Diaries and Intelligence Summaries are contained in F. S. Regs., Part II. and the Staff Manual respectively. Title pages will be prepared in manuscript.

VOL III

Page

WAR DIARY

~~or INTELLIGENCE SUMMARY~~

(Erase heading not required.)

OF 1st YORK LANCASTER

Army Form C. 2118.

Hour, Date, Place	Summary of Events and Information	Remarks and references to Appendices
Jan 31.3.15. R.E. FARM.	Report to 83rd BRIGADE "Situation generally quiet. No movement or action of the enemy has been observed AAA Patrols have nothing to report 12S trench officer patrol searched all old trenches 13S a patrol sent along an old communication trench leading to German lines could not get thro' wire AAA Work done 11B parapet tightened communication trench about 40 yards dug requires draining total length about 70x 12S communication trench completed to R.E. FARM tightened parados 12 trench extended now within 40x of 13. – 13 traverse made right end of parados built behind extension 13S communication trench to R.E. FARM about 40x dug. – Communication trench 13S – 13 pumped dry. 14 traverse constructed on right, parapet improved communication trench parapet on NORTH side made & is bullet proof 14S fire trench completed AAA An air ship passed over 13 & 14 trenches at 3.50am at intervals it showed 3 green lights & a white one it disappeared to the NORTH at 4.30am." —	
12 noon 31.3.15. R.E. FARM.	Casualties during last 24 hours. Killed other ranks 1 Wounded " " 2.	
6 pm. 31.3.15 R.E. FARM.	6 pm Report to Brigade. "Situation generally quiet. No movement or action of the enemy has been observed No patrols have been sent out during the day. AAA Enemy fired heavily with rifles at our aircraft 11 am AAA Our artillery fire was accurate on German trenches in front of 11B AAA Enemy's artillery fire could not be observed AAA	

1247 W 3299 200,000 (E) 8/14 J.B.C. & A. Forms/C. 2118/11.

Vol. III page.

Instructions regarding War Diaries and Intelligence Summaries are contained in F. S. Regs., Part II. and the Staff Manual respectively. Title pages will be prepared in manuscript.

WAR DIARY
or
INTELLIGENCE SUMMARY

(Erase heading not required.)

OF. 1st BATTN. YORK. & LANCASTER REGt.

Army Form C. 2118.

Hour, Date, Place	Summary of Events and Information	Remarks and references to Appendices
	Enemy have a Captive Balloon or Kite about 3/4 Mile N of MESSINES	
7.30 pm. 31.8.15 R.E. FARM.	D Coy & C Coy were Relieved in fire & support trenches by B and A Coys	see Appendix 20
	The following points have been brought out during the Month.—	
	1. The more men are given to do when in the trenches the fitter they keep.—	
	2. The difficulty of bringing up stores etc to the trenches.— (This means there are not enough men to garrison fire trenches & carry up the quantities of stuff that is necessary) i.e. Sand Bags, Boards for trench bottoms, planks for Revetting, Ammunition, Rations, Water etc.—	
	3. The necessity when in trenches for constant Rifle inspections.— We have never had any trouble with our Rifles & have at least 4 or 5 inspections a day.— (Some Territorials were attached to us for two nights the first day their Bolts got caked with mud etc. the O.C. 'C' Coy to whom they were attached insisted on inspecting their Rifles several times & the 2nd day he had no trouble at all.—	
	4. Loopholes should never be made straight but at an angle & should be blinded this is most necessary when trenches are very close.—	
	5. The importance of taking cover from Aeroplanes.—	

Instructions regarding War Diaries and Intelligence Summaries are contained in F. S. Regs., Part II. and the Staff Manual respectively. Title pages will be prepared in manuscript.

WAR DIARY
or
INTELLIGENCE SUMMARY
(*Erase heading not required.*)

Army Form C. 2118.

Hour, Date, Place	Summary of Events and Information	Remarks and references to Appendices
	during the time the Battalion held the DRANOUTRE SECTION we always had at least 100 men sometimes 175 in R.E. FARM ~~[illegible]~~ orders were issued to the effect that there would be no fires lighted in the day time & no one was allowed out — we were never actually fired at by artillery, tho some shells fell close. —	
	6. Many drafts have come out, fire discipline is not the same as it was, but if great attention is paid to this by Company & Platoon Commanders this difficulty can be got over. ——	
	7. The difficulty in training signallers or telephone operators especially [illegible] is very great. — Signallers were taken from us for Communication Companies before we left India, several went sick in England since we have been out, they have had several casualties, & our numbers are now 14, some of these often have to be taken by the Brigade if they go sick. — More men ought really be trained in peace, tho' we had 36 after 2 months we are short handed. ——	

LIST OF APPENDICES TO VOL III

No OF APPENDIX	CONTENTS	AUTHOR
1	Brigade orders for Relief on 1.3.15 Operation order No 16.	83rd Brigade
2.	Rough Sketch to show position of Lieut Leen OUDERDOM	CAPT BAMFORD
3.	Copy of operation order No 17.	83rd Brigade
4.	Copy of operation order No 18	83rd Brigade
5.	SKETCH MAP OF DRANOUTRE SECTION	GEN STAFF
6	Sketch of telephone Line DRANOUTRE Section	Capt BAMFORD
7.	Copy of operation order No 19.	83rd Brigade
8	Copy of operation order No 20.	83rd Brigade
9	Copy of operation order No 21	83rd Brigade.
10	Copy of operation order No 3	1/YORK & Lancaster Rgt

No of APPENDIX	CONTENTS	AUTHOR.
11	Orders for Relief	1/ Loyal Lancashire Re.
12	operation order 22	83rd Brigade
13	operation order 23	83rd Brigade
14.	Roll of officers with Battn on 31. 3. 15.	Capt BAMFORD
15	Operation order 20 24.	~~Brigade~~ 83 Brigade
16.	operation order 204	1/Loyal Lancashire Re.

E Bamford Capt.

adjt 1/ Loyal Lancashire R

GUIDES	FROM TRENCH	TO BE AT	TIME	TO CONDUCT
2 per Coy	fire trenches AREA C	Bde H.Q.	7.45 pm	3 Coys 2/K.O.Y.L.I.
2 men	Dugouts in Rear of 33	" "	"	½ Coy K.O.S.B.
2 men	Dugouts in Rear of 35	" "	"	½ Coy K.O.S.B.
2 men	~~ZILLEBEKE Village~~	ZILLEBEKE village	8 pm	1 Coy 2/K.O.Y.L.I.
" "	38. 39			½ " Dukes of Wellington's
" "	40			1 " "
" "	43, 44, 45, 46,			½ " "
" "	47 48			½ " "
" "	49			1 " "
" "	50		8.45 pm	½ " "
" "	41 42			½ [illegible]
" "	51			½ " "

N.B. Where more than one trench is mentioned above on the same line 2 men only are Required (to Represent all these trenches) not two from Each

APPENDIX No I

Operation Order No 16 By
Brig General R.C. Boyle CB
Commanding 83 Infantry Brigade

Copy No 5

1st March 1915.

I The Brigade will be Relieved to night as under —

Area C. fire trenches by 2/K.O.Y.L.I
supports " K.O.S.B

Area D. fire trenches 38, 39 by 2/K.O.Y.L.I Remainder by Duke of Wellington's Regt & West Kent Regt.

In Each Case the Relieving Companys will arrive at fire trenches at 10 minutes interval Commencing on the Right of Each area at 9pm — Support trenches will be similarly Relieved immediately after the Reliefs have Reached all the fire trenches. —

II Incoming area Commanders will probably Reach HQ of areas at 8pm the attached form will be Completed & handed over to them. —

III Guides will be furnished in accordance with the attached Table. —

IV Companies will March to the GRANDE PLACE YPRES as soon as Relieved tea will be provided at that place after which Battalions will march thence (by Companies if desired by C.O's) to the huts South of VLAMERTINGHE, Each Battn to march independently. —

V One Ambulance Wagon will be at Bde HQ & tuileries for Conveyance of men unable to walk. —

VI Any periscopes which were taken into the trenches by troops of 83rd Bde or sent there during this Tour will be brought out & Retained by units using them. —

(Signed) J.F. Mumby Capt.
Brigade Major 83rd Infantry Bde.

Issued by orderly
Copy No 2 Kings Own Regt
" " 3 East Yorkshire Regt
" " 4 K.O.Y.L.I.
" " 5 North Lancashire Regt

True Copy. [signature]
Adjt North Lancashire

APP
TO POPERINGHE
VLAMERTINGHE
YPRES
HUTS
OUDERDOM
N
ROUGH SKETCH TO SHOW POSITION OF HUTS NEAR OUDERDOM SCALE ABOUT

ENDIA N°2

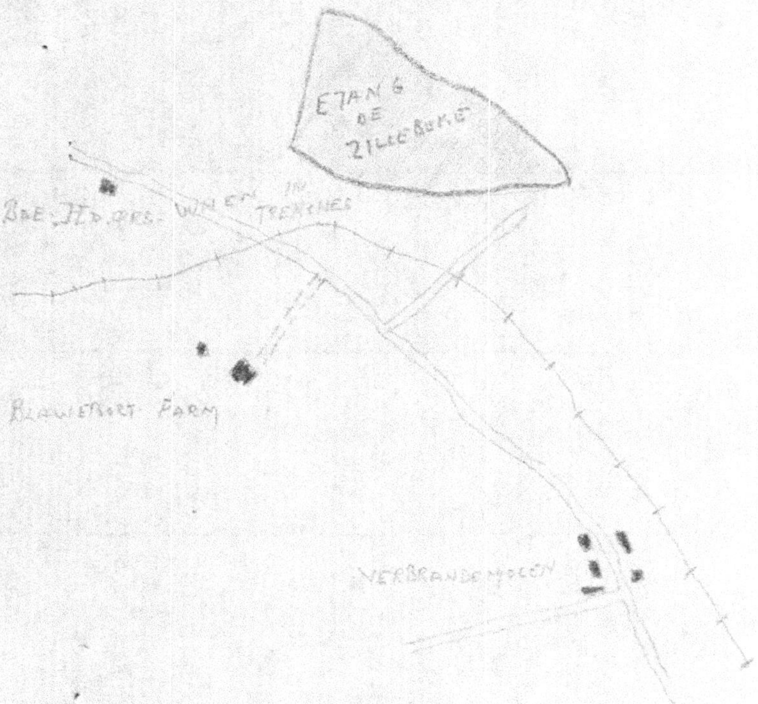
ETANG
DE
ZILLEBEKE
BDE. HD. QRS. WHEN IN TRENCHES
BLAWEPORT FARM
VERBRANDEMOLEN

Operation Order No 17 Copy No 5

By

Brigadier General R.C. BOYLE C.B

Commanding 83rd Infantry Brigade

Reference Map. FRANCE 28 1/40000. 2nd March 1915.

APPENDIX No 3

I The Brigade will march to BAILLEUL tomorrow by RENINGHELST, WESTOUTRE, CROIX DE POPERINGUE, starting point OUDERDOM.—

K.O.Y.L.I.	8 am
East Yorkshire Regt	8.20 am
Kings Own Regt	8.40 am
York & Lancaster	9 am

Bde Troops will join Rear of Column at RENINGHELST.— Halts will be made without orders for ten minutes duration at 10 minutes before each hour.—

II Transport to accompany units except supply waggons.—

III 1st York & Lancaster Regt to detail a platoon under an officer accompanied by the Regimental Medical Officer to act as Rear Guard.— To M.M.P will report to O.C. Rear Guard at the starting point.—

IV Billeting parties, who must be mounted on horses or bicycles and must include one officer per Battalion, will meet the Staff Captain at the starting point at 8.45 am.— The Brigade Headquarters orderlies have been ordered to accompany the Staff Captain.—

(Signed) J. P. Mackesy Capt.

Brigade Major 83rd Infantry Brigade

Copy No 2 Kings Own Regt.
" " 3 East Yorkshire Regt
" " 4 K.O.Y.L.I
" " 5 York & Lancaster Rt

True Copy. [signature] Captain

Adjutant 1/ York & Lancaster Rt

83rd Bde. Disposition in DRANOUTRE SECTION.

Unit	Area to be occupied	at present held by	Guides meet Relieving unit at
9th (Q.V.) Rifles	Sector "C" less 10 b Support & less half of 10 b.	10 b Support Div Gokn Coy	
1/York & Lancaster.	SECTOR D	1st Suffolk Regt. 9 (Q.V.) Rifles (14 A Support) Div Gokn (11 A)	Road Junction 100x S.E of BURNT FARM.
2/E Yorkshire	SECTOR E.	1st WELCH RGT.	TEA FARM.
1/K.O.Y.L.I	BUS. FARM AND LINDENHOEK Grand Farm	2nd Cheshire Rr.	
2/Kings Own Rr.	DRANOUTRE Village	2nd 5th Fusiliers	
1/1 Monmouth Rr. less 1 Coy & 1 Coy 9th (Q.V.) Rifles	present Billets of 1/Monmouth Rr		
1/3 Monmouth Rr.	present Billets (RAVETSBURG)		

OPERATION ORDER No 18 Copy No 5

By

Brigadier-General R.C. BOYLE

Commanding 83rd Infantry Brigade.

APPENDIX No 4

BAILLEUL
6th March 1915

Ref Map Belgium 28
and Sketch DANOUTRE SECTION

I The Brigade less the 5th Kings' Own Regt. will Relieve the 84th Brigade to-morrow

II Dispositions as per attached table.—

III The 9th (Q.V) Rifles and the 1/1 Monmouthshire Regt will be attached to the 83rd Brigade.—

IV The 5th Kings' Own Regiment will be accommodated in Billets from to-morrow on the BAILLEUL - St JEAN CAPPELLE Road and will move thence so as to be clear of BAILLEUL by 1 pm.—

V (a) The 2/East Yorkshire Regt and the 1/York & Lancaster Regt less S.A.A. Carts and blanket wagons will march in that order by the Lille Road to a point near NEUVE EGLISE which will be indicated, where teas will be served, starting point at St. ELOI at 2.30 pm.—

V (b) The 1/K.O.Y.L.I. less S.A.A. Carts and tool wagons will march by the LILLE Road ~~to a point~~ and NEUVE EGLISE so as to reach BUS FARM by 7.45 pm

(c) The 2/Kings Own Regt & Remainder of 1st Line transport of 1/K.O.Y.L.I. 2/East Yorkshire 1/York & Lancaster Rgt will march in that order, starting point the junction of the ZWADENMOLEN— BAILLEUL & LOCRE— BAILLEUL Roads at 2.30 pm.— The whole under the orders of O.C. 2/Kings Own Rgt.—

Route HAEGEDOORNE to DANOUTRE.—

The Baggage wagons may join the Rear of this Column at the farm N of the 2nd E in HAEGEDOORNE if required, by arrangement between C.O's and O.C 2o2 Coy A.S.C.—

VI O.C's 2/East Yorkshire Rgt. 1/York & Lancaster Rgt & 1/K.O.Y.L.I will reach their prospective head quarters one hour before their Battalions.—

VII The 15th Field Ambulance take over wounded at Battalion Dressing Stations.—

VIII Troops in fire & support trenches will stand to arms between 5.15 am & 6.15 am during the Ensuing tour of trench duty.—

IX G.O.C. 83rd Brigade assumes command at DRANOUTRE at 5 pm to-morrow.

H.Q. at DRANOUTRE.—

(Signed) L.P. Mundy Captain
Brigade Major 83rd Brigade.

Copy No 2	2/Kings own Rgt.	9. Divl. H.Q.
3	2. East Yorkshire	10 Brigadier
4	1/K.O.Y.L.I.	11 84 Bde
5	1/York & Lancaster	12 5/Kings Own Regt
6	1/3 Monmouth Rgt	
7	1/1	
8	9 Q.V. Rifles	

True Copy [signature] Capt.

APPENDIX No 5

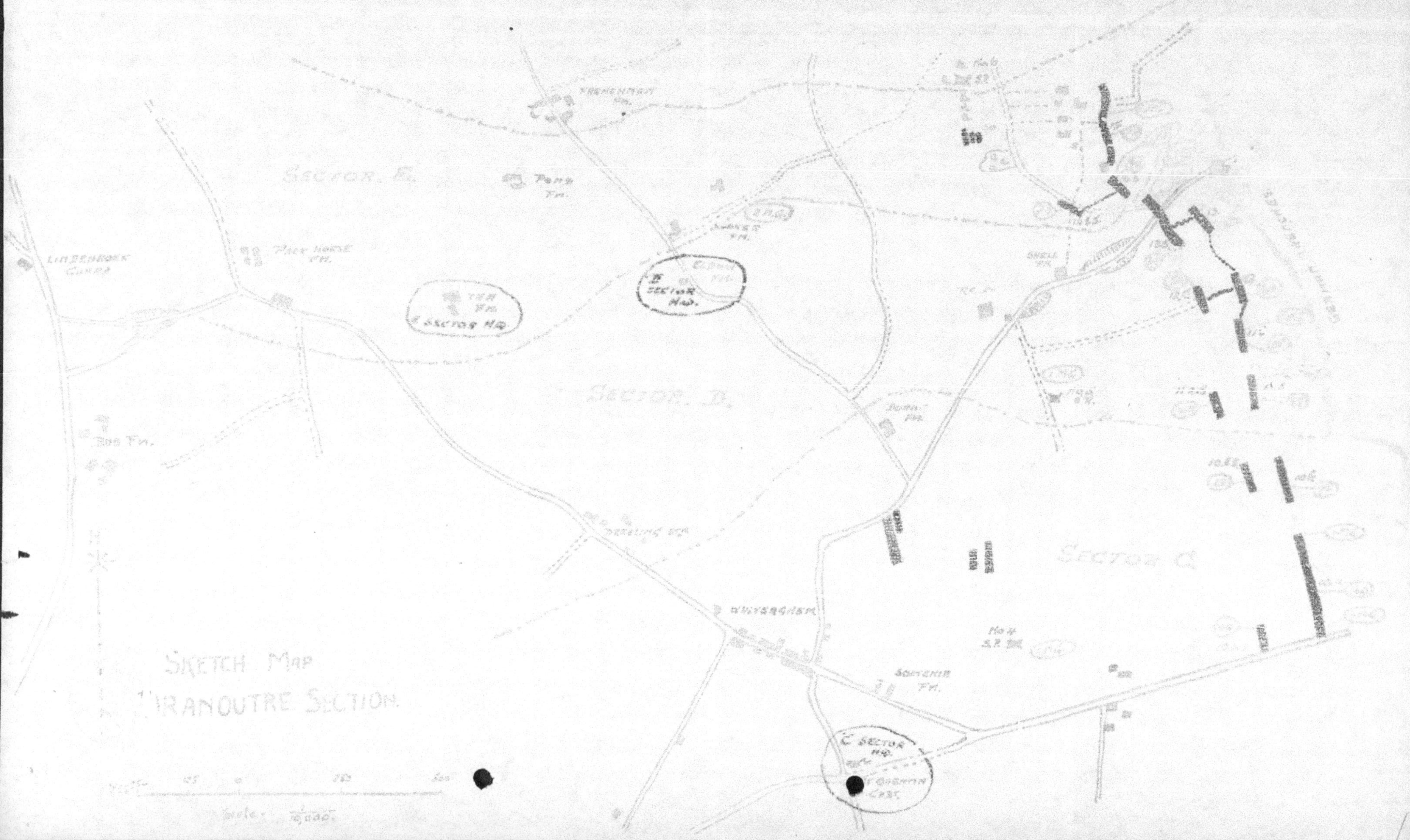

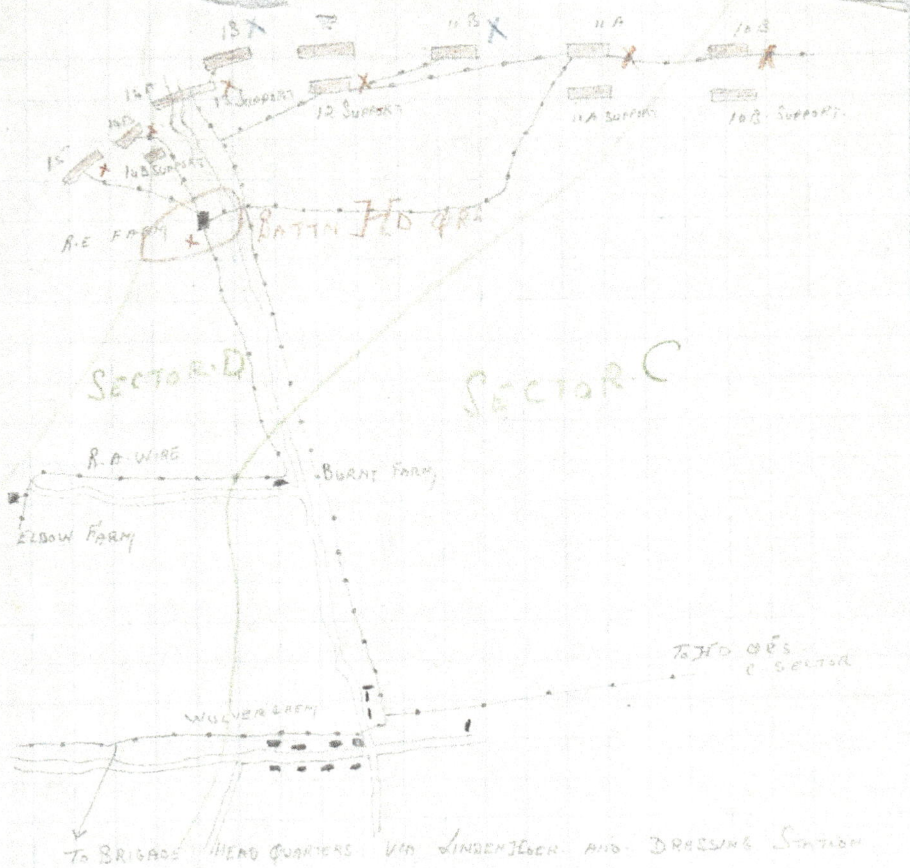

SKETCH NOT TO SCALE.
TO SHOW TELEPHONE COMMUNICATION
IN SECTOR D

X Denotes phonic instrument
X " Sounder "

Bamford. Captain
Adjutant 1/5th Lancaster Rgt.
18-3-15

APPENDIX 206

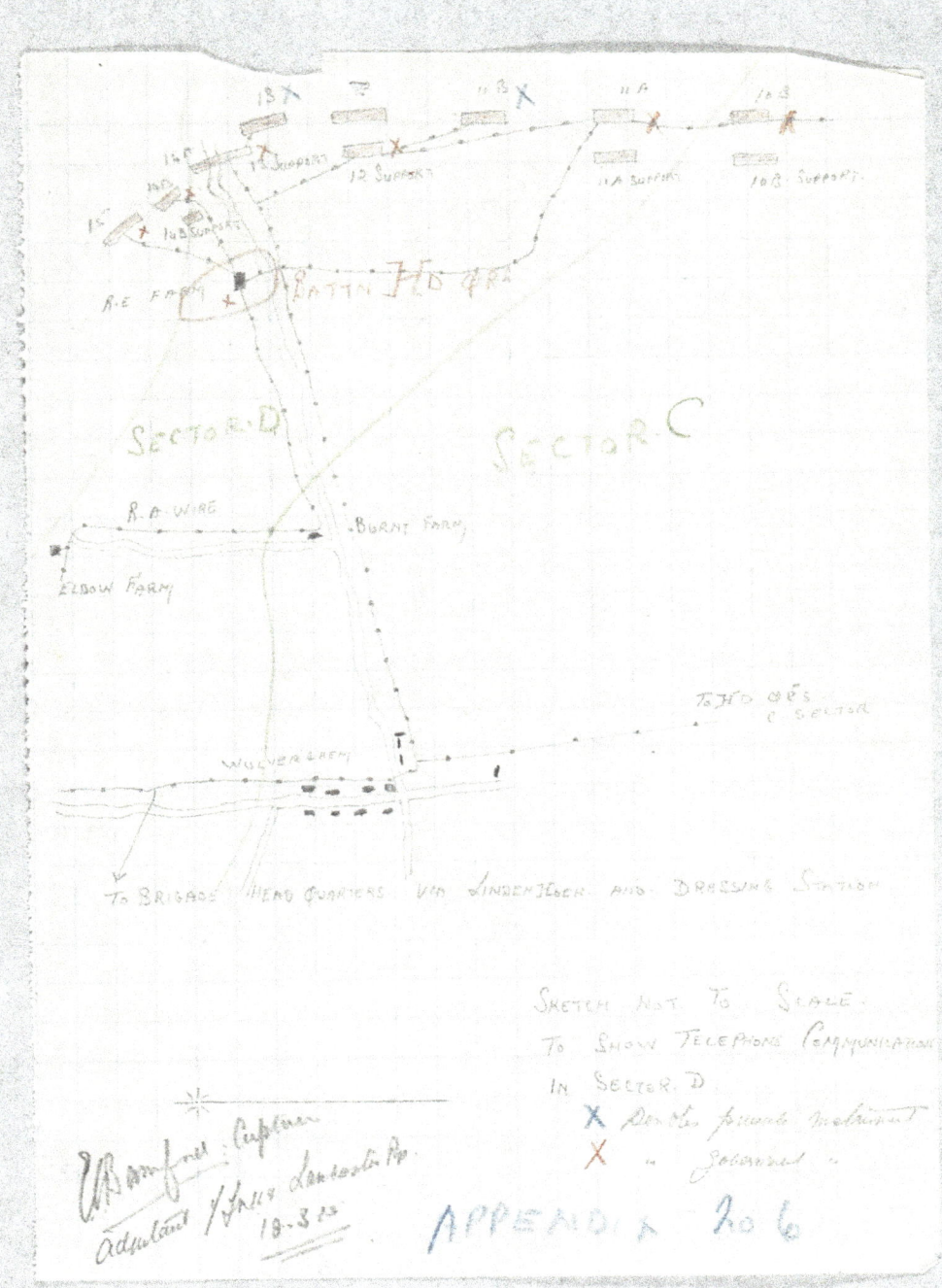

83rd Bde Dispositions Night 11/12 Issued with operation order Copy No 5

Unit taking over	Unit to be Relieved	Sector & Commander	Guides for trenches	to be at Place	Time
1/1 Monmouth Regt	9th Q.V. Rifles	Sector C OC 1/Mon Rgt	10A & B and Supports in SP4	Relief already taken place	
1 M.G. 2nd Kings Own	1 M.G. Q.V.R.				
1 KOYLI & 1 Coy 5/Kings Own	1/York & Lancaster & ½ Coy 1/3 Mon Regt	Sector D OC KOYLI	All trenches	R.E. FARM.	7.30 pm
			ELBOW FRM	DRESSING STN	7.15 pm
1 M.G. Detachment 2/E Yorks	Already in position		14A		
1 M.G. detachment 2nd E Yorks	Nil		RE FARM	to be arranged with O.C. York & Lancaster	
2nd Kings Own less 1 Machine Gun	2/East Lancashire	Sector E OC 2/Kings Own	14B, 14B Supp	WULVERGHEM	8 pm
			for Rest of Bn	TEA FARM.	6.30 pm

True Copy [illegible]

Signed J. E. Munby Capt
BM. 83rd Bde

APPENDIX No 7

OPERATION ORDER 2019 By
Brig. Gen. R.C. Boyle CB Comdg.
83rd Inf. Bde

Copy 2013

Ref. Sketch map of
DANOUTRE SECTION
and Map Belgium & France Sheet 28

DANOUTRE
10.3.15

I Relief will be carried out tomorrow as per attached Table.

II After Relief the 2nd East Lancashire Regt will occupy the Billets vacated by the 2nd Kings Own Regt and the 1/York & Lancaster Regt those of the K.O.Y.L.I. The 2nd Kings Own and the 1/K.O.Y.L.I. will provide guides (one per Company) to be at TEA FARM and DRESSING Stn respectively to conduct Companys to these Billets & will leave Representatives to hand these Billets over. —

III The 9th R.L. Rifles will march tomorrow 11th inst. at 2pm via BAILLEUL to occupy the billets vacated by the 5th Kings Own Regt & on arrival there will come under orders of 84th Bde. —

IV The 5th Kings Own Regt, less 2 Coys will march at 2.30pm to DANOUTRE via Road through second O in MEULEHOEK & just E of HAEGEDOORNE. —

Signed J. P. Brunby Capt
Bm. 83rd Bde.

True Copy J.H. Bamford Capt.
Adjt 1/York & Lancaster Regt.

APPENDIX No 8

OPERATION ORDER No 20.

By Brigadier General R.C. Boyle CB

Commander 83rd Infantry Brigade

DRANOUTRE.
23 15.

Reference Sketch Map of
DRANOUTRE Section

1 The third Division have orders to carry by assault the trenches opposite their Right flank, that Division will be supported by 2 Battalions 84th Brigade, whose orders are to assault the Mound & trenches opposite No 15.—

2 Consequently the following alterations will be made to the table of dispositions issued with operation order No 19.—

14 S Support Trench }
Dugouts in Rear of 15 } Are to be left vacant for use of
R.E. FARM } 84th Brigade.—

BURNT FARM to be Evacuated at once by the 1/1 Monmouth Regt & to be available for use of O.C. D Sector.—

3 Two Battalions 84th Brigade are expected to pass through DRANOUTRE at midnight & will be posted in the new dugouts near SHELL FARM & in all dugouts in Rear of 14 S & 15 trenches & in 14 S Support trench.—

4 A party of 240 men of the King's Own Lancaster Regt as already detailed will continue work (already in hand) on the new dugouts near SHELL FARM until arrival of 84th Brigade, & will reach BUS FARM by daylight.—

5 One Company 1/3rd Monmouth Regt as already detailed will reach WULVERGHEM by 8pm to night marching and returning by NEUVE EGLISE this Coy will be under orders of O.C. 59 Coy R.E.— It must return to its billets on completion of its work & be clear of NEUVE EGLISE by daylight.—

6. O.C. E Sector will at once commence the following work.—

A. Deepening Communication trench in rear of 15 trench to depth of 5 feet.

B. Deepening to 5 ft. the connecting trench between 15 trench & the Right hand fire trench of 5th Division (known as trench 16) or cutting new trench if required.

C. Commence sap from bottom end of 15 trench towards enemy's trenches.

7. The Company of K.O.Y.L.I. in BURNT FARM will be under the orders of the O.C. 59 Coy R.E. from 8 pm to-day, & under his orders will provide the working party to assist the 84th Brigade after the assault. O.C. 59 Coy R.E. will arrange for this Company to relieve the troops in para 6 if they can be spared for that work.—

Signed J. J. Mundy Captain
Brigade Major 83rd Brigade

True Copy.
C. J. Bamford Captain
Adjutant 2/ King's Own Lancaster R.

APPENDIX No 9.

Copy No 5

OPERATION ORDER No 21 By
Brigadier General R.C. BOYLE C.B. Commanding
83rd Infantry Brigade.

DRANOUTRE.
16.3.15

Reference. Sheet 28.
& Sketch DRANOUTRE Section

1. Reliefs will be carried out to-morrow as per attached table.— No troops will move East of LINDENHOEK – NEUVE EGLISE Road before 6.30pm — Guides to be furnished as 2 per trench & 2 per Machine Gun.—

2. The 2/ Kings Own Regiment will maintain a Machine Gun and detachment in S.P.4 & the 1st K.O.Y.L.I. will maintain a Machine Gun and detachment in R.E. FARM.

3. The drafts of the 2nd East Yorkshire & 1st York & Lancaster Regiment will accompany their Battalions.—

4. The 2nd East Yorkshire Regt will march by HAEGEDOORNE to DRANOUTRE so as to clear the Road junction in S 9A by 3 pm.— The 5th Kings Own Regt (less 2 Coys) will march by MEULEHOEK to the [illegible] & will not reach the Road junction in S.9.A before 3 pm.— Both these Battalions will halt for teas in their old billets.—

5. The Coy 2nd Kings Own Regt attached to 1/K.O.Y.L.I will rejoin its Battn in sector "C" as soon as relieved and will rendezvous at BURNT FARM.— The Coy 5th Kings Own Regt attached to 2nd Kings Own will be billeted in DRANOUTRE.—

6. After being relieved the 2nd Kings Own and 1st K.O.Y.L.I will be accomodated in their old billets in DRANOUTRE & BUS FARM respectively.— The 3rd Monmouth Regiment will be billeted in the huts on the DRANOUTRE– HAEGENDOORNE Road.—

7. The farm about 150x S.E of PACK HORSE FARM on the LINDENHOEK GUARD — WULVERGHEM Road will be known in future as C.B. FARM.— This farm is in the area occupied by the BUS FARM Battalion.—

8. The telephone operators at present in C.B. will rejoin their Battalion, & be relieved by the incoming unit — O.C. 3rd Monmouth will leave operators to cover the remainder of the sector.

9. The 3rd Monmouth Regiment will detail a fatigue party of 50 men to report to O.C. 2nd (H.C.) Field Coy R.E at 7.30 pm tomorrow at WULVERGHEM Church.

(Signed) J.P. [illegible] Captain
Brigade Major 83rd Brigade

True Copy [illegible] Capt
Adjt 1/ York & Lancaster Regt

Issued with Operation Order No. 21 Copy No. 5.

Unit taking over	Unit to be relieved	Trenches or farms to be occupied	Leading Company and Snipers to arrive at: Place	Time
Headquarters & 3 Coys 5/King's Own Regt with 2 M. Guns (4.10 am)	3/Monmouth Regt.	10A – 10B. S.P. 4 – Dejardins Farm Souvenir Farm	Wolverghem Church	9 pm
1/4th Lancaster Regt with 4 M. Guns	3 Monmouth Regt, K.O.Y.L.I. & 1 Coy 5/King's Own Regt, 1 M.G. 2/East Yorkshire, 2/King's Own Regt. –	10B & 10 B.S; 11A & 13 & 13 S, R.E. Farm, Elbow Farm, Dressing Station, Pack Horse Farm	Wolverghem Church; Dressing Station	8 pm; 7.45 pm
2/East Yorkshire Regt with 3 M. Guns	1/K.O.Y.L.I.; 2/King's Own Regt.; 1 Coy 5/King's Own Regt.	14 A, 14 B. 14 B.S; 15, 15 S, Cooker Farm, Tea Farm	R.E. Farm; Tea Farm	7.45 pm; 7 pm

True Copy. C. H. Bampfield Capt.
Adjt. 1/4th Lancaster Regt.

Signed J. S. Mansby Captain
Brigade Major 83rd Brigade

OPERATION ORDER No 3 By
Lieut. Colonel A. J. Burt Commanding
1st Sussex Lancashire Regt

BUS FARM
17.3.15

Appendix No 1b

1. The Battalion is ordered for duty in the trenches and will take over trenches to night as follows —

A COMPANY

10 B & 10 B Support from 3rd Monmouth Regt
This party will arrive at WULVERGHEM CHURCH at 8 pm —
11 A 11 A Support 11 B from K.O.Y.L.I
This party will arrive at the DRESSING STATION at 7.45 pm —

B COMPANY

12. 12 Support 13, 13 Support from K.O.Y.L.I or 5th Kings Own Regt —
This party will arrive at DRESSING STATION at 7.45 pm

C COMPANY

DRESSING STATION

To arrive at DRESSING STATION at 8pm. —

D COMPANY

1 officer 55 men in Trenches & Support point
Remainder of Company at R.E. FARM.

MACHINE GUNS

Machine Guns will be distributed as follows. — One in 11 A
" " 11 B
" " 13
1 at " 5 Support

they will arrive at the DRESSING STATION at 7 45 pm —

2. Immediately Trenches have been taken over trench Commanders will Report by telephone or orderly to the Adjutant that they have taken over. —

3. Reports & Returns

12 Noon daily
Return of Casualties incurred during previous 24 hours. —

3 am

Return of work done during previous 24 hours 12 Midnight to 12 Midnight. — This Return must also show —

a Numbers in each trench.

B Any place where Sapping has been carried out.

C Improvement of fire support and communication trenches —

D If any bombs or Rifle Grenades have been used if so with what results —

E All information as to the Enemy's action movements Artillery fire Sniping etc during previous 24 hours —

F Patrols sent out etc. —

G If wire along the front is satisfactory —

H List of stores etc Required to be sent up during following night —

5 pm

By telephone short summary of work done during the day also any ~~[struck out]~~ movements etc on the part of the enemy effects of our own or enemy's artillery fire & what they have been observed during the day —

P. F. Bamford Captain

Adjutant 1/5th K.O.R. Lancaster Re.

By orderly at 11 am.

The Garrisons of trenches etc are as follows

TRENCH	NUMBERS
10 B	90
10 B Support	35
11 A	35
11 A Support	25
11 B	35
12	60
12 Support	75
13	50
13 Support	80
R.E. FARM	1 Co [illegible] 55 [illegible]
DRESSING STN	1 Company
No 5 Support point	55

P.L. Bamford. Capt

Adjt / [illegible] Lancashire Regt

Issued with Operation orders No 3.

APPENDIX No 11

To. The Officer Commanding
Company
1/South Lancashire Regt.

19.3.15

Reliefs to night will be as follows.—

I C Company will Relieve A Company in trenches No 10B, 10 B Support 11 A, 11 support and 11B.—
Relief to Commence at 11.30 pm or later if trench stores Etc have not been carried up from the DRESSING STATION by C Coy.—
After Relief A Company will move to DRESSING STATION.

II D Coy will Relieve B Coy in trenches No 12, 12 Support, 13 & 13 Support, Relief to Commence at 11 pm.—
After Relief ~~the~~ B Coy will occupy
No 5 Support point 55 men.
R.E. FARM Remainder of Company.—

C.L. Bamford Captain
Adjt. 1/South Lancashire Regt.

APPENDIX No 12

OPERATION ORDER No 22 By
Brigadier General R.C. BOYLE C.B.
Commanding 83rd Infantry Brigade

Copy No 5

20th March 1915.

Reference Map 28
and Sketch DRANOUTRE Section

1/ From to-morrow onwards the Brigade will hold the line from 8 to 14 B, both trenches inclusive. —
Troops in trenches will be disposed of as per attached table. —

2/ Garrisons for the several trenches will reach the Guides Rendezvous at 10 minutes interval. —
Care will be taken that there is no delay at this Rendezvous. —
Guides detailed to be at R.E. FARM will wait at the gate of that farm for the parties whom they are to conduct. —

3 The Billeting area for the Brigade will be NEUVE EGLISE
Brigade headquarters at WESTHOF FARM. (T.19.A) after 9pm.

4/ To-morrow night Rations &c will be conveyed by ~~transport~~ as usual to TEA FARM for the East Yorkshire Regt, and to DRESSING STN for the York & Lancaster Regt & may be expected there by 7pm. —

5 One Company 5th Kings Own Regt will be billeted in NEUVE EGLISE to-morrow night. — No other troops in this area till the next Relief. —
The 3rd Monmouth Regiment will march not later than 8pm to their old billets in RAVETSBURG. —

(Signed) J.P. Murphy Captain
Brigade Major 83rd Brigade

Copy No 2 2/ Kings Own
" " 3 2/ East Yorkshire
" " 4 1/ K.O.Y.L.I.
" " 5 1/ York & Lancaster
" " 6 5/ Kings Own
" " 7 3/ Monmouth R.
" " 8 5/ Division

True Copy. [signature] Capt
Adjt 1/York & Lancaster R.

Issued with Operation Order No 82 Copy No 5

UNIT TAKING OVER.	UNIT TO BE RELIEVED	TRENCHES OR FARMS TO BE OCCUPIED	Guides (two per trench or farm) to be at — PLACE	TIME
5/King's Own Regt	14th Brigade	S. 9 2/3 of 10A (Garrison 200 men) 10 A Support S.P. 4 Souvenir Farm Brigade Hqrs S.P. 4	No 9 trench	9.30 pm
2/East Yorkshire Rgt	5/King's Own Regt	A Quenten Cabaret 1/3 of 10A (Garrison 100 men)	Wulverghem Church	10 pm
	1/York & Lancaster R.	10 B to 11 B both inclusive	R.E. Farm	9 pm
	" " "	Burnt Farm Dressing Stn Elbow Farm		
" " " 1 M. Gun " " " 1 M. Gun	" " "	11 B } 11 A }	R.E. Farm	9 pm
1/York & Lancaster Re.	2/East Yorkshire Rgt	14A. 14B. 14 B Support	R.E. Farm	10 pm
	" " "	Tea Farm		
	5/King's Own	Pack Horse Farm. Brigade T.5.B		
" " " 1 M.G.	2/East Yorkshire R	in 14 A	RE Farm	10 pm
" " " 1 M.G.	1/K.O.Y.L.I.	R.E. Farm		

True Copy. [signature] Capt. York & Lancaster R.

Signed P.? Capt. Brigade Major 83rd Bde.

APPENDIX 13

OPERATION ORDER. No 23 By
Brigadier General R.C. Boyle CB
Commanding 83rd Infantry Brigade

COPY No 5

DRANOUTRE.
22nd March 1915.

Reference Sheet 28 & Situation
Map DRANOUTRE Section

I Reliefs will be carried out tomorrow as per attached table. An interval of 10 minutes must be allowed between Companies moving E of the LINDENHOEK Ridge or NEUVE EGLISE.—

II The 2nd Kings Own Regt will not move E of the LINDENHOEK Ridge before 6.30 pm.—

The 1st K.O.Y.L.I. will march by CROIX DE POPERINGUE & DRANOUTRE so as not to reach the BAILLEUL–LOCRE Road before 4.30 pm or DRANOUTRE before 5.30 pm.— They will halt for tea if desired at BLUE FARM but must leave the LINDENHOEK–NEUVE EGLISE Road clear for traffic between 7.15 pm & 7.45 pm.—
Not to be East of TEA FARM before 8 pm

The 3rd Monmouth Regt will march by NEUVE EGLISE halting for teas (if desired) immediately South of that place on the TROIS ROIS Road. Leading Company not to move East of NEUVE EGLISE before 8.30 pm.—

III The transport of the 2nd Kings Own Regt & 1st K.O.Y.L.I will be billeted from tomorrow night in NEUVE EGLISE that portion not required to accompany the troops towards the trenches will leave DRANOUTRE at 6 pm & will keep clear of the roads until that time.—

IV. After Relief the—
2/3rd East Yorkshire Regt will occupy No 2 HUTMENTS at NEUVE EGLISE
1st York & Lancaster R " " No 1 " " "
5th Kings Own will be billeted in RAVETSBERG Area & the Company (less one platoon) of 5th Kings Own Regt now in NEUVE EGLISE will move thither so as to be clear of NEUVE EGLISE by 8.30 pm.—

V The platoon 5th Kings Own Regiment on guard on Road junction T10a will be relieved by 3rd Monmouth Regt at 9.30 pm.—

VI Trench 7 is held by the Royal Warwickshire Regiment with headquarters at LA PLUS DOUCE farm.—
Trench 15 is held by the 5th Fusiliers with headquarters at LINDENHOEK CHALET

VII Batteries are permanently in support of sections as under.—

Right Section	119th	Centre Section	52nd
Left "	80th		

VIII The R.A.M.C will take over wounded from the Centre & left sections at DRESSING ~~Station~~ FARM which will be the dressing station for both these sections

(Signed) [illegible] Captain
Brigade Major 83rd Infantry Bde

True Copy [signature] Capt.
[illegible] Lancaster R

Issue with Operation Order 13 Copy No 5

UNIT TAKING OVER.	UNIT TO BE RELIEVED	TRENCHES OR FARM TO BE OCCUPIED	GUIDES (TWO PER TRENCH OR MACHINE GUN) TO BE AT: PLACE	TIME
RIGHT SECTION				
3/Monmouth Rgt.	5/Kings Own Rgt.	8, 9 & 8 & 9 support	10 A.	
		½ 10 A	Nil	
		10 A Support.	"	
		S.P 4	"	9.30 pm
		X Rgt (near S.P.4)	"	
		SOUVENIR FARM	"	
		ST QUENTIN CABARET.	"	
		WATERMILL FARM	"	
			"	
CENTRE SECTION				
2/Kings Own Rgt.	2/East Yorkshire Rgt.	½ 10 A to 11 A both inclusive	WULVERGHEM CHURCH	7 pm.
	1/York & Lancaster Rgt	S.P.5.	"	"
	2/East Yorkshire	BURNT FARM		
		DRESSING FARM	"	"
		ELBOW FARM	Nil	Nil
		BUS FARM & farm buildings known as Bus Farm.	WULVERGHEM CHURCH	7 pm
" " 1 M. Gun	2/East Yorkshire	11 A	Nil	Nil
" " 1 M. Gun	1/York & Lancaster	S.P. 5	Nil	Nil

Issued with operation order No. [illegible]

UNIT TAKING OVER. LEFT SECTION.	UNIT TO BE RELIEVED.	TRENCHES OR FARMS TO BE OCCUPIED	GUIDES (2 per trench & Machine Gun) to be at PLACE	TIME
1/ K.O.Y.L.I	2/ East Yorkshire Regt	11 B	Nil	Nil
	1/ York & Lancaster Rr	12 to 14 B both inclusive	"	"
	" " "	R.E. FARM.	"	"
	" " "	TEA FARM	BUS FARM	7.45 pm
	" " "	PACK. HORSE FARM.	Nil	Nil
	2/ Kings Own Regt.	COB FARM	"	"
	" " "	LINDENHOEK GUARD & adjoining Linen	"	"
" " 1 M. Gun	1/ York & Lancaster Rr	14 A	"	"
" 1 M. Gun	2/ East Yorkshire.	11 B	"	"
" 1 M. Gun	1/ York & Lancaster	R.E. FARM	"	"

1st Bn York & Lancaster Regt APPENDIX 14

Roll of officers present on 31st March 1915

Rank & Name			Appointment	Remarks
Lieut Col.	Burt	A.G.	In command	
Major	Gresson, DSO	T.T.	Senior Major	
-"-	Colston	H.K.		
Capt	Wedgwood	G.H.		
"	Palmer	A.E.		
"	East	H.J.		
"	Collins	P.H.E.		
"	Bamford	E.S.	Adjutant	Aa
"	Walker	K.P.	Transport officer	
Lieut	Gauntlett	H.G.		
-"-	Rousada	B.C.	M Gun officer	
-"-	Lethbridge	N.B.		
-"-	Kent-Lemon	A.L.		
-"-	Chamier	C.K.		
-"-	Cowley	R.B.		Special Reserve
Hon. Lt.	Gilliard	W.T.	Quartermaster	
2/Lieut.	Howard	H.C.M.		
"	Brickwood	A.C.		
"	Battle	E.E.		
"	Connors	D.		
"	Gibbs	H.W.		
"	Briscoe	F.J.		Special Reserve
"	Bedford	H.S.		-do-
"	Webster	S.		-do-
"	Parry	N.C.		-do-
"	Boyd	J.W.B.		-do-
	Attached			
Lieut	Geo	A.J.	R.A.M.C.	

E. Bamford Captain
Adjutant, 1st York & Lancaster Regt

1.

APPENDIX No 15

OPERATION ORDER No 24 By Copy No 5
BRIGADIER-GENERAL R.C. BOYLE C.B
Commanding 83rd Brigade

Reference Sheet 28
and diagram of trenches

WESTHOF FARM.
28th March 1915

1. The following Reliefs will take place tomorrow
2nd East Yorkshire Reg will take over centre section from the 2nd Kings Own Regt —
1st Kings Lancaster Regiment will take over left section ~~from~~ (11B from 2nd Kings Own Regt) Remainder from 1st K.O.Y.L.I)

2. Intervals of a Quarter of an hour to be allowed between Companies Marching on the same Road E or N of NEUVE EGLISE —

3. 1st King's Lancaster Regiment will march so that the leading troops pass NEUVE EGLISE at 7pm — troops for TEA FARM or near thereof and wheel transport march by BUS FARM remainder direct to WULVERGHEM. —

4. The 2nd East Yorkshire Regiment will march, wheel transport by BUS FARM, troops by any Route desired, leading Company not to pass NEUVE EGLISE before 7.45pm. —

4 The 1st K.O.Y.L.I. will occupy ALDERSHOT Camp and the 2nd Kings Own Regiment BULFORD Camp after being Relieved. –

(Signed) J. P. [illegible] Captain

Brigade Major 83rd Infantry Brigade.

By orderly at 4.45 pm

True Copy P. [illegible] Bamford Captain

Adjutant 1/ [illegible] Lancaster Regt

APPENDIX No 16

App 20

Operation Order No. 4 By
Lt Colonel A.J. Best Commanding
1st Battn York & Lancaster Rgt.

HUTMENTS
NEUVE EGLISE.
Apl. 3.15

1. The Battalion is warned for duty in the trenches & will take over the left section of the defence to night.—

2. Companies will take over trenches as follows —

11B 12 12 Support	B. Company
13 13 Support 14 A 14 B 14 B Support	C Company
R.E FARM Dugouts near Swell FARM	A Company

TEA FARM
LINDENHOEK GUARD } B Company.

3. The Battalion will march by Companies as follows

"C" Company to pass "NEUVE EGLISE" Church at 7 pm & will march by the NEUVE EGLISE — WULVERGHEM Road. —

"D" Company to pass NEUVE EGLISE Church at 7.15 pm & will march by the NEUVE EGLISE — WULVERGHEM Road. —

"B" Company will pass NEUVE EGLISE at 7.10 pm & will march by the BUS FARM Road —
All Wheel transport will march by the BUS FARM Road. —

A Company to pass NEUVE EGLISE Church at 7.30 pm & will march by the NEUVE EGLISE - WULVERGHEM Road. —

The Machine Gun Section will move by the BUS FARM ROAD to BURNT FARM.
Men of the detachment will march with "A" Coy —

4. Reports & Returns will be sent in as follows. —

12 noon daily (by telephone)

Statement of Casualties occurred during previous 24 hours —

5 pm daily (By telephone)

All Information Regarding Movements or action of the Enemy, effect of the own or Enemy's artillery fire, if all quiet or otherwise —

8 AM. By orderly

A written Report showing the following —

(A) Work done during previous 24 hours

(B) Numbers in each trench or farm

(C) Any improvement to fire support or Communication trenches. —

(D) If Hand or Rifle grenades have been used if so with what Result. —

(E) All information on the Enemy's actions movements artillery fire sniping etc during previous 24 hours. —

(F) List of trench stores Ammunition etc Required +

(If Ammunition is Required it can be sent up any time during the night)

(G) If any patrols have been sent out & with what Result —

NB The above Report must be at

Battn Headquarters by 3am at the latest & should be sent in as soon after 12 midnight as possible.—

5

Battalion Headquarters will be at R.E. FARM. Where Reports should be sent —

E H Bamford. Captain

Adjutant 1st North Lancashire Regt.

The numbers given below are the minimum garrisons which must be maintained. —

TRENCH	NUMBERS
11 B	40
12	60
12 Support	50
13	60
13 Support } 14 A }	60
14 B	25
14 B Support	25

R.E FARM will take 200
TEA FARM " " 120.

C.W. Bamford Captain
Actg. [illegible] Lancashire [illegible]

Issued with operation order No 4

83/28

1/ York & Lancs.

April

1915

20th Infantry Brigade No 20/BM/362

Subject: Re 6th Gordon Highlanders

Action taken	BA or BF	Date
To 4th Division		30/12/15

Vol IV

Page 1

Instructions regarding War Diaries and Intelligence Summaries are contained in F. S. Regs., Part II. and the Staff Manual respectively. Title pages will be prepared in manuscript.

Army Form C. 2118.

WAR DIARY ~~or~~ ~~INTELLIGENCE~~ SUMMARY of 1st York & Lancaster Rgt.

(Erase heading not required.)

Hour, Date, Place	Summary of Events and Information	Remarks and references to Appendices
7am 1/4/15 R.E. FARM	Situation generally quiet. No movement or action of the enemy observed. Patrols sent out have nothing to report. The bright moon renders patrol work very difficult AAA Work done 11B New communication trench practically completed. Extension of parapet to 11A work continued & new bay started last night. Traverse on right completed. 12 Extension of parapet to connect with 13 communication trench completed AAA 13 to R.E. FARM completed about 50x now dug of communication trench 13S to R.E. FARM 13S New ammunition shelter dug – 14 Improvement of parapet right side very much strengthened. Dugout constructed in parados. Communication trench 14 to 14 Support parapet ~~strengthened~~ AAA A lot of repairs carried out.	Report to 83rd Brigade 7 am.— for sketch see appendix No1.
12 noon 1.4.15 R.E. FARM	Casualties during previous twenty four hours Nil.—	
6pm 1.4.15 R.E. FARM	No movement or action of the enemy observed during the day AAA No patrols have been sent out during the day AAA Our artillery and enemy's have at times been fairly active AAA Enemy shelled 11A & B at 4pm all shells were close one hitting parapet of 11A direction from which shells were coming 15 degrees N of E taken from left of 11B. 80th Battery R.F.A. informed. Shells were common shell AAA Enemy also shelled 14 support but went over AAA Our artillery fire fairly ~~[illegible]~~ accurate on enemy's trench opposite 11A. Some shells were also seen fall in MESSINES AAA At 3pm an air ship of sorts was seen in the distance going N bearing from right of 14 trench 100°	Report to 83rd Brigade at 6 pm.—
6.45 pm 1.4.15 R.E. FARM	Guides left to bring up 5th N STAFFORDS.—	See appendix No. 2. and 3

1247 W 3299/200,000 (E) 8/14 J.B.C. & A. Forms/C. 2118/11.

Instructions regarding War Diaries and Intelligence Summaries are contained in F. S. Regs., Part II. and the Staff Manual respectively. Title pages will be prepared in manuscript.

WAR DIARY or ~~INTELLIGENCE~~ SUMMARY of 1st York & Lancaster Regt

Army Form C. 2118.

(Erase heading not required.)

Vol IV Page 2.

Hour, Date, Place	Summary of Events and Information	Remarks and references to Appendices
8.50pm to 9.50pm 1.4.15 RE FARM	Relief by 5th North Staffordshire and East Yorkshire took place. Battalion marched by Companies to BAILLEUL via NEUVE EGLISE.— C.H.B. Capt	See appendices 2 & 3.
2am 2.4.15 BAILLEUL	Report sent to 83rd Brigade that Battn is billeted in BAILLEUL. C.H.B. Capt	
3pm 3.4.15 BAILLEUL	Battalion left BAILLEUL and marched to WESTOUTRE via Croix de Poperinghe	See appendix No 4
6.30pm 3.4.15 WESTOUTRE	83rd Brigade informed Battalion is billeted in farms N of WESTOUTRE. C.H.B. Capt	" " " 5.
1.30am 4.4.15 WESTOUTRE	the Battalion marched to WESTOUTRE for Church parade, after the Service the Brigadier read a complimentary letter from Sir Charles Fergusson Commanding, congratulating the Brigade on the good work done since it had been with the Vth Division.—	
6.4.15 YPRES	Captains Wedgwood Palmer, Post, Collier, Bamford & Lieut Savage saw the trenches occupied by the 146th (3rd Battn) (French) Regiment to the trenches occupied by them.— & spent 24 hours with them.— C.H.B. Capt	
11am 7.4.15 WESTOUTRE	The 83rd Brigade was inspected by Sir Horace Smith-Dorrien Commanding. — C.H.B. Capt	
6.15pm 8.4.15 WESTOUTRE YPRES	The Battn left WESTOUTRE for YPRES arriving there at 8pm. to take over trenches from the 3rd Battalion 146th Regiment (French).—	See appendix No 6 " " 7

1247 W 3299 200,000 (E) 8/14 J.B.C. & A. Forms/C. 2118/11.

Vol IV Page 3

Instructions regarding War Diaries and Intelligence Summaries are contained in F. S. Regs., Part II. and the Staff Manual respectively. Title pages will be prepared in manuscript.

WAR DIARY
or
INTELLIGENCE SUMMARY
(Erase heading not required.)

Army Form C. 2118.

Hour, Date, Place	Summary of Events and Information	Remarks and references to Appendices
9 pm 8.4.15 YPRES	The Battalion left YPRES via the PONT DE MENIN and marched via POTIJZE to FREZENBERG where guides were met belonging to 3rd Battn 146th Regiment (French) – Companies were led to trenches as follows A. B. D. C. – Trenches were occupied as follows: A Company Right; B " Centre (1 Machine Gun); C " Left (1 Machine Gun); D " Support; 2 Machine Guns to Support. The trenches can not be called good in few places is the parapet bullet proof, the communication trenches being especially bad – the distance from the enemy was from 10 x to 100 x – the left trench is especially bad being enfiladed from both sides also the Rear – the traverses are very poor in fact very little repairs had been done for a considerable time. –	See appendix No 48.
3 am 9.4.15 Near ZONNEBEKE	Relief completed (O.C. 3rd Batt 146th Regt left. Batt. H.Qrs) The Relief passed off quietly 2 men were slightly wounded going in to the trenches. –	
7 am 9.4.15 Near ZONNEBEKE	Report to Brigade 'Situation quiet Nothing to Report –	
	The Germans threw a message attached to a stone into our left trench	See appendix No 1

Vol [illegible] page 4.

Instructions regarding War Diaries and Intelligence Summaries are contained in F. S. Regs., Part II. and the Staff Manual respectively. Title pages will be prepared in manuscript.

WAR DIARY
or
INTELLIGENCE SUMMARY

Army Form C. 2118.

(Erase heading not required.) 1st Battn York & Lancaster Regt.

Hour, Date, Place	Summary of Events and Information	Remarks and references to Appendices
12 Noon 9.4.15 Trenches near ZONNEBEKE	Casualties during last 24 hours were Killed 3 Wounded 3 (other Ranks). —	
6 p.m. 9.4.15 Trenches near ZONNEBEKE	Report to 83rd Brigade Situation generally quiet. No movement of Enemy observed AAA Enemy Artillery shelled left trench between 4.45 pm and 5.10 pm, also used trench mortar on left trench at 11 am. Our artillery were informed AAA Our artillery fired on Enemy trenches in front of my left trench very accurately & put a stop to the Enemy's fire. — The numbers in trenches are as follows. — Left 210 Centre 213 Right 210 Supports 202 Machine guns 40.	(These were supplied by French artillery.) —
[illegible] 10.4.15 Trenches near ZONNEBEKE	During the night D Coy relieved C Coy.	see appendix No 1
5.30 a.m. 11.4.15 Trenches near ZONNEBEKE	Situation quiet nothing to report. At 1 pm the Enemy shelled our left trench with a trench mortar but did no damage, artillery were informed & they shelled the Enemy's trenches in front of left trench with great accuracy, making 2 breaches in the Enemy's parapet of about 25 yards. — After this the Enemy did not continue to use their mortar. —	(French Artillery)
12 Noon [illegible].4.15 Trenches near ZONNEBEKE	The casualties during the last 24 hours were other Ranks Killed 4 Wounded 7.	

1247 W 3299 200,000 (E) 8/14 J.B.C. & A. Forms/C. 2118/11.

Instructions regarding War Diaries and Intelligence Summaries are contained in F. S. Regs., Part II. and the Staff Manual respectively. Title pages will be prepared in manuscript.

Vol IV

Page 4.

WAR DIARY or INTELLIGENCE SUMMARY

(Erase heading not required.)

of 1st Yorks Lancaster Regt.

Army Form C. 2118.

Hour, Date, Place	Summary of Events and Information	Remarks and references to Appendices
12 pm 10.4.15. Trenches near ZONNEBEKE.	Report to 83rd Brigade. Situation quiet AAA. Our Artillery shelled enemy's trenches in front of my left trench with accuracy, French artillery officer reported result of each shot direct to Battery AAA. A sentry in left trench reported that several of the enemy ran to support trench when artillery began firing AAA Enemy's artillery fire unobserved. —	
6.30 pm 10.4.15 Trenches near ZONNEBEKE.	Report to Brigade. Situation quiet. No movement of the enemy observed AAA. Our artillery fired on enemy's trench in front of left trench with accuracy. Artillery officer reported result of each shot to Battery AAA. Enemy threw a few bombs into my right trench AAA At 4.45 pm a few shells fell near Battalion Headquarters. —	
5.30 am 11.4.15 Trenches near ZONNEBEKE.	Report to Brigade. Situation quiet. No movement of the enemy observed AAA At 11 pm enemy fired on my left trench with a Mortar. Artillery were informed AAA Artillery fired very accurately & knocked down about 20x of enemy parapet AAA at 5 am enemy again fired on my left trench with heavy Mortar. Within 3 minutes the artillery opened fire & enemy immediately ceased. —	
12 noon 11.4.15 Trenches near ZONNEBEKE. —	Situation quiet. No movement of the enemy observed. [Enemy's artillery set a house on fire about 2000x S.E. of my Battn Hd Qrs.] At 11.20 am Enemy continued to fire bombs at my left trench causing several casualties. At 1 pm they ceased firing when shelled by our artillery. — Casualties during last 24 hours were, other Ranks. Killed 6 wounded 12. —	

1247 W 3299 200,000 (E) 8/14 J.B.C. & A. Forms/C. 2118/11.

Vol IV Pages

Instructions regarding War Diaries and Intelligence Summaries are contained in F. S. Regs., Part II. and the Staff Manual respectively. Title pages will be prepared in manuscript.

WAR DIARY
or
~~INTELLIGENCE SUMMARY~~ OF 1st BATTN YORK & LANCASTER REGT

(Erase heading not required.)

Army Form C. 2118.

Hour, Date, Place	Summary of Events and Information	Remarks and references to Appendices
4 pm 11.4.15. ~~[illegible]~~ trenches near	Report to 83rd Brigade Situation Quiet Nothing to Report —	
11 pm 11.4.15. LONNEBEKE.	Report to 83rd Brigade All Quiet Nothing to Report – Enemy's Air Craft have been very active. —	
5 am 12.4.15. trenches near LONNEBEKE.	5 am. Report to Brigade. All Quiet Nothing to Report —	
	At 6 am. the O.C. Right trench (Captain Palmer) Reported that a working party in his trench had been considerably worried by Rifle fire & [illegible] to stop this he threw three hand grenades into the Enemy's trench, this was returned by about six from the Enemy. — he then threw about 11 hand grenades, after that all was quiet. —	
1 pm 12.4.15 trenches near LONNEBEKE	Nothing to Report to Brigade — Casualties during last 24 hours other Ranks Killed 1 Wounded 1. Lieut N.B. LETHBRIDGE was wounded in the head in the left trench the 2 N.C.O's belonging to the Royal Engineers were also wounded in the left trench. —	
9 pm		
4 pm	Nothing to Report to Brigade HQ	
11 pm	Nothing to Report to Brigade HQ. Handed over the line to 2nd Batt the King's Own (Royal Lancaster) Regt	For Reliefs see Appendices Nos 9 & 10. —
3 am. 13.4.15	And went into Billets in YPRES. — the last platoon arrived in at 6 am. —	
13.4.15	Captain [illegible] Reported his arrival from Royal Flying Corps. —	

1247 W 3299 200,000 (E) 8/14 J.B.C. & A. Forms/C. 2118/11.

Instructions regarding War Diaries and Intelligence Summaries are contained in F. S. Regs., Part II, and the Staff Manual respectively. Title pages will be prepared in manuscript.

WAR DIARY
or
INTELLIGENCE SUMMARY
of 1st York and Lancaster Regt

(Erase heading not required.)

Army Form C. 2118.

Hour, Date, Place	Summary of Events and Information	Remarks and references to Appendices
11 pm. 13·4·15 ZONNEBEKE.	2/Lt S. WEBSTER 3rd York and Lancs Regt attached to the Bn was wounded whilst coming back with a fatigue party from the trenches.	
7 pm 15·4·15 YPRES	Orders were received that the Bn was to be ready to move at a moment's notice to POTIJZE (Reliable information has been received by the 28th Div that the Enemy intended to attack in front of YPRES tonight, and in case this attack took place or YPRES was badly shelled, these orders were issued)	See Appendix 13
11 am 16·4·15 YPRES	Sir H. Plumer visited our billets and expressed his satisfaction with our work.	
6·30 pm 16·4·15 YPRES	Bn left YPRES to relieve 2/Kings Own Regt in the Trenches. Relief completed 3.30 a.m.	See Appendix 14
3 am 17·4·15 ZONNEBEKE	Report to Bde "Have taken over left section from Kings Own Regt. - all quiet" Two men were killed and four wounded during the relief.	
9.30 am to 10.40 am "	Enemy shelled extreme left of H trench with a howitzer which seemed to enfilade the trench, causing 13 casualties.	
11 am "	Report to Bde "Situation Quiet. AAA. Between 9.30 a.m and 10.30 a.m Enemy's guns shelled our left trench causing 13 casualties. Position of guns cannot be ascertained but enfilading our left trench. AAA. Enemy is using H.E. Shell from howitzer."	
12 noon "	Casualties during previous 24 hrs. Killed Other ranks 5 wounded 2/Lt H.C.M. Howard Other ranks thirteen.	
4 pm "	Report to Bde 'All Quiet.'	
7.30 to 7.45 pm	In accordance with instructions received from Bde rapid fire was opened on the enemy and a demonstration made to make them think attack is imminent.	

Instructions regarding War Diaries and Intelligence Summaries are contained in F. S. Regs., Part II. and the Staff Manual respectively. Title pages will be prepared in manuscript.

WAR DIARY or INTELLIGENCE SUMMARY of 1st York Lanc Regt

(Erase heading not required.)

Army Form C. 2118.

Hour, Date, Place			Summary of Events and Information	Remarks and references to Appendices
17-4-15	10pm	ZONNEBEKE.	Information rec^d that attack of 5th Div. was successful.	
	11pm.	"	Report to Bde "All quiet."	
	11-50pm	"	C.O. visited F trench.	
18-4-15	2am	"	Senior Major and Adjt. visited G and H trenches.	
	5 am	"	Report to Bde 'All quiet – nothing to report.'	
	8.20 am	"	Very heavy shell fire heard to our left both rifle machine guns and artillery. Afterwards found out the enemy had attacked part of the 84th Bde.	
	11 am	"	Report to Bde "All quiet nothing to report"	
	12 noon.		Casualties during previous 24 hrs. Other ranks killed 1 wounded 3.	
	4 pm	"	Report to Bde 'All quiet nothing to report.'	
	9.30pm		G.O.C. 83rd Bde arrived at Bn H.Q.	
	11 pm.	"	Report to Bde 'All quiet nothing to report.'	
19-4-15	5 am	"	Report to Bde 'All quiet nothing to report.' During the night 500 lbs of gunpowder was brought up to blow up the house in front of F trench where the enemy are so very close. The mine has apparently been prepared sometime before by the French. It was found however that the mine did not go far enough and that it would have to be deepened before anything could be done.	

1247 W 3299 200,000 (E) 8/14 J.B.C. & A. Forms/C. 2118/11.

Instructions regarding War Diaries and Intelligence Summaries are contained in F. S. Regs., Part II. and the Staff Manual respectively. Title pages will be prepared in manuscript.

WAR DIARY
or
INTELLIGENCE SUMMARY
(Erase heading not required.)

Army Form C. 2118.

Hour, Date, Place		Summary of Events and Information	Remarks and references to Appendices
19-4-15	11 am ZONNEBEKE.	Report to Bde "Situation quiet nothing to report."	
	4 pm. "	Report to Bde "Situation quiet nothing to report."	
	5.20 pm to 6 pm "	Very heavy firing heard in the direction of VERBRANDENMOLEN as near as could be judged. The first part of the night was very quiet there being practically no firing. After midnight however there was a good deal of rifle fire on the part of the Enemy. The first part of the night was so quiet that we thought the Enemy may have been conducting his relief.	
	11 pm "	Report to Bde "Situation quiet nothing to report."	
		2nd in Command visited F trench. G and H were visited by Adjt.	
20.4.15.	5 am "	Report to Bde "Situation quiet nothing to report."	
		The left of No 8 trench was shelled and the parapet damaged by a tree being knocked down.	
	11 am "	All quiet.	
	12 noon "	Casualties during previous 24 hrs. Other ranks 2 wounded.	
	4 pm "	Report to Bde "Situation quiet. AAA Enemy shelled left detached part of 8 trench but not effectively. AAA Enemy have been slightly more active in firing in front of 11 and 12 trenches.	
	5.30 to 6.30 pm "	Very heavy fire heard about 3 miles ... to our right.	
	8 to 9.15 pm	Ditto.	

1247 W 3299 200,000 (E) 8/14 J.B.C. & A. Forms/C. 2118/11.

Instructions regarding War Diaries and Intelligence Summaries are contained in F. S. Regs., Part II. and the Staff Manual respectively. Title pages will be prepared in manuscript.

WAR DIARY

or

~~INTELLIGENCE SUMMARY.~~

(Erase heading not required.)

Army Form C. 2118.

2/York Lanc Regt

Hour, Date, Place	Summary of Events and Information	Remarks and references to Appendices
	The Machine Gun Section under Lieut Lousada moved from the farm behind C Coy. and took up a position behind hedge A. From there it opened fire at 1200 Yards on the ridge where the German posn was supposed to be — covering the advance of the Companies attacking.	
	A very heavy and accurate shell and rifle fire met the companies after hedge B and, although very scanty temporary cover could be obtained behind dungheaps, losses were exceedingly heavy.	
	During the rush from hedge B to the stream C (about 300x) the men were in full view of the enemy and a devastating machine gun and shell fire met them here. Some efforts were made at reorganization at this stream but many Officers and N.C.O's were disabled and the fire so deadly and accurate that a further advance was ordered to hedge D.	
	This last advance necessitated a rush across absolutely open ground and uphill for some 350x and the losses were again very great.	
	It was apparent here that with such a small number of men and exhausted as they were it would be impossible to rush the final posn so it was decided not to push home the assault.	
	It was at this hedge that both the Colonel and Adjutant were hit, the former being killed and the latter mortally wounded. [Both their bodies were safely [illegible] to the rear.]	

(9 29 6) W4141—463 100,000 9/14 H W V Forms/C. 2118/10

Army Form C. 2118.

Instructions regarding War Diaries and Intelligence Summaries are contained in F. S. Regs., Part II. and the Staff Manual respectively. Title pages will be prepared in manuscript.

WAR DIARY
or
INTELLIGENCE SUMMARY.

(Erase heading not required.)

Hour, Date, Place	Summary of Events and Information	Remarks and references to Appendices
21·4·15. 1 a.m. ZONNEBEKE	Bn was relieved by 2nd King's Own. Relief was completed at 2 a.m. and Bn arrived in huts outside YPRES at 4 a.m.	See Appendix 15.
22·4·15. 6 p.m. HUTS nr YPRES	Very heavy firing heard to the north.	
7 p.m.	French troops came down all roads in great disorder saying the Germans had advanced overwhelming them with asphyxiating gases. The Bn "Stood to."	
23·4·15. 1-15 a.m. "	Orders were received from 28th Div: to move Bn to ST JEAN and there to come under command of Col GEDDES the Buffs. Bn left camp by Coys. in the following order B. D. A. C. with intervals of 300x between. On arrival at ST JEAN we heard 2 kilometres of French trenches had been rushed. Bn occupied some trenches to N of ST JEAN. while the Buffs. 5/King's Own. 3rd Middlesex tried to join up the gap made in the line.	
23·4·15. 5·30 a.m. ST JEAN.	Bn ordered to move forward and take up a posn. N.W. of WIELTJE. During this movement which was executed by small detached parties the Bn experienced a severe shelling by shrapnel and high explosives, causing a few casualties. The Bn dug itself in in some disused trenches and was heavily shelled most of the morning. –	See Appendix 16

(9 29 6) W 4141—463 100,000 9/14 H W V Forms/C. 2118/10

Instructions regarding War Diaries and Intelligence Summaries are contained in F. S. Regs., Part II. and the Staff Manual respectively. Title pages will be prepared in manuscript.

WAR DIARY
or
INTELLIGENCE SUMMARY.
(Erase heading not required.)

Army Form C. 2118.

Hour, Date, Place	Summary of Events and Information	Remarks and references to Appendices
23.4.15 4 pm. Near St JEAN.	Orders were received for Bn to participate in an attack on the German posn.	See Appendix 17.
4.5 pm. "	Orders were issued by C.O. to Company commanders.	See Appendix 18
4.10 pm "	Companies marched independently to the farm and the attack debouched from behind it under very heavy rifle and machine gun fire.	See Appendix 19.
	A Coy moved off first followed by C Coy.	
	On arrival at hedge B Lieut Chavier was sent forward with Nos 1 and 2 and Capt Palmer with 2/Lt Connors followed with Nos 3 and 4 platoons close behind. No 5 platoon under Capt Cowley moved off with A Coy, having become detached from B Coy before the attack started.	
	At about the same time C Coy. moved out to the right of A; Nos 11 and 12 platoons leading under Capt. Sandy Wilmot and Lieut. Briscoe followed by Nos 9 and 10 platoons under Lt Gaunlett.	
	A and C coys were followed by D and B coys also moving in small parties as far as hedge A. Here D Coy. followed the line of A at about 250x distance in the following formation :- Nos 13 and 14 platoons under Capt Collins and Lieut Kent Lemon followed by Nos 16 and 15 under Lieut Boyd and 2/Lt Battle.	
	B Coy followed the line of C Coy, No 7 platoon leading under 2/Lt. Gibbs followed by Nos 6 and 8 under Capt. East and Lieut. Parry.	

Instructions regarding War Diaries and Intelligence Summaries are contained in F. S. Regs., Part II. and the Staff Manual respectively. Title pages will be prepared in manuscript.

Army Form C. 2118.

WAR DIARY
or
~~INTELLIGENCE SUMMARY.~~

(*Erase heading not required.*)

York Lanc Regt

Hour, Date, Place	Summary of Events and Information	Remarks and references to Appendices
	During the advance of the infantry and after the last two Coys. had passed hedge A, the machine gun section took up a second position along the hedge B where 2 Canadian Machine Guns were already in action. From this post the guns opened fire on the Sama ridge at 1000x. The remainder of the country in front was so open that the guns were not advanced further until the fighting had considerably diminished and darkness had fallen when they were sent to the forward line in anticipation of a possible counter-attack by the Germans.	
6 pm.	Under cover of darkness Capt. Wedgwood who had assumed command of the Bn. decided that the Regt had been so weakened that he could not hold such an advanced post.	
	After consultation with officers of other Regts up there he decided to fall back and the Bn. dug themselves in along a position corresponding to the hedge A and continued to the left. Three machine guns were placed in position along this line and one in the farm behind. This had to be withdrawn on the following day owing to very heavy shell fire.	

Instructions regarding War Diaries and Intelligence Summaries are contained in F. S. Regs., Part II. and the Staff Manual respectively. Title pages will be prepared in manuscript.

WAR DIARY
or
INTELLIGENCE SUMMARY. 1/4 York and Lancs Regt

(*Erase heading not required.*)

Army Form C. 2118.

Hour, Date, Place	Summary of Events and Information	Remarks and references to Appendices
24.4.15. Nr ST JEAN.	The Bn remained in their posn exposed to heavy shell fire.	
25.4.15 "	Ditto.	
26.4.15 3 a.m "	Bn was withdrawn and marched to POTIJZE WOOD. where it came under the orders of the 27th DIVISION. – forming part of a composite Brigade under COL TEWSON. D.C.L.I.	
	The Bn dug themselves in in this wood.	
27.4.15. POTIJZE.	Bn remained dug in the wood.	
4.30 p.m.	Brigade was ordered to move out in support of the Sirhind Bde who had suffered a temporary check to the right of the YPRES-PILCKEM ROAD.	
	Bn moved out along hedge rows in single file following the D.C.L.I. and advanced under heavy shell and rifle fire to the ridge X. Companies took up posn in the following order: A coy on the left with its left resting on the road, under Lieut Gamblett; D Coy. Lieut Briscoe. B coy. Capt East. C coy. Capt Collins. Here the Bn dug themselves in.	X Ridge is shown in Map Belgium 28 joining 2 farms across the road in Square C21C. Road leads due N. from LA BRIQUE
28.4.15 2 a.m. Nr WIELTJE	D and C coys were relieved by the Sirhind Bde and took up a second position parallel to the road ST JEAN - WIELTJE and 300x from it.	
3 a.m "	A and B coys. were relieved, B coy prolonging this line and A coy returning to POTIJZE.	

(9 29 6) W 4141—463 100,000 9/14 H W V (Forms/C. 2118/10

Instructions regarding War Diaries and Intelligence Summaries are contained in F. S. Regs., Part II. and the Staff Manual respectively. Title pages will be prepared in manuscript.

WAR DIARY

or

~~INTELLIGENCE SUMMARY.~~ York Lanc Regt

(*Erase heading not required.*)

Army Form C. 2118.

Hour, Date, Place	Summary of Events and Information	Remarks and references to Appendices
28.4.15. N^r St JEAN.	Bn remained dug in throughout the day. Lt Wylie joined from 3rd Bn.	Note There is no appendix 20.
28.4.15. 10 p.m "	Orders were received to rejoin our Bde and return to huts near YPRES	See appendix 21.
	Bn marched by companies and were all in by midnight.	
	Draft of 209 men awaited us in Camp.	
29.4.15. 8 a.m. N^r YPRES	Br Lt Col Islerwood arrived to assume Command.	
	Special order received from H M the King.	See appendix 22
	" " " " C in C.	" " 23
	Following were Casualties in the week's fighting:- Officers	
	Killed. Lt Col. A G Bart.	
	Missing Major H K Colston	
	Lt C K Chancier	
	Died of wounds Capt Adjt E S Bamford	
	Wounded but at duty Lieut B C Lousada.	
	Wounded. Capt. Earley Wilmot	
	Capt. A E Palmer.	
	Capt. R B Cowley.	
	Lt. A L Kent Lemon.	
	Lt. J W D Boyd.	
	Lt K S Besford.	
	Lt N C Parry.	
	2/Lt D Connors.	
	2/Lt H W Gibbs	
	2/Lt E E Battle	
	Other Ranks	
	Killed 2 + 58	
	Wounded 10 + 283	
	Missing 2 + 82	

(9 29 6) W4141—463 100,000 9/14 H W V Forms/C. 2118/10

Instructions regarding War Diaries and Intelligence Summaries are contained in F. S. Regs., Part II. and the Staff Manual respectively. Title pages will be prepared in manuscript.

WAR DIARY
or
~~INTELLIGENCE~~ SUMMARY. ~~York~~ ~~Lanc~~ Regt

(*Erase heading not required.*)

Army Form C. 2118.

Hour, Date, Place		Summary of Events and Information	Remarks and references to Appendices
30-4-15.	YPRES	2/Lt TAYLOR and 2/Lt DODWELL arrived from Training College. Bailleul and were posted to D and A Coys. respectively.	
		C.O. inspected the draft and the camp.	
	11 p.m.	Shrapnel shells and high explosives burst near and over the camp for about an hour without doing any damage.	

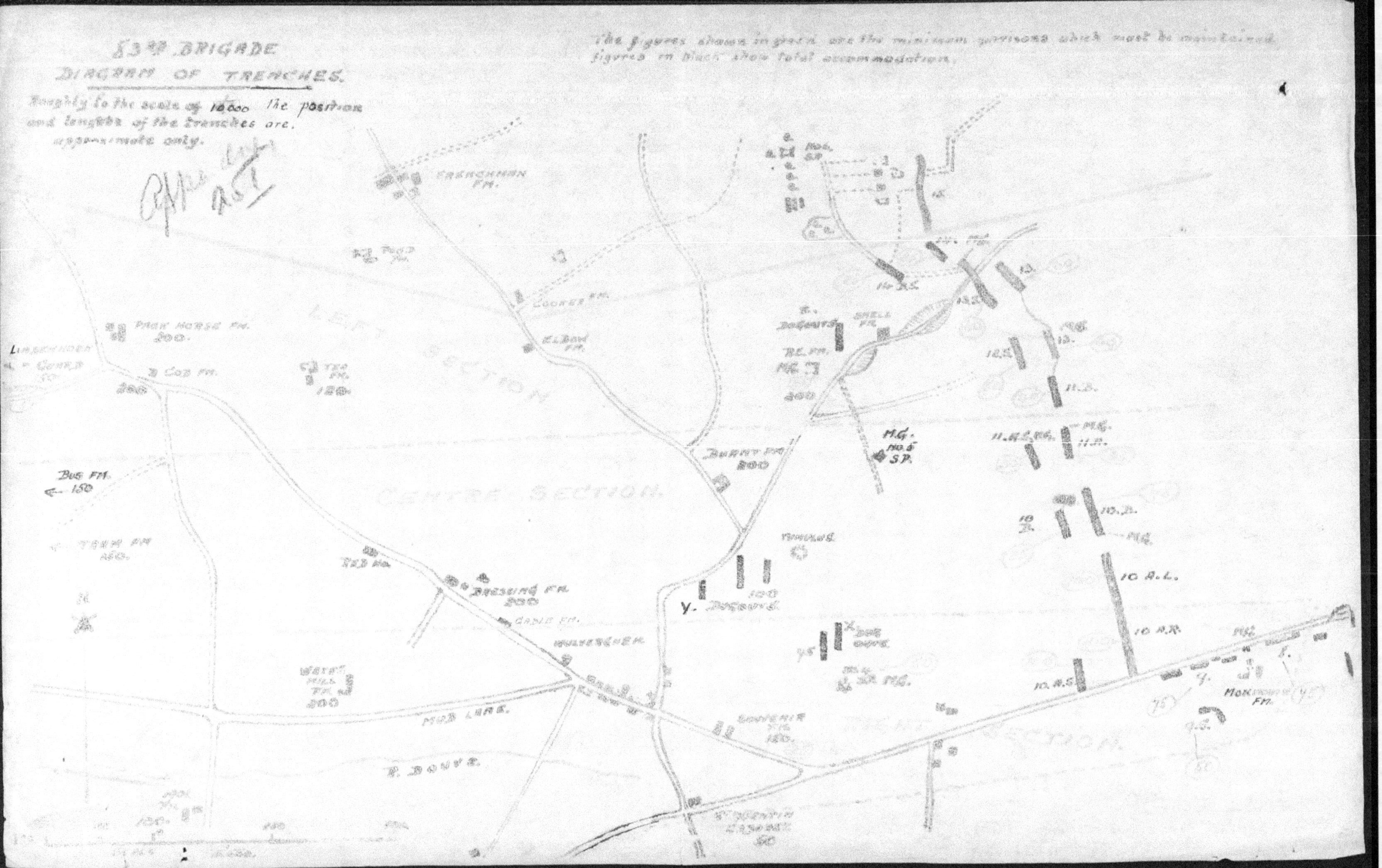

53rd BRIGADE
DIAGRAM OF TRENCHES.
Roughly to the scale of 1/10,000 the position and lengths of the trenches are approximate only.
The figures shown in green are the minimum garrisons which must be maintained; figures in black show total accommodation.
FRENCHMAN FM.
PACK HORSE FM.
200
COOKER FM.
ELBOW FM.
LEFT SECTION
CENTRE SECTION
BURNT FM.
200
M.G.
No. 5
S.P.
Y. DUGOUTS
100
DRESSING FM.
200
CADIE FM.
MUD LANE.
R. DOUVE.
SOUVENIR FM.
ST QUENTIN CABARET
SECTION
10 A.L.
10 A.R.
10 A.S.
10.B.
11.B.
12.S.
13.
M.G.
MONMOUTH FM.
TEA FM.
120
BUS FM.
150
200

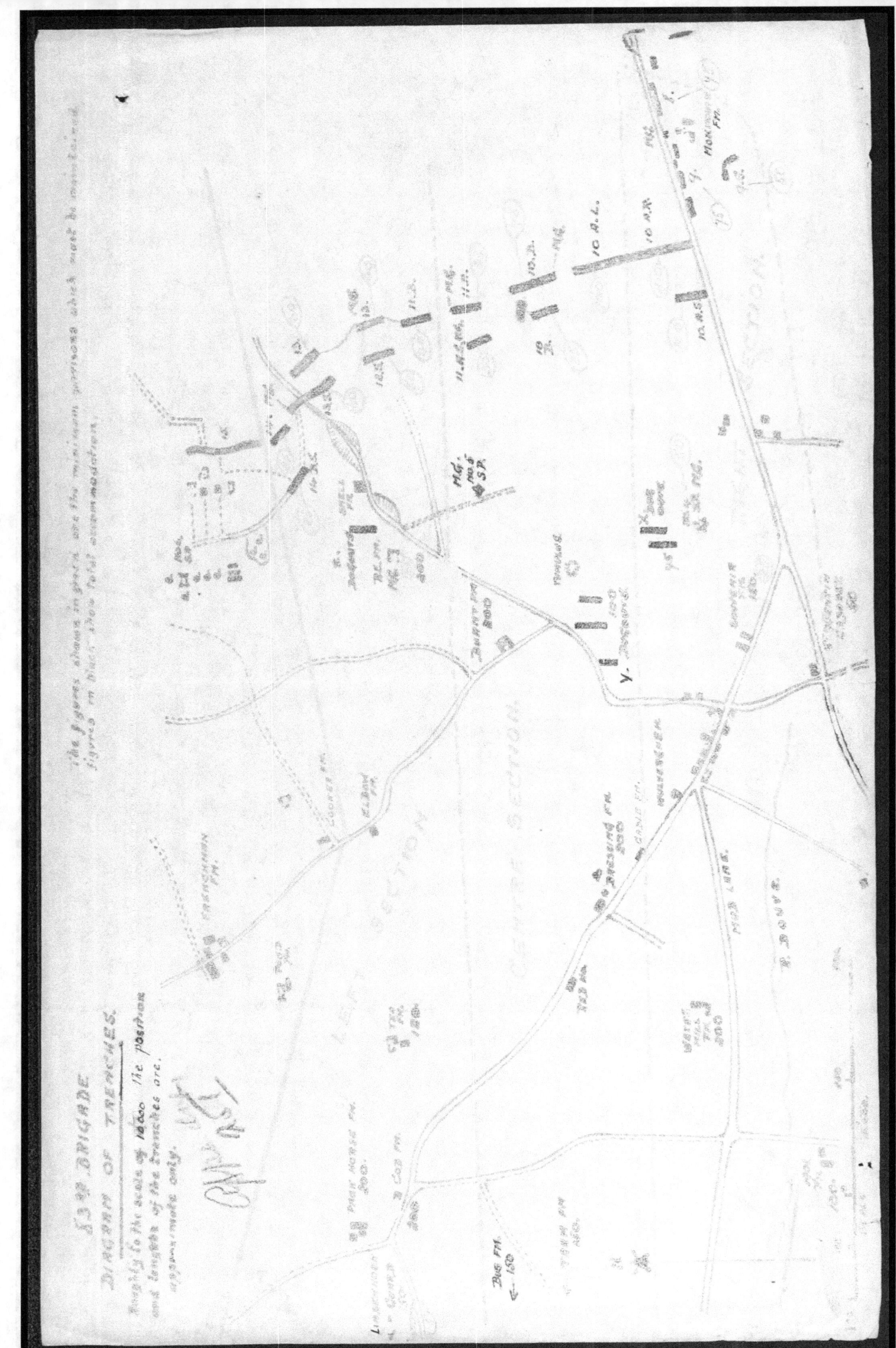

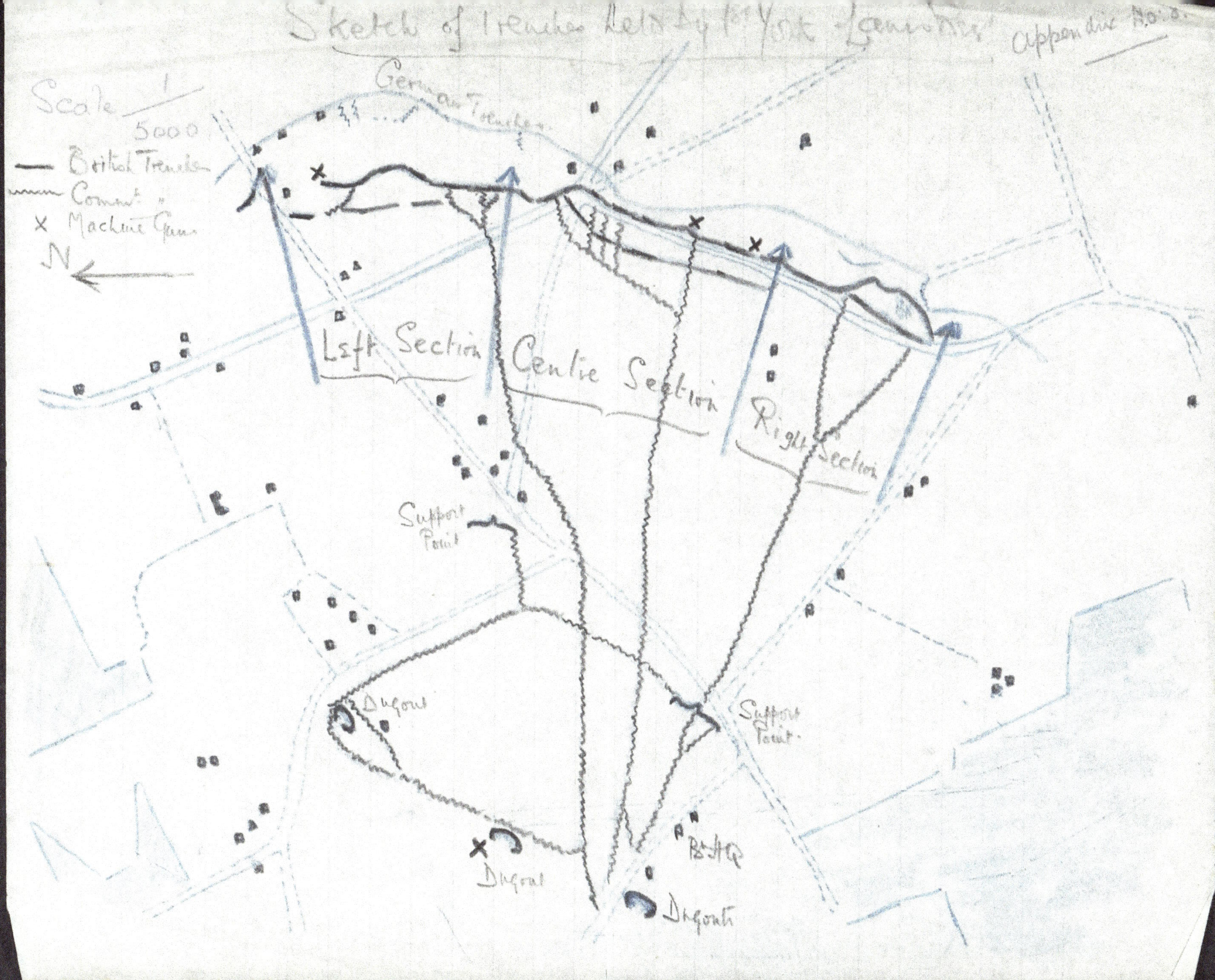
Sketch of Trenches held by 1st York & Lancasters
Appendix No. 8.
Scale 1/5000
British Trenches
Comm: "
x Machine Guns
N
German Trenches
Left Section
Centre Section
Right Section
Support Point
Support Point
Dugout
Dugout
Dugout
Bn HQ

Rough Sketches of
Trenches occupied by
1st York Lane
near Zonnebeke
April 1915

Appendix No 2 Copy No. 5.

Operation Order No 25 By
Brigadier General R. C. BOYLE C.B Commanding
83rd Infantry Brigade

WESTHOF PARK.
1st April 1915

Reference Map HAZEBROUCK 5A

1. The Brigade will move in accordance with the attached table. –
2. The following Battalions will march to BOESCHEPE to morrow – Starting point the Square BAILLEUL

2nd Kings Own Regiment	3.45 pm
5th Kings Own Regiment	4 pm
1st K. O. Y. L. I	4.15 pm

Baggage Waggons to accompany units
3. On arrival they will be billeted as follows
2nd Kings Own Regiment in farms between BOESHEPE and ABEELE. –
5th Kings Own Regt in farms between BOESHEPE and WESTOUTRE. –
1st K. O. Y. L. I. in BOESCHEPE. –
Billeting parties will meet the Staff Captain at the Southern Entrance to BOESCHEPE to-morrow. –
4 The 2nd Royal Irish Regiment will hand over the Centre Section trs 11a to 5th

Battalion South Staffordshire Regiment. Guides for each trench machine gun or farm to be at WULVERGHEM CHURCH at 4.50 pm and will hand over 14 & 16 Support to the 84th Brigade at 9 pm. – (20 Guides Required). –
After Relief the 2nd East Yorkshire Regt will march to BAILLEUL via DRANOUTRE.

B The 3rd Monmouth Regiment will hand over the Right sector to the 5th South Staffordshire Regt. Guides as in A. to be at WULVERGHEM Church at 8.30 pm. –
After Relief the 3rd Monmouth Regiment will march to BAILLEUL by NEUVE EGLISE. –

C. The 5th South Staffordshire Regiment will maintain Machine Guns in S.P. 4 & in 10 B. –

5.

The Brigadier Commands the line now held by the Brigade until completion of the Relief to morrow. –
After that time Brigade headquarters will be at BOESCHEPE. –

(Signed) S. T. Mundy Captain
Brigade Major 83rd Bde.

True Copy. J. Bamford Captain
actg [illegible] Commander Bde.

83rd Infantry Brigade Table of halting places Issued with operation order No 25

DATE	BAILLEUL	BOESCHEPE AREA	WESTOUTRE AREA
Night of 1st April	2nd Kings Own Regiment 1st York & Lancaster Regiment		
" " 2nd April	2nd East Yorkshire Regiment 1st York & Lancaster Regiment 3rd Monmouth Regt	2nd Kings Own Regt 1st K.O.Y.L.I 5th Kings Own Regt	
" " 3rd April	3rd Monmouth Regt (Remains there for present)		2nd East Yorkshire Regiment 1st York & Lancaster Regiment

True Copy [illegible] Captain
Adjt 1/York & Lancaster Re.

Signed J.E. [illegible] Captain
Brigade Major 83rd Brigade

Appendix No 8

Copy No.

Operation Order No 5 By
Lt Colonel A. G. Burt Commanding
1st Battn York & Lancaster Rt.

R.E FARM.

1.4.15

1. The Battalion will be Relieved to night by the 5th N. Stafford Regt and 2/East Yorkshire Regt. in accordance with the attached table. —

2. Shovels pick axes, hand axes felling axes hammers periscopes & fishing Reels in accordance with attached Memo to be Brought out. —

3. After Relief the Battalion will March by Companies or Complete platoons to BAILLEUL via NEUVE EGLISE.

4. Trench Commanders will Report as soon as they have handed over their trench if possible by telephone. —
When passing R.E FARM, the written Report of work done Etc will be handed to the Adjutant. —

[signature] Captain
Adjutant 1/York & Lancaster Rgt

TABLE OF RELIEFS 1ST APRIL 1915 -- Issued with Operation Order No 4

TRENCH.	HELD BY.	UNIT RELIEVED BY.	GUIDES TWO PER TRENCH OR MACHINE GUN TO MEET RELIEVING UNIT AT	TIME
11B. 12. 12S	B Company	5th North Stafford Regiment	WULVERGHEM CHURCH.	7.30pm
13 13S	A Company	5th North Stafford Regiment	WULVERGHEM CHURCH	7.30pm
14 14S	A Company	2/ East Lancashire Regt.	Will be notified later	

E. Bamford Captain
Adjutant ~~North~~ Lancaster Regt.

Appendix No. 8

Copy No.

Operation order No. 5 By
Lt. Col. A. J. Bird Commanding
1/ York & Lancaster Regt.

8. 4. 15
BAILLEUL

1. The Battalion will move to WESTOUTRE today.

2. The Battalion will form up at the LUNATIC ASYLUM at 2.50 pm in the following order A. B. C. D. Coys Machine guns ~~Transport~~ — Transport including supply waggons will follow the unit.—

3. A Billeting party consisting of 1 sergeant per Company & 1 N.C.O for M.G. Section will leave Bath Lodge under Lieut. Lancaster at 12.45 pm today.—

4. All Baggage & Blankets must be Ready for loading by 1.15 pm

5. Billets must be left thoroughly Clean

(sd) E.S. Bamford Captain
Adjutant 1/ York & Lancaster Re

A second day's Ration will be issued at the GRAND PLACE YPRES. & carried to the trenches. —

5. Cooks Carts will march to Ypres after teas to-day —

[illegible] Captain

Adjutant 1/ North Lancashire R.

Copy No.

Appendix No 6

app 6

Operation Order No 6 by
Lt Colonel A.J. Hart? Commanding
1st Battn [illegible] Lancashire [illegible]

1. The Battalion will move from billets at present occupied to-day & is warned for duty in the trenches —

2. The Battalion less Transport Machine guns Cooks? Carts & 2 platoons D Coy & pioneers will ~~move~~ move in accordance with the attached table to YPRES —

3. At FREZENBERG one guide per Company from the 3rd Battalion 146th Regiment (French) to lead Companies to Battalion Head Quarters — At Battalion Head Quarters one guide per platoon will lead platoons to trenches — Companies will leave FREZENBERG at intervals of ½ hour

The Battalion is due to arrive at FREZENBERG at 11 pm —

4. The following stores will be issued at FREZENBERG & carried to the trenches

Sandbags 2 per man
SAA 24 Boxes per Coy
Shovels 25
Picks 20
Hand grenades } 10 Boxes per Coy
Detonators }
Coke & Charcoal

Appendix No 5

Copy No 2

Operation Order No 6 by
Brigadier General R.C. Boyle CB
Commanding 83rd Infantry Brigade

WESTOUTRE
7th April 1915

Reference Map HAZEBROUCK
& Sheet 28

1. The Brigade will relieve the 146th Regiment in the trenches to-morrow.—

2. Troops for the trenches less 1st K.O.Y.L.I. & 5th Kings Own Regiment & less Machine Gun detachments will move in accordance with the attached table to-morrow.—
Busses are to hold 25 each, any men for whom accommodation in Busses is not available will march with the transport.—

3. Guides at the rate of 1 per Company & one per pair of Machine Guns meet troops at FREZENBERG.— additional guides at the rate of 1 per platoon meet the troops at Battalion Headquarters.—

4. The O.C. 2nd Kings Own Regiment will detail one Company to report at FREZENBERG to each of the Battalions going into the trenches as soon as those Battalions arrive there.— These Companies will be employed on carrying work under the orders of the O.C. Battalion to which they are attached & will return to FREZENBERG when dismissed by him.—

5. After passing FREZENBERG an interval of ¼ hour must be allowed between Companies.—

6. All available S.A.A. in charge of ~~Battalions~~ the Brigade will be taken into the fire trenches, now that ~~[illegible]~~ carried in the men not in those trenches. Allotment of ammunition is given below.— Battalions for the trenches to take their own Regimental tools.—

7. Until 12th instant the Brigade will be supported by artillery of the 36th French Division.— Each Battalion in the trenches is in communication with one Battery by wire from Battalion Headquarters, & also from the fire trenches.— The French will continue to give operators for these wires till the above date.—

8. Brigade Headquarters will be at the present Headquarters of the 146th Regiment.— Square D26. C.5.1.— The officer Commanding that Regiment commands the line until the relief is complete.—

9. The Battalions in the trenches will stand to arms between 3.45 and 4.45 am.—

10. A. Machine Gun detachments transport, & vehicles less Cooks & supply wagons of the 2nd East Yorkshire Regt. 3rd Monmouth Regt & 1st York & Lancaster Regiment, also the S.A.A wagons of all units & any other vehicles which the Officer Commanding 2nd King's Own Regiment may wish to send, will march under Command of the Senior transport officer to billets to morrow which will be pointed out by the Staff Captain.— Starting from Brigade Headquarters 1 pm.—

The S.A.A. Carts of the 1st K.O.Y.L.I will be attached to 2/East Yorkshire
" " " " 5th King's Own " " " 3/Monmouth Rr.
" " " " 2nd " " " " 1/York & Lancaster Rr

B. Vehicles containing Ammunition & other Reserves in the trenches will accompany units from YPRES. but will not proceed further East than Square D 26 A.—

(Signed) J. E. Munby Captain
Brigade Major. 83rd Brigade

True Copy. E. J. Bamford Captain
Adjutant 1/York & Lancaster R.

83rd Infantry Brigade March table 8th April

Issued with Operation order No 26

Copy No 5

UNIT	EMBUS at PLACE	EMBUS at TIME	No of BUSSES	DEBUS at PLACE	DEBUS at TIME	REACH FREZENBERG AT	RELIEVE
2nd Kings Own Regiment less 1 Company	BOESCHEPE	4 pm	25	VLAMERTINGHE	6 pm	8.30 pm	Reserve Battalion at FREZENBERG.–
2nd East Yorkshire Regt.	WESTOUTRE	4.30 pm	27	YPRES	7 pm	8.30 pm	1st Batt. 146th Regt.
3rd Monmouth Regt.	Where Junction Cross WESTOUTRE & BOESCHEPE Roads	5.30 pm	28	YPRES	8 pm	9.30 pm	2nd Batt. 146th Regt.
1st York & Lancaster Regt.	Batt HQ. RENINGHELST.	6.30 pm 7.30 pm	9 25	YPRES	9 pm 9.30 pm	11 pm	3rd Batt. 146th Regt.

Signed S. P. Mumby Captain

True Copy P. S. Bamford Captain

Adjutant 1st York & Lancaster Regt.

Appendix No 9.

A/9

OPERATION ORDER No: 27
By
Brigadier General R.C. Boyle, C.B.
Commanding 83rd Infantry Brigade.

11th April 1915.

Reference Map 28.

1. Tomorrow - 2nd Kings Own Regt will relieve 1st York Lancaster Regt
5th Kings Own Regt will relieve 3rd Monmouth Regt
1st K.O.Y.L.I. will relieve 2nd East Yorkshire Regt

2. Relief to be carried out by Companies from the right of Battalions; companies to leave YPRES at quarter of an hour intervals.

1st K.O.Y.L.I. leading company to pass MENIN Gate 7-15 pm
5th Kings Own Regt. " —— " —— " - " —— " —— " - 8-15 pm
2nd Kings Own Regt. - —— " —— " - " —— " —— " —— 9-15 pm.

3 Transport will not march with Battalions but will pass MENIN Gate at 7 pm. and march to dumping ground at road junction on the ZONNEBEKE Road, D.26. A.2.4. This dumping ground will be just clear of the road on the South Side.

Companies must call at this place for their stores

4. Guides, two per Company, provided by the outgoing Battalions and accompanied by the guides belonging to the incoming battalions who are already in the trenches will be ready to meet companies at the FREZENBERG Guard, C.30. C.7.3. —
for the 1st K.O.Y.L.I —— at 8-15 pm
" " 5th Kings Own Regt - " 9-15 pm
" " 2nd Kings Own Regt - " 10-15 pm

5. Twelve guides of each outgoing Battalion will remain attached to the incoming Battalions (who will provide rations) for two days.

They will be composed as follows:—
2 per Company
4 per Battalion Headquarters

They will work with guides of incoming Battalions and accompany them on all journeys

They will rejoin their Battalions on the evening of the 14th instant.

6. Sick are taken over by the R.A.M.C. bearers at the Battalion Dressing Stations.

P.T.O.

7. The 3rd Brigade, R.F.A. relieves the French Field Artillery tomorrow night.

One Battery is in co-operation with each Battalion.

8 The FREZENBERG Guard at C. 30. C.7. 3. will be taken over by the 2nd Kings Own Regt. at midnight, strength 2 N.C.Os. and 6 men

(Sd.) J.E. Munby, Captain,
Brigade Major,
83rd Infantry Brigade.

No: 8

Appendix No: 10

Operation Order
By
Lieut. Colonel A.G. Burt
Commanding 1st York + Lancaster Regt

Headquarters, Left Sector
12-4-1915

Reference Map 28

1. The Battalion will be relieved tonight by the 2nd Kings Own Regt

2 Companies will send the following guides to Battalion Headquarters:—
2 guides per Company to report to the Adjutant at Bn. Hdqrs. at 8-15 pm.
2 guides per platoon to report to the Adjutant at Bn. Hdqrs. at 11-pm.

3. Relief will be carried out by Companies from the right:—
After relief the Battalion will march by Companies or complete Platoons to YPRES, Guides to lead Companies to their Billets will be at the MENIN Gate
O.C. Companies or Trenches will report by Telephone as soon as their Company or trench has been relieved and will report at Battn Hdqrs. when passing

4. A receipt will be obtained from the Officer taking over a trench, for all stores handed over. A seperate receipt will be obtained for tools now in trenches (they are regimental one.)

All tools etc will be left in trenches

5 Each Company will leave 2 guides with the Kings Own Regt. They will remain with the Kings Own Regt. for two days and will be rationed by them.

6 The attached report on work done will be completed and sent to Battn Headquarters as soon as it is dark enough to night

Copy No: 1 to D Coy,
2 " B "
3 " A "
4 " C "
5 " R.H. Eleames.

E. Bamford.
Captain,
Adjutant, 1st York & Lancaster Regt.

Appendix No 11

11

Operation Order No 7 By
Lt. Col. A. J. Burt. Commanding
1/ King's Lancaster Regt.

10.4.15

1. The following Relief will take place to night. —
D Coy will Relieve C Company in left fire trenches.
After Relief "C" Company will occupy support dugouts. —

2. Before Relief takes place D Company will supply the following fatigue parties
A. 2 platoons to carry up trench stores to trenches from Battn HQ.
B. as many men as O.C. D Company Considers necessary to bring up stores left at FREZENBERG last night. —
when the above fatigues have

99

been Carried out Relief will take place. — fatigue parties will move as soon as possible after dark. —

3. the O.C. "C" Company will send 2 guides per platoon to be at Battn Head Quarters at 12 midnight to night, to guide D Coy to trenches. —

4. the O.C. D Company will draw Rations before Relief. O.C. C. Coy after Relief. —

5. Fatigue parties should Commence work as soon as possible after dark.

C.E. Bamford. Captain
Adjutant 1/York & Lancaster Regt

Issued at 7.45 pm by orderly.

Copy	No	1	to	A	Company
"	"	2	"	B	"
"	"	3	"	C	"
"	"	4	"	D	"
"	"	5	} Retained		
"	"	6			

Appendix No 12 12

Braves Camarades.—

Nous Regrettons Que Ce territoire n'Est pas neutre pour y tenir Conversation et pour Echanger des nouvelles de guerre.—
En nous Savant de la poste d'ane et vous envoier les journaux, si vous prie de faire le même Systeme.—
Ne Croyez vous pas de mieux servir a votre patrie si vous allez avec nous Contre les Anglais? Savez bien cette guerre terrible ne finira pas avant que l'Angleterre sera detruit.—
Nous n'avons pas detaire pour le franco Malen votre Rele de Revange Alsole même la Lane Malie Contre l'Angleterre oubliez la Revange et devenez votre Alhes.—

9.4.15

True Copy

[illegible]

[illegible]

Secret
G.511

Appendix 13

Appendix 13

In the Event of YPRES being heavily shelled troops of the 28th Division will assemble in the open ground North of YPRES – POTIJZE Road and West of the ST. JEAN – POTIJZE Road. –

Troops will be formed up round fields & kept under hedges & trees. – Rendezvous will be reached as follows –

1. Battalion occupying ~~ECOLE DES DAMES DE ROOSBRUGGE will move by streets to the North of the RUE ELVERD~~ LUNATIC ASYLUM in RUE DE THOUROUT will move via the RUE DE THOUROUT, thence by the Cross Roads in I 2 d 1.2., & Cross Roads 800 yards North EAST of MENIN Gate to Rendezvous. —

2. Battalion occupying ECOLE DES DAMES DE ROOSBRUGGE will move by streets to the North of the RUE ELVERDINGHE ~~as~~ in By the open ground North East of the prison and thence by the RUE DE THOUROUT to Rendezvous. —

3. Battalion occupying ECOLE COMMUNALE will move ~~as~~ by the same Route as the Battalion from ECOLE DES DAMES DE ROOSBRUGGE. –

4. R.E in Rue de DIXMUDE will follow the Battalion from LUNATIC ASYLUM. – Troops in the Prison will follow the Battalion from ECOLE DES DAMES DE ROOSBRUGGE – R.E from CATTLE MARKET will follow the Battalion from

ECOLE COMMUNALE.—

5. Various headquarters and other small units will take cover in Cellars in or near their Billets.— Reconnaissances should be made & each individual told where he is to go.—

6. If the YPRES–POTIJZE Road is being shelled, troops will move from RUE DE THOUR OUT to the Rendezvous across country.—

7. All Battalions will leave orderlies at Cross Roads RUE DE THOUR OUT (Square I.2.d.1.2) who know where their headquarters are to be found.—

To the Officer Commanding
K.O.R. Lancaster R.

Signed P.C. [illegible] Captain
for Brigade Major 83rd Infantry Brigade.

BM 20 58.

Signed [illegible] [illegible] [illegible] O.C. 2/[illegible]
[illegible]

Appendix 14

Operation Order No 9 By
Lt Col A. G. Bent. Commanding 1st/4th R. Reg

YPRES. 16.4.15.

Reference Belgium Sheet 28
1/40000.

1. The Bn is warned for duty in the trenches and will take over the line now held by the 2nd Kings Own Regt tonight.

2. The Bn will march by Companies as follows — A B. C. D. Machine Guns with 5 minutes interval.

3. Blankets must be ready for loading by 4 p.m.

4 The Dumping Ground is near the Stream on the YPRES - ZONNEBEKE ROAD Square D 26. a5.

5. 1 officer and 2 N.C.Os per Coy will report at Bn H.Q. at 5.30 pm to go to reconnoitre the Subsidiary Line.

True copy
[illegible]

E. S. Bamford Capt.
Adjt. 1st/4th York Lancs Regt.

Issued with Operation Order Number 6. 8.4.15. —

COMPANY	NUMBERS OF BUSSES	PLACE TO MEET BUS	TIME
A	9	REINGHELST	7.15 pm
B	10	REINGHELST	7.15 pm
C	{81 {58	REINGHELST. Battn Hd qrs.	7.15 pm 6.15 pm
D	5	REINGHELST.	7.15 pm
Hdqrs.	1	Battn Hdqrs.	6.15 pm.

The Battalion will debus at YPRES, & will march to FREZENBERG & is timed to reach the latter place at 11 pm. —

E. Bamford Captain
Adjutant 1/ York & Lancaster Regt.

Appendix 15

Operation Order No 11 By
Lt. Colonel A. G. Burt Commanding
1st Battn York & Lancaster Regt.

Reference Belgium
Sheet 28.

Near ZONNEBEKE
20.4.15

1. The Battalion will be relieved to night by the 2nd Kings Own Regt. —

2. Companies will be relieved in the following order. C.D.A. —

3. 2 Guides per platoon will report to the Adjutant at Battn Hdqrs at 10 pm. Company Commanders will please inform the Adjutant in what order they wish relieving platoons to arrive —

4. After relief the Battalion will march by Companies or complete platoons to Billets — the exact position is not known but Guides will meet the Battalion on the YPRES – POPERINGHE – Road near the Railway Crossing at 11 am

46

Guide Companies to the Site N of Road somewhere near that point.—

5. The following are the only places on the POPERINGHE — YPRES Road where 10 minute halts are allowed.—

Going East. Off the main Road in a farm S. of the Road at the point H.8 b 7.—

Going West. Off the main Road ~~in the~~ ~~[illegible]~~ to a farm lane North of the Road in H.10 a

6. Receipts for trench stores will be handed to the Senior Major when passing Battalion H.Q.—

7. Company & [illegible] Commanders will report to [illegible] [illegible] Batt. H.Q. that they have been relieved.—

8. The Medical Officer will be at the dressing station [illegible] the Batt. in [illegible] of ZONNEBEKE.

[illegible] Capt.

Adjt [illegible] [illegible] [illegible] Lancashire R.

48

"A" Form. Army Form C. 2121.

MESSAGES AND SIGNALS. No. of Message

Prefix Code m.	Words	Charge	This message is on a/c of:	Recd. at m.
Office of Origin and Service Instructions.	Sent		Service.	Date
	At m.			From
	To			
	By		(Signature of "Franking Officer.")	By

TO YORK LANCASTERS. appendix 16

Sender's Number	Day of Month	In reply to Number	AAA
GK 12	23rd.		

Move	your	battalion	to	between
the	roads	NW	of	WIELTJE
about	22 D 28 B	AAA	HQ	move
to	WIELTJE	AAA	Buffs	Third
Middlesex	Fifth	KORL	informed	

True copy

[illegible]

From COL GEDDES

Place

Time 5.10 am

The above may be forwarded as now corrected. (Z) HMM Crichton Capt

Censor. Signature of Addressor or person authorised to telegraph in his name

* This line should be erased if not required.

8350 S. B. Ltd. Wt. W4843/541—50,000. 9/14. Forms C2121/10.

"A" Form.

Army Form C. 2121.

MESSAGES AND SIGNALS.

No. of Message

Code m. Origin and Service Instructions.	Words / Charge / Sent At m. To By	This message is on a/c of: Service. (Signature of "Franking Officer.")	Recd. at m. Date From By

TO EAST YORKS
YORK & LANCS

appendix 17

Sender's Number	Day of Month	In reply to Number	AAA
GK 36	23rd.		

The 13th Brigade crosses by the pontoon bridge at 3 p.m. and advances to the attack at 3.45 p.m. with its right on the YPRES-PILCKEM ROAD AAA. First objective PILCKEM AAA O.C East Yorks will send an officer at once to report to Gen. O'Gowan at pontoon bridge C19C AAA. The East Yorks and York and Lancs will cooperate with this attack east of the PILCKEM-YPRES ROAD East Yorks with left on that road and maintaining touch with 13th Bde. York and Lancs will move ~~with~~ on right of E Yorks. Two battalions 27th Divn will cooperate in the attack on the right of York and Lancs AAA Buffs and Third Middlesex will hold their present line. 5th KORL (less 1 coy) will follow the attack in reserve moving with its left on the PILCKEM-YPRES RD AAA. Each Bn will move on a front of 500 yards AAA

From HQ will remain for the present at WIELTJE
Place where reports should be sent.
Time

COL GEDDES 3-20 p.m

The above may be forwarded as now corrected. (Z) HMM Crichton Capt

Censor. Signature of Addressor or person authorised to telegraph in his name

* This line should be erased if not required.

8350 S. B. Ltd. Wt. W4843/541—50,000. 9/14. Forms C2121/10.

"A" Form. Army Form C. 2121.

MESSAGES AND SIGNALS. No. of Message

Prefix Code m. Office of Origin and Service Instructions.	Words / Charge / Sent At m. To By	This message is on a/c of: Service. (Signature of "Franking Officer.")	Recd. at m. Date From By

TO O.C. Companies YL offenders 18

Sender's Number	Day of Month	In reply to Number	AAA

The 13th Brigade will attack at 3-45 p.m. with its right on the PILCKEM - YPRES road. First objective PILCKEM. East Yorks will move with their left touching 13th Brigade York and Lancasters on right of East Yorkshires.

The Bn will move in 4 lines Each Company in 2 lines.

A and C coy will be in first line A coy on left keeping touch with East Yorks followed by D on the left B on the right.

E S Bamford Capt
Adjt York Lanc Regt

True copy [illegible]

Lines to be about 200x apart.

From
Place
Time

The above may be forwarded as now corrected. (Z)

Censor. Signature of Addressor or person authorised to telegraph in his name

* This line should be erased if not required.

8350 S. B. Ltd. Wt. W4843/541—50,000. 9/14. Forms C2121/10.

Appendix 19
D
C
B
A
Sketch map of country over which attack was made Apr 23' 1915.
The farm shown is that shown on Map Belgium 28 Square C 21 C 1.8.
Farm

"A" Form. Army Form C. 2121.

MESSAGES AND SIGNALS.

No. of Message

Prefix Code m. / Office of Origin and Service Instructions.	Words / Charge / Sent At m. / To / By	This message is on a/c of: Service. / (Signature of "Franking Officer.")	Recd. at m. / Date / From / By

TO SIRHIND BDE appendix 21

Sender's Number	Day of Month	In reply to Number	AAA
G 401	28th	—	

Plumers force moves begins: the Battalions at present forming Composite Bde attached to Lahore Divn will return to their proper formations tonight under arrangements between Divisions concerned and Lahore Divn AAA.

1st York and Lancs and 5th Kings Own to move to new huts in Square H5. Ends AAA When will you be ready to move.

From Advanced Lahore Division
Place
Time 7 35 pm

The above may be forwarded as now corrected. (Z)

Censor. Signature of Addressor or person authorised to telegraph in his name

* This line should be erased if not required.

8350 S. B. Ltd. Wt. W4843/541--50,000. 9/14. Forms C2121/10.

Appendix 22

Special Order of the Day

The F.M. Commanding-in-Chief has received the following from the Secretary War Office.

To Sir John French. General HQ.

24th April 1915

His Majesty sends the following message:—
"During the past week I have followed with admiration the splendid achievements of my troops including the Capture and retention of Hill 60 after heavy fighting and the gallant conduct of the Canadian Division in repulsing the enemy and re-capturing four heavy guns.
I heartily congratulate all units who have taken part in these successful actions.

True copy
[illegible]

"A" Form. Army Form C. 2121.

MESSAGES AND SIGNALS. No. of Message

Prefix Code m.	Words Charge		Recd. at m.
Office of Origin and Service Instructions.	Sent	*This message is on a/c of:*	Date
	At m.	*Service.*	From
	To		
	By	(Signature of "Franking Officer.")	By

TO All Units and 3rd Bde RFA

appendix 23

Sender's Number	Day of Month	In reply to Number	AAA
* BMB 104	26th		

Following message received begins: The Commander-in-Chief wishes to express to all ranks of the 28th Division his appreciation of the manner in which the 28th Division has borne itself under the strain of the last few days AAA He feels confident that they will stubbornly hold their ground for the short time that the call is made on them and add fresh laurels to their regimental records AAA The Corps Commander desires to endorse the commendation of the Commander-in-Chief AAA Major General Bulfin congratulates the 28th Divn on the well merited praise they have won AAA To be communicated to all ranks Ends

True copy [illegible]

From	83rd	Bde	
Place			10.5 pm
Time			

The above may be forwarded as now corrected. (Z)

Censor. Signature of Addressor or person authorised to telegraph in his name

* This line should be erased if not required.

8350 S. B. Ltd. Wt. W4842/541—50,000. 9/14. Forms C2121/10.

83rd Bde.
28th Div.

1st YORK & LANCS.

APRIL 1915

M A Y 1 9 1 5

Apps. 1 to XIV.

Instructions regarding War Diaries and Intelligence Summaries are contained in F. S. Regs., Part II. and the Staff Manual respectively. Title pages will be prepared in manuscript.

WAR DIARY
or
~~INTELLIGENCE SUMMARY.~~
(Erase heading not required.)

1st York + Lancaster Regt.

Army Form C. 2118.

Hour, Date, Place	Summary of Events and Information	Remarks and references to Appendices
1st May Autiments YPRES	Letter Received from Brigadier Gen. Boyle	App. I
2nd "	Orders received to relieve 2nd Kings Own in the trenches. The Btn moved off at 8pm + marched under very heavy shell fire to the new line at VERLORENHOEK which we took up at about 10 pm. A + B coys held front line, C + D in dugouts in reserve	App. II
4pm 3 May Btn H.Q dugout	Orders received to move 2 coys in support of the Rifle Bde who were hard pressed E of St JULIEN. These with 2 coys 5th K.O.R.L. Regt under the command of Lt Col Isherwood moved in open order under a moderate shell fire. On arrival the E Lancs had turned up to help the Rifle Bde + we returned to VERLORENHOEK + occupied the line of trenches. The front line retired through us during the night, making us into the front line	App. III
9am 4th May Btn H.Q dugout	Enemy's patrols were seen in front of our line. Report to Bde "Patrols in front of my line of trenches report isolated patrols of Germans advancing down Rly line + opposite our right AAA Shots have been exchanged + enemy's patrols have retired" Ends	
10.30 AM " "	Report to Bde. K 516	App. IV – VIII
11 5 am " "	" " K 517	
11 30 am " "	" " K 518	
12 noon "	Casualty Report K 519	
~~4 pm~~	~~Report to Bde K 521~~	

(73989) W4141—463. 400,000. 9/14. H.&J.Ltd. Forms/C. 2118/10.

Instructions regarding War Diaries and Intelligence Summaries are contained in F. S. Regs., Part II. and the Staff Manual respectively. Title pages will be prepared in manuscript.

WAR DIARY
or
INTELLIGENCE SUMMARY.
(Erase heading not required.)

Army Form C. 2118.

Hour, Date, Place	Summary of Events and Information	Remarks and references to Appendices
2 pm 4 May/15 H.Q. Dugout	Report to Bde. "Cannot the Artillery fire at houses round the chapel in J I b. & opposite our left AAA It is believed that the enemy are placing machine guns in these houses which will command all our trenches.	
2.30 pm	Report to Bde. "Left trench report enemy massing about 400ᵡ down Rly from ARRET AAA Adjt E YORK Regt confirms this report AAA I have posted a Machine gun near Rly.	
3.55 pm	Report to Bde:- Left trench reports thousand Germans with transport moving through ZONNEBEKE in a S.E. direction AAA. Transport about 8 carts in rear AAA Troops are also reported moving down ZONNEBEKE-YPRES Rd, close to FREZENBERG"	
	An exceptionally heavy bombardment continued from 4 pm till 6 pm, when things quietened down considerably	
8 pm	C.O. visited trenches.	
9 am. 5 May B.H.Q dug out.	Report to Bde:- All communication wires with my Coys are cut by shell fire AAA Report by hand says enemy have blown in trenches in many parts AAA. Heavy artillery support urgently needed.	

(73989) W4141—463. 400,000. 9/14. H.&J.Ltd. Forms/C. 2118/10.

Instructions regarding War Diaries and Intelligence Summaries are contained in F. S. Regs., Part II. and the Staff Manual respectively. Title pages will be prepared in manuscript.

WAR DIARY

or

~~INTELLIGENCE SUMMARY.~~

(*Erase heading not required.*)

Army Form C. 2118.

Hour, Date, Place	Summary of Events and Information	Remarks and references to Appendices
9.15 am 5th May H.Q. Dugouts	Report to Bde "We are suffering heavy losses & trenches are being destroyed by heavy shell fire AAA We are in urgent need of support if possible AAA"	
11 am " "	Situation report rendered: Left companies satisfactory. Right companies suffered very heavily & had their trenches partially destroyed AAA Our artillery fire accurate, but H.E. shell needed against buildings AAA. Party of E Yorks arrived here report about ½ mile of their trench blown away & enemy advancing on their left AAA Capt Collins reports he has had to retire from Right centre trench AAA The support Coy is lining edge of wood behind it.	
4.35 pm	Enemy advanced in large numbers on left of Rly. Later, a German Battery was observed coming into action, also cavalry on the ~~[illegible]~~ FREZENBURG Rd. Reports rendered to Bde.	
11 am 6 May	Our Artillery had kept enemy quieter today. We have opened bursts of Rapid fire on parties working on trenches.	
11 am & 6 pm 7 May	Enemy artillery active but ineffective No movements of the enemy observed. Btn Relieved during the night by 1st KOYLI & marched back to the huts. Relief passed off quietly.	
	Lt Gen E A Alderson's report	App VII

(73989) W4141—463. 400,000. 9/14. H.&J.Ltd. Forms/C. 2118/10.

Instructions regarding War Diaries and Intelligence Summaries are contained in F. S. Regs., Part II. and the Staff Manual respectively. Title pages will be prepared in manuscript.

WAR DIARY
or
INTELLIGENCE SUMMARY.
(Erase heading not required.)

1st YORK & LANCASTER Rgt

Army Form C. 2118.

Hour, Date, Place		Summary of Events and Information	Remarks and references to Appendices
7th may		In the evening the Battalion was relieved by the K.O.Y.L.I. who took over the trenches held by us at ZONNEBEKE; and marched back to the huts at YPRES	
8th may.	In Huts at YPRES 1.30 am	The Battalion arrived at the huts and found there a draft of 487 N.C.Os & men	
	11.30 am	The draft paraded for inspection by the C.O.	
	11.35 am	Battalion ordered to "Stand to"	
	12.15 pm	Battalion left the huts under orders to retake the trenches from which the KOYLI had had to withdraw at ZONNEBEKE. The Battalion advanced in lines of Platoons towards ZONNEBEKE with its right flank resting on the railway line	
	5 pm	About this time the Battalion had halted and was in the Support trenches S.E of FREZENBERG (Sheet 28 D.25C) under heavy shell fire. Here Capt Collins was wounded and the casualties numbered between 30 & 40	
	7 pm	Company Commanders received orders from Col ISHERWOOD to advance at 8pm.	Lt-Col ISHERWOOD, Lt LOUSADA, Lt WYLIE, 2nd Lt DODWELL } were subsequently reported "as missing"
	8 pm	The attack was pushed almost up to the German trenches but owing to the very heavy casualties in officers & men, it did not achieve its object. All the Officers were put out of action with the exception of Lt Briscoe who was able to get together the remnants of the Battalion next day. Capt EAST was killed. Lt-Col ISHERWOOD, Lt LOUSADA, Lt GAUNTLETT, Lt WYLIE, 2nd Lt TAYLOR, 2nd Lt DODWELL, 2nd Lt MORGAN were wounded.	1/Capt COPLEY 1st Y&L Rgt states that he, with a party, carried Lt WYLIE to the dressing station at the white chateau POTIJZE and handed him over to the M.O.
	about 11 pm	Sgt SOUTH brought 30 men back to the Support trenches where he met Sgt TAYLOR with 45 men.	
9th may	12.30 am	The Brig.-General came along the trench and ordered the Battalion to reform and continue the attack. The Battn then numbered 83 men commanded by Sgt SOUTH. On this being reported to the Brigade, the Brigade Major ordered	

Instructions regarding War Diaries and Intelligence Summaries are contained in F. S. Regs., Part II. and the Staff Manual respectively. Title pages will be prepared in manuscript.

WAR DIARY

or

INTELLIGENCE SUMMARY.

(Erase heading not required.)

1st YORK & LANCASTER RGT. Army Form C. 2118.

Hour, Date, Place		Summary of Events and Information	Remarks and references to Appendices
9th May		the Battalion back into the support trenches and regot in touch with the regiment on their right. There they found the MIDDLESEX Regiment. Lt O'RILEY took command and sent back for reinforcements from his own regiment.	
	about 3.30am	Two platoons of the Middlesex regiment came up.	
	" 5. am	Lt Briscoe rejoined with 17 men from Batt H.Q. and took over command of the Battalion. All day the Battalion remained in the support trenches under heavy shell fire.	
	about 11 pm	Capt. H. Swales Johnson arrived in the trenches and took over command from Lt Briscoe.	
10th May	4am	Lt Briscoe was killed	
		In the evening the details of the Battalion were formed into a Company under Capt Forster. This Company was part of a Composite Battalion which relieved the Welsh Regiment.	
11 May	12.30am	The Battalion was relieved and marched back to the huts at YPRES where they remained all day	
	9 pm	Left the huts and marched back to a wood near VLAMERTINGHE.	
12th May	5.30am	The details under Capt Forster rejoined the Battalion in the bivouac in the wood	
	6. pm	Marched to POPERINGHE where the Battalion was billeted in sheds surrounding a farm.	
13th May	POPERINGHE	Lt Norris joined with a draft of 340 men	These men were sent to the 3rd Batt" from the 3rd N. Staffs and proceeded to the 1st Batt" within a week of joining the 3rd Bn
14th "		In the afternoon the Battalion was ordered to "stand to" to be ready to move at a moments notice	
	5. am	marched out of billets to a farm near VLAMERTINGHE as part of Army Reserve. the Batt" stood to for 3 hours out of every 12	
15th "	VLAMERTINGHE	At rest	
16th "	"	At rest	

(73989) W4141—463. 400,000. 9/14. H.&J.Ltd. Forms/C. 2118/10.

Instructions regarding War Diaries and Intelligence Summaries are contained in F. S. Regs., Part II. and the Staff Manual respectively. Title pages will be prepared in manuscript.

WAR DIARY
or
~~INTELLIGENCE SUMMARY.~~
(*Erase heading not required.*)

1st YORK + LANCASTER RGT

Army Form C. 2118.

Hour, Date, Place	Summary of Events and Information	Remarks and references to Appendices
17th May. Farm VLAMERTINGHE	Maj C.E. BAYLEY D.S.O took over the Command from Capt H SWALES-JOHNSON. He arrived from the 2nd Battalion accompanied by Capt E. BUCKLEY	
18th May	Battalion rested in farm.	
19th "	Battalion route marched to billets near WINNEZEELE starting at 10.45 am.	
20th " H.Q Farm WINNEZEELE	and, after a halt of 1½ hours at midday, reached the farms about 6 pm rested in Billets	
21st " "	83rd I.B was inspected by the C. in C. in pouring rain at 11.30 am at WINNEZEELE. For extract of speech see	App. VIII
	Battalion left billets at 3.15 pm and marched to the aerodrome near POPERINGHE	
	At 9pm Company Officers + adjutant went to inspect support dug-outs of the LEINSTER + 5th YORKS. REGTS 82nd I.B. in SANCTUARY WOOD	
22nd " POPERINGHE	The Battalion left aerodrome at 3.45 pm and marched through YPRES. At a halt near Bde H.Q. (ECOLE de BIENFAISANCE) a shell fell among the men of No 12 Platoon 'C' Coy, killing 3 and wounding 10. The men were lying down on the right hand side of the road and the shell fell in the right ditch. The men behaved very well considering that, for the majority, it was their first experience under fire. The Companies took over the dug outs in SANCTUARY WOOD at 11pm	
23rd " H.Q dugout SANCTUARY WOOD	Men chiefly occupied in cleaning up the wood which was left in a very dirty state. The officers visited the fire trenches held by the KLI, 2nd KOLR, 5th KOLR, + 2nd East YORKS.	
24th 3.am	Heavy firing. Enemy attacked ~~the~~ Brigades on our left after using a large quantity of Gas.	
3.30 "	9th Lancers report that they are weak through their men being gassed. Capt Buckley sent a platoon to support them.	
4. am	Capt WALKER & Capt BUCKLEY sent to investigate position in trenches	
5.15 am	Heavy firing continues	
7.30 "	Cavalry Brigade report that section of their line NORTH of HOOGE badly gassed and fire trenches lost. Capt WALKER with "D" Coy was sent to reinforce 18th Hussars at HOOGE.	

(73989) W4141—463. 400,000. 9/14. H.&J.Ltd. Forms/C. 2118/10.

Instructions regarding War Diaries and Intelligence Summaries are contained in F. S. Regs., Part II. and the Staff Manual respectively. Title pages will be prepared in manuscript.

WAR DIARY or INTELLIGENCE SUMMARY.

(*Erase heading not required.*)

1st YORK & LANCASTER REGIMENT.

Army Form C. 2118.

Hour, Date, Place		Summary of Events and Information	Remarks and references to Appendices
24th May	10. am	Capt FORSTER with "A" Coy were sent to occupy ZOUAVE WOOD, supported by two Machine Guns under Lt LAWS. Lt LAWS was wounded in the back and carried to dressing station at Bn HQ	This officer subsequently died from wounds in hospital at YPRES on the following day.
	11.10 am	Capt FORSTER reports " My patrol from my front reports only wounded men of the BUFFS and LANCERS are retiring. On my left flank in the wood are the 15th HUSSARS, and on their left flank a company of D.L.I."	
	11.20 am	Capt FORSTER reports " A 11th Hussar man has come in on my right flank and reports that the 9th Lancers are still in their trench on my right flank."	
	12. noon	Report from 83rd I.B. see	App. IX
	12.5 pm	Capt FORSTER reports " The 9th Lancers are on my right front. On my left flank are the 15th Hussars, lining part of the wood and on their left flank are the D.L.I. I will go down the line West and get out patrols. The Road on my immediate front appears to be clear of the enemy. There are men in the dug outs in the wood on my front	
	12.15 "	2nd Lt HILDRED reports " I have retired my two guns to door corners of HATHE COPSE, one on each flank of the Squadron there. The position on our left rear flank was enfiladed from three sides.	
	1.30 "	Capt BUCKLEY reports " Unable to get in touch with Capt WALKER, as we are separated by 2 Companies of the BUFFS. Cannot see anything of North side of MENIN ROAD. My position is N.W. Corner of I 24 B	See map App IX
	1.50 "	2/Lt H.A.K. HALCOMB reports " I am in Square I. 18 with "D" Coy; 200 yds inside the wood S of the farm. Capt WALKER halted us here at 8.30 am & he went on ahead to ascertain the exact position of the trench we were to reinforce (15th Hussars). Since then we have not seen him again. Can you please state the exact position of the trench so that I can take the company there if necessary. I am sending out a patrol now to try & pick up communication" Lt HALCOMB was ordered to attach himself to Capt FORSTER who was in the same wood.	

Instructions regarding War Diaries and Intelligence Summaries are contained in F. S. Regs., Part II. and the Staff Manual respectively. Title pages will be prepared in manuscript.

WAR DIARY
or
INTELLIGENCE SUMMARY.
(*Erase heading not required.*)

Army Form C. 2118.

Hour, Date, Place	Summary of Events and Information	Remarks and references to Appendices
24th May 2 pm	Casualty report 2 men killed, Lt LAWS & 15 men wounded.	
2.20 pm	2nd Lt HILDRED reports " I went out of MAPLE COPSE past the place vacated by my guns this morning and advanced a quarter of a mile towards the MENIN ROAD which is about 2800x from MAPLE COPSE, but had to return because (1) They are shelling the open ground between the COPSE and MENIN ROAD (2) They are firing from HILL 60, covering the ground & hitting the wounded who leave MAPLE COPSE en route for YPRES. Four were killed just now. It might be possible to advance towards dusk.	
2.40 pm	Capt ROSTRON B Squadron 5th DG reports " I have orders to withdraw from MAPLE COPSE if I have not definite information of a German attack coming from the rear. I propose to withdraw on the return of my Patrols unless they have definite information of the enemy in force	
3.35 pm	Capt FORSTER reports " My patrol along the MENIN ROAD towards the WEST reports that there are Germans on the MENIN ROAD westwards.	
4.10 pm	83rd Brigade order "Counter attack is being made by 84th Bde between railway and MENIN road to regain trenches lost there. Cooperate by fire from your position" We tried but failed to get in touch with the counter attack. It failed to reach our lines	
4.10	Capt FORSTER reports 5th DLI. on my left flank report that their first patrol out west has not returned. The second patrol sent out by them has returned and reports numerous snipers in the long grass west of the wood and East of the Buildings"	
4.35	83rd Brigade order sent to Capt FORSTER	
5.15	Capt FORSTER reports " I have recalled "D" Coy and suggest that two platoons should face North towards MENIN road and the other two platoons East to support trenches in front of them. This has been done and I am now rejoining 'A' Coy	

Instructions regarding War Diaries and Intelligence Summaries are contained in F. S. Regs., Part II. and the Staff Manual respectively. Title pages will be prepared in manuscript.

WAR DIARY
or
INTELLIGENCE SUMMARY.
(Erase heading not required.)

1st YORK & LANCASTER REGIMENT.

Army Form C. 2118.

Hour, Date, Place		Summary of Events and Information	Remarks and references to Appendices
24th May	5.25 pm	Lt WORKMAN report. Capt FORSTER has gone over to 'D' Coy leaving me in charge. I cannot support counter attack at present, so I am sending out patrols to get in touch with the counter-attack & to find out from the officer in charge how it is possible to assist him. I have sent your letter, re counter attack, on to Capt FORSTER so I expect he will return soon. I have communicated the contents of your letter to the O.C. 5th D.L.I on my left, who has orders not to move without orders from the Colonel of the 9th Lancers.	
	8.pm	Capt FORSTER instructed to clear the ground up to the MENIN road and start the attack at dusk. See report	App. X
	11.45	Report to Bde	App. XI
	12 midnight	Capt WALKER arrived at Bn H.Q wounded in the shoulder. He was hit shortly after he left his Company at 8.30 am. The two Companies under Capt FORSTER were relieved by the Q.O. OXFORDSHIRE HUSSARS. The enemy were reported to be still in a wood North of the MENIN.	
25th May. H.Q. dugouts SANCTUARY WOOD	5.am	Situation normal, nothing to report.	
	12 noon	OXFORDSHIRE HUSSARS report. "The Enemy are occupying a copse North of the H in HOOGE on North side of MENIN road."	Letter from Col Pitman Cmdg 3rd Cav. Corps App XII
	5 pm	Situation normal, nothing to report	
	9.30 pm	all quiet.	
	11.45	Capt Buckley's three platoons were relieved.	
	2.pm	Casualty report 2 killed, 23 wounded 7 missing	
26th May	5 am	Situation report. The three platoons in the fire trenches were relieved last night	
	11.45 am	Brigade order about relief	App XIII
	12. 12 pm		App. XIV
	2. pm	C.O & Coy officers visited trenches held by East YORKS.	
	3 pm.	2nd Lt Roberts, who had gone with 2nd Lt Highfield to visit C.H.Q. dugouts early on morning of May 24th and who has been missing since then was reported by the Brigade as having been admitted into Field Ambulance, suffering from shock.	This officer was reported as wounded in Papers on June 7th under date May 30.

(73989) W4141—463. 400,000. 9/14. H.&J.Ltd. Forms/C. 2118/10.

Instructions regarding War Diaries and Intelligence Summaries are contained in F. S. Regs., Part II. and the Staff Manual respectively. Title pages will be prepared in manuscript.

WAR DIARY *or* ~~INTELLIGENCE~~ SUMMARY.

(*Erase heading not required.*)

1st YORK + LANCASTER REGT

Army Form C. 2118.

Hour, Date, Place	Summary of Events and Information	Remarks and references to Appendices
26 May	Casualty report 3 killed 3 wounded 2 missing	
11 pm	as our Companies were stronger than those they were relieving, 170 men under 2nd Lt White were left in SANCTUARY WOOD and also a garrison of 22 men for Support Point C. Three Companies held the fire trenches and one was in support near the H.Q dug-out.	
27th May H.Q Dug-out behind trenches 5.A.M	Situation normal nothing to report after considerable trouble all the Battalion was supplied with black respirators. Lt H.H. DAVIS RAMC took over from Lt YEO. RAMC.	
2 pm	Casualty report 1 killed 2 wounded	
5 pm	Situation normal, nothing to report.	
28th May ... 5 am	" " " "	
2 pm	Casualty report 1 killed 2 wounded.	
5 pm	Situation normal " "	
6.30 "	Four large bombs for a Trench mortar were dropped near our right trench. The force of the explosion shook the hill, but no one was hurt	
10 pm	The Trench discipline was considerably better than on the previous nights; the men had more confidence and kept their heads well above the parapet when on Sentry.	
29th May ... 5 am	Situation normal nothing to report	
2 pm	Casualty report 1 wounded.	
5 pm	Situation normal, " "	
30th May ... 5 am	" " " "	
2 pm	Casualty report nil	
5 "	Situation normal less activity than usual on the part of the enemies aircraft.	
11 "	The Battalion was relieved by the EAST YORKS and returned to SANCTUARY WOOD. The relief was carried out without any casualties. Garrisons were found for Support Points A. B. E.	
31st May ... 5 am	Situation normal, nothing to report.	
9 pm	Two Cavalry officers were attached for the night and were shewn round the trenches by the Adjutant. Lt LOCAS & 2nd Lt Adsetts. Corwing & ELLISON came up with the Transport from details.	
1st June.	Two more Cavalry officers were attached for the day and were shewn round the trenches	
2 pm	Casualty Report 1 wounded.	

(73989) W4141—463. 400,000. 9/14. H.&J.Ltd. Forms/C. 2118/10.

Appx I

May

Appendix 1

May 1st

Dear Colonel Sherwood,

I am writing to you to say how my sympathies are with your Battalion in the heavy casualties you have sustained during the last ten days.

I am afraid your Battalion is sadly depleted [illegible] over 400 casualties [illegible] the line.

Please convey to the officers and men my sympathy in their losses and my appreciation of their good work in the past.

Yours sincerely,

R. C. Boyle

App 2

To 83rd Bde.
O.C. - East Yorks
O.C. York. Lancs
O.C. 5th Kings Own.

Appendix 2

G. 127 Second

The E. Yorks, York and Lancs and 5th King's Own will march this evening at 5.30 pm via N. of Ypres to Verlorenhoek. under orders of senior O.C. aaa.
Due precautions to be taken against moving in large formations to avoid shelling aaa
83rd Brigade to send Staff Officer to meet and direct Battalions to places they should go. aaa.
All Battalion Commanders and 83rd Brigade to acknowledge.

28th Divn.

app 3

"A" Form. Army Form C. 2121.

MESSAGES AND SIGNALS.

No. of Message

Prefix ______ Code ______ m. | Words | Charge

Office of Origin and Service Instructions

Sent
At ______ m.
To
By

This message is on a/c of: ______ *Service.*

(Signature of "Franking Officer.")

Recd. at ______ m.
Date
From
By

TO Appendix 3

Sender's Number.	Day of Month.	In reply to Number	AAA
* BM 28	Third		

Rifle	Brigade	in	square	D 14 B
and	D 14 D	are	in	urgent
need	of	help	AAA	~~Take~~
~~your~~	Two	companies	York	and
Lancaster	and	one	company	Fifth
Kings	Own	to	march	at
once	to	assistance	of	Rifle
Brigade	or	any	other	part
of	the	line	held	by
the	eleventh	Bde	AAA	Detachment
to	be	under	command	of
Colonel	ISHERWOOD	York	and	Lancaster
AAA	The	company	Fifth	Kings
Own	lately	reported	to	be
in	square	D 20 D	will	~~[struck out]~~
also	come	under	Colonel	ISHERWOODS
orders	if	found		

From 83 Bde
Place
Time 3.15 pm

The above may be forwarded as now corrected. (Z) J. C. Munby Capt

Censor. Signature of Addressor or person authorised to telegraph in his name.

* This line should be erased if not required.

Wt. 11400-2015. 50,000. 2-15. H. M. & S., Ltd.

App 4

"A" Form. Army Form C. 2121.

MESSAGES AND SIGNALS.

No. of Message

Prefix Code m. Office of Origin and Service Instructions.	Words Charge Sent At m. To By	This message is on a/c of: Service. (Signature of "Franking Officer.")	Recd. at m. Date From By [illegible]

TO 83rd Bde Appendix

Sender's Number	Day of Month	In reply to Number	AAA
K 516	4th		

Enemy	have	appeared	opposite	our
left	within	100	yards	of
a	trench	among	the	buildings
AAA	Others	are	advancing	from
wood	S	of	WESTHOEK	AAA
Cannot	get	any	artillery	support

From
Place YORK LANCASTERS [illegible]
Time

The above may be forwarded as now corrected. (Z) [illegible]

Censor. Signature of Addressor or person authorised to telegraph in his name

* This line should be erased if not required.

8350 S. B. Ltd. Wt. W4848/341—50,000. 9/14. Forms C2121/10.

App: 5

"A" Form. Army Form C. 2121.

MESSAGES AND SIGNALS. No. of Message

Prefix SM Code LA m.

Office of Origin and Service Instructions.

YL

Words | Charge

Sent
At 11 10 a m.
To ZHCR
By Lc Barker

This message is on a/c of:
[illegible] Service.

(Signature of "Franking Officer.")

Recd. at m.
Date YL
From 4/5/15
By

TO 83rd Brigade App 5

Sender's Number	Day of Month	In reply to Number	AAA
K 517	4th	—	

Enemy are massing behind houses in square J 1 d just in front of our trenches AAA Please get artillery to fire at them AAA Can you possibly send up more machine gun ammunit as Kings Own still have 24 boxes of ours and we are likely to run short.

From
Place YORK LANCASTERS 11. 5 am
Time

The above may be forwarded as now corrected. (Z) [illegible]

[illegible] Censor. Signature of Addressor or person authorised to telegraph in his name

* This line should be erased if not required.

8350 S. B. Ltd. Wt. W4843/341—50,000. 9/14. Forms C2121/10.

App 6

"A" Form. Army Form C. 2121

MESSAGES AND SIGNALS. No. of Message

Prefix	Code	m.	Words	Charge	This message is on a/c of:	Recd. at	m.
Office of Origin and Service Instructions.			Sent		Service.	Date	
			At	m.		From	
			To				
			By		(Signature of "Franking Officer.")	By	

TO 83rd Brigade App. 6.

Sender's Number	Day of Month	In reply to Number	AAA
K 518	4th	—	

Enemy are entrenching themselves on a line running from J1d5.5 to where the railway leaves J1b AAA Artillery shells have not fired a round to dislodge them

From
Place YORK LANCASTERS 11 30 a.m.
Time

The above may be forwarded as now corrected. (Z) B C Johnston Lt

Censor. Signature of Addressor or person authorised to telegraph in his name

* This line should be erased if not required.

8350 S. B. Ltd. Wt. W4843/541—50,000. 9/14. Forms C2121/10.

App VII

28th Division.

I forward herewith an extract from my report on the operations at YPRES during the period 22nd April to 4th May, 1915.

I am most grateful to the Geddes' Detachment for the gallant work they did.

I regret that the work in which my Division has been engaged since the operations referred to has prevented my sending you this extract at an earlier date.

28.5.1915. sd/ E.A. Alderson, Lieut-General,
Commanding 1st Canadian Division.

Appendix No 1
Chemin de fer
Eglise
ZONNEBEKE.
Molenaarelstaan
DUGOUTS
DUGOUTS
DUGOUT
DUGOUTS
DUGOUT
Polygone
de
Zonnebeke

VIII

App VIII

(Issued with 2nd Army Routine Order No. 94, dated 22nd May, 1915).

Precis of speeches delivered by Field-Marshal Sir John French, G.C.B., O.M., etc., Commander-in-Chief of the British Forces in the Field, to Brigades of the 27th and 28th Divisions on the 21st and 22nd May, 1915.

"I came over to say a few words to you and to tell you how much I, as Commander-in-Chief of this Army, appreciate the splendid work that you have all done during the recent fighting. You have fought the second Battle of Ypres, which will rank among the most desperate and hardest fights of the war. You may have thought because you were not attacking the enemy that you were not helping to shorten the war. On the contrary, by your splendid endurance and bravery, you have done a great deal to shorten it. In this, the second Battle of Ypres, the Germans tried by every means in their power to get possession of that unfortunate town. They concentrated large forces of troops and artillery, and further than that they had recourse to that mean and dastardly practice hitherto unheard of in civilised warfare, namely the use of asphyxiating gases. You have performed the most difficult, arduous and terrific task of withstanding a stupendous bombardment by heavy artillery, probably the fiercest artillery fire ever directed against troops, and warded off the enemy's attacks with magnificent bravery. By your steadiness and devotion, both the German plans were frustrated. He was unable to get possession of Ypres—if he had done this he would probably have succeeded in preventing neutral powers from intervening—and he was also unable to distract us from delivering our attack in conjunction with the French in Arras - Armentieres district. Had you failed to repulse his attacks, and made it necessary for more troops to be sent to your assistance, our operations in the South might not have been able to take place and would certainly not have been as successful as they have been. Your Colours have many famous names emblazoned on them, but none will be more famous or more well-deserved than that of the Second Battle of Ypres. I want you one and all to understand how thoroughly I realise and appreciate what you have done. I wish to thank you, each officer, non-commissioned officer and man for the services you have rendered by doing your duty so magnificently, and I am sure that your Country will thank you too."

1st Printing Co., R.E. 2nd Army Section. 63

VIII

IX

"A" Form. Army Form C. 2121.

MESSAGES AND SIGNALS.

No. of Message

Prefix SB Code MOR m. Words 92 Charge

Office of Origin and Service Instructions.

2 HC

Sent

At m.

To

By

This message is on a/c of:

Service.

(Signature of "Franking Officer.")

Recd. at m.

Date

From

By

TO ~~[illegible]~~ YORK and LANCASTER

Sender's Number	Day of Month	In reply to Number	AAA
BM343	24		

Enemy	reported	having	broken	our
line	north	of	MENIN	ROAD
AAA	There	are	five	platoon
and	two	machine	guns	York
and	Lancaster	on	north	edge
of	wood	in	I 18 c	AAA
4 R	D G's	occupy	a	line
in	the	open	about	200
yards	south	of	MENIN	road
facing	north	in	I 17 a	AAA
Send	the	two	companies	now
in	GHQ	line	to	reinforce
4 R D G	and	come	under	orders
of	O C	4 R D G	AAA	These
companies	to	move	at	once
AAA	Addressed	Hogge	repeated	York
and	Lancaster			

From 83 Bde

Place

Time 12 noon

App IX

The above may be forwarded as now corrected. (Z)

Censor. Signature of Addressor or person authorised to telegraph in his name

* This line should be erased if not required.

158 S. B. Ltd. Wt. W5673/619—50,000. 10/14. Forms C2121/10.

Copy. Report on the action near ZOUAVE WOOD on 24th May 1915.

On the report from the Cavalry Bgde. on our left that the enemy had broken through HOOGE on to the MENIN ROAD I detached a company, plus one platoon to ZOUAVE WOOD accompanied by two M. Guns with instructions to hold the Northern edge of the wood, with one M. Gun on the Eastern edge.

I had previously sent one Company to re-inforce the 18th Hussars and three platoons to the 9th Lancers.

About midday the Company in ZOUAVE WOOD was supported by another Company - Captain Forster being in command of the two Companies

He was ordered to push out patrols at all costs to the MENIN Road and if possible to advance and take up a more advanced position

Owing to the enemy being in buildings and the ditches on both the NORTH and SOUTH sides of the ROAD he was unable to get his patrols forward. Four patrols were all shot but one Corporal, though wounded and having his companion killed came back and gave very useful information. It was on information received from this Corporal and Captain Forster that I decided it was of vital importance to hold on to ZOUAVE WOOD and to extend his left flank more to the SOUTH to secure our left flank as it appeared as if the enemy were working round our left rear

Captain Forster was instructed to do this but the OC 11th Hussars had already done this. I therefore sent two M Guns to take up a position covering our left rear

Captain Forster was given instructions to act as a flank guard and cover any possible withdrawal of our troops SOUTH of the MENIN Road

The two Companies in ZOUAVE WOOD held on all day under a heavy shell fire till the evening when I sent orders to Captain Forster to attack the enemy on the MENIN ROAD, dislodge him from all the buildings and drive him back so as to make our left flank secure, as I feared that if we delayed he would bring up M-Guns and establish himself during the night and turn our flank. Captain Forster was also instructed to endeavour to get in touch with the counter attack on the NORTH of MENIN Road

As soon as it was dusk Captain Forster moved forward from the WOOD with one Company leaving the other in support and getting in touch with the left flank on MENIN ROAD he worked WESTWARDS down the ROAD clearing all houses and ditches, killing several and driving them back, at the same time he had a patrol working down the NORTHERN side of MENIN ROAD clearing the ditch where some of the enemy had dug themselves in

4

As the enemy retired their own men sent up flares and opened fire on them.

Captain Forster sent out a patrol well to the North of MENIN Road but they did not succeed in getting touch with the counter attack.

Lieut Workman was in charge of the patrol and he ably seconded Captain Forster in the attack which was quite successful.

The company afterwards returned to LOUVAIN WOOD and were relieved during the night. Our casualties were comparatively slight. Several identity marks taken off dead Germans were forwarded to the Brigade.

27/6/1915

(Sd.) G.E. Bayley, Major,
Comdg. R. York Lancaster Regt.

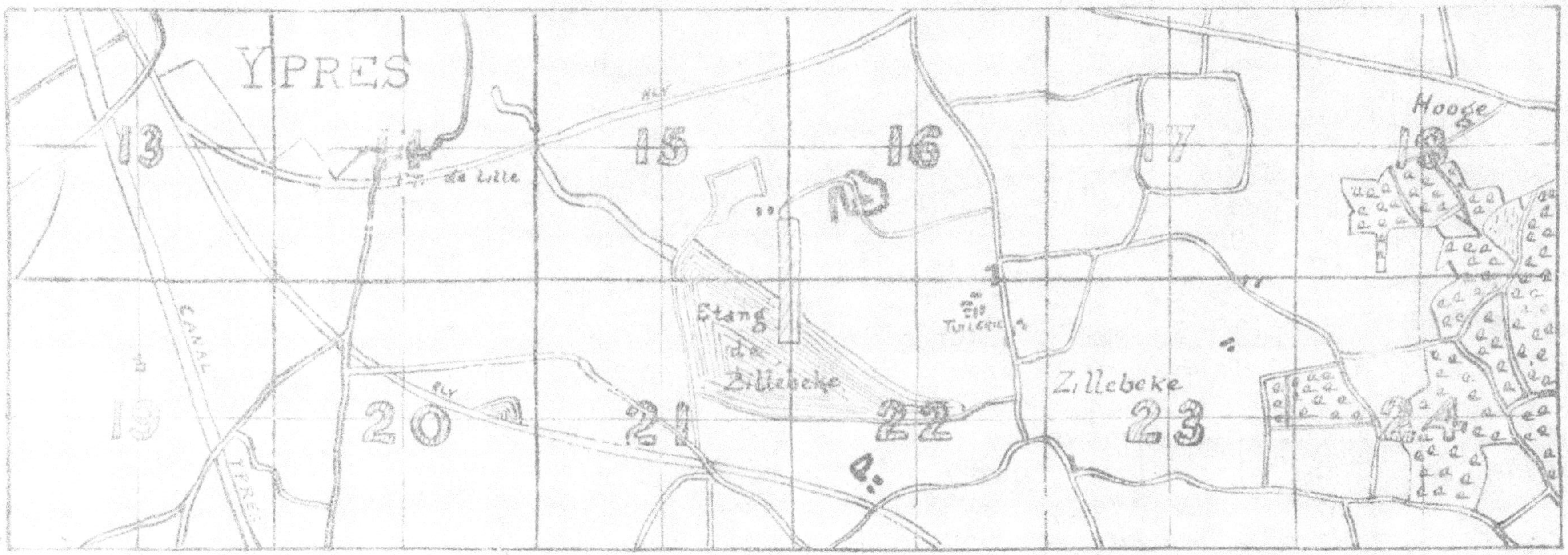

YPRES
Hooge
Etang de Zillebeke
Zillebeke
Tuilerie
CANAL
YPRES
13
14
15
16
17
18
19
20
21
22
23
24

XI

"A" Form. Army Form C. 2121.

MESSAGES AND SIGNALS.

No. of Message

Prefix ___ Code ___ m.	Words	Charge	This message is on a/c of:	Recd. at ___ m.
Office of Origin and Service Instructions.	Sent		___ Service.	Date
	At ___ m.			From
	To			By
	By		(Signature of "Franking Officer.")	

TO 83rd I B

Sender's Number	Day of Month	In reply to Number	AAA
KS1	24/5/15		

Our attack on the MENIN Road has been successful AAA All the enemy have been driven back as far as the point at which our left flank rests AAA The Companies have now withdrawn to ZOUAVE WOOD after leaving a post on the MENIN ROAD facing north AAA Patrols have been pushed on to the north to try and get in touch with the Cavalry attack but these patrols will now be withdrawn and the OXFORDSHIRE HUSSARS will be asked to send out similar patrols AAA Some of the enemy have been killed and the papers and identity marks will be sent to the Brigade as soon as possible

From O C 1st Y & L Regt
Place
Time 11.45 pm

Appx XI

The above may be forwarded as now corrected. (Z) [illegible]

Censor. Signature of Addressor or person authorised to telegraph in his name

* This line should be erased if not required.

5350 S. B. Ltd Wt. W4842/511—50,000. 9/14 Forms C2121/10.

XII

Letter from Col Pitman 11th Hussars 73
Cmdg 3rd Cavalry Corps

Dear Bailey

May 25

I wish to thank you very much for all the assistance you gave me throughout the day yesterday. and I must apologise for not having sent those 50 men back last night, it was entirely my fault in the hustle of trying to get all the reliefs carried out before dawn that I quite forgot them. Will you please tell the officer commanding the half company that I am very sorry and I hope he got back to you all right.

Yours sincerely

T T Pitman

App XII

XIII

"A" Form. Army Form C. 2121.

MESSAGES AND SIGNALS.

No. of Message

Prefix ✓ Code m.	Words	Charge	This message is on a/c of:	Recd. at 12.20 P m.
Office of Origin and Service Instructions.	Sent		Service.	Date 26/5/15
2HC Trinity	At m.			From 2HC
	To			
	By		(Signature of "Franking Officer.")	By L/C Barker

TO YORK AND LANCASTER

Sender's Number	Day of Month	In reply to Number	AAA
10M 378	26th		

York and Lancaster will relieve East Yorkshire tonight AAA Time and method to be arranged between Commanding Officers AAA Owing to difference in strength it is suggested that York and Lancaster put surplus men into redoubt I 30 b 9.9 or into the support trench I 24 C if considered desirable AAA Very ~~gu~~ pistols to be handed over by East Yorkshire AAA Report when relief complete and exact ~~dist~~ distribution

From 83rd Bde

Place

Time 11.45 AM

App XIII

The above may be forwarded as now corrected. (Z)

Censor. Signature of Addressor or person authorised to telegraph in his name

W Barker Lt

* This line should be erased if not required.

S. B. Ltd. Wt. W4848/541—50,000. 9/14. Forms C2121/10.

XIV

"A" Form. Army Form C. 2121.

MESSAGES AND SIGNALS. No. of Message

Prefix SM Code 12.11P m.	Words	Charge	This message is on a/c of:	Recd. at 12.55P m.
Office of Origin and Service Instructions.	Sent		Service.	Date YL 26/5/15
2HC	At m.			From E
	To			By Lt Barker
	By		(Signature of "Franking Officer.")	

TO York and Lancs

*Sender's Number	Day of Month	In reply to Number	AAA
BM 382	26th		

Reference 381 Brigadier considers desirable to occupy redoubt I20A9.9 and part of trench in I24C by night at any rate with a minimum garrison of twenty men each and a machine gun in redoubt AAA Garrisons should be employed in improving these places an if R E are working there the garrison must work under their orders

From E [illegible]
Place
Time 12.11PM

XIV

The above may be forwarded as now corrected. (Z)

Censor. Signature of Addressor or person authorised to telegraph in his name

* This line should be erased if not required.

[illegible] B. Ltd Wt. W4843/541—50,000. 9/14 Forms C2121/10.

EXTRACT FROM REPORT BY LIEUT-GENERAL E.A.H.ALDERSON,C.B.
ON OPERATIONS EMBRACED IN THE PERIOD 22nd APRIL to 4th MAY
BOTH DATES INCLUSIVE

-----------:-------------

Colonel Geddes Detachment.

2nd D. of Corn. L.I. 9th Royal Scots (T).	27th Division.
5th R. Lancs R. (T) 2nd E. Yorks R. 1st York & Lancs R. 2nd E. Kent R. 3rd Middx. R.	28th Division.

This detachment was the first of the reinforcements to arrive, and, though it was hastily formed into a Brigade and was composed of seven different battalions, it did excellent work from the23rd April until it was withdrawn on the morning of the 28th April.

I much regret the loss of Colonel Geddes who was killed just as his detachment was withdrawing. I regret also that, owing to his death, and to his Acting Brigade Major being wounded, I have no record of any special services rendered by the Units of his Command. I can, however, testify to the gallant conduct of the officers and men of the 3rd Middlesex Regiment which took part in the counter-attack East of the Canal on the evening of the 23rd April.

----------------- : ---------------

83rd Bde.

28th Div.

WAR
DIARY

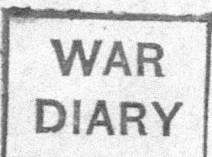

1st YORK & LANCS.

J U N E

1 9 1 5

Appendices I to XVIII

Instructions regarding War Diaries and Intelligence Summaries are contained in F. S. Regs., Part II. and the Staff Manual respectively. Title pages will be prepared in manuscript.

WAR DIARY
or
INTELLIGENCE SUMMARY.
(Erase heading not required.)

1st YORK & LANCASTER REGT

Army Form C. 2118.

Hour, Date, Place		Summary of Events and Information	Remarks and references to Appendices
2nd June	SANCTUARY WOOD 8 am	Heavy bombardment of ZOUAVE WOOD	
	11 am	Bombardment continues	
	1.45 pm	Operation Orders received	App. I
	3 pm	Casualty return 8 wounded	
	4 pm	Very heavy bombardment of ZOUAVE WOOD & [illegible] on MENIN road.	
	6 pm	Report Bde.	App. II
	7.30 "	" " Batt'n still intact, will report if anything happens.	
	8.30 "	" " "	App. III
3rd June	12.15 am	" " York & Lancaster Regt relieved	
	4.10 am	" " The Batt'n is now in the huts.	
	In the Huts.	Operation orders No 23	App. IV
	7 pm	Arrived at billets at WINNEZEELE. Generally tired.	
4th June	H.Q. Farm WINNEZEELE	Rested in Billets	
5 June	" "	" " "	
		Programme of training while at rest [illegible] orders and	App. V
6 June	" "	at rest. Maj ROBERTSON [illegible] left as second in command.	
7th	" "		
8th	" "	Maj [illegible] [illegible] [illegible]	
9th	" "		
10th	" "	[illegible] [illegible] 12th.	
11	" "		
12	" "	Battalion Route March from 9 am - 12.30 pm	
13	" "		
14	" "	Left WINNEZEELE district at 1.45 pm and marched to H.Q. between LOCRE and LA CLYTTE arriving at 8 pm.	
		Brigade operation orders	App. VI
15	H.Q. Farm RENINGHELST	Battalion At Rest.	App. VII

(73989) W4141—463. 400,000. 9/14. H.&J.Ltd. Forms/C. 2118/10.

Instructions regarding War Diaries and Intelligence Summaries are contained in F. S. Regs., Part II. and the Staff Manual respectively. Title pages will be prepared in manuscript.

WAR DIARY
or
INTELLIGENCE SUMMARY.
(*Erase heading not required.*)

1st York & Lancaster Regt

Army Form C. 2118.

Hour, Date, Place	Summary of Events and Information	Remarks and references to Appendices
16th June H.Q. farm nr 2000s	Major G. E. Bayley DSO, having commanded the Battalion for 30 days, took the rank of temp Lieut-Colonel. Bde. Routine order No 377. The Commander in Chief has awarded the medal for Distinguished Conduct in the Field to No 20054 Corporal C Bromley 1st York & Lancaster Rgt. Action for which commended For gallant conduct when on patrol near H000 E on 24th May 1915. His companion was killed, but he went on though wounded in the back. He, however, returned, and before being bandaged up, gave in his report to the officer Commanding his Company. It was chiefly due to his report that subsequent important action was taken. The Commanding Officer congratulates (B.O. June 16th) Corporal Bromley on his well earned distinction, which was gained for his gallant conduct on the 24th of May. The Commanding Officer takes this opportunity to congratulate the Battalion on the way they behaved on that occasion and it may be some satisfaction to them to know that the Cavalry Corps thanked the Battalion for their assistance and in addition the Brigadier expressed his satisfaction at the way the Battalion had behaved. The above honour serves to commemorate the occasion and is one which is shared by all the Battalion.	

(73989) W4141—463. 400,000. 9/14. H.&J.Ltd. Forms/C. 2118/10.

Instructions regarding War Diaries and Intelligence Summaries are contained in F. S. Regs., Part II. and the Staff Manual respectively. Title pages will be prepared in manuscript.

WAR DIARY
or
INTELLIGENCE SUMMARY.
(Erase heading not required.)

1st YORK & LANCASTER Rgt.

Army Form C. 2118

Hour, Date, Place	Summary of Events and Information	Remarks and references to Appendices
17th June Nr LOCRE	At rest.	
5.10pm	General BULFIN came to see rifle battery.	
6pm	Battalion on duty for the Brigade till 6pm the next day.	
18th June. Nr LOCRE	At 2pm Officers rode to KEMMEL to inspect the trenches held by the 138th Brigade (5th NOTTS & DERBY)	
19th June	Brigade operation orders No 35	
	Battalion " " No 2	see App VIII
	Notes by Brigadier General H.S.L. RAVENSHAW.	see App IX
	The Battalion took over the trenches occupied by the 5th Notts & Derby the relief was completed by 1.30am. The Companies were distributed as follows:-	App X
	A Coy 1 platoon in VIERSTRAAT. 1 platoon in Brigade dug out, 2 platoons in farms.	
	B Coy held trenches L_2 L_3 L_4 L_5 L_6 L_{7a}; the latter two only at night	
	C Coy " " L_7 K_{1B}, K_2, K_{2A}, K_{2B}, K_3.	
	D Coy " " M_1 & L_7. M_5 was not occupied	see App XI a rough map.
	The machine guns occupied emplacements in trenches M_1, L_5, K_{2B} and in VIERSTRAAT, while one was kept in Reserve at H.Q. which	
20th June HOWITZER FARM	was in Howitzer Farm three quarters of a mile from the head of the communication trenches on the KEMMEL - VIERSTRAAT Road. The dumping ground was at SANDBAG VILLA close to this road.	
4.30am	Reports to Brigade. Situation normal, wind slight drift N.E	
10.30am	The O.C 3rd F.A. Brigade paid Col Bayley a visit at Headquarters & arranged with him to test the telephone wires from the trenches to the Batteries. The Batteries supporting the trenches were the 18th 22nd and 62nd, from left to right.	
11 am	Report to Brigade. Situation normal, slight but increasing N.E wind The C.O and Major Robertson visited the trenches. Most of the day was spent cleaning up the trenches and making new sanitary arrangements. Flies abounded in enormous numbers	
12 noon	Casualty return. Killed other ranks three, wounded other ranks one. Two of these were due to men looking over the parapet by day, strictly against orders.	

(73989) W4141—463. 400,000. 9/14. H.&J.Ltd. Forms/C. 2118/10.

Instructions regarding War Diaries and Intelligence Summaries are contained in F. S. Regs., Part II. and the Staff Manual respectively. Title pages will be prepared in manuscript.

WAR DIARY 1st YORK & LANCASTER REGT.
or
INTELLIGENCE SUMMARY.
(Erase heading not required.)

Army Form C. 2118.

Hour, Date, Place		Summary of Events and Information	Remarks and references to Appendices
20th June HOWITZER FARM	3pm	The C.O. met Brigadier General Rawenstaw at the end of the FOSSE and conducted him round some of the trenches.	
	4.30pm	Report to Bde — Situation normal; wind N.E. slight.	
		During the night patrols were sent out to find out if the enemy were holding their line in strength. B & C Coys reported that the enemy's trenches were strongly held; while D Coy concluded that there were only a few men in the front trench.	
		The men were fully occupied all day cleaning up the trenches and making new sanitary arrangements. At night they worked on new fire trenches and converted communication trenches into fire trenches.	
21st June	4.30am	Report to Brigade — Situation normal; wind very mild E.S.E.	
	11 am	" " " ; wind still.	
	12 noon	Casualty report — Killed one; wounded one accidentally.	
	4.30pm	Report to Brigade — situation normal, wind still.	
		During the night the Companies had a practice alarm with the Batteries.	
		The "C" 2nd Battery fired one round 3 minutes after the alarm was given in K trench	
		The 22nd " " 2 " " " " " L "	
		The 15th Battery did not reply as the telephone communication was broken.	
22nd June	4.30am	Report to Brigade — Situation normal, wind still, no change in disposition of troops.	
	11 am	Situation unchanged; fair breeze N.E.	
	12 noon	Casualty report — nil	
	4.30pm	Situation normal, wind fresh N.E.	
		The Brigadier has tea at H.Q. farm.	
	6.30pm	Some shells fell near billet occupied by 2nd platoon of A Coy. One hit a shed killing a horse and wounding two civilians.	
23 June	4.30am	Report to Brigade — Situation normal, wind still, no change in disposition.	
	10 am	Brigade telephone instructions Col Bayley to meet Major Barrett 2nd YORKS at the head of the FOSSE.	
	11 am	Situation normal, wind N.E. fresh.	
	12 noon	Casualty report — nil	
	2 pm	Major Barrett and 3 officers arrived at H.Q. and arranged the details for the relief to be carried out that night.	

(73989) W4141—463. 400,000. 9/14. H.&J.Ltd. Forms/C. 2118/10.

Instructions regarding War Diaries and Intelligence Summaries are contained in F. S. Regs., Part II. and the Staff Manual respectively. Title pages will be prepared in manuscript.

WAR DIARY or INTELLIGENCE SUMMARY.

(*Erase heading not required.*)

1st York & Lancaster Rgt.

Army Form C. 2118.

Hour, Date, Place	Summary of Events and Information	Remarks and references to Appendices
23rd June Howitzer Farm	Brigade operation orders no 37	See App XII
	Battalion " " no 3	See App XIII
4.30pm	Relief & Brigade situation normal; Wind N.E. mild	
	The Battalion was relieved by 1 am and the Companies marched back to the Huts at SCHERPENBERG	See App XIV
24th June Farm at SCHERPENBERG	General Bulfin XXVIII Division visited Col Bayly. D Coy were relieved by the Northumberland Fusiliers and reached the camp at 4 am.	
25 June " "	Brigade operation orders no 38	See App XV
	Rested in billets. Two Companies always being ready to move off at an hours notice. In the evening the Battalion found working and carrying parties for the Brigade	
26th June " "	Rested in billets.	
	Brigade operation orders no 39	App XVI
	Officers & NCOs of C & D Companies reconnoitred G.H.Q line allotted to the Battalion	
27 June " "	Church Parade at Bn Headquarters at 11.30 am. Officers & NCOs of A & B Companies inspected G.H.Q line and a combined report was sent to the Brigade. Working & carrying parties were found as before.	
28th June " "	Rested in billets.	
29th June " "	Brigade operation orders no 40. Battalion operation orders no 4. The Battalion left the Huts at 8.30 pm At the halt on the LA CLYTTE - KEMMEL road it came on to rain very heavily, so the Battalion sheltered under the trees until the worst was over. The rain further delayed the relief which was completed by 11.40 pm, but not reported until 12.40 am owing to breakdown of [illegible]	

(73989) W4141—463. 400,000. 9/14. H.&J.Ltd. Forms/C. 2118/10.

Army Form C. 2118.

WAR DIARY
or
INTELLIGENCE SUMMARY.
(*Erase heading not required.*)

1st York & Lancaster Regt.

Instructions regarding War Diaries and Intelligence Summaries are contained in F. S. Regs., Part II. and the Staff Manual respectively. Title pages will be prepared in manuscript.

Hour, Date, Place	Summary of Events and Information	Remarks and references to Appendices
June 30th. HQrs YORK HOUSE KEMMEL.	The 2nd Kings Own had moved their Headquarters from HOWITZER FARM to a farm on the KEMMEL-VIERSTRAAT Road as the former was too far away from the trenches.	
	'C' Coy occupied the trenches K_{1B}, K_2, K_{2A}, K_{2B} and L_1	
	'B' " " " " L_2, 3, 4, 5, 6.	
	'D' Coy occupied the support trenches L_6 L_7 left, L_7 right & K_3	
	Two platoons of 'A' Coy went to HOWITZER FARM, one at SANDBAG VILLA and the other at a farm nearby.	
	The machine guns were placed in L_2, L_6, L_7 and K_{2B}	
4.30 am	Situation normal; Wind S.W. mild	
11. am	" " ; " S.W. by W. fresh	
12 noon	Casualty report wounded other ranks one	
12.35 pm	O.C. 'D' Coy reported [illegible] enemy had opened fire with Common shell but very little damage was done	
4.30 pm	Situation report Situation normal, slight shelling in K trenches; Wind S.W. by W.	
	The trenches had been left in a dirty state. Most of the day was spent in cleaning up. 'A' Coy worked on the dug outs near the new Sandbagged barn to make it safe for occupation. A working party of 50 from the KOYLI dug part of the new C. Trench from K_3 to Supporting Point No. 13	

Appx no 6
App I

Operation Order no...
by
Brigadier-General H.S.L. Ravenshaw. C.M.G.
Commanding 83rd Infantry Brigade.

ECOLE DE BIEN FAIRANCE.
2nd June. 1915.

Ref, Sheet 28. 1/40,000.

1. 9th Brigade will releive 83rd Brigade on night 2nd - 3rd June. 83rd Brigade, on relief, will march to huts in H. 14 to H. 19.

2. Battalions will be releived by the following units of 9th Brigade:-

(a) 2/East Yorkshire Regt by Liverpool Scottish.
(b) 1/York & Lancaster -"- by Scots Fusiliers and 2 coy's R. Fusiliers.
(c) K.O. Yorkshire Light Infantry by } Northumberland Fusiliers.
2/Kings Own Regt by }

3. One Officer per battalion, two guides per company and two guides for headquarters will be detailed to meet the releiving units as follows:-

(a) Guides of 2/East Yorkshire Regt 1/York & Lancaster Regt and 5/Kings Own Regt at road junction H. 18. d. 10. 5 at 8 P.M.
(b) Guides of 2nd Kings Own Regt and 1st K.O.Y.L.I. at Brigade headquarters at 8. 30 P.M.

Transport and M. GUNS- 4. Two guides for Transport and two guides for machine gun detachment will be detailed by each battalion to be at Brigade Headquarters by 8-30 P.M.

ROUTES 5. After relief battalions will march independantly by companies under arrangements of commanding officers to their destination Routes are allotted as follows:-

(a) YPRES - VLAMERTINGHE road - { 2/Kings Own Regt and 1st KOYLI -"-.

(b) ZILLEBEKE - KRUISSTRAAT - in cross-roads H. 16. d. - 5th Kings Own Regt, 2nd East Yorkshire -"-, 1st York & Lancaster -"-

No 2.

6. Guides from 1st line transport of battalions will meet them at H 14 b.
Units will report their relief by telephone and their arrival at the huts by orderly.

R S Follett Capt.
Bde major.
83rd Inf Brigade.

issued at .. 12-15 p.m.

Copy No 1 War Diary.
-"- -2. Operation File.
-"- -"-3 2nd Kings Own.
-"- -"-4 2nd East Yorkshire.
-"- -"-5 1st K.O.Y.L.I.
-"- -"- 6 1st York & Lancaster.
-"- -"- 7 5th Kings Own.
-"- -"- 8. 9th Infantry Brigade.

II

"A" Form.

Army Form C. 2121

MESSAGES AND SIGNALS.

No. of Message

Prefix	Code	m.	Words	Charge	This message is on a/c of:	Recd. at m.
Office of Origin and Service Instructions.			Sent		Service.	Date App II
			At m.			From
			To			
			By		(Signature of "Franking Officer.")	By

TO 83rd I. B

Sender's Number	Day of Month	In reply to Number	AAA
KS59	2/6/15		

Have	placed	one	company	at
disposal	of	officer	commanding	6th
Cavalry	at	his	urgent	request
for	a	reserve	Company	AAA.
Will	inform	you	if	they
are	used	AAA	Situation	at
present	is	that	report	came
that	enemy	made	half	hearted
attack	in	direction	of	HOOGE
AAA	all	quiet	in	front
AAA.				

From O.C.
Place 1st Y & L Regt
Time 6pm

The above may be forwarded as now corrected. (Z)

Censor. Signature of Addressor or person authorised to telegraph in his name: Thomas Shaw Lt, Adjutant 1st Y & L Regt.

* This line should be erased if not required.

8350 S. B. Ltd Wt. W4843/511—50,000. 9/14. Forms C2121/10.

III

"A" Form. Army Form C. 2121.

MESSAGES AND SIGNALS.

No. of Message

Prefix ___ Code ___ m.	Words	Charge	This message is on a/c of:	Recd. at ___ m.
Office of Origin and Service Instructions.	Sent		___ Service.	Date
	At ___ m.			From
	To			
	By		(Signature of "Franking Officer.")	By

TO 83rd I B

Sender's Number	Day of Month	In reply to Number	AAA
1561	2/8/15		

6th	Cavalry	Brigade	state
that	reliefs	are	in
abeyance	until	situation	is
cleared	AAA	2	that
[illegible]	AAA	The	officer
Commanding	6th	Cavalry	Bde
appears	to	think	that
my	Battalion	is	at
his	disposal	AAA	
at	present	all	quiet
along	our	front	AAA

From O. C.

Place 1st Y+L Regt

Time 8 30 pm

The above may be forwarded as now corrected. (Z) [illegible]

Censor. Signature of Addressor or person authorised to telegraph in his name [illegible]

* This line should be erased if not required.

8350 S. B. Ltd Wt W4843/541—50,000. 9/14 Forms C2121/10.

Copy No 6

App IV

OPERATION ORDER Nº 33

by

Brigadier General H S L Ravenshaw C.M.G

Commanding 83rd Infantry Brigade

Reference Sheet 28
and Hazebrouck 5A

Ouderdom
3 June 1915

1. The 83rd Brigade will march to WINNEZEELE according to the attached March Table

2. Starting point T road in H 13 d. 9·1

3. Route T road in H 13 d 9·1 cross roads G 6 d 4·0 – POPERINGHE – JANSTER DIEZEN – WATOU – WINNEZEELE.

4. Transport will accompany Battalions

5. Ten minute halts will take place at ten minutes before each clock hour.

6. Strict march discipline will be maintained especially amongst the transport and the ten minutes interval between units will be rigidly maintained

7. Battalions will occupy the same billets as when last in WINNEZEELE area except 2nd Kings Own.
Billeting party of 2nd Kings Own will report to Staff Captain at Brigade Headquarters at 9 am today

8. Numbers of men unable to march will be rendered to Brigade Headquarters by 9 am.

Issued at 3.45 am.

R.S. [illegible] Captain
Brigade Major 83 Bde

MARCH TABLE

UNIT	STARTING POINT	TIME
Brigade Headquarters	T road in H 13 d 9.1	1.10 pm
1st York & Lancaster Regt	T road in H 13 d 9.1	1.30 pm
2nd Kings Own Regt	do	1.50 pm
2nd East Yorkshire Regt	do	2.10 pm
5th Kings Own	do	2.30 pm
1st K.O.Y.L.I.	do	2.50 pm

A. 1896.

App V

83rd Infantry Brigade

Training when at "Rest"

1. Training should be progressive

2. Half hour's running and marching before breakfast each day (except Sundays)

3. Route marching 4 days a week, dress "drill order" two days, "marching order" two days, to be progressive, and up to 10 miles in marching order. Battalions need only march as a whole once a week.

   On all occasions strict attention will be paid to March discipline.

4. 1st Line Transport to be exercised regularly, and once a week to march with Battalion - loaded.

S. A. A. 5. ~~S.A.A.~~ Men are always to have in their possession 120 rounds. [The extra] ~~Spare~~ bandoliers [per man is] ~~are~~ to be collected ~~[illegible]~~, and kept ready for issue under regimental arrangements.

   Battalions will thus keep 170 rounds per man plus regimental reserve.

Parades 6. Musketry Parades and steady drill Parades (handling of arms included) will be held daily.

   Special attention should be paid to saluting and handling of arms when on guards.

7. Every endeavour will be made that each man fires 10 rounds rapid on the Rifle Range near CASSEL. Allotment of range will be notified later.

Machine Gun Class 8. Classes should be formed for machine gun instruction.

Each Battalion must be able to man 4 Machine guns, and have one spare team.

9. Bomb throwers 1 N.C.O. and four men per platoon should be instructed in use of bombs & throwing them.

Billets 10. All billets must be ~~left~~ kept clean, and all refuse, tins &c either buried or burnt.

Respirators 11. Attention is called to 28th Divisional Orders with reference to "Respirators". A Parade will be held daily to ~~[illegible]~~ inspect them, and see that each man understands how to adjust them.

12. An experimental trench will be dug and wired by each Battalion to demonstrate to young Soldiers the latest ideas on the subject.

13. Concerts should be arranged for the men under Regimental arrangements

R. S. Follett Captain
Brigade Major 83 Bde

4.6.15

App VI

SECRET.

COPY No. 5

VI

Operation Order No. 34.

by

Brigadier-General H.S.L.Ravenshaw, C.M.G.,

Commanding 83rd. Infantry Brigade.

Reference
Sheets 27 and 28

WINNIZEELE.
14th. June/15.

1. The Brigade will march to the area of ZEVECOTON today according to the attached march and billeting table.

2. Starting point. T road in J 12b9.1 sheet 27.

3. ROUTE. WATOU-POPERINGHE-RENINGHELST-ZEVECOTON.

4. Each battalion will furnish a rear-party under an officer, who will collect and bring on all stragglers in a formed body.

5. Water-bottles will be filled before starting.

6. All train wagons will report to O.C. No. 2. Coy. A.S.C. at the starting point at 3 p.m..

7. Billeting parties will report to Staff Captain at 2 p.m. at RENINGHELST CHURCH.

8. Guides from billeting parties will meet battalions at ZEVECOTON at 5 p.m..
Also Guides from billeting parties will meet train wagons of their units at the same place at 6 p.m..

B. [signature] Captain,

Brigade Major,

83rd. Infantry Brigade.

Issued at 5.30 a.m.

Copy No. 1. War Diary
" 2. 2nd. King's Own Regt.
" 3. 2nd. East Yorkshire Regt.
" 4. 1st. K.O.Y.L.I.
" 5. 1st. York & Lancaster Regt.
" 6. 2nd. Coy. A.S.C.
" 7. Staff Captain.
" 8. 5th. King's Own Regt.

MARCH TABLE.

****

UNIT.	STARTING POINT.	TIME.	DESTINATION.
Brigade Headquarters.	T road J.12b.9.1. sheet 28.	1-15 p.m.	LA CLYTTE.
1/ K.O.Y.L.I.	do.	1-30 p.m.	N.7a Sheet 28.
2nd. East Yorkshire Regt.	do.	1-45 p.m.	do.
2nd. King's Own Regt.	do.	2 p.m.	M.6a.2.7. Sheet 28
5th. King's Own Regt.	do.	2-15 p.m.	do.
1/ York and Lancaster Regt.	do.	2-30 p.m.	M.17b.9.8. Sheet 28.

VII

App VII

Operation Order No: 1.

by

Major G.E. Bayley D.S.O

Comdg. 1st York & Lancaster Regt.

1. The Battalion will march to its billeting area, M.17 b. 9. 8. sheet 28, today.
2. Starting point - The estaminet near A. Coy. Billet. J.30.a, 8.7 sheet 27. Time 1-45 p.m.
3. Route - WATOU - POPERINGHE, - RENINGHELST. ZEVECOTON.
4. Order of march - C. D A & B Coys, Machine Gun Sect. 1st Line Transport.
5. Billeting Party. O.C. Cos. will detail a N.C.O. to form a Billeting Party under 2/Lt H.L. Norris to report at Bn Hdqrs at 11.15 am.

This party will report to the Staff Captain at 2. pm. at the church at RENINGHELST.

6. O.C. B. Coy. will detail an officer and one N.C.O. to form a rear party to the Battn.
7. Water bottles will be filled before starting

T Knox Shaw Lt.
A/Adj. 1st York & Lancs Regt.

SECRET.

Copy No. 4

AH VIII

OPERATION ORDER No. 35

By

Brigadier General H.S.L. Ravenshaw C.M.G.,

Commanding 83rd Infantry Brigade.

LA-CLYTTE,

19th JUNE, 1915.

Ref. 1/10,000. VIERSTRAAT.

1. The Brigade will relieve the 139th Brigade on night 19th - 20th June.

(a) 2nd Bn. East Yorkshire Regt. relieve 7th Bn. Sherwood Foresters in right section.

(b) 1st York & Lancaster Regt. relieve 5th Sherwood Foresters in left section.

(c) 1/K.O.Y.L.I. relieve 6th Bn. Sherwood Foresters in KEMMEL Bivouac.

GUIDES. 2. (a) One Officer of 7th Bn. Sherwood Foresters, two guides per trench and two guides from the reserve company will meet 2nd Bn. East Yorkshire Regt. in the square KEMMEL village at 9.30.p.m.

(b) One Officer 5th Bn. Sherwood Foresters and a similar number of guides will meet 1st Bn. York & Lancaster Regt. at the Barrier LA-CLYTTE - KEMMEL road (square 20.b.10.5) at 9.45.p.m.

(c) One Officer 6th Bn. Sherwood Foresters and one guide per company will meet 1st Bn. K.O.Y.L.I. at LA-CLYTTE cross roads at 9.30.p.m,

MACHINE GUNS. 3. (a) One guide from each Battalion being relieved will meet the Machine Guns of the relieving Battalions at the times and places mentioned above.

These guides will conduct the limbers to the respective dumping grounds, where guides from each Gun Position in the trenches will be waiting.

(b) Two Machine guns and their teams of 5th Bn. King's Own Regiment will be permanently attached to 1st Bn. York & Lancaster Regiment to whom they will report at 4.30.p.m. to-day

(c) One Machine Gun and team 5th Bn. King's Own Regt. will be permanently attached to 2nd Bn. East Yorkshire Regt. to whom they will report at 4.30.p.m. to-day.

~~A copy of the latter will be sent to the Staff Captain by 10.a.m. 20th instant.~~

4. Log Books and a list of trench stores will be taken over by each Commanding Officer. a copy of the latter will be sent to the Staff Captain at 10.a.m. 20th Instant.

5. The 150th Brigade Mining Section will remain in charge of the mines at present.

6. Commanding Officers will be held responsible that all Officers under their Command are made fully acquainted with the line held by the Unit.

7. Completion of reliefs will be reported by telephone to Brigade Headquarters.

IN CASE OF ATTACK

FRONT LINE TRENCHES. 8. The line of trenches occupied by the Brigade will be held at all costs by the garrisons occupying them.

LEFT SECTOR RESERVE COY. 9. The platoon of the Reserve Coy of the Battalion garrisoning the LEFT Sector stationed in the Brigade Dug-outs will move up into VIERSTRAAT, and reinforce the platoon already there.

This half Company will then garrison VIERSTRAAT, which will be held at all costs. The remaining two platoons of this company will move into the subsidiary line, with their right where this line crosses the VIERSTRAAT - KEMMEL Road (Square N.17.a. 3.7.)

RIGHT SECTOR RESERVE COY. 10. The Reserve Company of the Battalion garrisoning the RIGHT SECTOR will move up into the Subsidiary Line in ROSSIGNOL WOOD.

BRIGADE RESERVE 11. The Battalion in Brigade Reserve at the KEMMEL BIVOUAC, will move up and occupy the Subsidiary Line between the North end of ROSSIGNOL Wood and where the line crosses the VIERSTRAAT -KEMMEL Road. The Head quarters of this Battalion will be at the Forge.

In coming up this Battalion will move by the least vulnerable route.

BRIGADE FIGHTING HEADQRS. 12. Brigade Head quarters will be in a Dug-out, 100 yards on the North side of SIEGE FARM, where the completion of the above moves will be reported to.

Two orderlies will also be sent from each Battalion to Brigade Head quarters. In normal circumstances Brigade Head quarters will be at Chateau KEMMEL.

R.S. Follett Captain.

19th June, 1915.

Brigade Major 83rd Infantry Bde.

Issued at 2p.m. to:-

1/York and Lancaster Regt.

IX

Operation Orders No: 2
By
Lt. Col. G.E. Bayley D.S.O.
Comdg. 1st Bn York & Lancaster Regt.
Saturday, 19th June 1915.

App IX

1. The Battalion will go into the trenches tonight.
Parade 8-30 p.m.
Order of march – A. D. B & C Cos followed by Machine Guns & transport.

2. Officers Kits will be collected by the Transport Officer at 6 p.m.

3. Trench Kits will be collected at 7 p.m.

4. Company Commanders and the Medical Officer will proceed to the trenches at 5-20 p.m. to take over.

5. On relief O.C. Cos will report by wire when their Companies are in. The M. Gun Officer will also report.

6. O.C. Cos will see that their men have their Respirators and Smoke Helmets ready as ordered. The Smoke Helmets will

IX

will be carried slung round the neck and the Respirator in the pocket.

7. Three Sand bags per man will be carried by B, C & D Cos. and the 2 platoons of A Coy going to VIERSTRAAT.
They will draw them from Headquarters at 7.30 p.m.

8. Two stretcher bearers and one medical orderly per Coy. will be attached to each Company while in the trenches.

9. Signallers will be attached as follows

A. Coy	–	2 Signallers
B "	–	4 –"–
C "	–	2 –"–
D "	–	2 –"–

10 Waterbottles will be carried filled. No water is to be taken from any so called springs in the trenches. Water will be issued under Bde arrangements to be notified later.

11. Each man will carry one day's rations

T Knox Shaw Lieut
A/Adj. 1st Yorks & Lancs. Regt.

App X

N O T E S

by

Brigadier General H.S.L.Ravenshaw, C.M.G.

Commanding 83rd Infantry Brigade.

****

1. Listeners Posts to be put out at once.

2. Second Line to be loop-holed at once.

3. If a forward trench is supposed to be mined as few men as possible to be left in it and the trench in rear to be manned and Machine Gun placed to cover ground over which enemy should advance.

4. Cover all dug-outs and support trenches as far as possible with branches.

5. Machine Guns not to fire over top of parapets but sited low down as possible and not to be visible from front.

6. Notice Boards at all dangerous spots in communication trenches and elsewhere.

7. Arrangements for water and Supplies and how carried up at night (best ways).

8. Where are Dressing Stations and First Aid Posts?

10. Each trench to be marked with its number so as to be seen by gunners (each end the best)

11. Aeroplane guards at Head quarters also at Battalions in reserve and dug-outs. No men to wander about and give the show away.

12. Lamp Signalling by day.

13. Test R.A. Signals and fire one round per gun and see how long it takes.

14. ~~Gunners~~ Germans can see down our trenches; so Officers must be careful how work is done in the dug-outs.

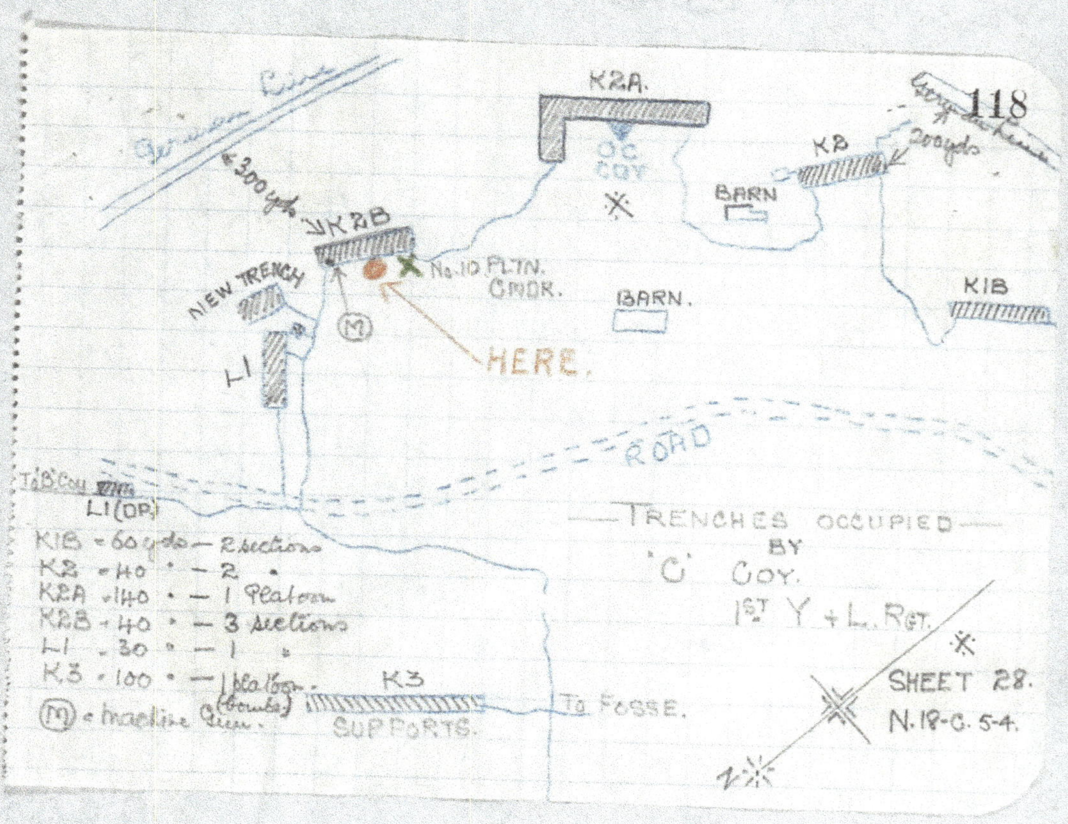
German Line
300 yds
K2A.
OC COY
K2
200 yds
BARN
K2B
No. 10 PLTN. CMDR.
BARN.
K1B
NEW TRENCH
L1
HERE.
ROAD
To 'B' Coy
L1 (OP)
TRENCHES OCCUPIED BY 'C' COY. 1ST Y + L. RGT.
K1B = 60 yds — 2 sections
K2 = 40 " — 2 "
K2A = 140 " — 1 Platoon
K2B = 40 " — 3 sections
L1 = 30 " — 1 "
K3 = 100 " — 1 platoon (bombs)
M = machine Gun.
K3
SUPPORTS.
To FOSSE.
SHEET 28.
N.18-C. 5-4.
N

Sheet 28. N. 18.

Trenches held by 1st Y + L Rgt from June 19–23

App XI

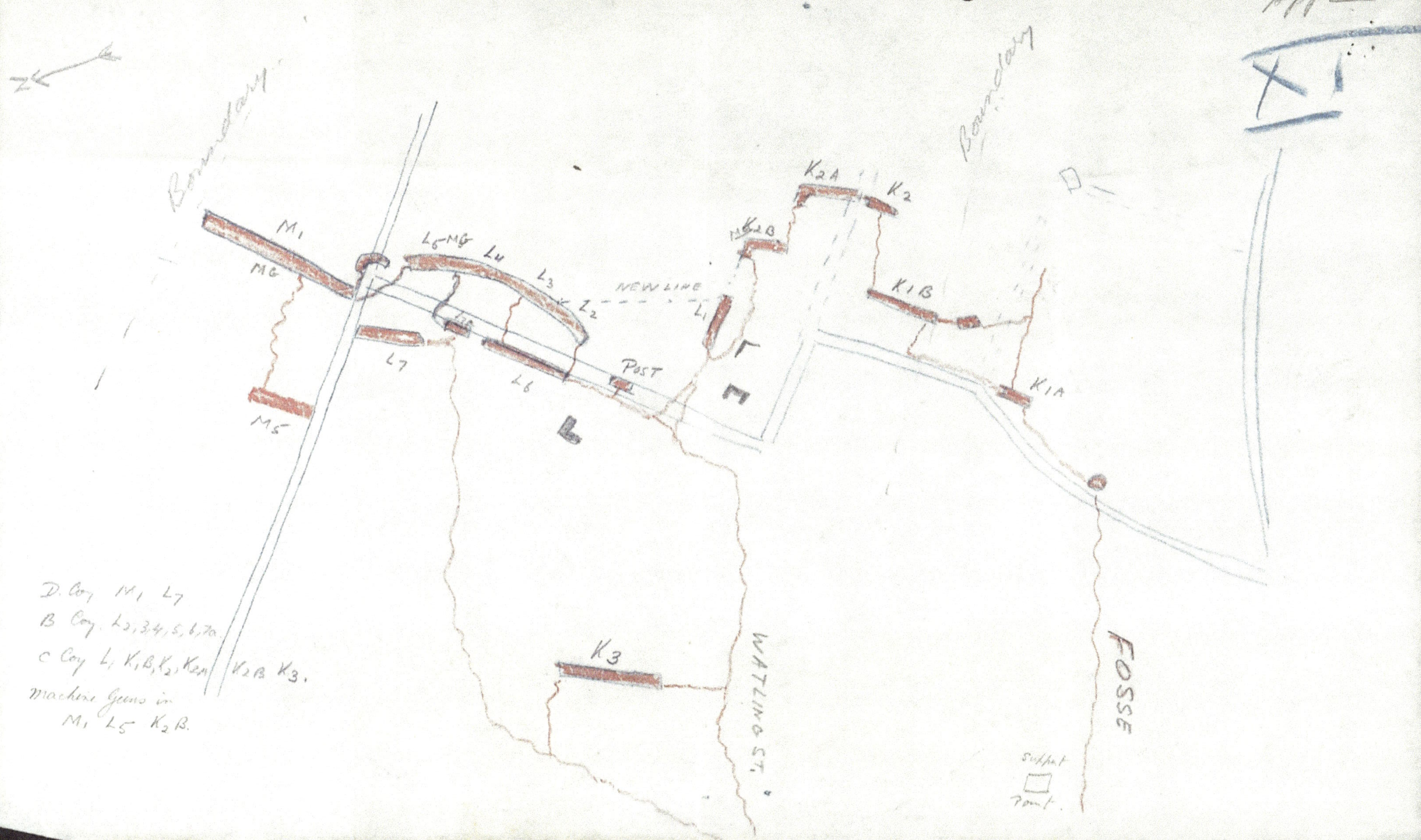

XII

Copy No. 5

App XII

SECRET.

OPERATION ORDER No. 37

By

Brigadier General H.S.L. Ravenshaw, C. M. G.

Commanding 83rd Infantry Brigade.

Reference Sheet VIERSTRAAT. 1/10000

KEMMEL.

23rd JUNE, 1915.

1. On night 23rd - 24th JUNE, the following reliefs will take place:-

(a). 1st Bn. K.O.Y.L.I. and one company 5th Bn. King's Own Regt. attached relieve 2nd Bn. East Yorkshire Regt. in the Right Section.

(b). 2nd Bn. King's Own Regt relieve 1st Bn. York & Lancs. Regt. in all trenches of left Section except M.1. and M.3., which will continue to be held by garrison of 1st Bn. York & Lancaster Regt.

This garrison will come under the Command of O.C. 2nd Bn. King's Own Regt. on completion of relief. This garrison will be relieved by 84th Brigade on night 24th - 25th June.

GUIDES. 2. (a). One Officer 2nd Bn. East Yorkshire Regt., two guides per trench and one guide per Machine Gun will meet 1st Bn. K.O.Y.L.I. at KEMMEL Church at 9.30.p.m.

(b). One Officer 1st Bn. York & Lancaster Regt., two guides per trench and one guide per Machine Gun will meet 2nd Bn. King' Own Regt. at the Barrier on LA CLYTTE - KEMMEL road (N.20.b.9.6.) at 9.30.p.m.

3. (a). The Officer Commanding 2nd Bn. East Yorkshire Regt. wil command Right Section until relief is completed.

(b). The Officer Commanding 1st Bn. York & Lancaster Regt. will command Left Section until relief is completed.

4. Machine Guns of 5th Bn. King's Own Regt. attached to 2nd Bn. East Yorkshire Regt. and 1st Bn. York & Lancaster Regt. will be transferred to 1st BN. K. O. Y. L. I. and 2nd Bn. King's Own Regt. respectively.

5. Reliefs will be reported by wire to Brigade Head quarters.

R.S. Follett Captain.

Brigade Major 83rd Infantry Brigade.

Issuedat :- 1.15.p.m.

Copy No. 1	War Diary.	Copy 5.	1/York & Lancs.
" 2	2/ King's Own.	" 6.	5/King's Own
" 3	2/E.York.R.	" 7.	28 Divn
" 4	1/K.O.Y.L.I.		
" 5			

XIII

Operation Orders No: 3

By App XIII

Lieut. Colonel G.E. Bayley, D.S.O

Comdg: 1st Bn York & Lancaster Regiment

Thursday, 23rd June 1915.

1. On night 23rd – 24th ~~of~~ June the following relief will take place.
2nd Bn Kings Own Regt relieve 1st Bn York & Lancaster Regt in all trenches of left section except M.1 and M5. which will continue to be held by "D" Coy. 1st York & Lancaster Regt.
This Coy. will come under the command of O.C. 2nd Bn Kings Own Regt. on completion of relief. This Company will be relieved by 3rd Brigade on night 24th – 25th June.

2. Lieut. F.L Norris with guides from Cos and Machine Gun as under will meet the 2nd Bn Kings Own Regt. at LA CLYTE Barrier at 9-30 p.m.

Guides from "C" Coy for K.1.b.
K.2.
K.2.a.
K 2 b
L.1
K 3.

From "B" Coy for – L.6. Detached Post
L.2
L.3
L.6.

P.T.O.

L. 4.
L. 5.

One guide of 'D' Coy for L. 7.
This platoon of 'D' Coy will be relieved tonight.

Machine Guns

One guide for each gun

These guides will be at the dumping ground but the Machine Gun officer will detail a guide to bring the teams and limbers to the dumping ground.

Lieut. E Workman will detail a guide to bring the Transport to Sandbag Villa.

A. Coy will detail 4 guides to bring the 4 platoons taking over from them.

The M.O. will detail one guide to show the relieving M.O. & Stretcher Bearers the way

Headquarters will furnish one guide for the relieving Headquarters.

All guides must be given a written pass showing the trench or place they are to take the relief to.

3. Reliefs will be reported by wire to Battn. Hdqrs. without delay.

4. Officers Kits etc. must be at the dumping ground by 9.30 pm.

5. Company Officers will obtain receipts for the stores handed over by them.

T Knox Shaw Lieut
a/Adj. 1st York & Lancaster Regt

HEADQUARTERS
Date 23-6-15
83rd INFANTRY BRIGADE

XIV

App XIV

Officer Commanding

1st York & Lancaster Regt.

1. The 1st K.O.Y.L.I., will leave a party at KEMMEL Bivouacs to hand over shelters to Battalion of other Brigade which is taking over. Receipt to be forwarded to this office.

2. On relief tonight :-

(a) 1st York & Lancaster will go into huts and shelters at SCHERPENBERG, taking shelters over from 85th Brigade.
Transport of 1st York & Lancaster will move tonight into lines previously occupied by them at SCHERPENBERG HUTS.

(b) 2nd East Yorks will move into huts previously occupied by them at LA CLYTTE, and also those occupied by 1st K.O.Y.L.I., except those East of the Officers' huts, viz:- between Officers' Huts and the LA CLYTTE - RENINGHELST ROAD
Transport 2nd East Yorks will move ~~int~~ tonight to the transport lines previously occupied by them at LA CLYTTE huts.

3. 5th King's Own will hand over to 2nd East Yorks shelters not now required by them owing to one Company going into the trenches tonight.

4. 5th King's Own(less one Company) will march at 8.30.a.m., tomorrow morning, and will occupy the huts at LA CLYTTE left vacant by the 2nd East Yorks. They will take the remaining shelters with them.
Transport will march at the same hour, and will bivouac in Square M 11 C.

5. Transport of 2nd King's Own will move at 10 a.m., tomorrow to the same field at SCHERPENBERG OCCUPIED by the transport of the 1st York & Lancaster.

Transport of the 1st K.O.Y.L.I., will move at 10 a.m. tomorrow to their old line at LA CLYTTE huts.

E C Gepp
Major,
Staff Captain. 83rd Bde.

23/6/15.

Copy has been sent to Q^rs

App XV

SECRET.

XV

Copy No. 4

OPERATION ORDER No. 38

By

Brigadier General H.S.L. Ravenshaw, C.M.G.

Commanding 83rd Infantry Brigade

KEMMEL,

Reference Sheet 28.

24th JUNE, 1915.

1. The company 5th Bn . King's Own Regt. (attached to 1/K.O.Y.L.I. will take over trenches H.1. and H.2. from 9th Bn. Durham Light Infantry, 151st Brigade on night 24th - 25th JUNE.

The company 1st Bn . York & Lancaster Regt. (attached 2nd Bn. King's Own will hand over trenches M.1. and M.3. to 2nd Bn. Northumberland Fusiliers, 84th Brigade on night 24th - 25th JUNE.

Reserve Company 2nd Bn. King's Own Regt. will handxxxx over VIERSTRAAT and dug-outs N.10.b.8.4. to 2nd Bn. Northumberland Fusiliers on night 24th - 25th JUNE.

GUIDES. 2. (a) One Officer 1st Bn. York & Lancaster Regt. will meet the Northumberland Fusiliers at the left end of M.1. at 9.30.p.m.

(b) One Officer and two guides each from VIERSTRAAT garrison and platoon in dug-outs N.10.b.8.4. will meet Northumberland Fusiliers at cross roads N.10.b. 8.4. at 9.30.p.m.

(c) Guides from 9th Durham L.I. will meet company of 5th Bn. King's Own Regt. (attached 1/K.O.Y.L.I.) at S.P.11. on VIA GELLIA at 9.45. p.m.

3. Trench stores will be handed over to relieving unit and taken over from unit relieved. Telephones will not be handed over.

A list of stores handed over and received will be sent to Brigade Office by 12.noon 25th instant.

4. Relief will be reported to Brigade Head quarters by wire.

5. From 10.p.m. this date BRIGADE HEADQUARTERS will be at LA CLYTTE.

P.S. Follett Captain.

Brigade Major 83rd Bde.

Issued at :- p.M.

Copy No. 1. War Diary.
" 2. 2/King's Own Regt.
" 3. 2/E.Yorks Regt.
" 4. 1/York & Lancs Regt.
" 5. 5/King's Own Regt.
" 6. 28th Division.
" 7. 84th Brigade.
" 8. 151st Brigade.
" 9.

Secret

XVI

Copy No. 4

App XVI

OPERATION ORDER No. 32
By

Brigadier General H.S.L. Ravenshaw, C. M. G.

Commanding 83rd Infantry Brigade.

****

LA CLYTTE,

26th JUNE, 1915.

Reference VIERSTRAAT Sheet - $\frac{1}{10000}$

BRIGADE AREA.

1. The area allotted to 83rd Brigade:-

NORTHERN BOUNDARY.
From Right of N.1. trench (exclusive) to junction of KEMMEL - VIERSTRAAT road and Subsidiary line point N.17.a.2.9. to track from N.15.b.10.7. to N.9. central (track inclusive).

SOUTHERN BOUNDARY.
From Right of trench H.1. (inclusive) to right of trench H.5. (inclusive)- to road South of wood N.22.a. (inclusive) - to junction of G.H.Q. line and KEMMEL & LA CLYTTE road (road inclusive) N.21.a.1.5.

2. (a) The Subsidiary line is allotted as follows;for the maintenance and improvement of works:-

2nd Bn.East Yorkshire Regt. & 1st Bn.K.O.Y.L.I.:-
From Southern boundary to track north of Fme. DESMEL (exclusive).

2nd Bn. King's Own Regt. & 1st Bn.York & Lancaster Regt.
From FME. DESMEL (inclusive) to Northern boundary.

(b) G.H.Q. line is allotted for maintenance and improvement of works:-
2nd Bn.East Yorkshire Regt. & 1st Bn. K.O.Y.L.I. - from Southern boundary to cross tracks (inclusive) N.15.c.6.9.

2nd Bn. King's Own Regt. & 1st Bn. York & Lancaster Regt. From cross tracks (exclusive) N.15.c.6.9. to Northern Boundary.

(c) The FOSSE is allotted to Right Sector and WATLING STREET to Left Sector, for maintenance and improvement.

3. Commanding Officers will arrange for all Officers and a proportion of N.C.O's to make themselves thoroughly acquainted with all works and country within their Sector East of the VIERSTRAAT - KEMMEL road when they are occupying the front line and of all works and country within their Sector west of the same road when they are at rest.

4. A reconnaissance will be made of their respective Sectors of G.H.Q. line by 2nd Bn. East Yorkshire Regt. and 1st Bn. York & Lancaster Regt. and a sketch (scale $\frac{1}{10000}$) and short report

report
report submitted to this Office by 6.p.m. 28th instant.

4. Battalions when at rest except 5th BN, King's Own Regt. will keep half a Battalion ready to move at an hour's notice.

5. Paragraphs 9,10, 11 & 12 of Operation Order No. 35 are cancelled.

~~[illegible]~~

IN CASE OF ATTACK.

(a) The Reserve Company holding Right Sector will occupy Subsidiary line from Southern Boundary (road inclusive) to N. end of ROSINGNOL wood.

(b) The Reserve Company of Battalion holding Left Sector will occupy Subsidiary line from Northern Boundary (road ~~inclusive~~ exclusive) to FME. PARENT (inclusive).

(C) Brigade Head quarters will move to dug-outs 100 yards W. of Farm N.21.b.7.10.
Units will be informed.

R.S. Follett Captain.

Brigade Major 83rd Infantry Brigade.

Issued at:-

Copy No. 1. War Diary.
" 2. 2/King's Own.
" 3. 1/K.O.Y.L.I.
4. 1/York & Lancs.R.
5. 5/King's Own. R.
6. 1/N. Midland Fd.Co.R.E.
7. 2/E-York R

L York & Lancs.

Copy No 4.

App XVII

XVII

SECRET.

OPERATION ORDER No. 40.
By
Brigadier H.S.L. Ravenshaw, C.M.G.
Commanding 83rd Infantry Brigade.

LA CLYTTE

Reference VIERSTRAAT 1/10000

28th JUNE, 1915.

1. Following reliefs will take place within the Brigade to-morrow night.

(a) 2/Bn. East Yorkshire Regt. and one Company 5th Bn. King's Own Regt. attached, will relieve 1st Bn. K.O.Y.L.I. and one Company 5th Bn. King's Own Regt. attached in the Right Sector.

(b) 1st Bn. York & Lancaster Regt. will relieve 2nd Bn. King's Own Regt. in the Left Sector.

2. Relieving units will pass cross roads N.20.b. 10.5. as follows:-

1st Bn. York & Lancaster Regt. - 9.30.p.m.
2nd Bn East Yorkshire Regt. with Coy. 5th Bn. King's Own attached - 9.45.p.m.

GUIDES. 3. Guides will be arranged between Battalion Commanders.

4. The garrisons for H.1. and H.2. trenches may use the VIA GELLIA.

5. The relief between companies of 5th Bn. King's Own Regt. will be under the direction of Commanding Officers of Battalions to which they are attached.

6. Major Heathcote, D.S.O. and Major Borrett, D.S.O. will command in the Right and Left Sectors respectively until the relief is completed.

7. Completion of reliefs will be reported by telephone to Brigade Headquarters.

R.S. Follett Captain.
Brigade Major 83rd Infy. Bde.

Issued at:- 9-30 p.m.

Copy No. 1. War Diary.
" 2. 2/King's Own.
" 3. 2/East Yorks.R.
" 4. 1/York & Lancs.R.
" 5. 1/K.O.Y.L.I.
" 6. 5/King's Own.
" 7. 28th Division.

XVIII

Operation Orders No: 4

App XVIII

By

Lieut-Col. G. E. Bayley D.S.O.

Comdg. 1st Bn. York & Lancaster Regiment

Tuesday, June 29th 1915.

1/

The Battalion will move into the trenches tonight.

Coy's. will parade on Coy. parade grounds ready to move off at 8.30 p.m. Order of march:- A. D. B. C. Cos. followed by Machine Gun, Stretcher bearers, and Transport.

2.

Guides will meet companies at the barrier (N 20. 6. 10. 6. Sheet. 28).

On arriving at the barrier the Machine Gun will leave first with their guides and transport.

3. Officers Kits must be handed into QM stores by 7 p.m.

4/

Trench kits must also be handed into Q.M. Stores by 7 p.m.

5/

Coy Commanders may proceed to the trenches in advance, to take over, if they think it advisable.

6. On relief O.C. Cos. will report by wire when their Cos. are in. The Machine Gun Officer will also report.

7.
Two sandbags per man will be carried by B. C & D.
They will be drawn from Hd. Qrs. by 6p.m.

8/
Two stretcher bearers and one medical orderly per coy. will be allotted to each Company while in the trenches.

9.
Signallers will be attached as follows:

"B" Coy — 3
"C" " — 3
"D" " — 5

10.
Water bottles will be carried filled.
O.C. Cos. will arrange to draw water from the dumping ground on completion of the move. This will be notified from Bn. Hd. Qrs. Until then no parties are to leave their posts.

11.
Each man will carry one days rations

12.
All shelters will be collected and handed over to the Qr. Mr. by 11 p.m.

13.
O.C. Cos. will see that their camp is left clean.

14. O.C. A. Coy. will furnish a guard for Bn. Hdrs.

This guard will report immediately on arrival in the trenches.

(Sd) T. Knox Shaw Lieut.,
a/Adj. 1st York & Lanc Rgt.

83rd Bde.
28th Division.

WAR DIARY

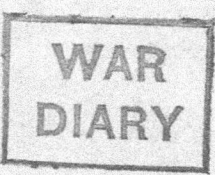

1st YORK & LANCS.

J U L Y

1 9 1 5

Appendices I to XXXI.

Instructions regarding War Diaries and Intelligence Summaries are contained in F. S. Regs., Part II. and the Staff Manual respectively. Title pages will be prepared in manuscript.

WAR DIARY
or
~~INTELLIGENCE SUMMARY~~

(Erase heading not required.)

1st York & Lancaster Regt

Army Form C. 2118.

Hour, Date, Place		Summary of Events and Information	Remarks and references to Appendices
1st July 1915	4.30 am	Situation report. Situation normal. Wind S.W mild	
	11 am	" " " " " "	
York House KEMMEL	12 noon	Casualty report wounded other ranks one	
	4.30 pm	Situation report Some shelling of communication trench between L_5 & L_7 otherwise situation normal, wind westerly mild During the day "A" Coy worked on WATLING ST and the dugouts at Headquarters. The 5th KORL supplied a working party of 50 to work of C.T from "K_3 cross roads" to S.P. 13.	
	9.30 pm	Two platoons of "A" Coy left HOWITZER FARM, and handed it over to a Trench Mortar Battery. One of the platoons under 2nd Lt COWING went back to the Transport lines at SCHERPENBERG to form part of a permanent working party under the C.R.E for improving the Subsidiary Line. The other platoon occupied the barn and dugouts near YORK HOUSE Two patrols were sent out to study the ground with a view to a bombing party later. Reconnoitring Reports 2nd Lt Ellison & 3 men went out on patrol at 11 pm. The party got down to the "dead" ground in front of L_3 and crossed over the old trench supposed to be occupied by a German listening post. They were fired on a little further on and one of the patrols was shot through the knee. A broken bayonet also temporarily injured another; so these two men returned to the trench. 2nd Lt Ellison then went on but about 20 yards further on, enemy machine guns & rifles opened fire. The patrol returned about 1.30 am. The night was very light for patrol work. Lt Halcomb's report We went out through the listening post South of K_2 and advanced 250 yds forwards up to the German barbed wire, which is 4'6" high and about	

Instructions regarding War Diaries and Intelligence Summaries are contained in F. S. Regs., Part II. and the Staff Manual respectively. Title pages will be prepared in manuscript.

WAR DIARY
or
INTELLIGENCE SUMMARY
(Erase heading not required.)

1st York & Lancaster Rgt

Army Form C. 2118.

Hour, Date, Place	Summary of Events and Information	Remarks and references to Appendices
	15 ft broad and very thickly interlaced. We followed the line of their wire for about 300 yds in the direction of L1 & returned to our lines via K2B. The grass in front up to within 30 yds of their trenches is about 2 ft high. We were under Machine Gun fire on our return. I do not think it possible to throw a bomb from our side of their wire into their trenches	
July 2nd YORK HOUSE 4.30am	Situation report Situation normal; wind westerly very mild	
11 am		
12 noon	Casualty report Killed O.R one; wounded O.R four	
4.30pm	Situation report Situation normal wind S.W mild	
9.pm	The KOYLI supplied a working party of 50 for the trench between K3 and SP.13. The Companies in the trenches worked hard at deepening and improving the fire trenches and communication trenches all the latter needed deepening, widening and boarding. In the fire trenches there was not much protection from shell fire as they consisted chiefly of breastworks. All these had to be altered by degrees.	
11.30pm	Divisional message forwarded by Brigade	App I
	In consequence of this order two patrols were sent out	
	Lt C.F Walls report.	App II
	Later Capt Johnson reported that his patrol were unable to identify hostile units. The N.C.O in charge of the patrol was killed. It was a light night and the message was received too late to organise a scheme likely to succeed.	
July 3rd 4.30am	Situation report. Situation normal, wind west mild	App III
7. am	Report to Brigade	
8.am	Situation report. Situation normal. wind S.W mild	
12 noon	Casualty report Killed one; wounded one	

1247 W 3299 200,000 (E) 8/14 J.B.C. & A. Forms/C. 2118/11.

Instructions regarding War Diaries and Intelligence Summaries are contained in F. S. Regs., Part II. and the Staff Manual respectively. Title pages will be prepared in manuscript.

WAR DIARY
or
~~INTELLIGENCE SUMMARY~~
(Erase heading not required.)

Army Form C. 2118.

pt yorks Lancaster Rgt-

Hour, Date, Place	Summary of Events and Information	Remarks and references to Appendices
July 3rd YORKHOUSE 4pm	Situation normal. The enemy fired common shell & shrapnel at new trench between 11.30am and 1.30pm. Wind S W slight.	
6pm	a shell fell near officers dug outs in L_3 and killed two of the servants two others being wounded.	
10pm	O.C. 'A' and 'C' Coy reported that there was a trace of gas in the air. It was found afterwards to be due to gas shells. 2nd Lieut G. H. HIGHFIELD was hit in the arm & chest while superintending the rebuilding of the parapet where it had been knocked down by a shell. He died of his wounds in the Dressing station.	
July 4th 4am	Situation normal, wind Westerly	
11 "	" " S E increasing	
12 noon	Casualty report 2nd Lieut G H Highfield died of wounds, killed one, died of wounds one, wounded four.	
2.50pm	Report from Brigade. East Yorkshire Rgt report that enemy transport distinctly heard about 11pm behind PETIT BOIS. Arrange to fire your rifle battery if the noise is heard tonight	
4.30pm	Situation normal wind S.E mild Report from Brigade. Following wire from 151 Brigade. "artillery have reported enemy noticed laying Sandbags and making a circular work at N.30A 4.4. Probably the work referred to is the prominent entrenchment in front of F5. artillery also report that close by work is a line of objects looking like drums or cylinders. Troops in F5 have been ordered to keep close watch. The Brigadier visited the trenches in the morning and remarked on the amount of work that had been done by the men. He was much impressed by the improvement in the trenches & complimented the Battalion its achievements.	
10pm	2nd Lt Highfield was buried at the Cemetery at KEMMEL. The C.O. Lt Wales, Lt Gribben & the Adjutant were present.	
[illegible] Bde	operation orders no 41	App IV
"	" " 42	App V

1247 W 3299 200,000 (E) 8/14 J.B.C. & A. Forms/C. 2118/11.

Instructions regarding War Diaries and Intelligence Summaries are contained in F. S. Regs., Part II. and the Staff Manual respectively. Title pages will be prepared in manuscript.

WAR DIARY
or
~~INTELLIGENCE SUMMARY~~
(Erase heading not required.) 1st YORK & Lancaster Rgt

Army Form C. 2118.

Hour, Date, Place	Summary of Events and Information	Remarks and references to Appendices
July 5th YORK HOUSE 4am	Situation normal. Wind S.E	
11 "	" " " S.W fresh & changeable	
12 noon	Casualty report nil	
4. pm	Situation report. The enemy's guns have been ranging on the K trenches since 2.30pm and have been firing constantly, situation otherwise normal. wind S.W mild	
	Brigade operation orders no 5	App VI
	The Battalion was relieved by the 2nd Kings Own.	
11.25pm	Reported to Brigade that relief was complete. The Companies marched back to SCHERPENBERG independently	
July 6th SCHERPENBERG	Rested in billets	
" 12 noon	Casualty report. Killed one, wounded two, one at duty.	
July 7th "	Rested in billets. Found fatigue parties at night	
July 8th	Rested in billets	
July 9th	" " "	
July 10th	" " "	
July 11th " 12 noon	Casualty report. one wounded	
	Brigade operation orders no 43	App VII
	Battalion " " no 6	App VIII
	The Companies left SCHERPENBERG independently starting at 8 pm. and relieved the 2nd Kings Own	
11.30pm	Relief reported to Brigade as complete	
11.40pm	Message from Bde Following reliefs take place on night 12th-13th 2nd East Yorks Regt take over all G trenches, SP 11, FOWLERS FARM + Bn H.Q from 5th L. North Lancs. and H_1 & H_2 trenches from 5th Kings Own Regt. 1st York & Lanc Regt take over K_1, all J trenches & H_3, H_4, H_5. 5th Kings Own take over all K trenches except K_1 & K_3 and take over S.P 12 & SP 13. 84th Bde take over all L trenches & K_3. Reconnaissance by officers of relieving units will take place on morning of 12th inst.	

1247 W 3299 200,000 (E) 8/14 J.B.C. & A. Forms/C. 2118/11.

Instructions regarding War Diaries and Intelligence Summaries are contained in F. S. Regs., Part II. and the Staff Manual respectively. Title pages will be prepared in manuscript.

WAR DIARY
or
INTELLIGENCE SUMMARY

(Erase heading not required.)

Army Form C. 2118.

Hour, Date, Place	Summary of Events and Information	Remarks and references to Appendices
July 11th. YORK HOUSE	The Surrender of a German in M1 trenches during the time of the relief led to the belief that a German Patrol was going out about 11 pm (Prisoners statement). Although Prisoner stated that the patrol was to go along VIERSTRAAT - WYSCHAETE road which is now, with about 20 yds to the right of it, manned by the Northumberland Fusiliers, Capt Buckley sent out a patrol beyond the wire & had a special listening patrol out to try & effect a capture. The large amount of hostile rifle fire & the flares sent up by the enemy convinced him that the patrol had gone in front of M1 trench as stated by prisoner.	
July 12. " " 4.30am	Situation normal. Heavy sniping during the night, but no artillery fire. 'B' Coy held trenches L2.3.4.5. 'D' Coy held L6 L7. L8 D.P and K3. 'C' Coy held K1B, K2, K2A, K2B & L1. 'A' Coy was in reserve. The Machine Guns were in L5 L6 L7 & K2B.	
10 am	Company officers went to the J trenches to make arrangements about the relief.	
	Brigade operation orders No 44.	App IX
	Battalion " " No 7.	App X
12 noon	Casualty report. wounded one self inflicted.	
4.30pm	Situation normal. No shelling.	
	Officers of 1st Suffolk Regt & 5th Kings own came to Bn HQ. to arrange about the reliefs.	
11.45pm	Reported to Brigade that 1st Suffolk Regt had taken of the L trenches and K3.	
11.5pm	O.C 5th Kings own reports he has taken over K1B K2. K2A. K2B and SP12. SP13.	
July 13th " " 1.20am	Reported to Brigade relief completed.	
4.30am	Situation quiet, about six trench mortars dropped right in front of J1 from corner of PETIT BOIS and some more on J3 new & on right of J3 right. Wind S W mild.	
	The Battalion was distributed as follows.	
	'B' Coy held H3 H4 H5 new & J1	
	'D' Coy held, J2, J3 Right, J3 new J10 and H5 old	
	'C' " " J3 left J4 K1 & K1A.	
	'A' Coy was in reserve.	

Instructions regarding War Diaries and Intelligence Summaries are contained in F. S. Regs., Part II. and the Staff Manual respectively. Title pages will be prepared in manuscript.

WAR DIARY
or
~~INTELLIGENCE SUMMARY~~
(Erase heading not required.)

1st York & Lancaster Regt.

Army Form C. 2118.

Hour, Date, Place	Summary of Events and Information	Remarks and references to Appendices
13th July YORK HOUSE.	The 5th Kings Own who were under Col. Bayley's Command held K,B, K2, K2A, K2B and SP12, SP13. The Machine Guns were placed in K1, J4, J1, K2B, SP 12 & SP13. Trench mortars were active all the morning	
11. am	Situation quiet. Trench mortars & rifle grenades have been fired from PETIT BOIS in front of J1. Wind S.W. mild	
12 noon	Casualty report. Died of wounds one, wounded one (result of mortar)	
4. 30pm	Situation unchanged. K1 shelled occasionally with 3" shells. As the Brigade considered the garrison of SP13 found by 5th Kings Own was weak, A Coy sent up a Sergeant & 12 men. A considerable amount of work was carried out during the night. Bombing parties were sent out from K1 & H4. The former found great difficulty, owing to the state of the ground which had been ploughed up by trench mortars, in pushing forward quietly. Lt Halcomb was badly shaken by one which exploded near him. Hostile rifle fire prevented them from causing much annoyance to the enemy. The party from H4 went towards S.W. corner of PETIT BOIS. It reached a point where it was possible to hear movement in what appeared to be a shell hole. This hole was bombed in the hope of getting an enemy listening post. All the parties returned safely.	
14th July " " 4.30 am	Situation unchanged. During early morning K1 & J1 suffered from Trench mortars. The rest of the day was quiet	
12 noon	Casualty report wounded other ranks 5.	
4.30pm	Situation unchanged wind S.W. mild.	
8.30pm	A mine exploded in front of G1 trench which was held by the 2nd East Yorkshire Regt (the Battalion on our right). The operator in J1 telephoned to H.Q that H3 trench had been blown up. At 9pm O.C "D" Coy reported that the enemy were attacking on right of "B" Coy who were holding H3 & H4 at the time.	

Instructions regarding War Diaries and Intelligence Summaries are contained in F. S. Regs, Part II. and the Staff Manual respectively. Title pages will be prepared in manuscript.

WAR DIARY
or
~~INTELLIGENCE SUMMARY~~
(Erase heading not required.)

1st Yorks Lancaster Regt

Army Form C. 2118.

Hour, Date, Place	Summary of Events and Information	Remarks and references to Appendices
14th July York House 9pm	Colonel Bayly, on receiving the news, instructed the 365th Battery to direct their fire on the right of J_3R and H_3. There was for a short time a general bombardment along the line. As soon as Colonel Bayly was able to get on to Captain Buckley he found out that the report that H_3 had been blown up was not correct and that the Germans were not attacking. He then telephoned to the Batteries to cease fire and by 9.30pm all was quiet. The East Yorkshire Regt reported later that the mine had made a huge crater 30 feet deep in front of the parapet and had knocked down part of the parapet, burying 11 of their men and 4 of the DLI who were mining in a sap at the time. As soon as the mine exploded the enemy shelled the G trenches with every conceivable kind of gun, but fortunately did not do much damage. Our guns did did some good execution. Lt Lynch reported that "immediately following the explosion of the mine to my right, the enemy began throwing trench-mortars onto the area of the explosion. From my position in J_3R I was able to locate one of these guns in right edge of PETIT BOIS. I was able to report this to our artillery when they shelled that spot and completely silenced the mortar". Captain Buckley also reported that as a result of the firing by our artillery on N W corner of PETIT BOIS, enemy's trench mortars were quiet during the night. The first few rounds on PETIT BOIS about 9.15pm must have been very close to the mortar which has fired on J_1 during the last few days.	
15 July 3.30am	<u>Captain Buckley's report</u> Explosion of mine in front of G_2 took place at 8.45pm followed by another explosion. Rifle fire was also opened on this point & on the parapets of J_1, H_3 & H_4. Machine guns of enemy from S. E. Corner of PETIT BOIS also enfiladed G Trenches from left, or so it appeared from observation in H_3 & H_4. Trench mortars, firing much bigger explosive than those in N.W corner of PETIT BOIS, also	

Instructions regarding War Diaries and Intelligence Summaries are contained in F. S. Regs., Part II. and the Staff Manual respectively. Title pages will be prepared in manuscript.

WAR DIARY
or
~~INTELLIGENCE SUMMARY~~
(Erase heading not required.) 1st Yorks & Lancaster Rgt

Army Form C. 2118.

Hour, Date, Place		Summary of Events and Information	Remarks and references to Appendices
15th July YORK HOUSE		fired. The enemy dropped some shells, as well, on road beside & in rear of J_{10} Trenches. Thinking that the enemy might be hoping to inflict loss on us by sweeping the parapet & not seeing any necessity to reply to enemy's rifle fire, I did not reply by rifle fire, but simply "stood to" until the disturbance subsided."	
[redacted]		Permanent Working Party. During the disturbance the Permanent Brigade working party was on its way to the LAITERIE. On passing SIEGE FARM, it came under Shrapnel fire. The two officers and 12 men were wounded, among which were 2nd Lt R.H. Cowing and two men of our regiment. 2nd Lt Cowing had a wound near his temple. He died at Bailleul on the following evening.	
	4.30 am	Situation quiet, no trench mortars	
	11 am	" " , " " wind S.W.	
		Brigade operation orders no 45	App XI
	12 noon	Casualty Report. Wounded 2nd Lt R.H. Cowing & two men.	2nd Lt Cowing died at BAILLEUL at 7pm
	4 pm	Battalion operation orders no 8	App XII
	4.30pm	Situation normal & quiet. Wind S.W.	
ROSSIGNOL ESTAMINET	8 pm	Battalion Headquarters moved to ROSSIGNOL Estaminet. The 2nd Kings Own relieved the 1st Suffolks in the L trenches and the 5th Kings Own in K_2A & K_2B. The 2nd Cheshires (84th I B) relieved the 2nd East Yorks in the G trenches.	
16th July " "	2 am	Reported relief complete to Brigade	
	4.30 am	Situation quiet. No trench mortars during the night. Distribution of troops unaltered except garrison of H_3 now occupies SP11 and garrison of H_4 is now in J_{11}. The Reserve Coy is in SIEGE FARM and the M Gun in K_2A is in SP11.	
	11 am	Situation quiet, wind Southerly fresh.	
	12 noon	Casualty Report Killed one; wounded two.	
	4.20pm	Situation normal, wind S W mild	
	8.30pm	Brigade operation orders no 46	App XIII
17th July "	4.30am	Situation normal. Sniping during the night slightly heavier than the previous night which was very quiet. AAA. The enemy had two bursts of rapid fire during the night. Four trench mortars were thrown at J_3 & J_2. no damage done. Wind S.W Fresh.	

Instructions regarding War Diaries and Intelligence Summaries are contained in F. S. Regs., Part II. and the Staff Manual respectively. Title pages will be prepared in manuscript.

WAR DIARY
or
INTELLIGENCE SUMMARY

(Erase heading not required.) 1st Yorks Lancaster Rgt.

Army Form C. 2118.

Hour, Date, Place		Summary of Events and Information	Remarks and references to Appendices
July 17th ROSSIGNOL ESTAMINET	11 am	Situation normal. Enemy fired 8 small trench mortars about 8.30am just over K1 trench. only one at a time was fired. Wind S W gusty.	
	12 noon	Casualty report wounded two.	
	1.30 pm	Brigade Operation orders no 47	App XV
	1 pm	Battalion operation orders no 9	App XIV
	4.30 pm	Situation normal. Wind S W strong	
	4.50 pm	Brigade operation orders no 48	App XVI
	6. pm	" " " 41a.	App XVII
	6.45 "	Battalion " " " 10	" XVIII
	10.35 "	Reported to the Brigade that the Battalion had been relieved by the 1st Bn K.O.Y.L.I. The Companies marched back independently to the Huts at SCHERPENBERG.	
July 18 SCHERPENBERG		Rested in Billets	
19th "		" " "	
20 "		Brigade Operation orders no 49	App XIX
		" " " 50	" XX
21 "		Rested in Billets	
	8 pm	Major Robertson went to YORK HOUSE to take over command of Left Sector, held by 5th Kings Own, one Company of 1st KOYLI & two platoons of 1st Bn Y & L Rgt. Lt Workman & 2nd Lt Adsetts marched their platoons to SANDBAG VILLA.	
	9 pm	4 N.C.Os & men of the 7th Battn Yorks Lancaster Rgt were attached for the night as they had lost their own Battalion.	
22nd "		Rested in Billets	
	4 pm	Brigade Operation orders no 51.	App XXI
23rd "		Battalion " " no 11.	App XXII
		The Companies left the Huts independently and relieved the 1st Bn KOYLI in the Right Sector. The Relief was complete by 10.30 pm. one platoon of 'C' Coy and two platoons of 'A' Coy held K1 B K2 K2A and came under Major Robertson O.C. Left Sector.	

Instructions regarding War Diaries and Intelligence Summaries are contained in F. S. Regs., Part II. and the Staff Manual respectively. Title pages will be prepared in manuscript.

WAR DIARY
or
~~INTELLIGENCE~~ SUMMARY.
(*Erase heading not required.*)

1st York & Lancaster Regt

Army Form C. 2118.

Hour, Date, Place	Summary of Events and Information	Remarks and references to Appendices
24th July ROSSIGNOL ESTAMINET	Situation report & Distribution of Troops.	App XXIII
4.30am	Enemy began shelling over C.T between J10 & H5 at 9.45 am otherwise quiet	
11 am	Casualty report nil	
12 noon / 3 pm	Two platoon officers of 10th Bn WEST YORKSHIRE Rgt & two from the 7th East Yorks came to reconnoitre trenches before taking up their platoons for 24 hours	
4.30 pm	Enemy's artillery active between 1 & 2.30pm, number of rounds about 25 shells no damage done.	
9.pm	Two platoons of 10th West Yorks and two platoons of 7th East Yorks attached for 24 hours.	
25th July " " 4.30 am	Situation quiet no mortars Sniping quiet in front of PETIT BOIS	
11 am	Situation very quiet	
12 noon	Casualty report wounded one	
3 pm	Six more officers of 50th Brigade arrived at Headquarters	
4.40 pm	Situation normal wind westerly fresh	
7 pm	General Pilcher Cmdg 17th Division while inspecting the trenches of left sector with Col Bayley was slightly wounded in the head a "whizz-bang" pitched a yard over the CT from K2B to L6 close to the party	
9.pm	Four more platoons of West & East Yorks came to relieve the others in the fire trenches	
26 July " 4.30 am	Situation normal quiet night	
12 noon	Casualty report. Wounded other Ranks three	
3.30 pm	Officers of Cheshire Regt came to reconnoitre the trenches	
4.30 pm	Situation normal one shell fell in J2	
9 pm	Four platoons of West and East Yorkshire Rgt came in for instruction	
27 July " 4.30 am	Situation normal Heavy Sniping during the night	
12 noon	Casualty report. Killed other ranks 3 wounded other ranks 6	
1 pm	Brigade Operation Orders No 52	App XXIV
4 pm	Battalion " " No 12	App XXV
	Letter of thanks from OC 10th West Yorkshire Rgt.	App XXVI
	The Battalion was relieved by the 2nd Cheshire Rgt at 11.30pm and marched back to billets at LOCRE with the exception of "C" Coy and two platoons of "A" Coy which remained under Capt Forster in left Sector	

Army Form C. 2118.

Instructions regarding War Diaries and Intelligence Summaries are contained in F. S. Regs., Part II. and the Staff Manual respectively. Title pages will be prepared in manuscript.

WAR DIARY
or
~~INTELLIGENCE~~ SUMMARY.
(*Erase heading not required.*)

1st York & Lancaster Rgt.

Hour, Date, Place		Summary of Events and Information	Remarks and references to Appendices
28th July	H.Q at LOCRE	Rested in billets. Capt Swales Johnson was admitted into hospital with influenza	
	11 pm	operation orders (Brigade) no 53	App XXVII
29th July	11.15 pm	Battalion operation orders no 13.	App XXVIII
	2.30 pm	The Battalion left LOCRE and marched to the Huts at SCHERPENBERG	
		Lt Col. Bayley left the Battalion for five days casual leave to England and left Capt Buckley in Command	
	Farm at SCHERPENBERG 5.30 pm	Brigade operation orders no 54	App ~~[illegible]~~ XXIX
30th July	"	Rested in Billets. Major Robertson and the Six platoons from the trenches reached the Camp early in the morning.	
31st July	"	Rested in Billets	
	6 pm	Brigade operation orders no 55	Appx XXX
	8 pm	Captain Lynch marched "D" Coy to SIEGE FARM in accordance to Battalion operation orders no 13a	Appx XXXI

(9 29 6) W 4141—463 100,000 9/14 H W V Forms/C. 2118/10

I

"A" Form

Army Form C. 2121.

MESSAGES AND SIGNALS.

No. of Message

Prefix SB Code LCp m.	Words 68	Charge	This message is on a/c of:	Recd. at m.
Office of Origin and Service Instructions.	Sent		ZHC Service.	Date YE
ZHC	At m.			From 2-7-15
	To		11·24	
	By Priority		(Signature of "Franking Officer.")	By WCox

TO 2/East Yorks
1/York and Lancs Regt

Sender's Number	Day of Month	In reply to Number	AAA
BM 942	2nd		

Following from twentyeighth division begins AAA at least one Bavarian division appears to have been with=drawn from our front AAA Special efforts should be made tonight to capture prisoners or obtain corpses to identify hostile units AAA Ends AAA make every effort to comply with this order tonight and report results tomorrow morning by 7·30 am

From 83rd Bde
Place
Time 11·10 pm

The above may be forwarded as now corrected. (Z)

Censor. Signature of Addressor or person authorised to telegraph in his name

App I

* This line should be erased if not required.

8350 S. B. Ltd Wt. W4843/541—50,000. 9/14. Forms C2121/10.

App. II

III

From Lt. C. E. Wales
1st York & Lanc. Rgt.

To. Capt. E. Buckley
1st York & Lanc. Rgt.

At 12.45 a.m. this morning 3/7/15 I went out on a patrol accompanied by Lt. Lynch, 1 Sgt. & 1 man.
We left the trenches at the junction of L5 & M1 & proceeded in the direction of the German trench opposite.
We proceeded along the hedge running on the north side of the VIERSTRAAT WYTSCHAETE road. The idea of this was to get up to & assault the ~~two~~ carts on the edge of the road known to have been used as a listening post by the enemy. We reached the carts but found them unoccupied. These carts are 30 yds from the German fire trench. We found no signs of a listening post near here. We heard digging operations near so proceeded back along the hedge & 29

crossed the road in order to get into the field South of the road. When in this field we proceeded along the hedge again as far as the carts but could find no one digging here but could distinctly hear it all the time so gathered it was a sap running below this road.
It was by this time 1.30 a.m. & almost light so we returned to M1. trench

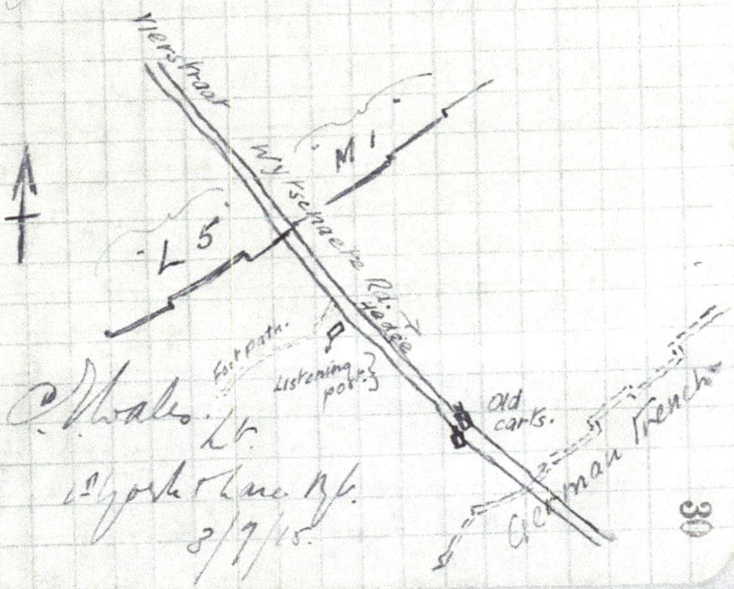

C. Wales.
Lt.
1st York & Lanc. Rgt.
3/7/15. 30

III

"A" Form. Army Form C. 2121.

MESSAGES AND SIGNALS.

No. of Message

Prefix ____ Code ____ m.	Words.	Charge.	This message is on a/c of:	Recd. at ____ m.
Office of Origin and Service Instructions.	Sent		____ Service.	Date
	At ____ m.			From [illegible]
	To			
	By		(Signature of "Franking Officer.")	By

TO 83rd I. B

Sender's Number	Day of Month	In reply to Number	AAA
KS 164	3	BM 242	

	Two	patrols	went	out
last	night,	but	were	unable
to	get	into	the	enemy's
trenches	or	find	a	listening
post	AAA	one	N.C.O	was
killed	AAA	The	night	was
too	light	for	patrol	work

From	O.C.	
Place	1st	K.O.Y.L.I. Regt
Time		7 am

The above may be forwarded as now corrected. (Z) [signature]

Censor. Signature of Addressor or person authorised to telegraph in his name

* This line should be erased if not required.

(24473). M.R.Co.,Ltd. Wt.W4843/541. 50,000. 9/14. Forms C2121/10.

1/York & Lancs

IV

SECRET. OPERATION ORDER NO.41. Copy No. 5

App IV

By

Brigadier General H.S.L. Ravenshaw, C. M. G.

Commanding 83rd Infantry Brigade.

****

Ref: VIERSTRAAT 1/10000 and BELGIUM 28.

LA CLYTTE

3rd July, 1918.

1. The Battalion at La Clytte will be ready to move forward at two hour's notice during daylight and at one hour's notice during the night.

This Battalion will take up position on the Subsidiary Line as follows:-

One Company about FME PARRET.
One Company about FME DESMEL.
One Company south of track running S.E. from LAITERIE.
One Company ROSSIGNOL WOOD.
One Machine Gun FME PARRET.
-do- -do- Emplacement 200 yds. N.E.FME DESMEL.
-do- -do- COETHALS FME.
-do- -do- N.E. corner - ROSSIGNOL WOOD.

Working and carrying parties from this Battalion, which may be working up in front, in case of alarm, will proceed to their appointed places in the Subsidiary Line and await the arrival of their Battalion.

All Officers and N.C.O's of 2nd Bn. East Yorkshire Regt. and 1st Bn. K.O.Y.L.I. will reconnoitre this line so that the position of each portion of their unit may be known to all subordinate Commanders.

2. The Reserve Companies of the Battalions holding Right and Left Sectors will be at the disposal of their C.O's for the purpose of counter-attacking and strengthening the front line.

3. The Battalion at SCHERPENBERG and half Battalion ~~5th~~ 5th King's Own Regt. at LA CLYTTE form the Brigade Reserve and will be ready to move at two hour's notice by day and at one hour's notice by night.

4. All previous Orders on this subject are cancelled.

R.S. Follett Captain.

Brigade Major 83rd Brigade.

Issued at 2.30 p.m.

Copy No. 1. War Diary.
" 2. 2/King's Own.
" 3. 2/E.Yorks R.
" 4. 1/K.O.Y.L.I.
" 5. 1/York & Lancs.
" 6. 5/King's Own.

1/York & Lancs.

V

Copy No. 4

App V

OPERATION ORDER NO. 42.

SECRET.

By

Brigadier General H.S.L.Ravenshaw, C.M.G.

Commanding 83rd Infantry Brigade.

LA CLYTTE,

Ref: VIERSTRAAT. 1/10000

4th JULY, 1915.

1. Following reliefs will take place within the Brigade to-morrow night.

(a) 1/K.O.Y.L.I. with 2 Companies and one Machine Gun Team 5/King's Own Regt attached will relieve 2/East Yorkshire Regt. with 2 Companies and one Machine Gun Team 5/King's Own Regt. attached in the Right Sector.

(b) 2nd Bn. King's Own Regt. will relieve 1/York & Lancaster Regt. in the Left Sector.

2. Relieving Units will pass cross roads N.20.b.10.6, as follows:-

2/King's Own Regt.	9.15.p.m.
1/K.O.Y.L.I. with 2 Companies and one Machine Gun Team 5/King's Own Regt. attached	9.30.p.m.

3. Guides will be arranged between Battalion Commanders.

4. Reliefs for N.1. N.2. and N.3. trenches may use VIA ~~GELLIA~~ GELLIA.

5. Signallers of relieving Units will be at their stations at 4.30.p.m. 5th instant.

6. Major Bogle and Lt. Colonel Bayley will command in the Right and Left Sectors respectively until the relief is completed.

7. Completion of the reliefs will be reported by telephone to Brigade Head quarters.

R.S. Follett Captain.

Issued at 11.p.m.

Brigade Major 83rd Brigade.

Copy No. 1. War Diary.
" 2. 2/King's Own.
" 3. 2/East Yorks.R.
" 4. 1/York & Lancs.R.
" 5. 1/K.O.Y.L.I.
" 6. 5/King's Own.
" 7. 28th Division.

83rd. Bde.

B.M.A.251.

VI

App. VI

ARTILLERY SUPPORT.

Officer Commanding,

1/ York & Lancaster

CONFIDENTIAL. This complete table must not be taken into the trenches.

TRENCHES.	BATTERY.	GUNNER TELEPHONE AT	VISUAL SIGNALLING FROM.
H.	62nd.	H2.	H.5.
J.	365th.	J.2.	
		J.4.	
K.	22nd.	K.1.	K.1.
		K.2a.	
L.	18th.	L.5.	

R.S. Follett

Captain,

28/6/15. Brigade Major,

83rd. Infantry Brigade.

Copy No. 4 VII

App VII

SECRET   OPERATION ORDER NO. 48

by

Brigadier General H.S.L.Ravenshaw, C.M.G.

Commanding 83rd. Infantry Brigade.

REF: VIERSTRAAT.   LA CLYTTE

$\frac{1}{10000}$ 10th July 1918.

1. Following reliefs will take plase within the Brigade tomorrow night:.

(a) 2/East Yorkshire Regt. with 2 companies and one Machine Gun Team 5/Kings Own Regt. attached will relieve 1/K.O.Y.L.I. with 2 companies and one Machine Gun Team 5/King's Own Regt. attached in the Right Sector.

(b) 1/York & Lancaster Regt will relieve 2/King'sOwn Regt. in the Left Sector.

2. Relieving Units will pass cross roads N.20.b.10.4, as follows:-

1/York & Lancaster Regt.	9.15.p.m.
2/East Yorkshire Regt. with 2 Companies and one Machine Gun Team 5/King's Own Regt. attached	9.30.p.m.

3. Guides will be arranged between Battalion Commanders.

4. Reliefs for N.1. N.2.and N.3. trenches may use VIA GELLIA.

5. Signallers of relieving Units will be at their stations at 3.p.m. 11th. instant.

6. Lt.Col.Morris and Lt.Col.Heathcote will command in the Right and Left Sectors respectively until the relief is completed.

7. Completion of the reliefs will be reported by telephone to Brigade Headquarters.

R S Follett
Captain

Issued at 10.45 p.m.   Brigade Major 83rd Brigade.

Copy No. 1. ~~War Diary.~~
" " 2. ~~2/Kings Own.~~
" " 3. ~~2/East Yorks.R.~~
" " 4. 1/York & Lancs.R.
Copy No.5. ~~1/K.O.Y.L.I.~~
" " 6. ~~2/King'sOwn~~
" " 7. ~~28th. Division.~~

VIII

No. 5 Operation Orders
By
Lieut-Colonel G.E. Bayley. D.S.O.
Commanding 1st Bn York & Lancaster Regt.
Monday, 5th July 1915.

1. The Battalion will be relieved tonight by the 2nd King's Own Regt.
2. O.C. Cos. & the M. Gun Officer will ~~[illegible]~~ report to Headquarters by telephone as soon as they are relieved.
3. On relief, Companies will march back independently under Coy. arrangements to the Huts at SCHERPENBERG Sheet 28, M.17. b.4.4.
   The Machine Gun teams will rendezvous at SANDBAG VILLA and march back in one body under Lieut. E. Gribben.
4. Officers trench kits and all water tins must be at SANDBAG VILLA by 9 p.m.
5. O.C. Cos will send in their "Handing over" and "Work" reports by 8 pm today, and their receipt for trench stores by 10 am tomorrow.
6. No guides will be required.

T Knox Shaw Lieut.
A/Adjt 1st York & Lanc Regt.

Issued at 2.15 pm. 5.7.15

App VIII

VIII

No 6 Operation Orders App VIII

By

Lieut-Colonel G E Bayley, D.S.O.

Commanding 1st Bn York & Lancaster Regt.

Sunday, 11th July 1915

1. The Battalion will move into the trenches tonight.

2. Cos. will parade on Coy Parade Grounds and move off independently under Coy Commanders at the following times:-

Machine Gunners with Machine Gun Limbers	8 p.m.
"B" Coy	8.10 p.m
"D" "	8.15 p.m.
"C" "	8.20 p.m
"A" " with Hdqs. Coy. and Stretcher Bearers	8.25 p.m.
Transport	8.30 p.m.

Each Coy will halt for 5 minutes at the spot about 3/4 mile from the ~~Bat~~ Barrier where the Battalion has halted on previous occasions.

There will not be any guides at the Barrier.

3. Officers Kits must be handed into the Quartermasters Stores by 7. p.m.

VIII

4. Trench Kits must be handed in to Quartermaster Stores by 7. p.m

5. Coy. Commanders with their Coy. Q.M. Sgts will proceed to the trenches in advance to take over.

6 On relief, O.C. Cos will report by wire when they have taken over. The Machine Gun Officer will also report.

7 Two sandbags per man will be carried by "B", "C" & "D" Cos. These will be drawn from the Quartermasters Stores at 4 p.m

8 Two stretcher bearers and one medical orderly per Coy will be attached to each Company while in the trenches.

9. Signallers will be attached as follows:-

"B" Coy	—	3
"C" "	—	3
"D" "	—	6

10. Water bottles will be carried filled. O.C. Cos. will arrange to draw water from the Dumping Ground on completion of the move. This will be notified from Bn Hdqrs. Until then no parties are to leave their posts.

VIII

11. Each man will carry one days rations

12. All shelters and blankets will be collected and handed into the Quartermasters Stores by 4 pm

13. O.C. Cos. will render written reports to the Adjutant before leaving that their lines and huts are clean.

14. O.C. "A" Coy will furnish a guard for Bt. Hdqrs. which will be mounted on arrival

T Knox Shaw Lieut
A/Adjt. 1st York & Lancaster Regt

Issued at 3.15 pm.

IX

Copy No. 5

SECRET

OPERATION ORDER NO.44
by
Brigadier General H.S.L.Ravenshaw C.M.G.

Commanding 83rd Infantry Brigade

Reference Sheet,

VIERSTRAAT
&
KEMMEL - WYTSCHAETE
1
―――――
10,000

LA CLYTTE

12th July 1915

1. Reliefs will take place tonight according to the attached Programme.

2. Times for relief and guides will be arranged between officers Commanding Battalions, except as stated in para. 5 & 6.

3. Signallers of relieving Units will take over at 8 p.m.

4. The officer commanding the unit to be relieved will command until the relief is complete.

5. The two companies 5/King's Own will come under the command of O.C. 1/York & Lancaster Regt. These two will pass the Barrier on KEMMEL-LA CLYTTE road at 8.30 p.m. & will report at Hqrs. of Left Sector.

6. One officer per company two guides per trench & one guide per machine gun will meet 1/Suffolk Regt. at junction of WATLING St. & KEMMEL-VIERSTRAAT road at 8.45 p.m.

7. Headquarters of Right Sector move to Doctor's House. Hqrs. Left Sector remain as at present. Dressing Stations do not move.

8. Completion of relief will be reported by wire.

Issued at 1.30 P.M.

R.S. Follett Capt.

Brigade Major
83rd Infantry Brigade

War Diary Copy No.1.
2/King's Own " " 2.
2/East Yorks " " 3.
1/K.O.Y.L.I. " " 4.
1/York & Lcs. " " 5.
5/King's Own " " 6.
28th Divn. " " 7.
84th Brigade " " 8.
181st. " " " " 9.
Northumbrian
Field Coy. " 10.

App IX

In substitution for incorrect copy issued R.G.H.

IX

1/York & Lancaster Regt.

TRENCH GARRISON.

Trench	Garrison	M.G.	Unit Handing Over	Unit Taking Over
G.1.	70	1	8/Loyal N.Lancs.	2/E.Yorks Regt.
G.2.	75	1	-do-	-do-
G.3.	50	1	-do-	-do-
G.4.) G.4a.)	210	1	-do-	-do-
S.P.11.	25		-do-	-do-
FOWLER's Fm.	30		-do-	-do-
Doctors Ho. (Battn.H.Q.)			-do-	-do-
H.1) H.2.)	105	X 1 (on road)	2/King's Own.R.	-do-
H.3) H.4)	29	1	2/E.York.R.	1/York & Lancs.R.
H.5.	105		2/King's Own.	-do-
J.1.	90	1	2/East Yorks.R.	-do-
J.2.	37		-do-	-do-
J.3.(R)) J.3.(new))	58		-do-	-do-
J.3.(L)	12		-do-	-do-
J.4.	48	1	-do-	-do-
J.10	26		-do-	-do-
J.11.	50		-do-	-do-
S.P.12.	23	O X 1(York&Lancs)	-do-	2/King's Own.
S.P.13.	34	1(2/King's Own)	-do-	-do-
K.1.	46	1	-do-	1/York & Lancs.
K.1.a.	35		-do-	2/King's Own.
K.1.b.	27		1/York & Lancs.	-do-
K.2.	34		-do-	-do-
K.2.a.	50	X 1 (York & Lancs)	-do-	-do-
K.2.b.	59		-do-	-do-

X Continues to be found by 2/East Yorkshire Regt.

X Teams found by 1/York & Lancs.R.

O GUN found by 2/King's Own.

IX

(continued)

TRENCH.	Garrison.	M.G.	Unit handing Over.	Unit taking Over.
L.1.	11		1/York & Lancs.	1/Suffolk.R.
L.2.) L.3.)	76		-do-	-do-
L.4.	38		-do-	-do-
L.5.	58	1	-do-	-do-
L.6.	37	1	-do-	-do-
L.6. detached post.	-		-do-	-do-
L.7.(R)	34		-do-	-do-
L.7.(L).	42	1	-do-	-do-
Watling Street Com. Trench			-do-	-do-
VIA Gellia			-do-	-do-

R. S. Follett Captain.

Brigade Major 83rd Infantry Brigade.

X

No. 7. Operation Orders App I

By

Lieut Colonel G.E. Bayley. D.S.O.

Commanding 1st York & Lancaster Regiment

Monday, 12th July 1915.

1. Relief will take place tonight according to the following programme.
"B" Coy will take over Trenches H 3, H 4. J. 1. & H. 5 new from 2nd E. Yorks Regt.
"C" Coy. will take over Trenches K. 1., K. 1. a. J. 4 & J. 3. left from 2nd E. Yorks Regt.
"D" Coy. will take over Trenches J. 3, right J 3 new, J. 2, J. 10 & H. 5. old

2. The Machine Guns will be in J. 1. J. 4, K. 1, & K. 2 b. Spare Gun Team will be in S.P. 13 with a gun belonging to 5th K.O. Regt. which will be brought ~~by~~ from H 3. by 2nd E. Yorks Regt.

3. "B" & "D" Cos will be relieved by 1st Suffolk Regt.
"C" Coy will be relieved by 5th K.O. Regt with the exception of L. 7. which will be taken over by 1st Suffolk Regt.

4. The Machine Gun in L. 5, L. 6, & L. 7. will be relieved by 1st Suffolk Regt.

5. O.C. "B" Coy will find guides for L 2, L 3, L. 4, & L. 5 for the 1st Suffolk Regt. They

will be at junction of track between WATLING STREET and the FOSSE on the KEMMEL-VIERSTRAATE Road at 8.45 p.m.

6. O.C. 'D' Coy will find guides for K.3, L.6, L.7 left, L.7 right, for 1st Suffolk Regt. They will be at junction of track between WATLING STREET and the FOSSE on the KEMMEL-VIERSTRAATE Rd. at 8.45 pm.

7 O.C. 'C' Coy will find four guides for 5th K.O. Regt. to be at Bn Hdqrs at 8.30 pm. and also 1 guide from L.1, for 1st Suffolk Regt. to be at junction of track between WATLING St & the FOSSE on the KEMMEL VIERSTRAATE Rd. at 8.45 pm.

8. The M.Gun Officer will find guides for teams of 1st Suffolk Regt. from L.5, L.6, & L.7, to be at junction of track between WATLING St. and the FOSSE on the KEMMEL-VIERSTRAATE Rd. at 8.45 pm.

9. O.C. Cos will report by wire to Bn Hdqrs as soon as relief is completed.

10. (a) All empty water tins should be handed in at SANDBAG VILLA by 8.15 pm. The carrying parties will rejoin their Cos.

(b) Coy. Qr. Mr Sgts will take over rations at SANDBAG VILLA at 9.30 pm.

(c) Ration parties will be sent to draw rations immediately after relief is completed.

T Knox Shaw Lieut.
A/Adjt. 1st York Lanc Regt

Issued at 7-55 pm

(X)

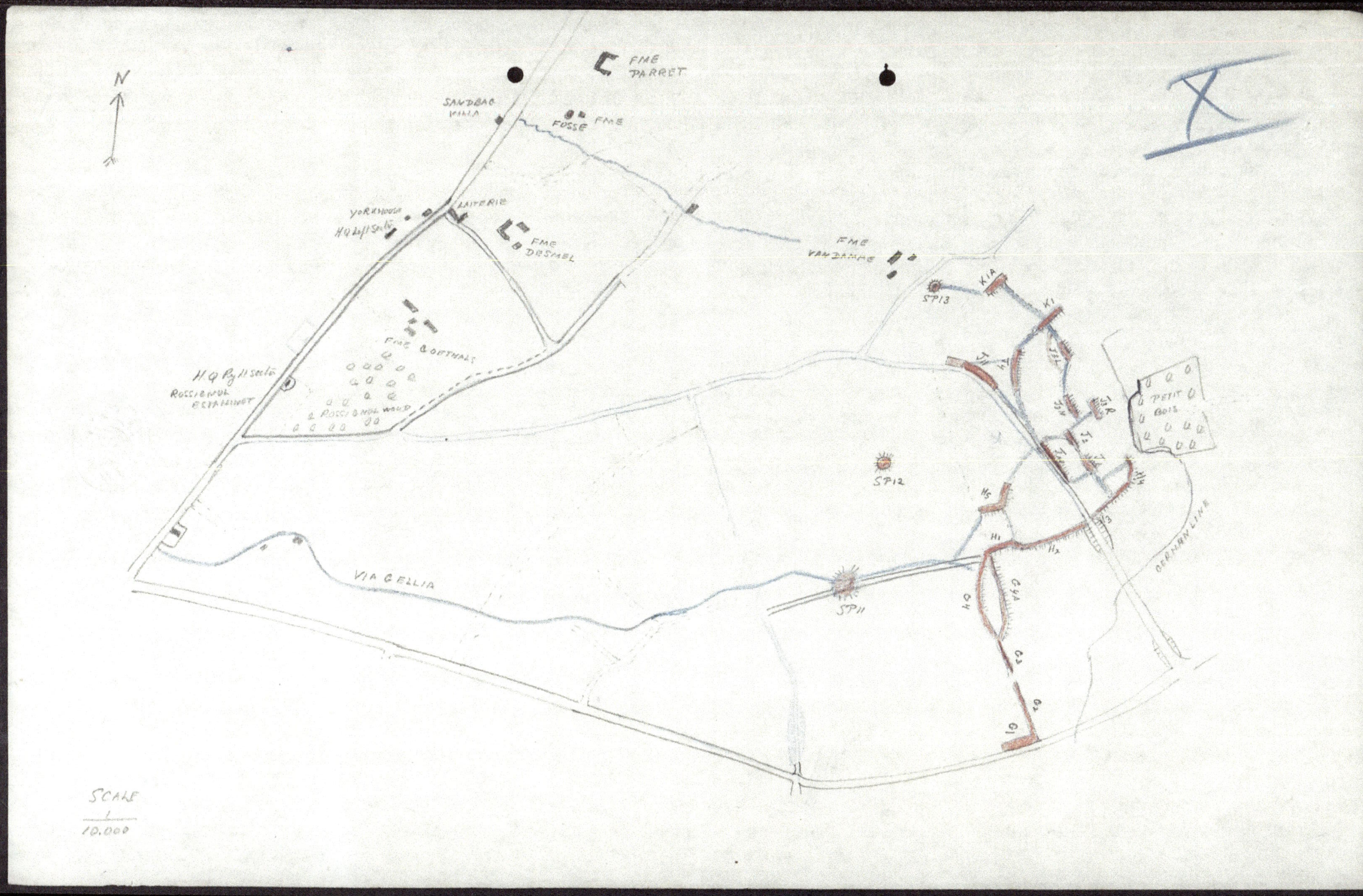
X
N
FME PARRET
SANDBAG VILLA
FME FOSSE
YORKHOUSE
H.Q Left Secto
LAITERIE
FME DESMEL
FME VANDAMME
FME GOETHALS
H.Q Ry II Secto
ROSSIGNOL ESTAMINET
ROSSIGNOL WOOD
SP13
K1A
K1
J1
J1L
J3R
J2
SP12
PETIT BOIS
H5
H1
H2
GERMAN LINE
VIA GELLIA
SP11
G4
G4A
G3
G2
G1
SCALE
1
10.000

XI App XI

SECRET

Copy No. 5

OPERATION ORDER No. 45
By

BRIGADIER GENERAL H.S.L. RAVENSHAW, C.M.G.

Commanding 83rd Infantry Brigade.

KEMMEL-WYATSCHATTE 1/10000

Ref:- VIERSTRAAT 1/10000

LA CLYTTE, 15th July, 1915

1. The following reliefs will take place on the night 15th - 16th July.

TRENCH.	Unit handing over	Unit taking over.
G.1.	2/E.Yorkshire R.	2/Cheshire Regt.
G.2.	-do-	-do-
G.3.	-do-	-do-
G.4.	-do-	-do-
G.4.a.	-do-	-do-
H.1.	-do-	-do-
H.2.	-do-	-do-
VIA GELLIA	-do-	-do-
S.P.11. (garrison can use VIA GELLIA)	-do-	1/York & Lancs.R.
H.3.	1/York & Lancs.R.	2/Cheshire Regt.
H.4.	-do-	-do-
K.2.a. K.2.b. (K.1b. K.2.)	5/King's Own Regt. & M. Gun Team 1/York & Lancs.R.	2/Kings Own Regt.
K.3.	1/Suffolk Regt.	2/King's Own Regt.
L.1.	-do-	-do-
L.2.	-do-	-do-
L.3.	-do-	-do-
L.4.	-do-	-do-
L.5.	-do-	-do-
L.6.	-do-	-do-
L.7.a.	-do-	-do-
L.7.	-do-	-do-
WATLING STREET	-do-	-do-

2. The garrisons of K.1.b. and K.2. found by 5/King's Own R. come under Command of 2/King's Own Regt. at midnight 15th-16th July. The Garrisons of S.P. 12 & 13 found by 5/King's Own R. remain under Command of O.C.1/York & Lancs.R.

3. Arrangements as to reliefs will be made between Commanding Officers of Battalions. No relieving unit will pass east of G.H.Q. second line before 8.30. p.m.

4. Officers Commanding units to be relieved will command in their Sectors until the relief is complete.

5. List of all trench stores handed over or received will be sent to this Office.

6. On completion of relief 1/Suffolk Regt. will rejoin 84th Brigade and 2/East Yorkshire Regt. will proceed to SCHERPENBERG Huts.

7. Completion of reliefs will be reported to this Office.

R S Follett Capt ~~Major.~~

Brigade Major 83rd Infantry Brigade.

Issued at 8-45 a.m.

Copy	No.1.	War Diary.
"	No.2.	2/King's Own.
"	No.3.	2/East Yorks.R.
"	No.4.	1/K.O.Y.L.I.
"	No.5.	1/York & Lancs.R.
"	No.6.	5/King's Own.R.
"	No.7.	1/Suffolk Regt.
"	No.8.	84th Brigade.
"	No.9.	28th Division.
"	No.10	2/1/Northumbrian Field Coy.
"	No.11.	3rd Brigade R.F.A.

No. 8

XII

App XII

Operation Orders
By
Lieut Colonel G. E. Bayley, D.S.O.
Commanding 1st Bn York & Lancaster Regiment
Thursday, 15th July 1915

1. BATTALION HEADQUARTERS	The Battalion Headquarters will move to RUSSIGNOL Estaminet, about 300 yards South of York House on the KEMMEL-VIERSTRAATE Road at 8 pm tonight. The Dressing Station will move from the LAITERIE to the Barn close to this Estaminet.
2. TAKING OVER TRENCHES.	The O.C. 'B' Coy. will take over Trench S.P. 11. from 2nd E. Yorks Regt. and occupy it with one platoon. He will also occupy J. 11 with one platoon. The 2nd Cheshire Regt. will take over H. 3. and H. 4. from the O.C. "B" Coy. The O.C. "A" Coy will take over SEIGE FARM from the detachment of 2nd East Yorks Regt. now in possession, and hand over SANDBAG VILLA, the dugouts and barn at YORK HOUSE and other billet to 2nd King's Own Regt. The 5th Kings Own Regt hand over K. 2. a. and K. 2. b. to the 2nd Kings Own Regt. and the garrisons of K. 1. b and K. 2. found by them come under the command of the OC. 2nd Kings Own Regt. at midnight 15th - 16th July. The garrisons of S.P. 12. and S.P. 13 found by the 5th Kings Own Regt. will remain under the command of O.C. 1st York & Lancaster Regt. Capt. Eaves, 5th King's Own Regt will arrange to relieve the section of one Sergeant and 12 men of 1st York & Lancaster Regt now in S.P. 13. and will increase the garrison to 34 men. The Machine Gun Team in K. 2. a. will go to SIEGE FARM on being relieved.

P.T.O.

3. DUMPING GROUND.	The Dumping Ground will be at Square N.21. B.9.2, Sheet 28. which is at corner of wood 1/4 mile South of YORK HOUSE on the KEMMEL — VIERSTRAATE Road.
4. TRENCH STORES.	O.C. Cos will render Receipts for Trench Stores to Bn Hdqrs by 8. am. 16th July.
5. REPORTS.	O.C. Cos. will report to Bn Hdqrs. by wire on completion of relief.
6. RATIONS.	O.C. Cos. will arrange to have all water tins at the new dumping ground and to draw their rations at the usual hour.
7. GUM BOOTS.	All gum boots must be returned to SANDBAG VILLA by 9 pm tonight.

T Knox Shaw Lieut.
A/Adjutant, 1st York Lancaster Regt.

XIII App XIII

OPERATION ORDER NO. 46 Copy No. 5

by

BRIGADIER GENERAL H.S.L.RAVENSHAW, C.M.G.,

Commanding 83rd Infantry Brigade.

****

La Clytte.

18th July, 1915.

Ref: VIERSTRAAT
and
KEMMEL - WYTSCHAETE

1

10.000

1. The following reliefs will take place within the Brigade tomorrow night :-

1st K.O.Y.L.I., will relieve the 1st York & Lancaster Regt., in the Right Sector.
5th King's Own Regiment will relieve their present garrisons in K 1 b, K 2, S.P.12, S.P. 13, and the Machine Gun Team in S.P., 13 by similar garrisons and fresh machine gun team.

2. Relieving units will pass the cross roads N 20 b 10.6 as follows :-

1st K.O.Y.L.I., 8.30.p.m.
5th King's Own. 8.45.p.m.

3. All details of reliefs will be arranged between Battalion Commanders.

4. Signallers of relieving units will be at their stations by three p.m.

5. Lieut.Col.Bayley will Command in the Right Sector until the relief is completed.

6. Relief for S.P. 11 will use the VIA GELLIA.

7. The garrisons of 5th King's Own in S.P. 12 and S.P.13 come under the command of O.C., 1st K.O.Y.L.I. The garrisons of K 1 b, and K 2 come under the command of O.C., 2nd King's Own.

8. Completion of relief will be reported by telephone to Brigade Headquarters.

9. On relief the 1st York & Lancaster Regiment will proceed to Scherpenberg Huts.
The 2nd East Yorkshire Regiment will march at 9 p.m. to LA CLYTTE Huts from their present position.

E C Lypp Major for Captain.
Brigade Major, 83rd Bde,

Issued at p.m.

Copy No. 1. War Diary.
2. 2nd King's Own
3. 2nd East Yorks
4. 1st K.O.Y.L.I.
5. 1st York & Lancs
6. 5th Kings Own.

XIV

App XIV

No. 9.

OPERATION ORDERS.

BY

Lieut. Col. G. E. Bayley D.S.O.,
Comd'g. 1st Bn. York & Lancaster Regt.,
Saturday 17th July 1915.

1/ Relief.	The Battalion will be relieved tonight by the 1st Bn. K.O.Y.L.I. and 5th Kings own will relieve their present garrisons in S.P.12, and S.P.13. These two garrisons will come under the command of the O.C. 1st K.O.Y.L.I.
2/ Reports.	O.C. Cos. and the Machine Gun Officer will report to Bn. Hd. Qrs. by telephone as soon as relief is completed.
3/ Return to Billets.	On relief, Cos. will march back independently under Coy. arrangements, to the huts at SCHERPENBERG, Square M.17. 6.4.4, Sheet 28. The Machine Gun teams will rendezvous at the Dumping Ground of the Right Sector and march back in one body under Lieut. E. Gribben.
4/ Kits.	Officers trench Kits and all water tins must be at the dumping ground, Right Sector, by 9 p.m.
5/ Guides.	O.C. "B" Coy. will furnish one guide from H.5. new. " "D" — " — — " — " — H.5. old. O.C. Detmt. 5th Kings Own will furnish guides from S.P.12, & S.P.13. All guides will report at Bn. Hdqrs. at 8.30 p.m.
6/ Returns.	O.C. Cos. will render "Handing Over" and "Work Reports" by 8 p.m. today, and their receipt for trench stores by 10 a.m. tomorrow.
7/ Officers Chargers.	Officers Chargers will be at KEMMEL BARRIER, except that for O.C. "A" Coy. which will be at SIEGE FARM.

T Knox Shaw Lieut.,
A/Adjutant 1st York & Lancaster Regt.

Issued at 1 PM.

XV

App XV

SECRET

Copy No. 5

OPERATION ORDER No. 47.
by
BRIGADIER GENERAL H.S.L.RAVENSHAW C.M.G.

COMMANDING 83rd INFANTRY BRIGADE

REF; $\frac{1}{20,000}$
SHEET 28 S.W.(B Series)

17th July 1915.

1. Paragraph 9 of Operation Order No. 46 as regards the 2/East Yorkshire Regt. is cancelled.

2. The 2/East Yorkshire Regt. with 1st.Line Transport and Train will march at 4 p.m. to-day to DRANOUTRE via LOCRE and will there come under the orders of the 85th Inf.Brigade

3. Under orders from the 85th Inf.Brigade officers 2/East Yorks. will reconnoitre Trenches to-night with a view to taking them over on the night 18/19 inst.

Issued at / p.m.

E.C. Gepp Major for
Brigade Major
83rd Infantry Brigade

Copy No.1.War Diary
" " 2.2/King's Own R.
" " 3.2/East York R.
" " 4.1/K.O.Y.L.I.
" " 5.1/York & Lancs.R.
" " 6.5/King's Own R.
" " 7.28th Divn.
" " 8.85th Brigade
" " 9.O.C.No.2.Coy.A.S.C.

XVI

Copy No. 4

App XVI

OPERATION ORDER NO. 48

BY

BRIGADIER GENERAL H.S.L.RAVENSHAW, C.M.G.

Commanding 83rd Infantry Brigade.

****

Ref. VIERSTRAAT and KEMMEL WYTSCHAETE 1/10,000

17th July, 1915.

1. Operation Order No. 46 of the 16th instant is cancelled.

2. Reliefs will take place tonight in accordance with attached table.

3. 1st K.O.Y.L.I., will pass cross roads N 20 b 10'6 at 8.30 p.m.

4. All details of relief will be arranged between Battalion Commanders.

5. Lieut.Col.Bayley will command in the Right Sector until relief is completed.

6. Completion of relief will be reported by telephone to Brigade Headquarters.

7. On relief Company of 5th King's Own to LA CLYTTE HUTS. 1st York & Lancaster to SCHERPENBERG HUTS.

8. Receipts for trench stores to reach this office by 11 a.m., 18th instant.

E C Gripp Major,
for Brigade Major, 83rd Bde.

Issued at 3 50 p.m.

Copy No. 1 War Diary.
2. 2nd King's Own.
3. 1st K.O.Y.L.I.
4. 1st York & Lancaster Regt.
5. 5th King's Own.
6. 84th Brigade.
7. 28th Division.

Unit handing over	Unit taking over	Trenches.
1st York & Lancaster Regiment.	1st K.O.Y.L.I.	All trenches now held by 1st York & Lancaster Regiment, except S.P. 11.
1st York & Lancaster Regiment	84th Infantry Brigade.	S.P., 11 and 1 Machine gun.
5th King's Own	1st K.O.Y.L.I.	S.P., 12 and 1 machine gun, and S.P., 13 and 1 machine gun (Team of K.O.Y.L.I., gun of 5th King's Own)
5th King's Own	2nd King's Own	K 1 b. and E 2.

XVII

App XVII

SECRET

COPY No. 4

OPERATION ORDERS No. 41a

by

BRIGADIER GENERAL H.S.L.RAVENSHAW, C.M.G.

Commanding 83rd Infantry Brigade.

****

Saturday, 17th July, 1915.

Ref. VIERSTRAAT
and
KEMMEL - WYTSCHAETE
1
10,000

1. Reference operation order No. 41, and the addition thereto issued on the 18th instant.

2. After relief tonight for Battalion "at LA CLYTTE" read 1st York & Lancaster.

For Battalion " at SCHERPENBERG" read 5th King's Own.

3. Necessary reconnaisance will be carried out.

E C Gepp Major,
for Brigade Major, 83rd Brigade.

Issued at p.m.

Copy No. 1 War Diary.
2. 2nd King's Own.
3. 1st K.O.Y.L.I.
4. 1st York & Lancaster.
5. 5th King's Own.

COPY. No. 5.

SECRET

The following Addition is made to Operation Order No.41. para. 1. of 3rd. Instant.

1. One machine gun from battalion at SCHERPENBERG to machine gun emplacement on South side of ROSSIGNOL WOOD, N.22.a.5.2.

P One machine gun from battalion at SCHERPENBERG to FME. DESMEL.

The teams of these two guns come under orders of Officer Commanding the battalion occupying Subsidiary Line.

3. The necessary reconnaissance will be carried out by 1/York & Lancaster Regt. and 2/King's Own Regt.

E. C. Gepp Major

Captain
Brigade Major
83rd Infantry Brigade

16th. July 1915.

Copy No. 1. War Diary
2. 2/King's Own R.
3. 2/East Yorks R.
4. 1/K.O.Y.L.I.
5. 1/York & Lancs.
6. 5/King's Own R.

XVIII

App XVIII

Copy No. 1

Operation Orders No. 10

By

Lieut Colonel G.E. Bayley, D.S.O.

Commanding 1st Bn York & Lancaster Regt.

Saturday, 17th July 1915.

1. Relief. Operation Order No. 9/1 of this date is cancelled and the following substituted:—

The Battalion will be relieved tonight by the 1st Bn K.O.Y.L.I.

The Garrison of S.P. 11 with 1 Machine Gun will be relieved by 2nd Cheshire Regt., 84th I. Bde.

The Garrison of S.P. 12 and ~~S.P. 13~~ 1 Machine Gun and S.P. 13 and 1 Machine Gun (team found by 1st K.O.Y.L.I. and gun found by 5th King's Own Regt.) will be relieved by 1st K.O.Y.L.I.

On relief the 5th King's Own Regt. will march back to the Huts at LA CLYTTE.

T Knox Shaw Lieut.

A/Adjutant, 1st Bn York & Lancaster Regt.

Issued at 6.45 p.m.

Copy No. 2. to O.C. "B" Coy.

" No. 3 to O.C. 5th Kings Own Regt.

" No. 4 to O.C. Det. 5th King's Regt.

XIX

COPY No. 5

App XIX

OPERATION ORDER No. 49

by

BRIGADIER GENERAL H.S.L.RAVENSHAW, C.M.G.

Commanding 83rd Infantry Brigade,

****

Reference 1/10000 B Series.Sheet 28, S.W. and VIERSTRAAT 1/10000

Tuesday, 20th July, 1915.

The following lines are allotted to this Brigade:-

1. SUBSIDIARY LINE from 20 yards S. of the road running along S. edge of wood in Square N.22.a. to point 20 yards W. of where the trench line crosses the KEMMEL-VIERSTRAAT road about Square N.17.a.2.7.
G.H.Q. LINE from Cross Roads Square N.15.c. (road inclusive) to point where trench line crosses road about Square N.9.d.10.2. (road inclusive)

2. IN CASE OF ALARM.
Any Battalion, out of the trenches, may be ordered to occupy the Subsidiary Line, and will place its machine guns in the following positions :-

One S. edge of ROSSIGNOL WOOD, Square N.22.a.
One N.E. of ROSSIGNOL WOOD, Square N.22.a.
One CORTHALS FARM, Square N.22.b.
One just S. of FARM DESMIL, Square N.16.d.

Two additional machine guns will be ordered from another Battalion, out of the trenches, to occupy the following positions :-

One 200 yards N.E., of FARM DESMIL.
One at FARM PERRET, Square N.17.a.

3. Working and carrying parties, which may be working up in front, will proceed to their appointed places in the Subsidiary Line and await the arrival of their Battalions.

4. Reserve Companies of Battalions holding Right and Left Sectors will be at the disposal of their Commanding Officers for the purpose of counter attacks etc.

5. Battalions out of the trenches will be prepared to move at two hours" notice by day and one hour's notice by night.

6. All previous orders on this subject are cancelled.

Issued at 11.45 a.m.

E C Cepp Major,
for Brigade Major, 83rd Bde.

Copy No. 1. War Diary.
2. 2nd East Yorks
3. 2nd King's Own
4. 1st K.O.Y.L.I.
5. 1st York & Lancs
6. 5th King's Own
7. Brigade M.G.Officer
8. Signals 83rd Brigade.

XX

COPY No. 5

OPERATION ORDER No. 50

by

BRIGADIER GENERAL H.S.L.RAVENSHAW, C.M.G.,

Commanding 83rd Infantry Brigade.

App XI

****

Reference 20th July, 1915.

VIERSTRAAT $\frac{1}{10000}$

1. Reliefs will take place on night 21-22 July in accordance with attached table.

2. Relieving parties will pass Cross Roads N.20.b.10.6., at 8.30.p.m.

3. All details of relief will be arranged between Battalion Commanders and Major E.C.Robertson, 1st York & Lancaster Regt.

4. Lieut.Col.E.M.Morris will Command in the Left Sector until relief is completed.

5. Completion of relief will be reported to Brigade Headquarters.

6. Signallers of 5th King's Own will take over Left Sector Headquarters, K 2 a, L 6, L 5, and K 3 by 3 p.m., on 21st July.

7. On relief 2nd King's Own Regiment to LA CLYTTE huts.

8. Dispositions and receipts for trench stores to reach this office by 11 a.m., 22nd instant.

E.C. [signature] Major,
for Brigade Major, 83rd Bde.

Issued at 1.30 p.m.

Copy No. 1. War Diary.
2. 2nd King's Own.
3. 2nd East Yorks.
4. 1st K.O.Y.L.I.
5. 1st York & Lancs
6. 5th King's Own.
7. Major E.C.Robertson, 1st York & Lancs.
8. 28th Division.
9. Signals, 83rd Brigade.
10. Brigade Machine Gun Officer.

Unit Handing over	Unit Taking over	Trenches etc	Machine Guns taken over by	Officer Commanding the whole of Left Sector after relief
2nd King's Own	5th King's Own	All L's K 2 b, K 3.	L 5, Team & Gun 5th King's Own. L 6 do. L 7 do. K 2 a, Team and Gun 2nd King's Own.	Major E.C. Robertson. 1st York & Lancs
2nd King's Own	1st K.O.Y.L.I.	K 1 b, K 2. K 2 a.		
2nd King's Own	2 Officers, and 100 other ranks. 1st York & Lancs	SANDBAG VILLA		
2nd King's Own	Roserve Coy, 5th King's Own	Dug Outs, York House		

XXI

App XXI

COPY No. 5

OPERATION ORDER No. 51

by

BRIGADIER GENERAL H.S.L.RAVENSHAW, C.M.G.

Commanding 83rd Infantry Brigade.

Reference VIERSTRAAT 1/10000

22nd July, 1915.

1. Reliefs in accordance with attached table will take place on night 23rd-24th July.

2. Relieving parties will pass Cross Roads N.20.b.10.6. at 8.30 p.m.

3. All details of relief will be arranged between Battalion Commanders and Major E.C.Robertson, 1st York & Lancaster Regiment, Officer Commanding Left Sector.

4. Lieut Colonel C.E.Heathcote, D.S.O., will command in the Right Sector until relief is completed.

5. Completion of relief will be reported to Brigade Headquarters.

6. Signallers of relieving Battalion will take over by 3 p.m., on 23rd July.

7. Second King's Own Regiment will move at 8.15.p.m., 23rd instant into SCHERPENBERG Huts.
On relief 1st K.O.Y.L.I., to bivouacs now occupied by 2nd King's Own. 7.15,

8. Dispositions and receipts for Trench Stores to reach this office by 11 a.m., 24th instant 7.20. 7.25 73

E.C. Gepp.
Major.
for Brigade Major, 83rd Inf. Bde.

Issued at 3.45 p.m.

Copy No. 1, War Diary.
2, 2nd King's Own
3, 2nd East Yorks.
4, 1st K.O.Y.L.I.
5, 1st York & Lancs.
6, 5th King's Own
7, Major E.C.Robertson, 1st York & Lancs
8, 28th Division
9, Signals, 83rd Inf. Bde.
10, Brigade Machine Gun Officer

26.

TRENCHES ETC

Trenches etc	Unit Handing over	Unit taking over	
All trenches etc in Right Sector	1st K.O.Y.L.I.	1st York & Lancs	
K 1 b. K 2. and K 2 a.	1st K.O.Y.L.I.	1st York & Lancs	Garrisons come under command of O.C.. Left Sector.
SANDBAG VILLA	2 Officers. and 100 other ranks. 1st York & Lancs	2 Officers and 100 other ranks 2nd King's Own.	do.

MACHINE GUNS

Position	Unit handing over	Unit taking over	
J 1.	1st K.O.Y.L.I.	1st York & Lancs	Gun and team
J 4.	"	" "	" "
K 1.	"	" "	" "
S.P. 12	"	" "	" "
S.P. 13	"	Team 1st York & Lancs.	Gun, 5th Kings Own
K 2 a.		Gun and Team 2nd King's Own will not be relieved.	

Operation Orders No: 11 Copy No: 1.
By
Lieut Colonel G.E. Bayley, DSO.
Commanding 1st York & Lancaster Regiment.
Friday, 23rd July 1915.

App XXII

XXII

---

1. The Battalion will move into the trenches tonight and take over trenches as per attached table.

2. Cos. will parade on Coy. parade grounds and move off independently under Coy. Commanders at the following times:-

4 Machine Gun Teams with limber	7.15 pm.
"C" Coy. with garrison of S.P.13 from "D" Coy and Machine Gun Team for S.P.13.	7.20 pm
"D" Coy	
"B" "	7.25 pm.
"A" Coy (2 platoons) with Hdqrs. and Stretcher bearers will march to SIEGE FARM via MILLECRUISO (Sheet 28. N.2.C.2.1.)	7.30 pm.
	7.35 pm.
Transport	
	8.10 pm.

Each Coy. will halt for 5 minutes en route.

3. Guides for S.P.12 and S.P.13 will be found at junction of KEMMEL-VIERSTRAATE Road and road to trenches.

4. Officers Kits must be handed into the Quartermasters Stores by 6 pm.

5. Trench Kits must be handed into the Quartermasters Stores by 6 pm.

6. O.C. "B" "C" & "D" Cos. will arrange that an officer with their Coy. Q.M.S. proceed to the trenches in advance to take over.

7. On relief O.C. Cos. & Machine Gun Officer will report when they have taken over.

8. Two sandbags per man will be carried by "B C & D" Cos. These will be drawn from the Quartermasters Stores at 4 pm.

9. Two stretcher bearers and one Medical orderly per Coy. will be attached while in the trenches. The stretcher bearers for the two platoons of "A" Coy in Left Sector will march with "C" Coy.

10. Signallers will be attached as follows:-

"A" Coy. for stations in	K.2.a and S.F.
"B" " " "	J.1.
"C" " " "	K.1.
"D" " " "	J.2 and J.4.

P.T.O.

11. Water bottles will be carried filled.

O.C. Cos. will arrange to draw water from the dumping ground on completion of the move. This will be notified from Bn. Hdqrs. Until then no parties are to leave their posts

12 Each man will carry one days rations

13. All shelters and blankets will be handed into the Quartermasters Stores by 5 p.m.

14. O.C. Cos will render written reports to the Adjutant before leaving that their lines and huts are clean.

15. O.C. 'A' Coy. will furnish a guard for Bn Hdqrs. which will be mounted on arrival.

T. Knox Shaw Lt
a/Adjutant
1st York & Lancaster Rgt

Issued at 6.45 p.m.

Copies 1 & 2 War Diary.
Copy 3 O.C. 'A' Coy
" 4 " B "
" 5 " C "
" 6 " D "
" 7 Machine Gun Section
8 Major E.C. Robertson.

Trenches	Coy. Taking Over	Remarks
H.5. Old & New. J.1. J.10. S.P. 12.	'B' Coy. —"— —"— —"—	
J.3. Right & J.3. New J.2. J.4. J.11. S.P. 13.	'D' Coy —"—	
J.3. left. K.1. K.1.a. K.1.b.	'C' Coy —"— —"—	Garrisons come under Command of O.C. left Sector.
K.2. K.2.a.	'A' Coy.	" " " "

MACHINE GUNS.

J.1. J.4. K.1. S.P. 12.
S.P. 13 Team with M. Gun. found by 5th King's Own.

XXIII

"A" Form. Army Form C. 2121.

MESSAGES AND SIGNALS. No. of Message

Prefix Code m. | Words | Charge | This message is on a/c of: Service. | Recd. at m.

Office of Origin and Service Instructions.

Sent At m. To By

(Signature of "Franking Officer.")

Date

From [illegible]

By

TO 83rd I B

Sender's Number.	Day of Month	In reply to Number	AAA
* KB87	24		

Situation	quiet	AAA	no	trench
mortar	nor	artillery	fire	during
night	AAA	Wind	S. W	fresh.
Distribution	of Troops.			
J_1	officer	one	other Ranks	59
J_{10}	"	1	" "	33
H_5 old & New	"	1	" "	76
SP12	"	1	" "	30
SP13	"	1	" "	35
J_{11}	"	0	" "	24
J_4	"	1	" "	31
J_2	"	1	" "	45
J_3 New	"	1	" "	31
J_3 Right	"	0	" "	14
J_3 Left	"	1	" "	30
K_1	"	2	" "	64
K_{1A}	"	1	" "	46

From machine Guns in K_1 J_1 J_4 SP12 SP13

Place OC

Time Y+L 4 am

The above may be forwarded as now corrected. (Z) T Knox Shaw Lt

Censor. Signature of Addressor or person authorised to telegraph in his name.

* This line should be erased if not required.

(688-9) — McC. & Co. Ltd., London.— W 14142/641. 250,000. 4/15. Forms C 2121/10.

XXIV

SECRET. OPERATION ORDER No. 52. COPY No..4...

by

BRIGADIER GENERAL H.S.L.RAVENSHAW. C.M.G.

Commanding 83rd Infantry Brigade.

****

Reference VIERSTRAAT 1/10000

Sheet 28 1/40000

27th July 1915.

1. The following reliefs take place tonight.

To 2/Cheshire Regt 84th Brigade.
Machine gun emplacements in J.1. J.4. & S.P.12.
Trenches H.5. J.1. J.2. J.3(right) J.3(new) J.3(left) J.4. J.10. J.11. S.P.12. & ROSSIGNOL ESTAMINET.

The 1/York & Lancaster R. evacuate SIEGE FARM but this farm does not pass to 84th Brigade.
1/York & Lanc'r R. relieve M-gun Detachment 2/King's Own R. in K.2.a.

2. On relief 1/York & Lancaster Regt. move to huts M.29.a. (sheet 28 Belgium).

3. The garrisons of 1/York & Lanc.R. in K.1. K.1.a. K,1.b. new fire trench K.1. to K.2. K.2. and K.2.a. will come under the orders of O.C.Left Sector at 9 p.m.

4. All trench stores will be handed over and receipts forwarded to this office. The ammount of ammunition handed over will also be reported.

5. All details as to relief will be arranged between O.C. 2/Cheshire Regt. and O.C. 1/York & Lancaster R. the latter will inform 83rd Brigade Hqrs. by wire of the time and place at which relieving units will be met by guides.

6. Lieut-Colonel Bayley D.S.O. will Command in the area to be handed over until the relief is complete.

7. Completion of relief will be repeated to Brigade Hqrs. by wire.

Issued at 12.10 p.m.

R. S. Follett
Captain
Brigade Major.
83rd Infantry Brigade.

Copy No.1. War Diary
2. 2/King's Own R.
3. 1/K.O.Y.L.I.
4. 1/York & Lancr.R.
5. 5/King's Own R.
6. 28th Divn.
7. 84th Brigade.
8. 2/1 Northumbrian Fd.Co.
9. No.2 Coy. A.S.C.
10. 3rd Brigade R.F.A.

App XXIV

Copy No: 1

No: 12.

App XXV

XXV

OPERATION ORDERS

by

Lieut-Col. G. E. Bayley D.S.O.
Comdg. 1st Bn York and Lancaster Regt.
Tuesday 27th July 1915.

1. The following reliefs will take place to-night.
The 2nd Cheshire Regt. 84th Bde. will take over trenches J.1. J10. H5. S.P.12. from 'B' Coy.
J.2. J.4. J.11. J.3. right, J.3. New. from 'D' Coy.
J.3. left from 'C' Coy.
The Machine Gun emplacements in J.1. J4. & S.P.12.
Hd. Qrs. and ROSSIGNOL ESTAMINET.

2. O.C. Coy. will arrange to relieve the garrison of 'D' Coy. in S.P. 13.

3. The Machine Gun & Team in S.P.12. will ~~be set~~ ~~back~~ relieve the Machine Gun and team of 2nd Kings Own in K.2.a.

4. O.C. 'A' Coy. will evacuate SIEGE FARM at 9.30 p.m. but will not be relieved

5. On relief the Cos. will form up by the Church in KEMMEL and march to ~~[illegible]~~ LOCRE. (M.29.a, Sheet 28). under Coy. Comdr's. by the road through M.24.
The Hd. Qr. Coy. will march under the Sergt.-Major.
The Machine Gun Teams will march under the M. Gun Sgt.

6. Lieut Gibben will take charge of the M. Guns in K.1. K.2.a. & S.P.13.

7. Capt. J.C. Forster will relieve Capt. H.S. Johnson and Command the Detmt of 1st Y&L. Regt. in K.1. K.1.a. K.1.b. K.2. K2.a. S.P.12. & New fire trench K.1.b K.2. This Detmt. will come under the orders of O.C. left Sector at 9.p.m.
The rations and water for this Detmt. will be sent to SANDBAG VILLA.

8. O.C. Cos. will arrange to send guides from each trench to be taken over by 2nd Cheshire Regt. who will report ~~to~~ at Bn. Hdqrs. at 8.30.p.m.
The Machine Gun Officers will send guides from J.1. J.4. & S.P.12. who will report at Bn Hdqrs at 9 p.m.

9. Trench stores will be handed over and the receipts will be forwarded to Bn. Hdqrs. with handing over report and work report by 8 p.m. The amount of Ammunition handed over will also be ~~[illegible]~~ forwarded by 8 p.m.

10. Officers trench kits and all water tins must be at dumping ground by 9 p.m.

11. Coy. Officers Charge ~~ts~~ will be at KEMMEL CHURCH.

12. ~~13~~ O.C. Cos. and Machine Gun Officer will report by wire to Bn. H.qrs. when relief is completed.

13. The attached Platoons of 10th W. Yorkshire Regt. and 7th E. Yorkshire Regt. will leave the trenches as soon as it is dusk, so as to be clear before the relieving units arrive.

14. Cos. will occupy billets in LOCRE and will meet their Quarter Masters Sergts. at LOCRE. CHURCH.

~~Sd~~ T Knox Shaw Lieut,
A/Adj 1st York & Lancaster Regt.

Copies 1. & 2. War Diary
Copy 3. O.C. A Coy.
" 4 " B "
" 5 " C "
" 6 " D "
7 O C Left Sector
8 M.G. Officer

XXVI

24/7/15 App XXVI

10TH (SERVICE) BATTALION.
WEST YORKSHIRE REGT.

My dear Bayly (hope I have spelled yr name properly)

I cannot sufficiently thank you for the great help you have so kindly given to my novices - they must have been a great nuisance to you, but you seemed to find time somehow to tell them everything there was to be told - I can only wish you & yours Batts the best of good luck

& believe me that the 10th West Yorkshires will always remember the kindness shown by you & your Bn.—

Yours sincerely

JCKUmfreville

XXVII

OPERATION ORDER No. 53 COPY No. 4

by

BRIGADIER GENERAL H.S.L.RAVENSHAW, C.M.G.,

Commanding 83rd Infantry Brigade.

=============

Reference :- SHEET 28. Wednesday, 28th July, 1915.

1. At 1 p.m. tomorrow, the 2nd King's Own Regiment march from SCHERPENBERG via LOCRE - DRANOUTRE - CROSS ROADS S.5.b - CROSS ROADS S.6.b. - CROSS ROADS T.1.C - T road T.1.d.4.7. road junction T.1.d.9.1. - CROSS ROADS T.2.c.7.7., to Farm T.2.d.2.3., where they will come under the orders of the 85th Brigade.

2. At 2.30.p.m., the 1st York & Lancaster Regiment will march from LOCRE to huts at SCHERPENBERG.

R S Follett
Captain,
Brigade Major, 83rd Inf. Bde.

Issued at 10·30 p.m.

Copy No. 1. War Diary.
2. 2nd King's Own Regt.
3. 1st K.O.Y.L.I.
4. 1st York & Lancaster Regt.
5. 5th King's Own Regt.
6. 28th Division
7. 85th Brigade.
8. No. 2 Coy. A.S.C.
9. Signals. 83rd Brigade.

App XXVII

XXVIII

Copy No 1 —— No 13.

Operation Orders
By
Lt. Col. G.E. Bayley D.S.O.
Comdg. 1st Bn York & Lancaster Rgt.
Thursday 29th July 1915.

1/. The Battalion will march to the Huts at SCHERPENBERG at 2.30 p.m. today.
Order of March:- B, D, A, Hd. Qr. Coys.
Starting point A Coy. billet on the LOCRE – LA-CLYTTE ROAD.

2/. M. Gunners will march to the Huts after practice on the range at SCHERPENBERG at 2.30 p.m.

3/. O.C. Cos. will render a written statement to the Adjutant that the billets are left clean.

T Knox Shaw Lieut.
a/Adj 1st York & Lancaster Regt

Issued at 11.15 am.

Copies 1 & 2 War Diary
Copy 3 O.C. A Coy
" 4 " B "
" 5 " C "
" 6 " D "
" 7 M.G. Sgt.
" 8 O.C. Detmt.

App XXVIII

XXIX

SECRET OPERATION ORDER No. 54. Copy No. 3....

by

BRIGADIER GENERAL H.S.L. Ravenshaw C.M.G.

Commanding 83rd InfY Brigade.

Reference

VIERSTRAAT
1
―――
10,000

29th July 1915.

1. On the night 30th - 31st July 1/K.O.Y.L.I. with two companys two machine gun teams and two machine guns, 80th Brigade attached, will relieve 5/King's Own Regt. and all attached troops on 83rd Brigade front.

2. Details of relief will be arranged between Officer Commanding 1/K.O.Y.L.I. and Major Robertson 1/York & Lancaster Regt., Commanding Left Sector.

3. The detachment of 80th Brigade will report to O.C. 1/K.O.Y.L.I. at 7.30 p.m. ready to march off.

4. The relieving units will not pass barrier on LA CLYTTE & KEMMEL road N.20.b.8.7. before 8.30 p.m.

5. Signallers of relieving units will take over at 3 p.m.

6. Major H.C.Robertson will Command until the relief is Completed.

7. Completion of relief will be wired to this office.

8. On relief the 5/King's Own will move to Bivouacs at SCHERPENBERG.

Issued 4.15 p.m.

R S Follett
Captain
Brigade Major
83rd Infantry Brigade.

Copy No.1. War Diary
2. 1/K.O.Y.L.I.
3. 1/York & Lancaster R.
4. 5/King's Own R.L.R.
5. 28th Divn.
6. 80th Brigade
7. No.2 Coy. A.S.C.
8. Signals 83rd Bde.

App XXIX

XXX

S E C R E T   OPERATION ORDER No. 55.   Copy No. 3

by

BRIGADIER GENERAL H.S.L.Ravensham C.M.G.

Commanding 83rd Infantry Brigade

Reference VIERSTRAAT $\frac{1}{10,000}$ 31st July 1915

1. The troops of 50th Brigade attached to 1/K.O.Y.L.I. will return to the headquarters of their respective battalions tonight.

2. One company and two machine gun teams with guns 1/York & Lancaster Regt. will leave SCHERPENBERG at 8 p.m. and march to SIEGE FARM N.16.c.2.8. On arrival this detachment comes under the orders of O.C.1/K.O.Y.L.I. who will accommadate the company at SIEGE FARM and allot the machine guns and teams to emplacements in relief of machine guns of 50th Brigade

3. Completion of relief will be reported by wire to this office.

Issued at 5.45 p.m.

R.S. Follett
Captain.
Brigade Major.
83rd Infantry Brigade.

Copy No. 1. War Diary
2. 1/K.O.Y.L.I.
3. 1/York & Lanc'r R.
4. 5/King's Own R.L.R.
5. 28th Division.
6. 50th Brigade
7. Machine Gun Officer 83rd Bde.
8. Signal " " " ".

App XXX

Copy No. 1

No. 14-A Operation Orders
By
Major E. C. Robertson
Commanding 1st York & Lancaster Regt.
Saturday, 31st July 1915

appx XXXI

1. "D" Coy and 2 Machine Gun Teams, with Guns will parade at "D" Coy Billet at 8 pm. to-night and will march to SEIGE FARM.
The following will be attached:-
Signallers – 3
Stretcher Bearers – 2

2. On arrival this Detachment will come under the orders of O.C. 1st K.O.Y.L.I. who will allot places for the Machine Guns.

3. O.C. "D" Coy will report to O.C. 1st K.O.Y.L.I. as soon as the Farm has been taken over.

4. The Transport Officer will arrange transport for M. Guns, Officers Kits and rations.

5. Sick Wastage & Casualty Returns will be rendered to the Adjutant by O.C. "D" Coy direct, at the usual hours.

T. Knox Shaw Lieut.
A/Adjutant, 1st York & Lancaster Regt.

Copies 1 & 2 – War Diary
Copy 3. Transport Officer
" 4 M. Gun Officer
" 5 O.C. "D" Coy

83rd Bde.
28th Div.

WAR DIARY

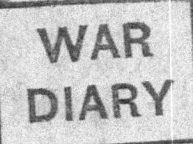

1st YORK & LANCS

AUGUST

1 9 1 5

On His Majesty's Service.

Instructions regarding War Diaries and Intelligence Summaries are contained in F. S. Regs., Part II. and the Staff Manual respectively. Title pages will be prepared in manuscript.

WAR DIARY
or
~~INTELLIGENCE SUMMARY.~~
(Erase heading not required.)

1st York & Lancaster Regt.

Army Form C. 2118.

Hour, Date, Place		Summary of Events and Information	Remarks and references to Appendices
August 1st		Rested in Billets	
FARM at SCHERPENBERG	Aug 2nd 3pm	Brigade operation orders no 56	App I
	6pm	" " amendment.	
Aug 3rd	11am	Battalion operation orders no 14.	App II
	7.30pm	The Battalion left the huts and marched to the trenches. Major Robertson was in Command as Lt Colonel Bayley was still on leave. The relief was complete by 11.50pm. The Welsh Regt 84th Brigade was on our right and the 1st KOYLI on our left. The trenches were dirty and the telephone wires were handed over in poor condition.	
Aug 4th ROSSIGNOL ESTAMINET	4.30am	Situation quiet. Very little Sniping from PETIT BOIS	
		Distribution of Troops see	App III
		Quiet all day. Col Bayley rejoined in the morning.	
	12 noon	Casualty report. wounded O R two.	
Aug 5th "	1.30am	Burst of rapid fire on our right following a report of a mine explosion	
		Situation, quiet all day.	
	12 noon	Casualty report nil	
Aug 6th " "	4.30am	Situation quiet all day	
	12 noon	Casualty report wounded. O R two.	
Aug 7th	4.30am	Situation quiet all day.	
	12 noon	Casualty report wounded O R one	
Aug 8th	4.30am	Situation quiet all morning	
	12 noon	Casualty report wounded O R one	
	4.30pm	Situation now normal. H_2 & H_3 shelled between 1.30 & 2.30pm	
		Causing some casualties. J_1 & J_{10} and between J_1 & J_2 shelled between 2 & 3pm damage slight.	
	7pm.	Heavy bombardment audible from the YPRES Salient.	
Aug 9th	2. am	Bombardment started all along line. Very heavy in HOOGE direction. It lasted till after 4am & recommenced again at 7am. The enemy did not reply to any extent on our front	
	4.30am.	Situation fairly Quiet in our trenches. Nothing to report.	
	12 noon	Casualty report killed O R 1 ; wounded O R 1.	

Instructions regarding War Diaries and Intelligence Summaries are contained in F. S. Regs., Part II. and the Staff Manual respectively. Title pages will be prepared in manuscript.

WAR DIARY
or
~~INTELLIGENCE SUMMARY.~~
(*Erase heading not required.*) 1st Yorks & Lancaster Rgt

Army Form C. 2118.

Hour, Date, Place		Summary of Events and Information	Remarks and references to Appendices
Aug 9th ROSSIGNOL HQ.	4.30pm	Situation quiet.	
	7pm	operation orders no 58	
	9pm	one Company of the 6th LEICESTER RGT 37th Division was attached to our Companies in the trenches for instruction. They were to remain in for 48 hours	App IV
Aug 10th	4.30am	quiet all day	
	12 noon	Casualty report wounded O.R one.	
	6.15pm	Brigade operation orders no 59.	App V
	11.50pm	Relief of 5th Kings own attached to our Batt" reported complete. During the night patrols were sent out to investigate the crater in front of H4 and to listen for sapping in front of J3 (right). Only negative information was gained.	
Aug 11th	4.30am.	quiet all day	
	12 noon	casualties nil	
	5.30pm	Bde operation orders no 60	App VI
		Batt" operation order no 15	App VII
		The 6th Leicesters who were attached for 48 hours left the trenches at dusk. The Batt" was relief by 2nd Kings own and marched to be bivouacs at SCHERPENBERG. The relief was complete at 12.10am	
Aug 12. SHERPENBERG		Rested in Billets.	
13th		Casualty report nil.	
14th		Rested in Billets	
15th			
16th	11.25pm	Brigade operation orders received no 62.	App VIII
17th		Battalion operation orders no 17	App IX

(9 29 6) W4141—463 100,000 9/14 H W V Forms/C. 2118/10.

Army Form C. 2118.

Instructions regarding War Diaries and Intelligence Summaries are contained in F. S. Regs., Part II. and the Staff Manual respectively. Title pages will be prepared in manuscript.

WAR DIARY
or
~~INTELLIGENCE SUMMARY.~~
(*Erase heading not required.*) 1st York & Lancaster Regt

Hour, Date, Place		Summary of Events and Information	Remarks and references to Appendices
17th August	7.30pm	The Battalion marched to the trenches and relieved the 2nd Kings own. The relief was carried out by 11.5 pm. The Companies were distributed according to attached scheme	App X
18th August ROSSIGNOL HQ		Quiet all day wind westerly Casualty report nil	
19th August "	" 4am	Situation quiet. no enemy mortars, enemy sniping less than usual.	
	12 noon	Casualty report. other ranks 2 wounded.	
		quiet all day	
	11.15pm	The Battalion practised an alarm	
	1.15am	Capt Lucas, Capt Lynch, C.S.M. Barlow & L/Cpl Hobson went out to far edge of the crater in front of J_3 (left) and threw grenades into the German trenches. Considerable alarm was caused. The enemy replied with mortars, rifle and hand grenades & rapid fire. The listening post in front of J_3 (left) report that they heard groans from the enemy's trenches shortly after the explosion of our second bomb.	
20th August		quiet all day.	
	12 noon	Casualties nil	
	9pm	2nd Lt J.M. HOLLIS joined from the 3rd Battalion	
21st "		quiet all day	
	12 noon	Casualties one wounded on Dumping ground	
		weekly return showing Battalion strength	App XI
	9.30pm	Brigade operation orders no 65 received	App XII
22nd August	10.30pm	fired a machine gun from up a tree S of ROSSIGNOL WOOD onto PETIT BOIS. All shots went well over our trenches, except a few which fell near J_3 (right). quiet all day. Casualties wounded one. The 25 men of 5th Kings own in H5 were relieved at 9.50pm by the 3rd Monmouth Regiment	

(9 29 6) W4141—463 100,000 9/14 H W V Forms/C. 2118/10

Army Form C. 2118.

Instructions regarding War Diaries and Intelligence Summaries are contained in F. S. Regs., Part II. and the Staff Manual respectively. Title pages will be prepared in manuscript.

WAR DIARY
or
~~INTELLIGENCE SUMMARY.~~

(Erase heading not required.) 1st York & Lancaster Rgt.

Hour, Date, Place	Summary of Events and Information	Remarks and references to Appendices
August 22 ROSSIGNOL H.Q 11.15pm	Lt Wales & Sgt Barker of D Coy went out in front of crater to left of J_3 (right) and bombed enemy's trench. Enemy replied with a few mortars which did no damage.	
	During the day enemy shelled S.P.13 knocking down parapet & two dug outs. The garrison moved into C.T. no one hit.	
August 23.	quiet all day.	
	casualties 3 wounded.	
12 noon		
3 pm	Battalion operation orders no 18.	App XIII
5.30pm	Enemy sent 40-50 rifle grenades over J_1; one fell in the trench & killed a sergeant & wounded 3 men	
11 pm	The Battalion was relieved by 2nd Kings own Rgt and marched back to the bivouacs at SCHERPENBERG	
August 24th SCHERPENBERG	Rested in Billets. casualties 1 killed. 6 wounded	
3 pm	Lts Workman, Morton & Gribben left to join the 2nd R Irish Rifles 3rd Division. Lt Coles took over duties of Machine Gun officer	
25th	Capt Vickerman & 2nd Lt Cole joined the Battn from 1st East Surrey Rgt. The former took over command of "D" Coy.	
	Report on observations by Lt L.A.K. Halcomb, Battn Intelligence officer	App XIV
26th	Rested in billets. Lt H.C.M HOWARD rejoined the Battn	
27th	Two companies worked on the subsidiary line all night.	App XV
28th	Brigade operation orders no 66	App XVI
29th	Return showing Battn strength etc	App XVII
	operation orders no. 19	
ROSSIGNOL H.Q	The Battalion relieved the 2nd Kings own in the centre sector at 9.45pm	
10 pm	listening Post in front of J_1 reported movement in front of German parapet, given away by rattling of tins. The listening post was withdrawn and rapid fire opened on the place from J_1 & J_2	

Instructions regarding War Diaries and Intelligence Summaries are contained in F. S. Regs., Part II. and the Staff Manual respectively. Title pages will be prepared in manuscript.

WAR DIARY
or
~~INTELLIGENCE SUMMARY.~~

(*Erase heading not required.*) 1st Yorks Lancaster Regt.

Army Form C. 2118.

Hour, Date, Place		Summary of Events and Information	Remarks and references to Appendices
Aug 29 ROSSIGNOL HQ	11pm	The listening Post on being relieved noticed a party of about 6 Germans away on the left going to the left. As soon as this was reported the enemy threw bombs between J_3 R & J_3 L Fire was immediately opened from J_1 in the direction of the smoke which could be clearly seen. No casualties on our side.	
Aug 30th	4.30am	Situation report "quiet".	
		Distribution of Troops according to attached scheme	App. XVIII
	12 noon	Casualty report. wounded other ranks two	
		A German working in a white coloured shirt on a CT NOTNW corner of PETIT BOIS at range of 400yds was hit by a Sniper from H4.	
	4pm	Situation quiet all day.	
		The Enemy shelled SP13 and knocked in a dugout during afternoon.	
Aug 31st	4.am	Situation quiet.	
	12 noon	Casualty report wounded. O.R. two	
	9pm	2nd Lt. Bates. 8092 Sgt Cooper. 2852 Pte Collier formed a patrol which went out in front of H4 to inspect enemy's wire south of PETIT BOIS. As far as could been seen, it consisted of low entanglements about 20 yards from parapet and 20 feet thick in good condition.	
		Mr Gullett, an Australian Press correspondent arrived at 6pm and after dining at H.Q went up to spend the night in the trenches. He crawled out through the parapet in J_3 Right into the crater and saw the [illegible] German line 20 yds away. After going round with the C.O in the morning, he left at 12.45pm	

(9 29 6) W4141—463 100,000 9/14 H W V Forms/C. 2118/10

SECRET OPERATION ORDER No. 56 Copy No....4....

by

BRIGADIER GENERAL H.S.L.Ravenshaw C.M.G.

Commanding 83rd Infantry Brigade

Reference
VIERSTRAAT
1

10,000

2nd August 1915

1. (a) On night 3rd - 4th Aug. the 1/York & Lancaster R. with two companies and two machine guns 5/King's Own R. attached will relieve 2/Cheshire Regt. 84th Brigade in all trenches held from H.2 to J.11 (vide attached schedule)
The 5/King's Own Regt. will garrison trenches H.2 H.3 and H.5 and their machine guns will be mounted in H.3 and S.P.12.

(b) On same night 1/York & Lancaster Regt. will relieve 1/K.O.Y.L.I. in trenches K.1 K.1 new K.1.a and S.P.13.

(c) Garrisons will be in accordance with attached schedule.

(d) The company 1/York & Lancaster Regt. now attached to 1/K.O.Y.L.I. will come under command of O.C. 1/York & Lancaster Regt. at 11 p.m.

2. The Hqrs. of Right Sector will be at ROSSIGNOL ESTAMINET. The reserve Coy. of Left sector at SANDBAG VILLA and YORK HOUSE. The reserve coy. of Right Sector at SIEGE FARM.

3. All details of relief will be arranged between O.C. 1/York & Lancaster Regt and O.C. 2/Cheshire Regt. OC KOYLI
The relieving Units will not pass barrier N.20.b.8.7 before 8.30 p.m.

4. Signallers of relieving units will take over at 3 p.m.3rd AUG.

5. The necessary reconnaissance will be carried out before relief.

6. O.C. 2/Cheshire Regt. will command until relief is completed; Completion of relief to be reported by wire to this office. 1 KOYLI

Issued at 2 p.m.

R.S. Follett
Captain
Brigade Major
83rd Infantry Brigade.

Copy No.1 War Diary
2 2/East York' R.
3 1/K.O.Y.L.I.
4 1/York & Lanca'r R.
5 5/King's Own R.L.R.
6 28th Division.
7 84th Brigade.
8 3rd Brigade R.F.A.
9 No 2 Coy. A.S.C.
10 O.C.Signals 83rd Bde.
11 M.G.O. 83rd Brigade .

App I

Copy No. 4

AMENDMENT TO OPERATION ORDER No 56

SECRET | 2nd Aug. 1915

Para 1.(d) add:-

The two machine guns and teams 1/York & Lancaster R. now attached to 1/K.O.Y.L.I. and garrisoning K.1 & S.P.13 will come under the orders of O.C. 1/York & Lancaster Regt. on the completion of relief.

Delete para 3 and substitute:-

All details of relief will be arranged between O.C. 1/York & Lancaster Regt. and O.C. 2/Cheshire Regt. and O.C. 1/K.O.Y.L.I.

Delete para 6 and substitute:-

O.C. 2/Cheshire Regt. will command in the sector occupied by his battalion until the completion of the relief by 1/York & Lancaster Regt.; similarly O.C. 1/K.O.Y.L.I. will command in those trenches now occupied by his battalion until they are relieved by 1/York & Lancaster R.

Insert new Para.

7. At 11 a.m. 3rd August 2/East Yorkshire Regt. will march from LOCRE to SCHERPENBERG where they will bivouac until the departure of the 1/York & Lancaster Regt. when they will take over their huts .

Issued at 5 p.m.

R.S. Follett
Captain
Brigade Major.
83rd Infantry Brigade

Copy No.1 War Diary
2 2/East Yorks R.
3 1/K.O.Y.L.I.
4 1/York & Lanc R.
5 5/King's Own R.
6 28th Division
7 84th Brigade
8 3rd Brigade R.F.A.
9 No2 Coy. A.S.C.
10 O.C. Signals 83rd Bde
11 M.G.O. 83rd Brigade.

DISTRIBUTION OF TROOPS IN TRENCHES

RIGHT SECTOR

Trench	Establishment	Distribution	Machine gun
~~H.2~~	~~80~~	K.O.	
~~H.3~~	~~45~~	K.O.	1.M.-G. (K.O)
H.4	50	B(1)	
~~H.5~~	~~75~~	K.O.	
J.1	50	B(2)	1.M.-G.
J.2	40	B(3)	
J.3 new	30	A(1)	
J.3 (r)	15		
-J.3 (L)	20	A(3)	
-J.4	50.	A(4)	1.M.-G.
-J.10	30	B(4)	
-J.11	50	A(2)	
-K.1	50	C(2)	(already in) 1.M.-G.
-K.1 new	40	C(1)	
-K.1.a	35	C(3)	
-S.P.12	25	A(3)	1.M.-G. (K.O)
-S.P.13	55	C(4)	(already in) 1.M.-G.
	700		

LEFT SECTOR

Trench	Establishment	Distribution	Machine gun
K.1b	25		
K.2	35		
K.2.a	65		1.M.-G.
K.2.b	50		
K.3	50		
L.1	15		
L.1 new	40		
L.2	45		
L.3	30		
L.4	35		
L.5	65		1.M.-G.
L.6	45		1.M.-G.
L.7 (r)	25		
L.7 (L)	40		1.M.-G.
	565		

Copy No. 1.

Operation Orders No. 14.

By

Major E. C. Robertson,

Commanding 1st Bn. York & Lancaster Regt.

Tuesday, 3rd August 1915.

1. The Battalion will march into the trenches tonight in the following order

Machine Guns with limbers	7-30 p.m.
"C" Company	7-35 p.m.
"A" ———	7-40 p.m.
"B" ———	7-45 p.m.
Two Companies of 5th King's Own Regt.	7-50 p.m.
Two Machine Gun Teams of 5th King's Own Regt. under Lieut. E. Gribben, 1st York & Lancaster Regt.	7-25 p.m.
Headquarters Coy under the Sergt. Major	7-50 p.m.
Transport	8. 0. p.m.

Cos. will halt for 5 minutes en route.

Reliefs will take place in accordance with the attached schedule.

2. Guides will be provided at the Barrier (N.20. b. 8.7. Sheet 28.)

3. Officers kits and trench kits will be handed into the Quartermaster Stores by 6 p.m.

4. O.C. Cos. will arrange for an officer and their Quarter-Master ~~Sergts~~ Sergeants to proceed to the trenches in advance to take over trench stores.

5. Two sandbags per man will be drawn from Quartermasters Stores at 4 p.m.

6. O.C. Cos. and the Machine Gun Officer will report to Bn. Hdqrs. by wire when relief is complete.

Appx. II

7. Signallers will be attached as follows:–

"A" Coy – 3 men for T.4. 6 each.

"B" – – 6 – " T.1 and T.2. trenches

"C" – – 3 " " K.1 trench

5th King's Own Regt. 6 men " H.2 and H.3 trenches

"D" Coy. – 2 men " Siege Farm.

8. Stretcher Bearers will be attached to each Company.

9. The O.C. "D" Coy. will detail parties to carry water to the trenches on completion of relief. Numbers of tins per Coy. will be notified later.

10. Water bottles will be filled and each man will carry one days' rations.

11. Shelters and blankets will be handed into the Qr. Mr. Stores by 5 p.m.

12. O.C. Coys. will render certificates to the Adjutant, before moving off that their lines are left clean.

13. The O.C. "D" Coy. will detail a guard of 1 N.C.O. and 3 men for Bn. Hdqrs. which will mount at 6.30 p.m.

Thos. Shaw Lieut.
A/Adjutant, 1st York & Lancaster Regt.

Copies No. 1 and 2. War Diary.
Copy " 3 O.C. "A" Coy
" " 4 " "B" "
" " 5 " "C" "
6 "D"
7 " M. Gun Section.
" 8 Transport Officer.
" 9 O.C. 5th King's Own Regt.
10 O.C. 1st K.O.Y.L.I.
11 O.C. 2nd Cheshire Regt

Schedule of Reliefs

Company	Trenches	Units handing over.
"A" Coy	T. 3 new. T. 3. right T. 3 left T. 4. T. 11 S.P. 12	2nd Cheshire Regt. (Guides for these trenches will be found at the barrier.)
B Coy.	T. 1. T. 2. T. 10. H. 4.	2nd Cheshire Regt.
"C" Coy.	K. 1. K. 1. new. K. 1. 0. S.P. 13.	1st K.O.Y.L.I.
5th Kings Own Regt.	H. 2. H. 3. H. 5.	2nd Cheshire Regt. (Guides will be found at the Barrier)
Machine Guns 1st York & Lancaster Regt.	T. 1. T. 4. K. 1. S.P. 13.	2nd Cheshire Regt. The present Guns will remain in. K. 1. and S.P. 13.
5th Kings Own Regt.	H. 3. S.P. 12.	2nd Cheshire Regt. (Guides will be found at the Barrier)

"A" Form. Army Form C. 2121.

MESSAGES AND SIGNALS.

No. of Message

Prefix ... Code ... m.	Words	Charge	This message is on a/c of:	Recd. at ... m.
Office of Origin and Service Instructions.	Sent		... Service.	Date
	At ... m.			From
	To			
	By		(Signature of "Franking Officer.")	By

TO 83rd I. B

Sender's Number.	Day of Month	In reply to Number	
* KS 4	4		AAA

Distribution of Troops

K_1	officer 1	other Ranks	43	C Coy under Capt LUCAS
K_1 new	" 1	" "	40	
K_1A	" 1	" "	45	
SP13	" 1	" "	45	
J_3 Left	" 1	" "	21	A Coy under Capt FORSTER
J_3 Right	" 0	" "	15	
J_3 new	" 1	" "	31	
J_4	" 1	" "	42	
J_{11}	" 0	" "	44	
SP12	" 1	" "	23	
J_1	" 2	" "	58	B Coy under Capt BOCKLEY
J_2	" 1	" "	43	
J_{10}	" 1	" "	45	
H_4	" 1	" "	43	
SIEGE FARM	" 4	" "	170	D Coy Capt LYNCH
H_3	" 2	" "	48	5th Kings Own
H_2	" 1		69	
H_5	" 1		85	

From

Place OC 4 KL

Time 4 30 am

The above may be forwarded as now corrected.

Censor.

(Z) T Knowles Lt.

Signature of Addressor or person authorised to telegraph in his name.

* This line should be erased if not required.

(688-9) —McC. & Co. Ltd., London.— W 14142/641. 225,000 4/15 Forms C2121/10.

App III

S E C R E T. COPY No. 2

OPERATION ORDER No. 58

by

Brigadier-General H.S.L.Ravenshaw, C.M.G.,

Commanding 83rd Infantry Brigade.

****

Ref. VIERSTRAAT $\frac{1}{10,000}$ Monday, 9th August, 1915.

1. a. On night of 10th August, 1915, the 5th King's Own Regiment will relieve their garrisons in H. 2., H.3., and H.5., trenches, and the machine gun detachments in H.3., and S.p., 12, attached to the 1st York & Lancaster Regiment.

b. Relieving units will not pass barrier on LA CLYTTE-KEMMEL Road before 8.30.p.m.

c. Signallers of relieving units will take over at 3 p.m., 10th instant.

d. All details of relief will be arranged between O.C., York & Lancaster Regiment and O.C., 5th King's Own Regiment.
Necessary reconnaisance will be carried out before relief.

e. Completion of relief to be reported to this office by O.C., 1st York & Lancaster Regiment.

R S Follett Captain.
Brigade Major, 83rd Inf.Bde.

Issued at 6 p.m.

Copy No. 1, War Diary.
2, 1st York & Lancaster Regt.
3, 5th King's Own Regt.
4, 28th Division.

S E C R E T   COPY No....5....

OPERATION ORDER No. 59.

by

BRIGADIER GENERAL H.S.L.Ravenshaw C.M.G.

Commanding 83rd Infantry Brigade

Reference
VIERSTRAAT
1 and Sheet 28
10,000 1/40.000

10th August 1915.

1. (a) On night 11th - 12th August 2/King's Own Regt. will relieve 1/York & Lancaster Regt. in the Right Sector.

(b) The two companies and two machine guns 5/King's Own R. now attached to 1/York & Lancaster Regt. will comm under the orders of O.C. 2/King's Own Regt. on completion of relief.

(c) All details of relief will be arranged between Officers Comdg. 2/King's Own Regt. and 1/York & Lancaster Regt. necessary reconnaissance will be carried out before relief. Relieving units will not pass barrier on LA CLYTTE - KEMMEL road before 8.15 p.m.

(d) Signallers of relieving units will take over at 3 p.m. 11th instant.

(e) O.C. 1/York & Lancaster Regt. will command in Right Sector until relief is completed. Completion of relief to be wired to this office.

2. On relief 1/York & Lancaster Regt. will take over bivouacs at SCHERPENBERG vacated by 2/King's Own Regt.

3. At 2 p.m. 11th August 5/King's Own Regt. will move to bivouac in square , M.11.c.4.5. with their transport in M.17.c.6.5.

4. At 4 p.m. 11August the 3/Monmouth Regt. join the Brigade and will bivouac in square M.22.d.4.6 with their transport in square M.22.c.9.6. These fields are now occupied by 5/King's Own Regt.

Issued at 4.45 p.m.

Copy No.1. War Diary
2. 2/King's Own
3. 2/East Yorks
4. 1/K.O.Y.L.I.
5. 1/York & Lancs.
6. 5/King's Own.
7. 3/Monmouths.
8. 28th Divn.
9. 84th Brigade.
10. 3rd Brigade R.F.A.
11. No 2 Coy A.S.C.
12. O.C.Signals 83rd Bde.
13. M.G.O.83rd Brigade.

R.S. Follett Captain
Brigade Major
83rd Infantry Brigade

App. V

S E C R E T   Copy No....6.....

OPERATION ORDER No.60.

by

BRIGADIER GENERAL H.S.L.Ravenshaw C.M.G.

Commanding 83rd Infantry Brigade.

Reference,
VIERSTRAAT 1/10,000 & Sheet 28 1/40,000

11th August 1915

1. (a) On night 12th - 13th August 1/K.O.Y.L.I. will relieve 2/East Yorkshire Regt. in the Left Sector.

(b) The company 6/Leicester Regt attached to 2/East Yorkshire Regt. will come under orders of O.C. 1/K.O.Y.L.I. on completion of relief.

(c) All details of relief will be arranged between Officers Commanding 2/East Yorks Regt & 1/K.O.Y.L.I. Signallers of relieving unit take over at 3 p.m. 12th inst.. 1/K.O.Y.L.I. will not pass barrier on LA CLYTTE - KEMMEL road before 8.15 p.m.

(d) O.C. 2/East Yorks Regt. will command until relief is completed. Completion of relief to be wired to this office.

2. (a) Brigade Headquarters move at 3 p.m. 12th inst,, to Farm square M.18.d.5.1.

(b) Trench stores on 12th inst will be drawn from this Farm. Wagons will approach from the West Via BRULOOZE Cross Roads Square M.24.a.

Issued at 4.30 p.m.

R.S. Follett
Captain
Brigade Major
83rd Infantry Brigade.

Copy No.1. War Diary
2. 2/King's Own
3. 2/East Yorks
4. 1/K.O.Y.L.I. - 6. 1/York & Lancs.
5. 5/King's Own
7. 28th Division
8. 3rd Brigade R.F.A.
9. No.2Coy A.S.C.

App VI

Copy No. 1.

Operation Orders No. 15.
by,
Lt-Col- G.E. Bayley D.S.O.
Comdg. 1st York & Lancaster Regt.
Wednesday 11th Aug 1915.

1. The battalion will be relieved by the 2nd Kings Own Regt tonight. On relief Cos. will rendevous at KEMMEL CHURCH and march back under Coy. Comdrs. to the bivuacs at SCHERPENBERG.

The M. Gun teams will rendevous at the DUMPING GROUND. and march back under the M. Gun Officer.

2. Coy. Comdrs. Chargers will be at KEMMEL CHURCH.

3. Officers trench Kits and all water tins must be at the DUMPING GROUND by 9 p.m.

4. The Coy. of 6th Leicester Regt. at present in the trenches will leave the trenches as soon as it is dusk and march back to their billets. Guides will be found by O.C. Cos. if necessary. The guides will report at Bn. Hd. Qrs. after the departure of Detm't. of 6th Leicestershire Regt. from the DUMPING GROUND.

5. The two Cos. and two M. Guns of 5th Kings Own Regt. now attached will come under the orders of O.C. 2nd Kings Own Regt. on completion of relief.

6. O.C. Cos. will detail one guide per trench to report at the KEMMEL BARRIER at 8·15 p.m.

The M. Gun Officer will detail one guide from each team to report at Bn. Hd. Qrs. at 8·45 p.m. The O.C. Detm't. 5th Kings Own Regt. will detail one guide for the platoon of 6th Leicestershire Regt. attached for 48 hours. The guide will report at KEMMEL BARRIER at 8·15 p.m.

App XII

7. O.C. Cos. and M. Gun Officer will report completion of relief to Bn. Hd. Qrs.

The guides to S.P. 12, and S.P. 13, will at once return to Bn. Hd. Qrs. to report relief as soon as they have conducted their parties to these places.

8. Handing over reports, Work reports, and receipts for trench stores will be rendered to the Adjutant by O.C. Cos. by 8 p.m.

9. O.C. "D" Coy. will furnish a guard for Bn. Hd. Qrs. which will mount as soon as the Coy. reaches the bivouacs.

T. Knox Shaw Lieut,
A/Adj. 1st B. York & Lancaster Regt.

Issued at p.m.

Copy No. 1 } War Diary
2 }
3 O.C. A Coy
4 - B -
5 - C -
6 - D -
7 M. Gun Officer
8 Transport Officer
9 Quartermaster
10 2nd Kings Own Regt.
11 O.C. 9 Kings Own Regt
12 O.C. Detmt. 5th Kings Own Regt.
13 O.C. - - 6th Leicestershire Regt.

"A" Form. Army Form C. 2121

MESSAGES AND SIGNALS. No. of Message

Prefix SM Code A.Sl m. | Words | Charge | This message is on a/c of: | Recd. at m.
Office of Origin and Service Instructions.

YL

Sent At 1.40 P m. To ZHC By Clange Pte

Service. (Signature of "Franking Officer.")

Date YL 11/8/15 From By

TO ~~O.C.~~ 83rd I. B.

Sender's Number	Day of Month	In reply to Number	AAA
BY 11	11		

In	view	of	G.O.C	28th
Divs	remarks	yesterday	following	may
be	of	interest	AAA	our
Snipers	in	J1	yesterday	morning
killed	two	Germans	working	on
their	parapets.	AAA.	above	shows
our	snipers	are	vigilant	and
only	fire	when	there	is
a	target	when	they	do
so	to	some	purpose.	AAA
I	do	not	report	such
small	bag	as	a	rule
and	only	do	so	now
in	view	of	above	reason.
AAA				

From O.C. 1 Y & L. Regt
Place
Time 1.20 A.m.

The above may be forwarded as now corrected. (Z) [signature]

Censor. Signature of Addresser or person authorised to telegraph in his name

* This line should be erased if not required.

8350 S. B. Ltd Wt. W4848/541—50,000. 8/14 Forms C2121/10.

S E C R E T. Copy No. 5

OPERATION ORDER No.62.

by

BRIGADIER GENERAL H.S.L.Ravenshaw C.M.G.

Commanding 83rd Infantry Brigade.

Reference, VIERSTRAAT 1/10,000
Sheet 28 1/40,000

16th August 1915.

1. (a) On night 17th - 18th August 1/York & Lancaster Regt., will relieve 2/King's Own Regt., in the present Right Sector, 5/King's Own garrison in H.5 & their Machine Gun team in S.P.12..

(b) 5/King's Own Regt., will hand over their Machine Gun in S.P.12 to 1/York & Lancs., and will leave 25 men in H.5, who will come under orders of 1/York & Lancaster Regt..

2. (a) On night 17th - 18th August 5/King's Own Regt. will take over from Northumberland Fusiliers 84th Brigade the following trenches:-

G.4	35 men
G.4.a	50 men
New Sap	65 men & 1 Machine Gun.
H.1	55 men
S.P.11	30 men & 1 Machine Gun,

and will still garrison trenches H.2 & H.3, the command of which will pass to O.C. 5/King's Own with 25 men in H.5 as in para 1.(b).

(b) Headquarters 5/King's Own Regt., will be at the Stables KEMMEL CHATEAU.

3. (a) All details of reliefs will be arranged between the Commanding Officers of battalions concerned.

(b) Signallers of relieving units will take over at 3 p.m. 17th instant.

(c) Relieving units will pass barrier N.20.b.6.8
5/King's Own Regt at 8 p.m.
1/York & Lancaster Regt at 8.15 p.m.

(d) On relief 2/King's Own Regt. move to bivouacs SCHERPENBERG

4. Lists of trench stores taken over from Northumberland Fus. will be sent to this office.

5. Completion of reliefs will be wired to this office.

6. On completion of relief 83rd Brigade front will be divided into three sectors:-
Right Sector 5/King's Own Regt.
Centre Sector 1/York & Lancaster Regt.
Left Sector 1/K.O.Y.L.I.

Issued at 10 p.m.

R.C. Follett Captain
Brigade Major
83rd Infantry Brigade.

Copy No.1	War Diary	
2	2/King's Own	
3	2/East Yorks	
4	1/K.O.Y.L.I.	
5	1/York & Lancs.	
6	5/King's Own	
7	3/Monmouths	11 No.2 Coy A.S.C.
8	28th Divn.	12 Staff Captain
9	84th Brigade	13 O.C. Signals 83rd Bde.
10	3rd Bde R.F.A.	14 M.G.O. 83rd Bde.

HP VIII

Copy No. 2. Operation Order No. 17.
by
Lt. Col. G.E. Bayley D.S.O.
Comdg. 1st York & Lancaster Regt.
Tuesday 17th Aug. 1915.

1.

The Battalion will relieve the 2nd Kings Own Regt. tonight. and take over trenches in accordance with attached schedule.

2.

Order of March:-

Machine Guns	7.15 p.m.
C Coy	7.20 "
D "	7.25 "
B "	7.30 "
A & Hd. Qr. Cos.	7.35 "
Transport	7.50 "

3.

O.C. Cos. will arrange to send, Officer & their Coy. Qr. Mr. Sgts. in advance, to take over trench stores.

4.

Officers Kits and trench Kits will be handed in to the Qr Mrs Stores by 6 p.m.

5.

O.C. B C & D Cos. will arrange to draw 2 sandbags per man from the Qr. Mrs. Stores.

6.

Water bottles will be carried filled.

O.C. A Coy will detail parties to carry the Water tins up to the trenches on completion of relief.

7.

Two stretcher bearers will be attached to each Coy.

8.

Signallers will be allotted for stations in K.1. J.4. J.1. J.2. SIEGE FARM and Headqrs.

9.

The 6th Kings Own Regt. will hand over their Machine Gun in S.P.12. and will leave 25 men in H.5. to be under the orders of the O.C. 1st York & Lancaster Regt.

10.

O.C. Cos. & Machine Gun Officer will report by wire to Bn. Hdqrs. when relief is complete

The relief of S.P.12. & S.P.13. will be reported direct to Bn. Hdqrs. by Coy. Orderlies.

11.

The sector held by the Battalion will in future be known as CENTRE SECTOR.

T Knox Shaw Lieut.
A/Adj. 1st York & Lancaster Regt.

Copy No 1 } War Diary
2 }
3 OC. 'A' Coy
4 - 'B' -
5 - 'C' -
6 - 'D' -
7 Transport Officer
8 OC. 2nd Kings Own
9 OC 6th Kings Own
10 Machine Gun Officer.

Company	Trenches taken over	Unit handing over	Remarks.
"A."	SIEGE FARM.	2nd King's Own Regt.	
"B"	H.11. J.1. J.2. J.10.	2nd King's Own Regt.	
"C"	K.1. K.1.a. K.1 new. J.3. left. S.P.13.	2nd King's Own Regt.	
"D"	J.3 right J.3. new. J.4. J.11. S.P.12.	2nd King's Own Regt	
	H.5.	5th King's Own Regt	25 men of 5th King's Own Regt. will remain.
Machine Guns and Teams.	K.1. J.4. J.1. S.P.13.	2nd King's Own Regt.	
Maxim Gun Team only.	S.P.12.	5th King's Own Regt.	

"A" Form. Army Form C. 2121.

MESSAGES AND SIGNALS.

No. of Message

Prefix ... Code ... m. | Words | Charge

Office of Origin and Service Instructions.

Sent At ... m. To ... By ...

This message is on a/c of: ... Service. (Signature of "Franking Officer.")

Recd. at ... m. Date ... From 4/Y&L ... By ...

TO 83rd I B

Sender's Number.	Day of Month.	In reply to Number	AAA
* KS42	18		

Distribution of Troops

	Officers	other ranks		Officers	other Ranks
J1	2	55	J3 right	0	14
J2	1 C Coy	50	J3 new	1	41
J10	1	45	J4	1 C Coy	31
H4	1 B	38	J11	0 A	23
			SP12	1	24
J3 left	0	22	H5	1	55 + 25 5th Kings own
K1	2 C Coy	30			
K (new)	1 D	44			
K1 A	0	25			
SP13	0	42			

SIEGE FARM
3 officers 184 other Ranks
of A Coy

machine guns in K1 J1 J4 SP13
Team in SP12 with gun of 5th Kings own

From O C
Place Y + L
Time 4.30 am

The above may be forwarded as now corrected. (Z) T Knox Shaw Lt
Censor. Signature of Addressor or person authorised to telegraph in his name.

* This line should be erased if not required.

(42265) Wt. W. 14142-641. 10,000. 4-15. H G.& S., Ltd.

App XI

1st Bn York & Lancaster Regt

Extracts from Battalion Returns for the week ending 21st Aug 1915

Total present	22 Officers	883 Other ranks
Details	2 Officers	88 Other ranks
Total Strength	24 Officers	971 Other ranks

TRENCH STRENGTH

Battalion Headquarters	4 Officers	14 Other ranks
Stretcher Bearers	—	20 — " —
Machine Gunners	1 Officer	41 — " —
Signallers	—	30 — " —
Rifles in trenches	15 Officers	690 — " —
TOTAL	20 Officers	795 — " —

Sick Wastage

Admitted to Hospital during week Other ranks 18

Discharges from — " — — " — 4

T Knox Shaw Lt
a/Adjutant
1 Y & L Regt

App XII

SECRET.

Copy No. 5

OPERATION ORDER No. 65.

by

BRIGADIER GENERAL H.S.L.Ravenshaw C.M.G.

Commanding 83rd Infantry Brigade.

Reference, VIERSTRAAT 1/10,000
Sheet 28 1/40,000

22nd August 1915.

1. (a) On the night 23rd - 24th August 2/King's Own Regt., will relieve 1/York & Lancaster Regt., in Centre Sector.

(b) The twenty five men of 3/Monmouth Regt., in H.5 will come under the orders of O.C. 2/King's Own Regt., on completion of relief.

2. On night 24th - 25th August 1/K.O.Y.L.I. will relieve 2/East Yorkshire Regt., in Left Sector.

3. (a) All details of above reliefs will be arranged between Commanding Officers concerned.

(b) Relieving units will pass barrier N.20.b.6.8 at 7.45 p.m.

(c) Signallers of relieving units will take over at 3 p.m. on the day of relief.

(d) Commanding Officers of Battalions to be relieved will command in their sectors until relief is completed. Completion of relief to be wired to this office.

Issued at 7.45 p.m.

R.S. Follett Captain
Brigade Major
83rd Infantry Brigade.

Copy No.1 War Diary
2 2/King's Own
3 2/East Yorks
4 1/K.O.Y.L.I.
5 1/York & Lancs
6 5/King's Own
7 3/Monmouths
8 28th Division
9 84th Brigade
10 3rd Bde R.F.A.
11 2/1 Northumbrian Fd.Co.R.E.
12 No.2 Coy.A.S.C.
13 O.C. Signals 83rd Bde
14 M.G.Officer 83rd Bde
15 Staff Captain.

Copy No. 1.   OPERATION ORDERS No. 18.

Lt. Col. G. E. Bayley D.S.O.
Comd'g. 1st Bn. York & Lancaster Regt.
Monday 23rd Aug. 1915.

1. The battalion will be relieved by the 2nd Kings Own Regt. tonight. On relief the Companies will march back independantly under Coy. arrangements, to the bivouacs at SCHERPENBERG.
The Machine Gun teams will rendezvous at the DUMPING GROUND and march back under the Machine Gun Officer.

2. Chargers of O.C. "B", "C", & "D" Cos. will be at the DUMPING GROUND and that for O.C. "A" Coy. at SIEGE FARM.

3. Officers Trench Kits and all Water tins must be at the DUMPING GROUND by 9 p.m.

4. The 25 men of 3rd Monmouthshire Regt. in H.5. will come under the Orders of O.C. 2nd Kings Own Regt. on completion of relief.

5. O.C. Cos. and Machine Gun Officer will report completion of relief to Bn. Headqrs.
Relief of S.P. 12. & S.P. 13. will be reported direct to Bn. Headqrs. by runners.

6. Handing over reports and Work Reports will be rendered to the Adjutant by O.C. Cos., by 8 p.m.; and receipt for trench stores as soon as possible.

7. O.C. "A" Coy. will furnish a guard for Bn. Headqrs. which will mount as soon as the Coy. reaches the bivouacs.

8. No guides are required.

T. Knox Shaw Lieut.,
A/Adj. 1st Bn. York & Lancaster Regt.

Issued at 1-45 pm

Copy No. 1 War Diary
2 —"—
3 O.C. "A" Coy.
4 " "B" "
5 " "C" "
6 " "D" "
7 M. Gun Officer.
8 Transport Officer
9 O.C. 2nd Kings Own.
10 " 3rd Monmouthshire Regt.

App XIII

App XIV

Report on Observations
by
1st BN York & Lancaster Regt.

(The Detached Post, referred to below as DP, is situated between K1B and K1 Trenches.)

(1.) From DP, at bearing 95° Mag: an Artillery Observation Station can be seen, on the brick-stack, on the ridge between the Grand Bois + Wytschaete wood - A thin slit revetted with planks is the look-out post. At 7 o'clock from this slit + nearly at the ~~bottom~~ of the stack a dug out can be seen also.

(2.) From DP, at bearing 80° Mag, a working party was seen, deepening their third line of trenches, about 800 to 900 yds range. The men worked without coats or equipment, but one man, who appeared to come + superintend at intervals wore a grey tunic and

2

round grey cap - He did not wear equipment. The men had beards as if they had been in the trenches a long time. A few yards (say 10) to the right of where these men were seen, the parapet was built up of 2 yellow, 2 pink, several black & the rest white sand-bags.

(3.) From the OP, bearing 85° mag, a working party was sighted, digging just inside the Grand Bois. They wore white shirts & no coats or equipment. Another man was also sighted just outside the Grand Bois, dressed in gray tunic, round gray cap with bright badge on it & no equipment. This man was quite young & very tall.

(4.) From Loop-hole at right hand end of Hadrian's Wall, adjoining J4 trench, bearing 140° mag. Point under observation is enemy's trench immediately in front of right-hand tree of the WYTSCHEATE WOOD – An opening has been cut here down the whole depth of the parapet, about 3 ft wide & seems to open onto an open sap in the grass in front. Behind the parapet long boards were lifted up out of the trench & thrown onto the parados. About a dozen boards, each say 15 ft long, were seen being thrown over. Digging is also going on at this point in the trench.

L. A. K. Halcomb. Lt.
"C" Company.
1st Bn. York Lanc. Regt.

23/8/15.

S E C R E T. Copy No....5.......

OPERATION ORDER No. 66.

by

BRIGADIER GENERAL H.S.L.Ravonshaw C.M.G.

Commanding 83rd Infantry Brigade.

Reference, VIERSTRAAT 1/10,000
Sheet 28 1/40,000

27th August 1915.

1. On night 28th - 29th August 5/King's Own Regt will relieve 3/Monmouth Regt in Right Sector and the Machine Gun teams 2/King's Own Regt & 1/K.O.Y.L.I.

2. On night 29th - 30th August 1/York & Lancaster Regt will relieve 2/King's Own Regt in centre sector.

3. On night 30th - 31st August 2/East Yorkshire Regt will relieve 1/K.O.Y.L.I. in Left Sector.

4.(a) All details of above relief will be arranged between Commanding Officers concerned.

(b) Relieving units will pass the barrier N.20.b.6.8 at 7.15 p.m.

(c) Signallers of relieving units will take over at 3 p.m. on day of relief.

5.(a) Officers Commanding battalions to be relieved will command in their sectors until the relief is completed.

(b) Completion of relief to be wired to this office.

Issued at 9.35 a.m.

Captain
for Brigade Major
83rd Infantry Brigade.

Copy No.1 War Diary.
2 2/King's Own
3 2/East Yorks
4 1/K.O.Y.L.I.
5 1/York & Lancs
6 5/King's Own
7 3/Monmouths
8 28th Division
9 84th Brigade
10 3rd Bde R.F.A.
11 No.2 Coy.A.S.C.
12 2/1 Northumbrian Fd.Co.R.E.
13 O.C.Signals 83rd Bde.
14 M.G.Officer 83rd Bde
15 Staff Captain.

App XV

Appx XVI

1st Bn York & Lancaster Regiment

Extracts from Battalion Returns 24. 8. 1915.

	Officers	Other ranks.
Total Strength	25	964.
On Command	1.	86

TRENCH STRENGTH

Distribution	Officers	other ranks	Remarks
Battalion Headquarters	4	14	
Stretcher Bearers	—	19	
Signallers	—	29	
Machine Gunners	1	40	
Rifles in Trenches.	17	693	
TOTAL	22	795	

SICK WASTAGE.

Admitted to Hospital during week 6 Other ranks

Discharged during week 6 — " —

28/8/1915.

T Knowles Shaw Lieut
A/Adjutant, 1st York & Lancaster Regt

Copy No. 1.

App XVII

Operation Orders No. 19.

By

Lieut. Colonel G.E. Bayley, DSO.

Commanding 1st Bn. York & Lancaster Regiment.

Sunday, 29th August 1915.

1. The Battalion will relieve the 2nd King's Own Regiment to-night and take over trenches in accordance with the attached schedule.

2. Order of march.

M. Gun Section	6-15 p.m.
"C" Coy.	6-20 "
"D" "	6-25 "
"B" "	6-30 "
"A" Coy & Hdqrs.	6-35 "
Transport	7 "

3. O.C. Cos. will arrange to send 1 officer and their Quartermaster Sergeants in advance to take over trench stores.

4. Officers Kits and trench Kits will be handed into the Quartermaster's Stores by 6 p.m.

5. O.C. "B" "C" & "D" Cos. will arrange to draw 2 sandbags per man from the Quartermaster's Stores.

6. Water bottles will be carried filled.
O.C. "A" Coy. will detail parties to carry the Water Tins up to the trenches on completion of relief.

7. Two stretcher bearers will be attached to each Company.

8. Signallers will be allotted to Stations in K.1., J.4., J

P.T.O.

J.2, H.5, SIEGE FARM and Battalion Headquarters.

9. O.C. Cos. and Machine Gun Officer will report by wire to Headquarters when relief is complete.
The relief of S.P. 12 and H.5. will be reported by wire from the latter Signal Station.
The relief of S.P. 13 will be reported by orderly.

10. O.C. 'A' Coy. will furnish a guard for Battalion Headquarters. This guard will mount immediately on arrival of the Company at SIEGE FARM.

11. O.C. Cos. will render a certificate to Orderly Room before leaving Bivouacs that their lines have been left clean.

T. Knox Shaw Lieut.
A/Adjutant, 1st Bn. York & Lancaster Regt.

Copies 1 and 2 War Diary.
Copy 3 O.C. 'A' Coy.
" 4. " B.
" 5. " C.
" 6. " D.
" 7. Transport Officer.
" 8. Quartermaster.
" 9. O/c M.Gun Section.
" 10. O.C. 2nd King's Own Regt.

Issued at 2-15. p.m.

Company.	Trenches to be taken over.	Unit handing over.	Remarks.
A.	SIEGE FARM.	2nd King's Own Regt.	
B.	H.4, J.1, J.2, J.10.		
C.	K.1, K.1.a., K.1. new. J.3. left. S.P.13.		
D.	J.3 right. J.3. new. J.4, J.11, S.P.12. H.5,		
Machine Guns & Teams.	K.1, J.4, J.1, S.P. 13.		
Team only	S.P. 12.		

"A" Form.

Army Form C. 2121.

MESSAGES AND SIGNALS.

No. of Message

Prefix ____ Code ____ m.	Words / Charge	This message is on a/c of:	Recd. at ____ m.
Office of Origin and Service Instructions.	Sent	____ Service.	Date
	At ____ m.		From Hpp XVIII
	To		
	By	(Signature of "Franking Officer.")	By

TO 83rd I B

Sender's Number.	Day of Month.	In reply to Number	AAA
* VS 3	30		

Distribution of Troops

H4	1	offrs	37 other ranks
J[illegible]	2	"	46 "
J[illegible]	1	"	45 "
J10	0	"	45 "
J[illegible] R	0	"	27 "
T[illegible] N	1	"	34 "
J[illegible]	2	"	32 "
J[illegible]	0	"	21 "
H5	1	"	34 "
SP12	1	"	14 "
J[illegible]	1	"	31 "
K1	1	"	41 "
K[illegible]	1	"	46 "
K1A	0	"	19 "
SP13	1	"	30 "

M guns in K1 J[illegible] J4 SP12, SP13.

One Company in SIEGE FARM

From

Place Y+L

Time 8 am

The above may be forwarded as now corrected. (Z) T [illegible] 21

Censor. Signature of Addressor or person authorised to telegraph in [illegible]

* This line should be erased if not required.

4-15. H G.& S.,Ltd.

83rd Bde.

28th Div.

WAR DIARY

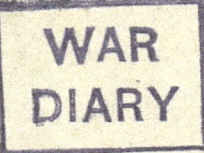

1st YORK & LANCS.

S E P T E M B E R

1 9 1 5

[redacted]

[redacted]

[redacted]

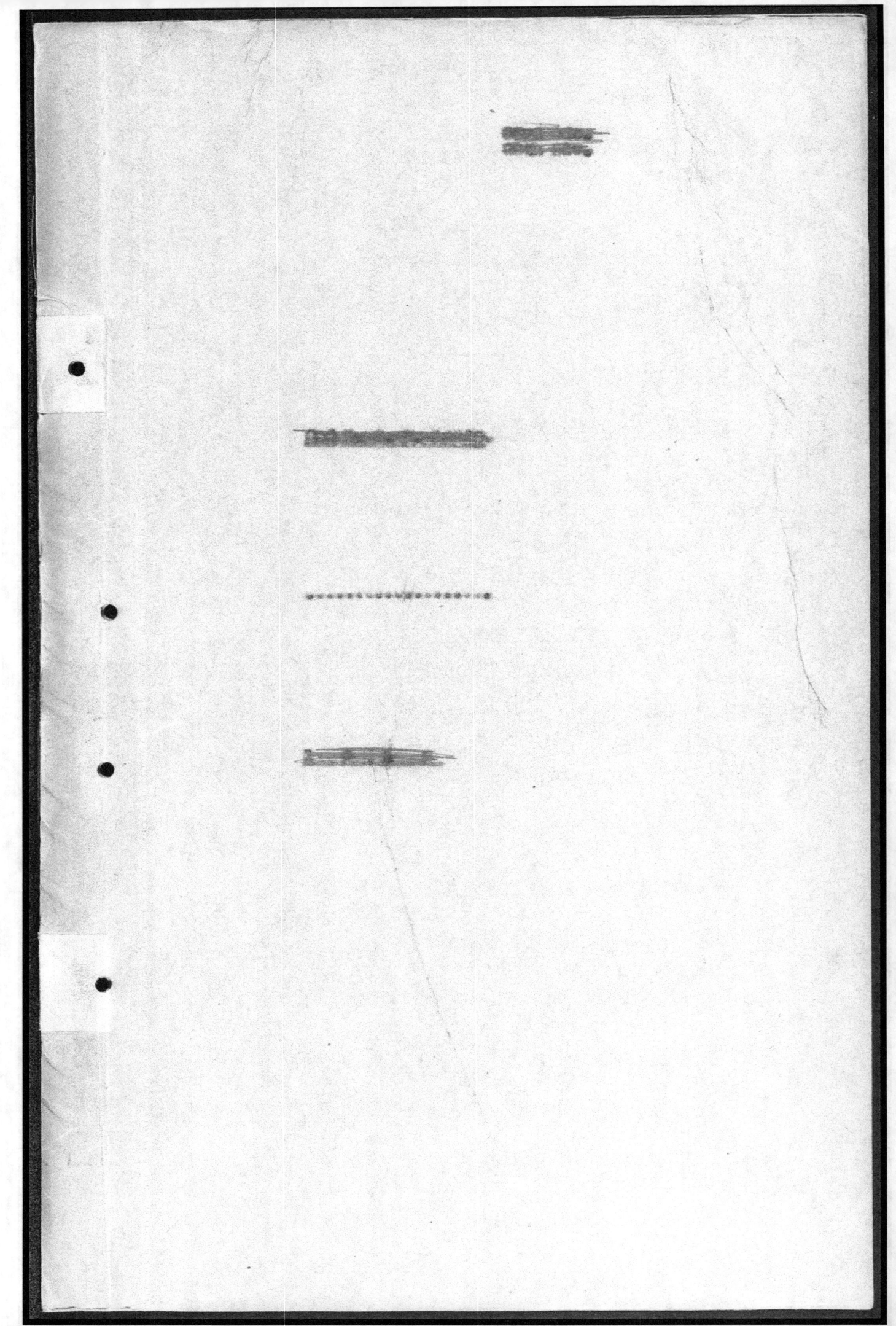

N O T E

Instructions regarding War Diaries and Intelligence Summaries are contained in F. S. Regs., Part II. and the Staff Manual respectively. Title pages will be prepared in manuscript.

WAR DIARY
or
~~INTELLIGENCE SUMMARY.~~
(Erase heading not required.)

1st York & Lancaster Regt

Army Form C. 2118.

Hour, Date, Place		Summary of Events and Information	Remarks and references to Appendices
Sept 1st ROSSIGNOL HQ	4.30am	Situation quiet	
	5.am	Capt. Buckley crawled out in front of H4 to inspect enemy wire. He lay in long grass & used a periscope.	
	12 noon	Casualty report. one killed; four wounded	
	3.20pm	Enemy sent three 5.9 high explosive shells into ROSSIGNOL WOOD	
	6.10pm	Enemy sent eight shrapnel shells which burst just over the KEMMEL - VIERSTRAAT road. Fortunately no working party was on the road at the time. Large working parties working by day on the Subsidiary Line must have been noticed by the enemy.	
	10pm	Capt Wales & Sgt Barker went out from J3 Right to reconnoitre enemy wire. They found bodies of many Royal Scots who had been out there since last year. Two bombing parties went out from K trenches at different times; composed as follows. Capt Lucas. 9136 L/c Hobson 20252 Pte Barrett and. 2nd Lt Hollis 9136 L/c Hobson, 9995 [illegible]	
Sept 2nd "	4.30am	Situation normal	
	12 noon	Casualty report three wounded	
	4.30pm	Quiet all day	
	11.55pm	Bde Operation Orders no 67	Appendix I.
Sept 3rd "		Quiet all day	
		Casualties nil	
	4pm	Battalion Operation Orders no 20	Appendix II
		Owing to the 3rd Monmouths leaving the Brigade, the Battalion had to hold a longer bit of the line. For one night the Companies did not make a complete	

Instructions regarding War Diaries and Intelligence Summaries are contained in F. S. Regs., Part II. and the Staff Manual respectively. Title pages will be prepared in manuscript.

Army Form C. 2118.

WAR DIARY
or
~~INTELLIGENCE SUMMARY.~~

(*Erase heading not required.*) 1st York & Lancaster Rgt

Hour, Date, Place		Summary of Events and Information	Remarks and references to Appendices
ROSSIGNOL H.Q.		but occupied the new trenches with platoons from support trenches. Two Companies of 5th Kings own came under the Command of Col. Bayley. The relief was complete by 7.5 pm	
4th Sept	4.30am	Situation normal. Enemy sniping much heavier during early part of night.	
	11. am	Brigade operation orders no 68	Appendix III
	12 noon	Casualties nil	
	1 pm	Battalion operation orders no 21	Appendix IV
		Return showing Battalion Strength etc	Appendix V
	6 pm	Captain Lynch was wounded in the head by a piece of shrapnel. He was able to walk to Bn. H.Q. to get it dressed and later on to the ambulance	
	9.45 pm	The Battalion was relieved by 2nd Kings own at 9.45 pm & marched back to billets in LOCRE.	
5th Sept	[illegible] LOCRE.	Rested in Billets Casualty return. Captain Lynch & two other ranks wounded	
Sept 6th		Rested in Billets	
Sept 7th		" " "	
Sept 8th		" " "	
Sept 9th	9 am	2nd Lt. H. N. Aston joined from the 3rd Battalion.	
	12 noon	The Battalion was inspected by Lt. General Sir H. Plumer. Cmdg II army in field occupied by "D" Coy. He was accompanied	

Army Form C. 2118.

Instructions regarding War Diaries and Intelligence Summaries are contained in F. S. Regs., Part II. and the Staff Manual respectively. Title pages will be prepared in manuscript.

WAR DIARY
or
INTELLIGENCE SUMMARY.

(*Erase heading not required.*)

Hour, Date, Place		Summary of Events and Information	Remarks and references to Appendices
LOCRE		by General Bulfin & Staff. Capt Jackson, his A.D.C was with him	
		Extract from Batt[n] orders No 128	
		Lt General Sir H Plumer Comdg II army expressed his satisfaction today at the smart appearance of the men. The Divisional Commander wishes all ranks to be told that he was extremely pleased at everything and said the Battalion fully came up to what he expected of it.	
		The Comdg. Officer congratulates all ranks on their general turn out and the handling of their rifles which left nothing to be desired and hopes they will continue to show increasing efficiency in the field.	
Sept 10th	10 pm	Brigade operation orders No 70 received	Appendix 6
	2 pm	Battalion operation orders No 22	Appendix 7
	5.45 pm	Battalion left LOCRE and marched to the trenches to relieve the 2nd Kings own. The relief was complete at 9.15 pm	
Sept 11 ROSSIGNOL	H.Q. 4.30 am	Situation quiet	
		Distribution of troops	appendix 8
	12 noon	Casualty report 1 wounded	
	12.5 pm	Enemy were crumping K1. our heavy artillery replied and silenced enemy.	
	4.30 pm	Quiet.	
	9 pm	2nd Lt. R.F. Halcomb Sergt Marshall & 20319 Pte Podmore went out from J3 Right and threw six bombs into enemy's trench	
		Return showing Battalion strength etc	appendix 9
Sept 12 " "	4.30 am	Situation quiet	
	12 noon	Casualty report 2 wounded.	
		Situation quiet all day.	

Instructions regarding War Diaries and Intelligence Summaries are contained in F. S. Regs., Part II. and the Staff Manual respectively. Title pages will be prepared in manuscript.

WAR DIARY
or
~~INTELLIGENCE~~ SUMMARY.
(*Erase heading not required.*) 1st York & Lancaster Rgt

Army Form C. 2118.

Hour, Date, Place		Summary of Events and Information	Remarks and references to Appendices
Sept 13 ROSSIGNOL ESTAMINET.		Quiet all morning	
	5 am	2nd Lt Pearman was wounded in the ear while trying to observed an enemy working party.	
		Enemy dropped 3 mortars into K1, only one did any damage.	
	12 noon	Casualty report, killed one, wounded officer one other ranks two.	
		Quiet all afternoon.	
Sept 14th		Very quiet all day	
	12 noon	Casualty report wounded one	
	5 pm	Brigade operation orders received	Appendix 10
		Very quiet all night	
Sept 15th		Quiet all day	
	11 am	Our heavy battery B/130 fired on enemy's trench and machine gun emplacement in front of Petit Bois good shooting	
	12 noon	Casualty report wounded one	
	3.30 pm	Enemy shelled K1A with H E and damaged the trench. Our artillery replied and silenced enemy	
	6 pm	Three officers, one from 9th and two from 10th K.O.Y.L.I. were attached for 24 hours	
	9 pm	5th Kings own relieved the two companies in right sector	
Sept 16th	4.30 am	Situation quiet	
	12 noon	Casualty report killed one, wounded four; (one killed & two wounded were caused by bomber carelessly playing with grenade)	
	3 pm	The attached officers left for Bde H.Q	
	9 pm	The Battalion was relieved by the 2nd Kings own and march back to their billets at LOCRE.	Appendix 11
Sept 17th LOCRE		Rested in billets. Found working parties for subsidiary line.	
	12 noon	Casualty report one killed. one wounded.	

(9 29 6) W4141—463 100,000 9/14 H W V Forms/C. 2118/10

Instructions regarding War Diaries and Intelligence Summaries are contained in F. S. Regs., Part II. and the Staff Manual respectively. Title pages will be prepared in manuscript.

WAR DIARY
or
INTELLIGENCE SUMMARY.
(*Erase heading not required.*) 1st Bn York & Lancaster Regt

Army Form C. 2118.

Hour, Date, Place		Summary of Events and Information	Remarks and references to Appendices
Sept 18th LOCRE		Rested in billets	
Sept 19th "		" "	
" 20th "		Brigade operation order no 72	appendix 12
Sept 21st "		Brigade operation orders no 73	appendix 13
22 "		" " " 74	" 14
23 "		Batt" " " 24	" 15
	9 am	The Batt" left LOCRE at 9 am; the Brigade band leading. The Brigade marched passed the Corps Commander (Gen. Ferguson) in the Square at BAILLEUL + reached billets between METEREN + OUTERSTEENE at 11.30 am	
Sept 24. near METEREN		Batt" went for Route march in morning + practised Physical exercises in afternoon. Brigade anxious to get men fit.	
Sept 25 near OUTERSTEEN		Bn Headquarters were moved to a farm near OUTERSTEENE, where Col Bayley had billeted his Company oct 15 1914.	
	6 pm	wire from Brigade. "You will hold yourself ready to proceed by Route march at two hours notice if ordered"	
Sept 26	3.20 am	Brigade wire All troops 83rd Bde will proceed by route march, lead of Column passing OUTERSTEENE 6 am.	
	3.45 am	Brigade operation order no 74	appendix 16
		Batt" " " 27	" 17
		The Batt" fell in on alarm post at 5.30 am and marched to MERVILLE where we expected to get billets and allow men to breakfast, but orders were received to march on to ROBECQ where the Batt" arrived at 11 30 am and found billets. about 60 men fell out on the way but rejoined later. as they had had no breakfast the march was most creditable.	
	12.30 pm	Orders received to continue march at 2 pm.	appendix 18
		Brigade operation order no 74 continued	

Instructions regarding War Diaries and Intelligence Summaries are contained in F. S. Regs., Part II. and the Staff Manual respectively. Title pages will be prepared in manuscript.

WAR DIARY
or
INTELLIGENCE SUMMARY.
(*Erase heading not required.*) 1st Bn York & Lancaster Rgt

Hour, Date, Place	Summary of Events and Information	Remarks and references to Appendices
Sept 26 ROBECQ	The march was continued at 2 pm. After going about 2½ miles the Brigade halted and after waiting an hour was ordered to return to ROBECQ where it rested for the night.	
	Brigade Operation Orders no 75	Appendix 19
7.50pm	Battn " " no 28	" 20
Sept 27th " 7.45am	Orders received to leave in Busses at 1 pm	
10.20am	Brigade Operation Order no 76	" 21
	Battn " " 29	" 22
12.30pm	As no motorbusses were available the Brigade went in motor lorries. The Convoy passed through BETHUNE and stopped at NOYELLE. The Battn bivouaced in a field half way between NOYELLE & VERMELLES.	
5pm	The C.O. Coy Comdrs & Adjutant went up the HULLOCK ROAD to H Q of Brigade to make arrangements to take over trenches. While there, the orders for relief were cancelled and our officers returned to Battn	
Sept 28th NOYELLE 2.6am	Brigade wire your battalion will move at once to Clark's KEEP VERMELLES to come under orders of 25th I.B. The 26th I B will have six guides at CLARKS KEEP at 2.30am to meet Battn and conduct it to CENTRAL BOYAU. This message was received at 2.30 am and by 2.50 am Battn was on the move. The guides were picked up at CLARKS KEEP, but they did not know what they had to do. The C O halted the Battn on arriving at the railway line and made the companies line the hedge while he went forward for instructions	

Instructions regarding War Diaries and Intelligence Summaries are contained in F. S. Regs., Part II. and the Staff Manual respectively. Title pages will be prepared in manuscript.

WAR DIARY
or
INTELLIGENCE SUMMARY.
(*Erase heading not required.*) 2nd Yorks & Lancaster Regt

Army Form C. 2118.

Hour, Date, Place	Summary of Events and Information	Remarks and references to Appendices
Sept 28 VERMELLES 4.45 am	The CENTRAL BOYAU was blocked by the Middlesex Regt going up. One of the guides led the C.O; Coy Comdrs & Adjutant to Brigade H.Q. Before leaving the following message was sent to 83rd I B.	
	"Left CLARKS KEEP 3.30 am with guides. Arrived at entrance to CENTRAL BOYAU and found it blocked by Middlesex Regt 85th Bde. Luckily discovered my Coys being wrongly led by guides. Have collected my Battn at entrance to CENTRAL BOYAU. Have received no instructions. Guides do not know where they are taking us. Am leaving my Battn at entrance to Central Boyau and going on myself with Coy Commanders to ascertain what is required of us"	
	After wandering for many hours we arrived at H.Q 85 Bde. The C.O of Royal Fusiliers was acting Brigadier. On reporting our arrival the Coy Officers returned and the C.O & Adjutant remained for orders, and rejoined the Batt about 10 am.	
11.25 am	85th Brigade wire "Please bring up your Battn and occupy front line of old British Trench"	
	The Battn filed up the Central Boyau. The narrow CT was hopelessly blocked by men of Highland 2 Division trying to get out. On arriving at old British front line, we found it full of troops, so the C.O took the Battn back to the Reserve Trench.	
12 noon	Casualty report Killed 7. wounded 3. wounded & missing 3.	

(9 29 6) W4141—463 100,000 9/14 H W V Forms/C. 2118/10

Instructions regarding War Diaries and Intelligence Summaries are contained in F. S. Regs., Part II. and the Staff Manual respectively. Title pages will be prepared in manuscript.

WAR DIARY
or
~~INTELLIGENCE SUMMARY.~~
(Erase heading not required.)

1st York & Lancaster Rgt

Army Form C. 2118.

Hour, Date, Place		Summary of Events and Information	Remarks and references to Appendices
Sept 28th	8 pm	85th Bde wire "Reported that Germans are attacking HOHENZOLLERN REDOUBT. Be prepared to give support. Can you move 2 of your Companies up to close support."	
	9.15 pm	85th Bde wire "The Buffs have so many casualties that they cannot hold on. Will you please send two Coys to relieve them in DUMP TRENCH. The Buffs on being relieved will occupy BIG WILLIE filling up gap between FUSILIERS Right in Redoubt and Middlesex left. The Buffs position is from the junction of South Face and DUMP TRENCH to the junction of BIG WILLIE and DUMP TRENCH." (Note. The Buffs did not hold this position only a small section of Dump trench near where it joins Big Willie was held by our troops.)	
	1.30 pm	The C.O. & Adjutant of Middlesex Rgt came to report weak situation of Buffs. Major Robertson Captain Forster & Buckley went back with them to BIG WILLIE to investigate and arrange to send back guides for A & B Coys to take them up to support the Buffs.	
Sept 29th	3 am.	As no guides had arrived A & B Coys set off to go to BIG WILLIE. Guides from the Middlesex Rgt were met on the way. On arrival about 5 am the Coys halted in the trench waiting for the parties sent out by C.O. of the Buffs to return and report on position of the Batt".	

(9 29 6) W4141—463 100,000 9/14 H W V Forms/C. 2118/10

Army Form C. 2118.

WAR DIARY
or
INTELLIGENCE SUMMARY.
(Erase heading not required.) 1st York & Lancaster Rgt

Instructions regarding War Diaries and Intelligence Summaries are contained in F. S. Regs., Part II. and the Staff Manual respectively. Title pages will be prepared in manuscript.

Hour, Date, Place	Summary of Events and Information	Remarks and references to Appendices
Sept 29 In trenches opposite HOHENZOLLEN REDOUBT.	about 6 am A Company advanced through BIG WILLIE and two platoons had entered the advance Trench when the Germans commenced a strong bomb attack on the left flank. The Buffs meanwhile were filing out & the trenches were very congested. The position at this stage was as follows	

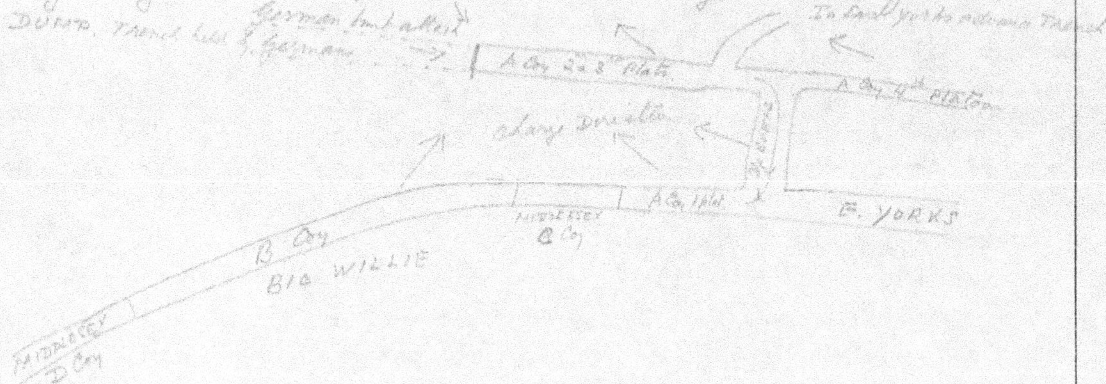

The order was given by the Adjutant of the Buffs to "about turn" but this was almost impossible owing to the congestion, although no 4 Platoon of "A" Coy was able to file into an empty trench to allow Buffs to pass.
Capt Buckley & 2nd Lt Ellison in response to a request for bombs lead the bombers of "B" Coy over the top & delivered an attack, returning when the supply of bombs was exhausted.
The wounded passing down made the trench more congested still & the order was given to charge.

(9 29 6) W4141—463 100,000 9/14 H W V Forms/C. 2118/10

Instructions regarding War Diaries and Intelligence Summaries are contained in F. S. Regs., Part II. and the Staff Manual respectively. Title pages will be prepared in manuscript.

WAR DIARY
or
~~INTELLIGENCE SUMMARY.~~
(*Erase heading not required.*) 1st York & Lancaster Rgt

Army Form C. 2118.

Hour, Date, Place	Summary of Events and Information	Remarks and references to Appendices
Sept 29th	The Charge was led by Major Robertson and Capt Forster & was successful in preventing the Germans coming over the top & also drove them back along their trench. All the platoons of "A" Coy and the nearest platoon of "B" Coy lead by Capt Buckley took part in the charge.	
	Major Robertson, Capt Forster, Lt Howard & 2nd Lt Cole were killed while Capt Buckley, 2nd Lt Ellison & 2nd Lt Aston were wounded	
	As all the officers of "A" Coy were casualties, Sgt Major Rickell ordered the men of "A" Coy to return to B.6.W 1421C and the Communication trench.	
	The position then was as under	

There was a lull in the fighting & A Coy was reorganised by Sgt Major Rickell. 2nd Lt B. A. Batts was instructed to take temporary command of "A" Coy and during the course of the morning he handed over to 2nd Lt A. C. Essex who arrived from Headquarters, where he had remained behind as he was sick. Shortly after his arrival "A" Coy occupied advance trench

After Capt Buckley was wounded, Lt Coles took command of "B" Coy & was reinforced by a platoon of D Coy under 2nd Lt R. R. Halcomb.

Instructions regarding War Diaries and Intelligence Summaries are contained in F. S. Regs., Part II. and the Staff Manual respectively. Title pages will be prepared in manuscript.

WAR DIARY
or
INTELLIGENCE SUMMARY.

(*Erase heading not required.*) 1st York. Lancaster Rgt.

Army Form C. 2118.

Hour, Date, Place	Summary of Events and Information	Remarks and references to Appendices
Sept 29	Lt Coles received an unintelligible message from the Adjutant of the Middlesex Rgt asking him whether he proposed to retire. Not understanding it, he went down the Trench to make enquiries. On the way he found some empty traverses which had previously been held by "D" Coy of Middlesex Rgt. He then returned & went to the O.C. "C" Coy Middlesex Rgt. to ask for an explanation & to state that he would not retire.	
	Meanwhile 2nd Lt Batts. C.S.M. Wigley & a few men went down to the left of the Trench to find out the situation. About 15-20 traverses were found empty and the Germans who had evidently crept up an unused Communication Trench were established in BIG WILLIE with a supply of bombs. The party withdrew to report & were ordered to return with bombs.	
	In the mean time the Germans had advanced up the Trench slowly and were assisted by gas fumes which emanated from a burning mop shaped apparatus which had been placed on our parapet.	
	There was a shortage of bombs and so Lt Coles went to the right to try to arrange for a supply which was eventually obtained through the E YORKS while 2nd Lt Batts superintended the operations on the left flank.	
	Messages explaining the situation were successfully carried across the open by Cpl Atkinson and delivered to Col Bayley.	

(9 29 6) W4141—463 100,000 9/14 H W V Forms/C. 2118/10

Army Form C. 2118.

Instructions regarding War Diaries and Intelligence Summaries are contained in F. S. Regs., Part II. and the Staff Manual respectively. Title pages will be prepared in manuscript.

WAR DIARY
or
INTELLIGENCE SUMMARY.
(Erase heading not required.)

Hour, Date, Place	Summary of Events and Information	Remarks and references to Appendices
Sept 29th	The bomb fight continued for 6 hours on the left flank and on two occasions charges were made, one of which was successful in dislodging the Germans from 6 Traverses. The East Yorks bomb officer & his men rendered invaluable assistance during the whole of this time. The Germans had been driven to the last Traverse when "D" Coy arrived and took up a position on the left causing the Germans to retire. During the morning "C" & "D" Coy occupied the old British front line trench. It was from this position that Pte Harvey gallantly carried box after box of bombs across the open under heavy rifle fire to the HOHENZOLLERN REDOUBT until he was wounded. At 1.40 pm 85th Bde wire was received saying "Send one Company immediately to ridge on right of E/Surrey trench" "C" Coy were then ordered to reinforce the right of the East Surrey's & moved into the advanced British fire trench just behind the Redoubt. At 5 pm there was a sudden panic in the Redoubt and about 50 men rushed over the top into our trench. The order was given to fix bayonets. About 5.30 pm Capt Lucas gave the order to charge. The left flank put out of action a bombing party which was stationed at the corner of the Redoubt and a communication trench.	

(9 29 6) W4141—463 100,000 9/14 H W V Forms/C. 2118/10

WAR DIARY
or
INTELLIGENCE SUMMARY.
(Erase heading not required.)

Army Form C. 2118.

Instructions regarding War Diaries and Intelligence Summaries are contained in F. S. Regs., Part II. and the Staff Manual respectively. Title pages will be prepared in manuscript.

Hour, Date, Place	Summary of Events and Information	Remarks and references to Appendices
Sept 29th	Capt Lucas & 2nd Lt HOLLIS were wounded in the charge. 'C' Coy were then moved to the right and finally occupied a portion of the advanced British front line trench. 2nd Lt Odsetts was wounded in the stomach about this time while working his Machine Guns.	
	About 6 pm 'D' Coy were ordered to get in touch with 'B' Coy in BIG WILLIE. They filed into the Redoubt and halted there among the Royal Fusiliers while Capt Vickerman went to report to Col Bayley. On returning he moved his Company up BIG WILLIE until he got in touch with 'B' Coy on his right. The Royal Fusiliers were on his left.	
	At 12.30 pm Capt Vickerman reported that all was quiet. During the night one Coy of 7th KOYLI under Lt Heath relieved the Middlesex & the few Buffs that remained in BIG WILLIE. They occupied a portion of the trench between 'A' Coy & 'B' Coy.	
	The casualties during the day among other Ranks were 6 killed, 20 wounded, 21 missing, 4 missing believed killed, 5 wounded & missing.	
Sept 30th	The Companies in BIG WILLIE worked hard at improving the trench and making fire steps. Parties were sent up the communication trenches leading towards the German line to make stops and fill in for 50 yards. 'A' Coy had to repel repeated bomb attacks from the Dump Trench and 'D' Coy were able to repel successfully	

Instructions regarding War Diaries and Intelligence Summaries are contained in F. S. Regs., Part II. and the Staff Manual respectively. Title pages will be prepared in manuscript.

WAR DIARY
or
INTELLIGENCE SUMMARY.
(Erase heading not required.)

1st York & Lancaster Regt

Army Form C. 2118.

Hour, Date, Place	Summary of Events and Information	Remarks and references to Appendices
Sept 30th	the bomb attacks on their left flank. The three Companies & the KOYLI in Big WILLIE were relieved by the Northumberland Fusiliers. Owing to one of the Companies losing touch the relief was considerably delayed, and the Companies did not start to file out much before 5 am. The Cheshire relieved the Royal Fusiliers on our left and left a gap of at least 100 yards in Big Willie. "D" Coy luckily vacated their [illegible] spreading out before any damage was done. "A" Coy filed out through the East Yorks and so missed a bomb attack made by the Germans on the Redoubt as our B Coy and KOYLI were filing through. The last two Platoons of B Coy were kept by the Cheshire to help in a counter attack. Owing to the congestion in the Trench the enemy bombs and mortars did considerable damage. The Coy of KOYLI lost heavily. The casualties during the day were as under O.R. Ranks. 12 killed, 15 wounded. 9 missing 10 missing believed killed 33 wounded & missing. Throughout the two days fighting no part of a trench was given up by our men although Regiments on our flanks did leave positions which we had to retake.	

Appendix I

SECRET

COPY No. 5

OPERATION ORDER NO. 67

by

BRIGADIER GENERAL H.S.L.RAVENSHAW, C.M.G.,

Commanding 83rd Infantry Brigade.

****

References. VIERSTRAAT 1/10000 BELGIUM, SHEET 28. 2nd September, 1915.

1\. a. The front of 83rd Brigade will be re-distributed on night 3rd - 4th September into a RIGHT and LEFT SECTOR ACCORDING TO THE ATTACHED TABLE, the Garrisons of 5th King's Own Regiment coming under the orders of Officer Commanding, 1st York & Lancaster Regiment.

b. All details of relief will be arranged between Commanding Officers of the present three Sectors.

c. The 5th King's Own Regiment (less two Companys and ~~three~~ four machine guns) will proceed to SCHERPENBERG on relief.

d. Completion of relief to be wired to this Office.

e. The present Headquarters of RIGHT SECTOR in KEMMEL will be vacated.

2\. a. On 3rd September, 3rd Monmouth Regiment will march via RENINGHELST and POPERINGHE to join 49th Division, passing Cross Roads M.17.c., at 9 a.m.

b. Guide from 49th Division will meet this Battalion at POPERINGHE.

c. Supply wagons will draw rations for consumption on Saturday and accompany the Battalion.

Issued at 9.45pm

R S Follett

Captain,

Brigade Major. 83rd Inf. Bde.

Copy No. 1. War Diary.
2. 2nd King's Own Regt.
3. 2nd East Yorkshire Regt.
4. 1st K.O.Y.L.I.
5. 1st York & Lancaster Regt.
6. 5th King's Own Regt.
7. 3rd Monmouth Regt.
8. 28th Division.
9. 3rd Brigade R.F.A.
10. 84th Infantry Brigade.
11. 2/1 Northumbrian Field Coy R.E.
12. No. 2 Coy A.S.C.
13. 52nd Brigade.
14. Staff Captain. 83rd Inf.Bde.
15. Machine Gun Officer, 83rd Inf. Bde.
16. Signals, 83rd Infantry Brigade.

G A R R I S O N S

	Trench	Garrison	Unit
RIGHT SECTOR	G.4.	35	5th King's Own Regt.
	G.4.a.	45	"
	H.1.a.	60	"
	H.1.	40	"
	S.P.11.	25	"
	H.2.	50	1st York & Lancs Regt.
	H.3.	40	"
	H.4.	40	"
	H.5.	50	"
	J.1.	40	"
	J.2.	40	"
	J.3.R.	15	"
	J.3.new	30	"
	J.3.L.	20	"
	J.4.	40	"
	J.10.	30	"
	J.11.	25	"
	K.1.	40	"
	K.1.a.	30	"
	S.P.12.	25	"
	S.P.13.	30	"
LEFT SECTOR	K.1.new.	40	2nd East Yorkshire Regt.
	K.1.b.	25	"
	K.2.	30	"
	K.2.a.	50	"
	K.2.b.	30	"
	K.3.) L.1.)	60	"
	L.1.new.	35	"
	L.2.	40	"
	L.3.	30	"
	L.4.	35	"
	L.5.	50	"
	L.6.	40	"
	L.7.R.	20	"
	L.7.L.	35	"

2/9/15.

MACHINE GUNS

	Trench	Guns	Unit finding gun	Unit finding Team
RIGHT SECTOR:-				
	H.1.a.	1	5th King's Own	5th King's Own
	S.P.11	1	do.	do.
	H. 3.	1	do.	2nd King's Own
	J. 1.	1	1st York & Lancaster	1st York & Lancaster
	J. 4.	1	do.	do.
	K. 1.	1	do.	do.
	S.P.12.	1	5th King's Own	do.
	S.P.13	1	1st York & Lancaster	do.
LEFT SECTOR:-				
	K.2.a.	1	2nd East Yorks	2nd East Yorks
	L.5.	1	do.	do.
	L.6.	1	do.	do.
	L.7.	1	do.	do.

Copy No. 1 Appendix II

OPERATION ORDERS No. 20.

By

Lieut-Col. G. E. Bayley D.S.O.
Comdg. 1st Bn York & Lancaster Regt.

Friday, 3rd Septr. 1915.

1. The following reliefs will take place this evening.

(i) O.C. "C" Coy. will withdraw the garrison in K,1, now, on being relieved by the 2nd East Yorkshire Regt, and distribute them in K,1, and K,1,a.

(ii) O.C. "D" Coy. will relieve the 5th Kings Own Regt. in H,2, with his garrison in H,5.

Reliefs to start at 6·30 p.m.

(iii) O.C. "B" Coy. will relieve the 5th Kings Own Regt. in H,3, with his garrison in J,10.

Relief to start at 6 p.m.

(iv) O.C. Cos. will arrange to take over French stores in advance.

2. The 2nd King's Own Regt. will find a team for the 5th Kings Own Regt's. Machine Gun in H,3.

3. Signallers will take over telephone in H,2.

4. The two Cos. of the 5th Kings Own Regt. will come under the command of O.C. 1st York & Lancaster Regt.

5. The CENTRE SECTOR will in future be called the RIGHT SECTOR.

6. Reliefs will be reported by wire to Bn. Hd. Qrs.

7. The 5th Kings Own Regt. will report their relief to their C.O.

T. Knox Shaw, Capt,
A/Adj. 1st York & Lancaster Regt.

Issued at 1 p.m.

Copies No. 1 & 2 War Diary.
Copy " 3. O.C. A Coy.
" " 4. " B "
" " 5 " C "
" " 6 " D "
" " 7 O.C. 2nd Kings Own Regt.
" " 8 " 2nd East Yorkshire Regt.
" " 9 " 5th Kings Own Regt.
" 10 Machine Gun Officer.

Appendix III

SECRET

Copy No. 5

OPERATION ORDER No. 68

by

BRIGADIER GENERAL H.S.L.RAVENSHAW, C.M.G.,

Commanding 83rd Infantry Brigade.

Reference :- VIERSTRAAT $\frac{1}{10000}$ BELGIUM, SHEET 28.

4th Sept. 1915.

1. The 2nd King's Own Regiment relieve the 1st York & Lancaster Regiment on night 4th - 5th September in all trenches of RIGHT SECTOR occupied by the latter Battalion (see table issued with Operation Order No. 67).

2. The 1st K.O.Y.L.I., relieve the 2nd East Yorkshire Regiment in LEFT SECTOR on night 5th - 6th September.

3.a. Signallers of relieving units will take over at 3 p.m., on the day of relief.

b. Relieving units will pass barrier N.20.b.6.8., at 7 p.m.

c. Completion of relief will be wired to this Office.

4. On relief 1st York & Lancaster Regiment proceed to Billets at LOCRE.

Issued at 9 a.m.

R.C. Follett Captain.
Brigade Major, 83rd Inf.Bde.

Copy No. 1, War Diary.
2. 2nd King'sOwn Regt.
3, 2nd East Yorkshire Regt.
4. 1st K.O.Y.L.I.,
5. 1st York & Lancaster Regt.
6. 5th King's Own Regt.
7. 28th Division,
8. 3rd Brigade R.F.A.,
9. 84th Infantry Brigade.
10, No. 2 Coy. A.S.C.
11. 2/1 Northumbrian Fld.Coy.R.E.
12, Staff Captain, 83rd Inf.Bde.
13. Machine Gun Officer, 83rd Bde.
14. Signals, 83rd Infantry Bde.

Copy No. 1

App IV

OPERATION ORDERS No. 31.
By
Lieut-Col. G.E. Bayley, D.S.O.
Comdg. 1st York & Lancaster Regiment
Saturday 4th Sept 1915.

1. The Battalion will be relieved tonight by the 2nd Kings Own Regt. On relief Cos. will rendezvous at KEMMEL CHURCH and march back to billets at LOCRE, via BRULOOZE, under Coy. Comdrs.

Machine Gun Teams will rendezvous at the DUMPING GROUND and march back under the Machine Gun Officer.

2. Chargers of O.C.s 'B' 'C' & 'D' Cos. will be at KEMMEL CHURCH and that for O.C. 'A' Coy at SIEGE FARM.

3. Officers trench kits and all water tins must be at the DUMPING GROUND by 8 p.m.

4. The two Cos. of 5th Kings Own Regt. will come under the orders of O.C. 2nd Kings Own Regt. on completion of relief.

5. O.C. Cos. and Machine Gun Officer will report completion of relief to Bn. Hd. Qrs.

Relief of H.6. and S.P.12. will be reported from H.6.

6. Handing Over Reports and Work Reports will be rendered to the Adjutant by O.C. Cos by 4 p.m. and Receipt for Trench Stores as soon as possible.

7. O.C. 'A' Coy will furnish a guard for Bn. Hd. Qrs. which will mount as soon as the Coy. reaches LOCRE.

8. No guides will be required.

T. Knox Shaw Capt,
A/Adj. 1st York & Lancaster Regt.

Issued at 1 p.m.

Copies 1 & 2 War Diary
Copy No. 3 O.C. 'A' Coy
" " 4 " 'B' "
" " 5 " 'C' "
" " 6 " 'D' "
" " 7 M.G. Officer.
" " 8 Transport Officer
" " 9 O.C. 2nd Kings Own Regt.
" " 10 O.C. 5th — " —
" " 11 O.C. Detmt. 5th Kings Own Regt.

Appendix V

1st Bn York & Lancaster Regt

Extracts from Regimental Returns

	Officers	Other ranks
Present with Battalion	23	864
Details	2	87
TOTAL STRENGTH	25	951

TRENCH STRENGTH

	Officers	Other ranks
Battalion Headquarters	4	14
Stretcher Bearers	-	20
Signallers	-	30
Machine Gunners	1	39
Rifles in trenches	16	671
TOTAL	21	774

Sick Wastage

Admitted to hospital during the week	9
Discharged from — " —	5

7/9/1915

T Knox Shaw Captain
a/Adjt 1st York & Lancaster Regt

Appendix 6

SECRET COPY No. 5

OPERATION ORDER No. 70

by

BRIGADIER GENERAL H.S.L.RAVENSHAW, C.M.G.,

Commanding 83rd Infantry Brigade.

****

References:- VIERSTRAAT $\frac{1}{10,000}$
BELGIUM, SHEET 28. Thursday, 9th September, 1915.

1. On night 10th-11th September, the 1st York & Lancaster Regiment will relieve 2nd King's Own Regiment in the RIGHT SECTOR.

2. On night 11th-12th September, 2nd East Yorkshire Regt., will relieve 1st K.O.Y.L.I., in the LEFT SECTOR.

3.a. Details of above reliefs will be arranged between Commanding Officers.

b. Signallers will take over at three p.m., on day of relief.

c. Relieving units will pass barrier N.20.b.6.8., at 6.45.p.m.

d. The present O.C., Sectors will command until the relief is complete. Completion of relief to be wired to this office.

4. On relief 2nd King's Own Regiment proceed to LOCRE. 1st K.O.Y.L.I., to SCHERPENBERG.

R S Follett
Major.
Issued at 9-15 p.m. Brigade Major, 83rd Inf. Bde.

Copy No. 1, War Diary.
2, 2nd King's Own Regt.
3, 2nd East Yorkshire Regt.
4, 1st K.O.Y.L.I.
5, 1st York & Lancas. Regt.
6, 5th King's Own Regt.
7, 28th Division.
8, 84th Brigade.
9, 3rd Brigade R.F.A.
10, No. 2. Coy, A.S.C..
11, 2/1 Northumbrian Field Coy R.E.
12, Signals, 83rd Inf. Bde.
13, Staff Captain, 83rd Bde.
14, Machine Gun Officer, 83rd Bde.

Copy No 1

Appendix 7.

OPERATIONS ORDERS No. 22.
By Lieut.Colonel G.E.Bayley.D.S.O.
Cmdg.1st.York & Lancaster Regt.

10/9/15%

(1) The Battalion will relieve the 2nd. King's Own Regt. in the trenches tonight, and occupy them as follows:-

C Coy.	D Coy.	B COy.
K.1	J.3.right.	H.2.
K.1.a.	J.3.new.	H.3.
J.3.left.	J.1.	H.4.
J.4.	J.2.	H.5.
S.P.12.	J.10.	
S.P.13.		

A Coy SIEGE FARM&

Machine Guns and teams in K.1.,J.1.,J.4.,S.P.13.
Teams only in S.P.12 and H.3.
Order of march:-

Machines Guns	5.15.pm.
D COy	5.20.pm.
C Coy.	5.25.pm.
B Coy.	5.30.pm.
A Coy & H.Q. Coy.	5.35.pm.
Transport	6. pm.

(2) O.C. Coy's will arrange that an Officer and their C.Q.M.S. proceed to the trenches in advance to take over.

(3) Officer's kits and trench kits must be ready to be fetched by transport by 4.pm.

(4) Completion of relief will be wired to Bn.H.Q.
Relief of S.P.12 will be reported from H.5.,S.P.13 from K

(5) On completion of relief the detachment of the 5th. King's Own Regt. will come under the command of O.C.1st. Y & L Rgt.

(6) O.C."A" Coy will arrange to provide carrying parties for water, and a Guard for Bn. Headquarters.

T Knox Shaw Captain.
A/Adjutant,1st.York & Lancaster Regt.

Copy No.1 & 2 War Diary
3 O.C. A Coy.
4 O.C. B Coy.
5 O.C. C Coy.
6 O.C. D Coy.

Copy No. 7 M.G.O.
8 O.C. 2nd. K.O.
9 O.C. Det. 5/K.O.
10 Transport Officer

"A" Form.

Army Form C. 2121.

MESSAGES AND SIGNALS.

No. of Message

Prefix Code m. | Words | Charge

Office of Origin and Service Instructions.

Sent
At m.
To
By

This message is on a/c of:
Service.
(Signature of "Franking Officer.")

Recd. at m.
Date Appendix 8
From
By

TO 83rd I.B.

Sender's Number.	Day of Month.	In reply to Number	AAA
* KS216	11		

Distribution of Troops.

K1	1	officer	C Coy	40	other Ranks
J3 left	0	"		22	" "
J4	1	"		22	" "
K1A	0	"		20	" "
SP12	1	"		20	" "
SP13	1	"	D Coy	30	" "
J1	1	"		35	" "
J2	2	"		43	" "
J3 R.	1	"		13	" "
J3 new	0	"		44	" "
J10	1	"		22	" "
H2	1	"	B Coy	52	" "
H3	1	"		45	" "
H4	1	"		45	" "
H5	1	"		31	" "
G4A	1	"		38	" "

From
Place
Time

The above may be forwarded as now corrected. (Z)

Censor. Signature of Addressor or person authorised to telegraph in his name.

* This line should be erased if not required.

(13265) Wt. W. 14141-641. 10,000. 4-15. H.G.&S.,Ltd.

"A" Form. Army Form C. 2121.

MESSAGES AND SIGNALS. No. of Message

Prefix ..... Code ..... m.	Words	Charge	This message is on a/c of:	Recd. at ..... m.
Office of Origin and Service Instructions.	Sent		..... Service.	Date
	At ..... m.			From
	To			
	By		(Signature of "Franking Officer.")	By

TO

Sender's Number.	Day of Month.	In reply to Number	AAA
*			

G4	1 officer	}		38	other Ranks
H1A	2 "	}	5th Kingsm	55	" "
H1	2 "	}		34	" "
SP11	1 "	}		42	" "
SIEGEFARM	5 "	A Coy		176	" "

Machine Guns on K1 J1 J4 H3 SP12 SP13. SP11 H1A

From VC

Place Y+L

Time 8.10 pm

The above may be forwarded as now corrected. (Z) W. Mac Bell

Censor. Signature of Addressor or person authorised to telegraph in his name.

* This line should be erased if not required.

(132651) Wt. W. 1414.-641. 10,000. 4-15. H. G. & S., Ltd.

Appx. 9

1st Bn York & Lancaster Regt

Extract from Regimental Returns dated 10th Sept 1915

Distribution	Officers	Other ranks	Remarks
Trench Strength			
Battalion Headquarters	4	13	
Stretcher Bearers	—	20	
Signallers		32	
Machine Gunners	1	39	
Rifles in Trenches	16	679	
	21	783	
Strength of Battalion			
Present with Unit	23	865	
Details	3	85	
Total strength	26	950	
Sick Wastage			
Admitted during previous week	1*	8	* Capt. Lynch wounded
Discharged — do —	—	6	

14/9/1915

[signature] Captain,

A/Adjutant, 1st Bn York & Lancaster Regt.

App 10

SECRET. Copy No. 5

OPERATION ORDER No.71.

by

BRIGADIER GENERAL H.S.L.Ravenshaw C.M.G.

Commanding 83rd Infantry Brigade.

Reference, VIERSTRAAT 1/10,000
Sheet 28 1/40,000

14th September 1915.

1. On night 15th - 16th Sept., 5/King's Own will relieve their garrisons and machine gun teams in the Right Sector.

2. On night 16th - 17th Sept., 2/King's Own Regt., will relieve 1/York & Lancaster Regt in Right Sector

3. On night 17th - 18th 1/K.O.Y.L.I. will relieve 2/East Yorkshire Regt. in Left Sector.

4. (a) All details of reliefs will be arranged between Commdg., Officers.

(b) Signallers will take over 3 p.m. on day of relief.

(c) Relieving units will pass barrier N.20.b.1 6.8. at 6.45 p.m.

(d) The present O.C. Sectors will command until the relief is complete. Completion of relief to be wired to this office.

5. On relief 1/York & Lancaster Regt., proceed to LOCRE; 2/East Yorkshire Regt., to SCHERPENBERG.

Issued at 4 p.m.

Copy No.1 War Diary
2 2/King's Own
3 2/East Yorks
4 1/K.O.Y.L.I.
5 1/York & Lancs
6 5/King's Own
7 28th Division
8 84th Brigade
9 3rd Bde R.F.A.
10 No.2Coy,A.S.C.
11 2/1 Northumbrian Fd.Co.R.E.
12 O.C. Signals 83rd Bde.
13 M.G.Officer 83rd Bde.
14 Staff Capt., 83rd Bde.

R S Follett Major,
Brigade Major,
83rd Infantry Brigade.

App. 11

Copy. No. 1. OPERATION ORDERS No. 23.

By

Lieut.Colonel G.E.Bayley. D.S.O.

Cmdg.1st.York & Lancaster Regiment.

Thursday. sept. 16th.1915.

(1) The Battalion will be relieved by the 2nd. King's Own Regt. tonight. On relief Companies will march back to LOCRE to their billets, under Coy. arrangemnets.
Machine Gun teams will rendezvous at the DUMPING GROUND and march back under the M.G.Officer.

(2) Chargers of O.C's B,C,D,Coys. will be at KEMMEL CHURCH and that for O.C. A Coy. at SIEGE FARM.

(3) Officer's trench kits and all water tins must be at the DUMPING GROUND at 7.30 pm. Servants will see kits are put on the Transports.

(4) The two Coys. of 5th. King's Own Regt. will come under the orders of O.C. 2nd. King's Own Regt. on completion of relief.

(5) O.C. Cos. and M.G.Officer will report completion of relief by wire to Bn. Headquarters.

(6) Handing over Reports and Work Reports will rendered to the Adjutant by O.C.Cos. by 4 pm. and receipts for Trench Stores as soon as possible.

(7) O.C. A Coy. will furnish a Guard for Bn. H.Q. which will mount as soon as the Coy. reaches LOCRE.

(8) No guides will be required.

T Knowshaw
Captain.
A/Adjutant.1st.York & Lanc. Regt.

Issued at 2 pm.

Copy No.1 & 2 War Diary.
3 O.C. A Coy.
4 " B "
5 " C "
Copy No.6 O.C. D Coy.
7 " M Guns.
8 Transport Officer.
9 O.C. 2/K.O.
10 O.C.5/K.O.
11 O.C.5/K.O.Det.

S E C R E T.

Copy No.......5

App 12.

OPERATION ORDER No. 72.

by

BRIGADIER GENERAL H.S.L.Ravenshaw C.M.G.

Commanding 83rd Infantry Brigade.

Reference, VIERSTRAAT 1/10,000
Sheet 28 1/40,000

19th September 1915.

1. (a) On night 20th - 21st Sept. eight platoons 25th Bn. 5th Canadian Bde., will be distributed throughout the fire and support trenches (exclusive of K.1, K.1.a & S.P.13) of Right Sector.

Eight platoons of 22nd Battn., 5th Canadian Bde., will be similarly distributed throughout Left Sector and in K.1. K.1.a & S.P.13.

(b) After the arrival of the above, 1 coy., 5/King's Own and one & a half coys., 2/King's Own & 1/K.O.Y.L.I. will be withdrawn (see para 3).

(c) The above platoons will be placed between platoons of 83rd Brigade. They will not garrison supporting points, H.4. J.3 right & left, K.1 or K.3.

(d) The Company Commanders & one other Officer of each of the half companies relieved (mentioned in sub para B) will remain in the front line.

(e) Machine Gunners of 5th Canadian Bde., will be allotted to emplacements by the Brigade Machine Gun Officer but will not mount their guns. Machine Gunners 83rd Brigade will not be withdrawn.

2. (a) O.C.Sectors will furnish an officer & guides at barrier N.20.b.6.8 to meet 22nd Battn., at 6.45 P.M. and 25th Battn., at 7.15 P.M.

(b) All details of reliefs will be arranged between Commanding Officers concerned. Completion of relief to be wired to this office.

(c) Officers of 83rd Brigade will continue to command in both the Sectors and trenches under their charge.

(d) VIA GELLIA will not be used before 8.15 P.M.

3. On relief the 2/King's Own will proceed to bivouacs in field M.22.d. at LOCRE. The 1/K.O.Y.L.I. will proceed to field near farm M.11.d.2.7 (K.O.Y.L.I. Headquarters).

Issued at 6.40 P.M.

R S Follett
Major,
Brigade Major,
83rd Infantry Brigade.

Copy No.1 War Diary
2 2/King's Own
3 2/East Yorks
4 1/K.O.Y.L.I.
5 1/York & Lancs
6 5/King's Own
7 28th Division
8 84th Brigade
9 3rd Bde R.F.A.
10 No.2 Coy A.S.C.
11 2/1 Northumbrian Fd.Co.R.E.
12 O.C. Signals 83rd Bde
13 M.G. Officer 83rd Bde
14 Staff Captain 83rd Bde
15 5th Canadian Brigade
16 52nd Brigade
17 22nd Battn. Canadian Bde
18 25th Battn. Canadian Bde

SECRET.

Copy No.......5

App 13

OPERATION ORDER No.73.

by

BRIGADIER GENERAL H.S.L.Ravenshaw C.M.G.

Commanding 83rd Infantry Brigade

Reference HAZEBROUCK 5a. 1/100,000

20th September 1915.

1. On 23rd September the Brigade will march to billets about OUTTERSTEENE via LOCRE - BAILLEUL - OUTTERSTEENE road.

2. Starting point LOCRE CHURCH.

Order of March.	TIME
Billeting parties of all units as a formed body under Captain Brazier 1/K.O.Y.L.I.	8 a.m.
Brigade Headquarters	8.58 a.m.
1/York & Lancaster Regt.	9. a.m.
2/King's Own Regt.	9.10 a.m.
2/East Yorkshire Regt.	9.20 a.m.
1/K.O.Y.L.I.	9.30 a.m.
5/King's Own Regt.	9.40 a.m.
2 Ambulances 84th Field Ambulance	9.50 a.m.
Clearing up parties of all units as a formed body under Captain Carew R.Dub. Fusiliers.	11. a.m.

3.(a) 5/King's Own will detail a rearguard of one Officer & 12 other ranks to march in rear of the ambulances & collect any stragglers falling behind the Brigade.

(b) One Officer per battalion & one N.C.O. per Coy., will march in rear of the 1st line transport of each unit to collect stragglers.

(c) No individuals or small parties will be allowed to march except as laid down in para 2 of this operation order.

(d) Attention is drawn to Standing Orders for marches issued on 13/6/15 and re-issued on 19/9/15.

(e) There must be no check when marching into billets. Billeting parties will meet their own units well back on the line of march & conduct companies transport vehicles etc direct to their appointed places, leaving the road clear for the battalion following them.

4. The Corps Commander will be in BAILLEUL to watch the Brigade pass through. Compliments will be paid to all General Officers.

5. Brigade Headquarters will be at OUTTERSTEENE on Conclusion of the march.

Issued at 10 p.m.

R.S. Follett
Major,
Brigade Major,
83rd Infantry Brigade.

Copy No.1 War Diary
2 2/King's Own
3 2/East Yorks
4 1/K.O.Y.L.I.
5 1/York & Lancs.
6 5/King's Own
7 No.2.Coy, A.S.C.
8 Staff Capt.83rd Bde
9 O.C.Signals83rd Bde
10 M.G.Officer83rd Bde

S E C R E T. Copy No....5.....

app. 14

OPERATION ORDER No. 74.

by

BRIGADIER GENERAL H.S.L.Ravenshaw C.M.G.

Commanding 83rd Infantry Brigade

Reference, VIERSTRAAT 1/10,000
Sheet 28 1/40,000

21st September 1915.

1.(a) On the night of the 21st - 22nd September the 5th Canadian Bde., will mount their machine guns in the following emplacements:- L.6. L.5. S.P.11. S.P.12. S.P.13. & H.1 (new).

(b) Two machine gunners of the 83rd Brigade will remain in each of the emplacements for instructional purposes, the remainder of the teams and guns will be withdrawn from the above mentioned emplacements and rejoin their first line.

(c) During the morning and afternoon of the 22nd inst, the 5th Canadian Bde., will mount their machine guns in the remaining emplacements.

(d) Two machine gunners of the 83rd Brigade will remain in each emplacement and the remainder of the teams and guns will be withdrawn and rejoin their first line.

2.(a) On the 22nd inst. the 25th Battn., will relieve the 2/King's Own & the 5/King's Own in Right Sector and the 22nd Battn., will relieve the 1/K.O.Y.L.I. in the Left Sector according to the following table:-

(b) TABLE OF RELIEFS.

UNIT	PLACE.	TIME.
1 Platoon "A" Coy 22nd Battn.	83rd Bde Hqrs.	9.45 a.m.
1 Platoon "A" Coy 22nd Battn.	-do-	10.30 a.m.
1 Platoon "B" Coy 22nd Battn.	-do-	11.15 a,m.
1 Platoon "B" Coy 22nd Battn.	-do-	12. Noon.

(c) 10 Guides from 1/York & Lancaster Regt will be at Brigade Hqrs at 9.45 a.m. 22nd inst. to conduct 2 platoons "A" Coy 22nd Bn. to Headquarters 2/King's Own Regt..

10 Guides from 2/East Yorkshire Regt. will be at Brigade Hqrs. at 11.15 a.m. to conduct 2 platoons "B" Coy 22nd Battn, to 1/K.O.Y.L.I. headquarters.

(d) 2/King's Own R. & 1/K.O.Y.L.I. will furnish trench guides to be ready to guide above platoons to their respective trenchos.

3.(a) On the night of the 22nd - 23rd inst. the 25th Battn. will complete the relief of the 2/King's Own R. and 5/King's Own R. in the Right Sector & the 22nd Battn. that of the 1/K.O.Y.L.I in the Left Sector. [Except the Reserve Companies. Orders reference these will be issued later.]

(b) An Officer and guides from each Sector will meet the relieving ~~one & a Half~~ [Three] Coys. at the barrier N.20.b.6.8. as follows:-
Right Sector 25th Battn. at 6.30 P.M. [2 Coys 25th Battn]
Left Sector 22nd Battn. at 6.45 P.M. [1 Coy 22nd Battn.]

4. All details will be arranged between Commdg. Officers concerned.

5. Completion of relief will be reported to this office by wire both by Sector commanders & the Officers relieving.

6. ORDERS FOR THE RELIEF OF 83rd BRIGADE TELEPHONES.

Operators of relieving units will be posted to telephone offices in the trenches during the daytime on the 22nd inst. under arrangements to be made between the Signal Officers 83rd Brigade & 5th Canadian Brigade.

The 83rd Brigade operators will however not hand over,
(a) In the trenches, until their company is entirely relieved.
(b) At Battalion headquarters until the relief of the whole Sector is complete.

All telephones and other signalling equipment & appliances, belonging to the 83rd Brigade (except the telephone wires) will be brought out of the trenchos by the units of the 83rd Brigade.

Issued at 4.40 P.M.

Copy No.1 War Diary
2 2/King's Own
3 2/East Yorks
4 1/K.O.Y.L.I.
5 1/York & Lancs
6 5/King's Own
7 3rd Bde R.F.A.
8 No.2 Coy A.S.C.
9 2/1 Northumbrian Fd.Coy.R.E.
10 3rd Canadian Bde.
11 5th Canadian Bde.
12 22nd Battn. 5th Canadn. Bde
13 25th BattN. " " "
14 52nd Brigade.
15 Staff Captain
16 O.C. Signals
17 M.G.Officer

[signature] Br General
for Major,
Brigade Major,
83rd Infantry Brigade.

Copy No: 2

Appx. 5

Operation Orders No:
By
Lieut. Colonel G. E. Bayley, D.S.O.
Commanding 1st Bn York & Lancaster Regt.
Wednesday, 22nd Sept 1915

Reference Map – Sheet 27 or HAZEBROUCK. Sheet 5.a

1. The Battalion will march to Billets near OUTTERSTEENE via BAILLEUL on 23rd Sept

Starting point – Locre Church
Time. – 9. am
Order of march. Signallers
"A" Coy.
"B" "
"C" "
"D" "
Stretcher Bearers
Officers servants, Coy Cooks, etc under the Sergt Master Cook
1st Line Transport

2/Lieut. R. A. Holcomb and one N. C. O. from each Coy. will form a rear party and march in rear of 1st Line Transport and collect Stragglers. This party will report at Orderly Room at 9. am.

Sanitary Squads will parade with similar parties from other units, in the field behind Bn. Hdqrs at 10.50 am and march off under Capt. Carew. R. Dublin Fusiliers.

3. The Coy. QM Sergts and a N.C.O. from M. Gun Section will parade at Locre Church at 8. am. and march under Capt. Brazier. 1st K.O.Y.L.I

This party will meet the Cos. well back on the line of march and conduct their Cos. direct to their Billets, leaving the road clear for the Battalion following behind. There must be no checks

3. The Brigade Band will march in front of the Battalion.

4. The Corps Commander will be in front of the Mairie in GRAND PLACE, BAILLEUL on the right of line of march to watch the Brigade pass through. Compliments will be paid to all General Officers.

5. Water bottles and water carts will be filled before marching off.

6. On arrival at billets a "Marching in" State will be rendered to the Adjutant.

(Sgd.) T. Knox Shaw Captain

Issued at 6.30 p.m.

Copies 1 & 2. War Diary
Copy 3 O.C. "A" Co.
4 " "B"
5 " "C"
6 " "D"
7 Transport Officer
8. Quartermaster

S E C R E T. Copy No.......5

app. 16.

OPERATION ORDER No. 74.

by

BRIGADIER GENERAL H.S.L.Ravenshaw C.M.G.

Commanding 83rd Infantry Brigade.

Reference, HAZEBROUCK 5a. 26th September 1915.

1. The troops in 83rd Brigade area will march via VIEUX BERQUIN & NEUF BERQUIN to billets about MERVILLE today according to attached table.

2.(a) O.C. 84th Field Ambulance will detail two ambulances to follow in rear of Echelon B 1st Line Transport to pick up men unable to march.

(b) O.C. 2/King's Own Regt. will detail a rear-guard of one officer and twenty other ranks to march in rear of above two ambulances to collect all stragglers.

3. All Train waggons of 83rd Inf. Brigade will join No.2.Coy., A.S.C. by 5 A.M.

4.(a) Billeting parties will meet Staff Captain at Cross roads due W. of B in LA BRIANNE 3/4 mile N.E. MERVILLE at 8.30 A.M.

(b) 2/East Yorkshire Regt., will approach starting point by METEREN - OUTTERSTEENE road.

Issued at 3.30 A.M.

Copy No.1 War Diary
2 2/King's Own
3 2/East Yorks
4 1/K.O.Y.L.I.
5 1/York & Lancs
6 5/King's Own
7 3rd Bde R.F.A.
8 84th Field Ambulance
9 No.2.Coy, A.S.C.
10 3rd Bde Ammunition Column
11 Capt. Poake 2/King's Own
12 Lt. White
13 Staff Captain
14 Bde M.G.Officer
15 O.C. Signals.

R.C. Follett Major,
Brigade Major,
83rd Infantry Brigade.

STARTING POINT OUTTERSTEENE CROSS ROADS.

Order of March,

Brigade Headquarters	6 A.M.
1/K.O.Y.L.I.	6.1. A.M.
2/East Yorkshire Regt.	6.7. A.M.
1/York & Lancaster Regt.	6.13 A.M.
2/King's Own Regt.	6.19 A.M.
5/King's Own Regt.	6.25 A.M.
Brigade S.A.A. Reserve	6.29 A.M.
Echelon B. 1st Line Transport	6.30 A.M.
3rd Brigade R.F.A.	6.35 A.M.
3rd Brigade-Ammunition Column.	6.55 A.M.
84th Field Ambulance	7.3. A.M.
No.2.Coy, A.S.C.	7.7. A.M.

App 17

Operation Orders No. 27
By
Lieut Colonel G.E. Bayley, DSO
Commanding 1st Bn York & Lancaster Regt
Sunday, 26th Sept 1915

1. The Battn. will march to billets at MERVILLE.
Battn. Alarm Post - Starting point.
Time. 5-30 am
Order of march -
Signallers
"A" Coy
"B" "
"C" "
"D" "
Machine Gun & Stretcher Bearers

2. Two ambulances will be detailed to follow in rear to pick up men unable to march.

3. O.C. "D" Coy. will detail one officer and O.C. Cos will detail one NCO each to form rear party behind the Battn.

4. Major Robertson & O.C. Cos & Machine Gun Officer and two guides detailed by O.C. Transport will form a Billeting Party.
They will meet the Staff Captain at Cross Roads due W of B in

in LA BRIANNE 8/4 N. E. MERVILLE
at 8.30 am.

Ref. Map HAZEBROUCK. Shee 5.A.

T Knox Shaw Captain,
A/Adjutant, 1st York Lancaster Regt

App 18

SECRET. COPY No. 5

OPERATION ORDER No. 74 Continued
by
BRIGADIER GENERAL H.S.L.RAVENSHAW, C.M.G
Commanding 83rd Infantry Brigade
****

Sunday, 26th Sept. 1915.

1. Troops will resume the March as follows :-

Starting Point, Bridge over Canal, S.E., of ROBECQ on ROBECQ-BETHUNE ROAD.

Order of March :-

Brigade H.Q.,	1.59.p.m.
1st York & Lancs	2 p.m.
1st K.O.Y.L.I.	2.6.p.m.
2nd E.Yorks	2.12.p.m.
2nd King's Own	2.18.p.m.
5th King's own	2.24.p.m.
Bde S.A.A. Reserve	2.28.p.m.
Echelon B,	2.29.p.m.
3rd Bde R.F.A.	2.34.p.m.
3rd Bde Ammn.Col.	3.4.p.m.
84th F. Amb.	3.12.p.m.
2 Coy A.S.C.	3.16.p.m.

2. The 2/1 Northumbrian Field Coy will join the Column in rear of No. 2 Coy A.S.C., at T Roads Mt. BERNENCHON on the ROBECQ-BETHUNE Rd at 3.40.p.m.

RS Follett
Major.
Brigade Major, 83rd Bde.

Issued at 1 p.m.

Copy No. 1 War Diary.
2, 2nd King's Own.
3. 2nd E.Yorks.
4, 1st K.O.Y.L.I.
5, 1st York & Lancs
6, 5th King's Own
7, 3rd Bde R.F.A.
8, 84th F. Amb.
9. No. 2 Coy A.S.C.
10. 3rd Bde Ammn. Col.
11, Capt. Peake.
12. 2/1 Northumbrian Fld Coy. R.E.

Appendix 9

SECRET Copy No. 6

OPERATION ORDER No. 75
by
BRIGADIER GENERAL H.S.L.RAVENSHAW. C.M.G.
Commanding 83rd Infantry Brigade.

****

REF:-. HAZEBROUCK 5a. Sunday, 26th Sept. 1915.

1. All units will be held in readiness to move at one hour's notice.

2. Each unit will select an alarm post.

3. Place of assembly, to which all units will move on receipt of orders will be ROBECQ-BETHUNE Road, with head of column at Bridge over canal half a mile S.E., of ROBECQ. except 2/1 Northumbrian Field Coy R.E., who will remain on their alarm post until receipt of orders. Units in same order as laid down for this afternoon's march.

4. A mounted officer from 3rd Brigade R.F.A., 2/1 Northumbrian Field Coy. R.E., No. 2 Coy A.S.C., and 84th Field Ambulance will report in future to the Brigade Major at the starting point, prior to the commencement of any march. This officer will accompany the Brigade Head-quarters on the march so as to carry direct any orders that G.O.C., Column may issue.

5. All units in the Brigade area will send a mounted or cyclist orderly to Brigade as soon as they have arrived in billets or bivouacs. This orderly will remain at Brigade Headquarters until it moves: he must bring his own rations.

6. Brigade Headquarters ~~is~~ are in ROBECQ near the Church on the LILLERS Road.

R S Follett Major,
Brigade Major, 83rd Bde.

Issued at p.m.

Copy No. 1. War Diary.
2. 2nd King's Own.
3. 2nd E.Yorks.
4. 1st K.O.Y.L.I.
5. 1st York & Lancs.
6. 5th King's Own.
7. 3rd Bde R.F.A.
8. 84th F.Amb.
9. No. 2 Coy A.S.C.
10. Capt. Peake.
11. 2/1 Northumbrian Field Coy R.E.

Copy No 7 Operation Orders No: 28 9/120

by

Lieut Col. G.E. Bayley D.S.O.

Commanding 1st York & Lancaster Regt.

Sunday, 26th Sept. 1915.

Reference map - HAZEBROUCK, Sheet 5.a.

1. The Battn. will be held in readiness to move at 1 hours notice.

2. The Battalion alarm Post will be on the ROBECQ - BETHUNE Road extending from A to H.Q. Billets.

All Cos. will close up to A and fall in in the following order.

Signallers

A Coy

B

D

C

Machine Guns & Stretcher Bearers.

on the order to assemble

3. Bde. Hdqrs are in ROBECQ near the Church on the LILLERS Road.

~~Capt.~~ Knox Shaw Captain

A/Adjutant, 1st York & Lancaster Regt

Issued at 7.50 pm.

Copy No: 1 A Coy. Copy No 2 B" Copy 3 C

" 4 D " 5 [illegible]

" 7 & 8 War Diary " 9 M.G. Officer

a/p21

Copy No...5..

SECRET.

OPERATION ORDER No.76.
by
BRIGADIER GENERAL H.S.L.Ravenshaw C.M.G.
ooooooooooo
Commanding 83rd Infantry Brigade

Ref:- HAZEBROUCK 5a. 27th Sept. 1915

1. Today the Brigade will proceed by bus to BETHUNE & march from there to BEUVRY where it will halt for the night.

(b) All 1st line transport will march under Capt Peake 2/King's Own to BEUVRY.

2. Embussment stations in order of move:-

Brigade Headqrs.	On	ROBECQ-BETHUNE road
1/York & Lancaster R.		-do- -do-
1/K.O.Y.L.I.		-do- -do-
2/East Yorkshire R.	On	ROBECQ-ST VENANT Rd.
2/King's Own R.		-do- -do-
2/King's Own R.	On	ROBECQ-MERVILLE Rd.

Busses arrive ROBECQ 12 noon.
Battalions will be drawn up ready to embus 12.30 P.M.

3.(a) No extra ammunition will be issued.
(b) Machine gunners will go in busses.
(c) Machine guns travel with 1st line transport.

4. All officers chargers will be sent to field opposite Brigade Hqrs. by 11.15 a.m. & proceed under 2/Lt P.J.C.Simpson 1/K.O.Y.L.I. to GRAND PLACE, BETHUNE to await the arrival of the Brigade.

5. At 1.30 p.m. the Brigade S.A.A. reserve & the whole of 1st line transport will be formed up on ROBECQ-BETHUNE road with head of column at ~~[illegible]~~ Bridge 1/2 mile S.E. of ROBECQ. Order of march same as yesterday

5.Continued

yesterday afternoon. Route MT BERNENCHON - BETHUNE - BEAUVRY.

Issued at 10.20 A.M.

R I Follett Major,

Brigade Major,
83rd Infantry Brigade.

Copy No.1 War Diary
2 2/King's Own
3 2/East Yorks
4 1/K.O.Y.L.I
5 2/York & Lancs
6 5/King's Own
7 No.2.Coy, A.S.C.
8 Capt. Peake 2/King's Own.

app/22

Operation Orders No: 24.

By

Lieut. Colonel G.E. Bayley D.S.O.

Commanding 1st Bn York & Lancaster Regt

Monday, 27th Sept. 1915.

1. The Battn. will proceed by bus to BETHUNE and march from there to BEUVRY where it will halt for the night.

2. The Battn. will fall in at Alarm Post ready to march off at 12 noon.

Order of march –

Party for 1st Hdqs. Bus.
A Coy
B
C
D
M Gun Section.
Stretcher Bearers
Pioneers.

3. All 1st Line Transport will march under Capt Peake 3rd King's Own to BEUVRY

4. Officers Chargers will be sent to a field opposite Bde. Hdqrs. by 11.15 a.m. and proceed to Grand Place, BETHUNE to await the arrival

of the Brigade.

5. Marching in States & Casualty States will be rendered to the Adjutant on arrival at Billets.

T Knox Shaw Captain
A/Adjutant, 1st York & Lancaster Regt

Issued at 11.15 a.m.

Copy No: 1 & 2	War Diary	Copy No: 3	A Coy		
" " 4	B Coy	" 5	C "		
" " 6	D "	" 7	Q.M.		
" " 8	M.G. Officer	" 9	T.O.		

83rd Bde.
28th Div.

WAR
DIARY

Division left for Salonika November 1915.

1st YORK & LANCS

OCTOBER

1 9 1 5

On His Majesty's Service.

Instructions regarding War Diaries and Intelligence Summaries are contained in F. S. Regs., Part II. and the Staff Manual respectively. Title pages will be prepared in manuscript.

Army Form C. 2118.

WAR DIARY
or
INTELLIGENCE SUMMARY.
(Erase heading not required.) 8th Yorks Lancaster Rgt

Hour, Date, Place		Summary of Events and Information	Remarks and references to Appendices
VERMELLES Oct 1st	6am	The Battalion was relieved by the Northumberland Fusiliers and went to the LANCASHIRE TRENCHES. Here the Battn bivouaced all day until relieved by the South Staffordshire Rgt in the evening.	
	Noon	Casualties killed 1, wounded & missing 1.	
	9pm	Battn marched to ANNEQUIN. Difficulty was experienced in finding billets as 22nd Bde were occupying houses in our area. Headqrs did not get settled till 2.30 am.	
Oct 2nd ANNEQUIN.		Cleaned up in billets. Total strength of Battn including Quartermaster & M.O was Officers 14, other Ranks 800.	
		The Battn was to be ready to move at 1 hours notice	
	10.20pm	Bde wire 53rd Bde relieve 84th Bde on night 3rd-4th inst. Reconnoitring Officers will be prepared to leave billets 11am on the 3rd. These officers will await the arrival of their Batt at BARTS	
Oct 3rd	8am	Bde wire Your Battn will march to Clarks Keep at 11am.	
	9.45am	Battn operation order no 30	appendix 1
	10am	Bde wire Your Battn will march to CLARKS KEEP at 1pm	
	12noon	casualties killed 1 wounded 6	
	1pm	The Battn marched off and on arriving at CLARKS KEEP found the road blocked by 2nd East Yorks. The C.O ordered the Battn to move along road till clear of KEEP and sit down while he went to reconnoitre BARTS TRENCH.	

(9 29 6) W 4141—463 100,000 9/14 H W V Forms/C. 2118/10

Instructions regarding War Diaries and Intelligence Summaries are contained in F. S. Regs., Part II. and the Staff Manual respectively. Title pages will be prepared in manuscript.

WAR DIARY
or
INTELLIGENCE SUMMARY.
(Erase heading not required.) 1st York & Lancaster Rgt

Army Form C. 2118.

Hour, Date, Place	Summary of Events and Information	Remarks and references to Appendices
Oct 3rd	After tea the Battn moved up to the Reserve Trench.	
Oct 4th HQ in Reserve Trench 1.45am	Copy of instructions given to 2nd East Yorks Rgt and 1st KOYLI with reference to the attack to be launched at 4.45 am	Appendix 2
3.15am	The Battn moved up into the Support Trenches C & D Coys on the right and A & B on the left of CENTRAL BOYAU.	
4.15am	There was no appreciable artillery bombardment.	
4.45am	The Germans clearly knew the attack was coming off, as they opened fire with Machine Guns before attack started. Neither Battn was able to get into the Redoubt.	
12 noon	Casualties wounded two	
	B Coy went to support the KOYLI and were placed in a Reserve trench in centre of their line.	
5 pm	C Coy was sent to relieve a Company of the 2nd Kings Own which were holding the fire trench on right of position occupied by KOYLI. This Coy of 2nd Kings Own had been sent to support the Coy of KOYLI which had lost heavily in the attack.	
Oct 5th	Situation was quiet all day in front line. Enemy shelled the CENTRAL BOYAU and Reserve Trench practically all day.	
12 noon	Casualty report wounded 5	

Instructions regarding War Diaries and Intelligence Summaries are contained in F. S. Regs., Part II. and the Staff Manual respectively. Title pages will be prepared in manuscript.

WAR DIARY
or
INTELLIGENCE SUMMARY.

(*Erase heading not required.*) 1st 4th/5th? Lancashire Regt

Army Form C. 2118.

Hour, Date, Place		Summary of Events and Information	Remarks and references to Appendices
Oct 5th	5 pm	Informed that 2/ Guards Brigade would relieve 83rd Bde	Appendix 3
	6 30 pm	Batt^n Operation Order no 31	4
		Owing to the congestion due to narrow communication trenches the relief was not over till 6 am. The Companies marched independently to ANNEQUIN	
Oct 6th ANNEQUIN	7.30 am	Headquarters reached billets at ANNEQUIN.	
	9 am	Brigade Operation Order no 77	Appendix 5
	10 30 am	Batt^n " " no 31	" 6
	12 noon	Casualty return wounded one	
	2 30 pm	The Batt^n marched to GONNEHEM after passing through BETHUNE an hours halt was made for tea. The Batt^n reached GONNEHEM at dusk (marching in strength 707), and was billeted in farms.	
Oct 7th GONNEHEM		Rested & cleaned up in billets. Lt WH Butler joined & took Command of "C" Coy	
Oct 8th	"	Batt^n commenced a system of training, particular attention being paid to bomb throwers: 50% of Batt^n being trained in bombs. 2nd Lt A F. HUGHES & 2nd Lt T W. MOORE joined from 3rd S. Lancs Rgt.	
Oct 9th	"	The Corps Commander (Gen Gough) inspected the Companies training. 2nd Lt F H CLAYDON joined from 10th S. Lancs Rgt.	
Oct 10th	"	Church Parade in morning. Two Coy dug trenches for bomb practice in afternoon	
Oct 11th	"	Batt^n practised attacking over trenches. Bombers practised working down C.T.s & bombing traverses, over ground previous prepared for practical demonstrations.	

(9 29 6) W 4141—463 100,000 9/14 H W V Forms/C. 2118/10

Instructions regarding War Diaries and Intelligence Summaries are contained in F. S. Regs., Part II. and the Staff Manual respectively. Title pages will be prepared in manuscript.

Army Form C. 2118.

WAR DIARY
or
INTELLIGENCE SUMMARY.
(Erase heading not required.) 1st York & Lancaster Rgt

Hour, Date, Place		Summary of Events and Information	Remarks and references to Appendices
Oct 12th GONNEHEM		Batt^n Route march & Training	
Oct 13th "	10 am	Brigade inspection by Gen Briggs G.O.C. 28th Division.	
		Afterwards the whole Batt^n practising trench warfare.	
Oct 14th "		2nd Lt Halcomb left Batt^n on sick leave. 2nd Lt Green joined	
		Batt^n from 2nd Middlesex Rgt.	
Oct 15th "		Route march in morning	
	3.30pm	Brigade operation order no 78	appendix 7
	4.20pm	Batt^n marched to BEUVRY and occupied billets previously	
		used by Bedford Rgt, arriving at 7.30pm	
		2nd Lt Trethowan & 2nd Lt Coppock joined from 11th Batt^n	
		2nd Lt Gibson joined from 3rd Batt^n. 2nd Lt Essex reported	
		sick and went to hospital	
Oct 16th BEUVRY	10.15am	C.O Coy Cmdrs Transport officer & adj. rode to Cambrin	
		to reconnoitre reserve trenches held by 2nd Warwicks	
	3pm	Brigade operation order no 79	appendix 8
	8.30pm	Batt^n " " no 31	appendix 9
		The following officers joined from 3rd Batt^n	
		Lt Angus, Lt Bedford, 2nd Lt Stedman	
Oct 17th	11.30am	Batt^n left BEUVRY and marched to HARLEY ST. CAMBRIN.	
		The 2nd Warwickshire Rgt was relieved by 12.30pm	
		Capt Hartley (Indian Cavalry) joined & took over duties of Senior Major	
Oct 18th		G.O.C 28th Division visited Batt^n in morning	
	12 noon	Casualties O.R one wounded.	

Instructions regarding War Diaries and Intelligence Summaries are contained in F. S. Regs., Part II. and the Staff Manual respectively. Title pages will be prepared in manuscript.

WAR DIARY
or
INTELLIGENCE SUMMARY.
(Erase heading not required.) 1st York & Lancaster Rgt

Army Form C. 2118.

Hour, Date, Place		Summary of Events and Information	Remarks and references to Appendices
Oct 19 VARLEY ST.		Visited by Gen Gough Corps Commander.	
Oct 20th "	2pm	Bde operation order no 80	Appendix 10
	9pm	Battn " " no 32	" 11
Oct 21st		The following honours were awarded for distinguished conduct during action on Sept 29th in BIG WILLIE.	
		2nd Lt R. A Bates Military Cross.	
		8336 Sgt J Brown, 15271 Pte A Street, 18271 Pte J Haw 18165 Pte T Jones, 17531 Cpl J. Atkinson. D.C.M.s	
	2pm	The Battn was relieved by 1st Kings Rgt 6th Bde and marched back to billets at Gonnehem.	
		Casualty report, O.R. 3 wounded by shell.	
Oct 22nd GONNEHEM		Preparation for move, [illegible] Smoke Helmets etc.	
Oct 23rd		Brigade order No 31	Appendix 12
		Battn order No 33	" 13
Oct 24th	5 am	"C" Coy and 1st Transport started for the Station, so as to be entrained when the rest of the Battn arrived.	
	7 am	Rest of Battn marched to [illegible] ... 24 at 9.30 am	
	4pm	The first stop was at L[illegible]	
		[illegible]	
25th TRAIN	4am	Arrived at VILLENEUVE [illegible]	
		Men served with tea [illegible]	
	[illegible]	Changed engines at [illegible]	

(9 29 6) W4141—463 100,000 9/14 H W V Forms/C. 2118/10

Instructions regarding War Diaries and Intelligence Summaries are contained in F. S. Regs., Part II. and the Staff Manual respectively. Title pages will be prepared in manuscript.

Army Form C. 2118.

WAR DIARY
or
INTELLIGENCE SUMMARY.
(*Erase heading not required.*) 1st York + Lancaster Rgt

Hour, Date, Place			Summary of Events and Information	Remarks and references to Appendices
24th oct	Train	7.30pm	Halted at MACON. Men had tea and were allowed to go to Buffet. Officers dined at buffet. Left at 8.30pm	
25th	"	9am	Halted at PIERRELATTE, where men had tea.	
		5pm	Arrived at MARSEILLES, about six hours late: due to an accident on line to a train in front of ours. Shunted back to another station where Batt. detained.	
		7pm	Marched away from station to Quay. Streets crowded with applauding populace	
		8½pm	Reached S. S BORNU and embarked. The horses and transport men were left behind under Lt Walker to come on afterwards. All the limbers were on board by 2 am	
26th	S S BORNU	11am	After shipping limbers of East Surrey Rgt. the boat left the harbour. Encountered rough sea in Gulf of Lyons. Some officers and many men incapacitated.	
27th		10am	Went round the ship with Captain. Men cheering up. Parties detailed for each boat. Alarm stations fixed. Coy on duty found eleven sentries and a platoon as a submarine guard.	
		9pm	Lights out	
			Wet day. Rounds at 10 am	

(9 29 6) W 4141—463 100,000 9/14 H W V Forms/C. 2118/10

Instructions regarding War Diaries and Intelligence Summaries are contained in F. S. Regs., Part II. and the Staff Manual respectively. Title pages will be prepared in manuscript.

WAR DIARY
or
INTELLIGENCE SUMMARY.

(Erase heading not required.) 1st York & Lancaster Regt

Army Form C. 2118.

Hour, Date, Place	Summary of Events and Information	Remarks and references to Appendices
Oct 29th S.S BORNU	Fine weather. Half hour physical exercise for men each day. Practised a fire alarm at 5 pm	
Oct 30th	Rigged up a bath for men. Getting much warmer	
Oct 31st	Usual routine. 3 men sick with diarrhoea.	
Nov 1st	After rounds practised standing to in boat parties	

Operation Order No. 30 Appendix 1.

By

Lieut Col G.E. Bayley, DSO

Commanding 1st Bn York & Lancaster Regt.

Sunday. 3rd October 1915

1. The Battn. will fall in on the Alarm Post ready to march to CLARKS KEEP, VERMELLE.
Starting Point – Battn. Hdqrs
Time 11. a.m.
Order of march – Signallers, A Coy, B Coy, C Coy, D Coy, M Guns, Pioneers, Stretcher Bearers, 1st Line Transport.

2. Officers Kits must be stacked at the Transport Lines at once.

T Knox Shaw Captain
A/Adjutant, 1st York & Lancaster Regt

Issued at 9.45 am.

Copy 1 & 2	War Diary	Copy 3	O.C. A Coy
" 4	O.C. B Coy	" 5	" C "
" 6	" D "	" 7	" M Guns
" 8	Quartermaster	" 9	Transport "

MESSAGES AND SIGNALS. No. of Message

Prefix ... Code ... m.	Words	Charge	This message is on a/c of:	Recd. at ... m.
Office of Origin and Service Instructions.	Sent		... Service.	Date
	At ... m.			From 4/2
	To			By
	By		(Signature of "Franking Officer.")	

TO 1/York & Lancaster Regt.

Sender's Number.	Day of Month	In reply to Number	AAA
* B.M. 644	4		

at 4-45 a.m. 4th Oct. 15 2/East
Yorks Regt and two coys
1/KOYLI with one coy 2/King's
Own Regt. attached will assault
HOHENZOLLERN REDOUBT AAA
First objective western face of
redoubt second objective THE
CHORD AAA The 4-15 a.m. the
[illegible] will be [illegible] heavily until
4-45 a.m. when they will lift
on to enemy communication
trenches AAA When the [illegible]
commences the first and second
lines of platoons will get
over the parapet advance
towards the enemy parapet and
lie down AAA Absolute silence

From			
Place			
Time			

The above may be forwarded as now corrected. (Z)

Censor. Signature of Addressor or person authorised t

* This line should be erased if not required.

(774-5) —McC. & Co. Ltd., London.— W 1789/1402. 150,000. 8/15. Forms C 2121/10.

"A" Form. Army Form C. 2121.

MESSAGES AND SIGNALS.

No. of Message ______

Prefix ____ Code ____ m. Office of Origin and Service Instructions.	Words	Charge	This message is on a/c of: ______ Service. (Signature of "Franking Officer.")	Recd. at ____ m.
	Sent At ____ m. To ____ By ____			Date ____ From ____ By ____

TO: 2/East Yorks Regt
1/K O Y L I

Sender's Number.	Day of Month	In reply to Number	AAA
* BM 644	4		

will be maintained until the enemy trench is reached AAA The assault of the CHORD will be undertaken without delay once the REDOUBT has been gained AAA All communication trenches leading from captured works towards the enemy will be filled in and blocked AAA Two sections RE will follow behind last platoons and dig communication trenches back from captured work to old British line AAA Signal Officer 83rd Brigade will arrange to place a telephone on western face of REDOUBT directly

From
Place
Time

The above may be forwarded as now corrected.

Censor.

(Z)

Signature of Addressor or person authorised to telegraph i[n his name]

* This line should be erased if not required.

(774-5) —McC. & Co. Ltd., London.— W 1789/1402. 150,000 8/15. Forms C 2121/10.

MESSAGES AND SIGNALS. No. of Message ....

Prefix ...... Code ...... m. Office of Origin and Service Instructions.	Words / Charge	This message is on a/c of: .... Service. (Signature of "Franking Officer.")	Recd. at ...... m.
	Sent At ...... m. To ...... By		Date ...... From ...... By ......

TO { 2/ East Yorks Regt
1/ K O Y L I

Sender's Number.	Day of Month	In reply to Number	AAA
* B M 44	4		

It is taken AAA 1/ York & Lancaster Regt. will move up to hold the front British line as it is vacated by 2/ East Yorks and 1/ K O Y L I. AAA Suffolk Regt will be in support trenches behind 1/ York and Lancs Regt AAA 2/ R Lancs Regt will be at CENTRAL KEEP in reserve.

From 83 Brigade
Place
Time 1-45 pm

The above may be forwarded as now corrected. (Z)

.... *Censor.* Signature of Addressor or person authorised to telegraph in his name. [illegible signature]

* This line should be erased if not required.

(774-5) —McC. & Co. Ltd., London.— W 1780/1402. 150,000. 8/15. Forms C 2121/10.

B.M. 2
2
Copy 3

1 – 21 Guards Brigade will relieve 83rd Brigade tonight in all trenches according to attached table –

2 – On relief battalions will march to NORTH ANNEQUIN; ~~company billeting~~ guides will meet them there & conduct them to their billets – Companies may march independently –

3 – Officers Comdg. battalions 83rd Brigade will command in their own sectors until relief is complete – Completion of relief to be wired to Brigade Hqrs –

4 –

R. Hollett Major

5 Sept 15 – Brigade Major 83rd Brigade

Copy No 1 – [illegible] 3 / K.O.Y.L.I.

[illegible] 4 [illegible]

[illegible] [illegible]

TABLE of RELIEFS.

1. 3/ Grenadier Guards relieve 2/King's Own Regt. in BIG WILLIE.

2 1/ Scots Guards will relieve 5/King's Own Regt and 1 coy 2/East Yorks Regt. from HULLUCK ALLEY to RIGHT BOYAU (exclusive).

3 2/ Irish Guards relieve 3 coys 2/ East Yorks Regt + 1 co. 1/ York + Lancs Regt. from RIGHT BOYAU to LEFT BOYAU (both inclusive)

4 1/ Coldstream Guards relieve 1/KOYLI from LEFT BOYAU (exclusive) to VERMELLES - AUCHY road (inclusive)

5 Guards Pioneer Battalion relieve Middlesex Regt in RESERVE TRENCH.

R. S. Follett
Major
Brigade Major
83rd Inf Brigade

5 Sept '15.

App 4

Operation Order No 31
By Lt Col. G. E. Bayley D.S.O
Cmdg 1st York & Lancaster Regt
Tuesday October 5th 1915

1. 2nd Guards Brigade will relieve 83rd Brigade in all trenches tonight

2. The Irish Guards will relieve "C" Coy: The Coldstream Guards "B" Coy. On completion of these reliefs. O.C. Coys will at once report by orderly to Batt^n H.Q.

3. The O.C. "D" & "A" Coys will be informed by orderly from Batt^n HQ when they can move as no batt^n will be going into their trenches.

4. Coy will march independently under their own Coy Cmdrs to NORTH ANNEQUIN where guides will meet & conduct them to their billets.

117

5. The M. Guns in front line as soon as relieved will rendezvous at the DUMP and march back with the transport

6. Officers chargers will meet them at CLARK'S KEEP

7. The March will be continued at 12 noon tomorrow. Coy Cmdrs will arrange for dinners before the start

8. There will be a halt for tea during the march.

8. The O.C transport will see that baggage wagons accompany the Batt^n on the march.

9. Transport officer will make the usual arrangements for officers kits

T Knox Shaw Capt
a/Adjutant
1st Y&L Regt

Issued at
6.30pm

106

SECRET   COPY No. 5

OPERATION ORDER No. 77   App 5

by

BRIGADIER GENERAL H.S.L.RAVENSHAW. C.M.G.
Commanding 83rd Infantry Brigade.

****

Ref. BETHUNE combined sheet.   Wednesday, 6th October, 1918.

1. The Brigade will march today independently by Battalions to billets in area Mt.BERNENCHON - GONNEHEM.

2. Starting point :- Cross Roads F.29.b.
Route :- SEUVRY-BETHUNE-OBLINGHEM-GONNEHEM.
Order of March :-

	Time
1st K.O.Y.L.I.	12 noon.
2nd East Yorks	1 P.M.
1st York & Lancs	1.30.p.m.
5th King's Own	2 p.m.
2nd King's Own	2.30.p.m.
3rd Middlesex Regt.	3 p.m.

3. a. 1st Line Transport and baggage wagons will accompany battalions.
b. Two ambulances will march in rear of each Battalion.
c. An Officer from each Battalion will report to Lt.Colman, Surrey Yeomanry at SKATING RINK. BETHUNE, to be shown place WEST of BETHUNE where Battalions will halt for Tea.
d. Billetting parties will meet Staff Captain at forked roads, GONNEHEM W.13.a.8.5., at 12 noon

4. Strict march discipline will be maintained.

5. Brigade Headquarters leave ANNEQUIN 2.15.p.m.

R B S Follett Major
B.M. 83rd Bde

Copy No. 1

Operation Orders No: 31

By

Lieut Colonel G.E. Bayley, D.S.O.

Commanding 1st Bn York & Lancaster Regt.

Wednesday, 6th October 1915

1. The Battn. will march to Billets in area MT BERNENCHON - GONNEHEM today.
Starting point - Battn Headquarters.
Time - 1-30 pm In position 1.25 pm.
Route - BEUVRY - BETHUNE - OBLINGHEM - GONNEHEM
Order of march - Signallers - C Coy, A Coy, B Coy D Coy M. Gun Section, Stretcher Bearers, 1st Line Transport and Baggage Wagons

2. The Battn. will halt WEST of BETHUNE for tea

3. Officers Kits will be collected at 11-30 am.

4. Lieut. L.A.K. Halcomb will report to Lieut Colman, Surrey Yeomanry at the SKATING RINK, BETHUNE and will be shown a place where the Battn will halt for tea

5. O.C. Cos. will detail 1 N.C.O. each and O.C. D Coy 1 officer to form a Rear Party which will march in rear of the Transport

T Knox Shaw Captain,
A/Adjutant, 1st York & Lancaster Regt.

Copies 1 + 2 War Diary Copy 3 O.C. A Coy
Copy 4 O.C. B Coy " 5 " C "
" 6 " D " " 7 " M. Gun
" 8 Transport Officer.

Appendix 7

S E C R E T.　　　　　　　　　　　　　　　　Copy No. 5

Operation Order No.7[illegible].

by

Brigadier General H.S.L.Ravenshaw C.M.G.
Commanding 83rd Infantry Brigade.

Reference, BETHUNE (Combined sheet) 1/40,000.　　　　　　15th October 1915.

1. The Brigade will march to Billetting area at 4 p.m.

2. Order of March:-

Brigade Headquarters	4 p.m.
2/King's Own Regt.	4.5 p.m.
1/K.O.Y.L.I.	4.10 p.m.
1/York & Lancaster R.	4.20 p.m.
5/King's Own Regt.	4.29 p.m.
~~84th Field Ambulance~~	~~4.37 p.m.~~

Starting point Forked roads V.23.b.9.9.

2/East Yorkshire Regt. will march independently via OBLINGHEM - BETHUNE to billets in ESSARS. Starting at 4.40 p.m.

3. The Brigade will be billetted as follows:-

2/King's Own Regt	LE PREOL
1/K.O.Y.L.I.	LE QUESNOY
1/York & Lancaster R.	BEUVRY
5/King's Own Regt.	FERME du ROI
2/East Yorkshire Regt.	ESSARS
~~84th Field Ambulance~~	~~BEUVRY~~

4. Guides from 9th Division will meet units at Forked roads F.8.b.8.7. to guide them to their billets. Guide will meet 5/King's Own at Forked roads E.11.b.5.9.

5. Brigade Headquarters will be at BEUVRY.

Issued at 　 p.m.

Copy no.1 War Diary
2 2/King's Own
3 2/East Yorks
4 1/K.O.Y.L.I.
5 1/York & Lancs
6 5/King's Own
7 84th Field Ambulance.

Major.
Brigade Major,
83rd Infantry Brigade.

B. A. C. S.

Four [illegible] on B Coy [illegible]

4-10-

Coy [illegible] closed up to B Coy by 4-10

Cartridges left in lines

Cyclist Orderly.

Appendix 8

SECRET. OPERATION ORDERS NO, 79 Copy No.....8

by

Brigadier General H.S.L.Ravenshaw, C.M.G.

Commanding 83rd Infantry Brigade,

Reference BETHUNE Combined Sheet, 1/40,000. 16th October, 1915.

1. The 83rd Brigade will relieve the 22nd Brigade tomorrow.

2. 1/K.O.Y.L.I. will relieve the 2/Queens and take over from THE LANE to HANOVER STREET exclusive.

2/King's Own will relieve the Welsh Fusiliers and take over from HANOVER STREET inclusive to CANAL.

3 1st York & Lancaster will relieve the 2/Warwicks and be in Reserve in HARLEY STREET.

2/East Yorks will move to LE PREOL, taking over billets from S.Staffords,

5/King's Own will move to LE PREOL, taking over billets now occupied by the 2/King's Own.

3. Units will march at the following times :- (~~by platoons.~~)

1/K.O.Y.L.I.	9,30 a.m.	guides at HARLEY STREET	11 a.m. } By platoons
2/King's Own	10.30 "	" " " "	11.30 a.m. }
1/York & L.	11.30 "	" " " "	12.15 p.m. }
2/East Yorks	10 a.m.	take over billets at	11 a.m.
5/King's Own	10.30a.m.	" " " "	11. 30 a.m.

4. 1/ K.O.Y.L.I. will find the Garrison for STAFFORD REDOUBT.

5. 1/York & Lancaster Regt. will place Machine Guns
Two in PONT FIXE
Onr in THE BULGE
One on Canal Bank, to sweep the front of the Brigade on the left.

6. The 34th Brigade R.F.A. will be covering the front of the Section.

7. 1st Line Transport of Bde. Hdqrs., 2/King's Own, 1/K.O.Y.L.I. and 1 /Y.& Lancaster Regts. will be parked about F.23 b. Brigade Transport Officer will select ground.
1st Line Transport 2/E.Yorks. & 5/ King's Own will remain with Battalions at LE PREOL.

8. Brigade Headquarters will move at 11 a.m. to CAMBRIN,A.19.d.6.3

Issued at 3 p.m.

Copy No.1 War Diary
2 2/East Yorks
3 2/King's Own
4 1/K.O.Y.L.I.
5 1/York & Lancaster R.
6 5/King's Own
7 28th Division
8 22nd Brigade
9 No.2 Coy.A.S.C.
10 84th Field Ambulance
11 C.O.Signals 83rd Bde
12 M.G.Officer 83rd Bde

[signature] Capt
for Major
Brigade Major
83rd Infantry Brigade.

Copy No: 1. Operation Orders No: 31. app 9.

By

Lieut. Colonel G.E. Bayley, D.S.O.

Commanding 1st Bn. York & Lancaster Regt.

Saturday, 16th October 1915.

1. The 83rd Bde. will relieve the 22nd Bde. tomorrow.

2. The 1st York & Lancaster Regt. will relieve the 2nd Warwickshire Regt. and be in reserve in HARLEY STREET.

3. Starting Point - Cross Roads South of Bde. HdQrs.
Time. 11-30 am
Order of march. Signallers, Pioneers, A B C & D Cos. Machine Guns & Stretcher Bearers.

4. Dennets will be issued in HARLEY STREET after taking over.

5 A limber will be provided for officers trench kits which must be stacked in the Square, BEUVRY by 10 am. except "D" Coy which will be collected by the limber.

6. Blankets will be collected and stacked by Cos. in the Square by 10 am.

7. Machine Guns will be placed as follows:-
2 in PONT FIXE
1 in THE BULGE.
1 on Canal Bank to sweep the front of the Bde. on left.

8. The 1st Line Transport will be parked about T.23.c. BETHUNE Combined Sheet.

9. O.C. Coys. will report to Battalion on completion of relief.

10. O.C. Cos. will detail 1 N.C.O. each and the O.C. "C" Coy. 1 officer to form a rear party which will march in rear of the Bn.

L. Halcourt. Lieut.
A/ Adjutant, 1st Bn York & Lancaster Regt.

Issued at 8-30 pm.

Copies	1 & 2	War Diary
Copy	3	O.C. "A" Coy
"	4	" B
"	5	" C
"	6	" D
"	7	Transport Officer
"	8	Quartermaster
"	9	M Gun Sergt.
"	10	Headquarters Coy.

appendix 10

S E C R E T. Copy No. 5

83rd BRIGADE OPERATION ORDER No.80.

Reference BETHUNE Combined Sheet 1/40,000.

October 20th 1915.

1. The 83rd Infantry Brigade will be relieved by the 6th Inf. Brigade on October 21st.

2. The reliefs will be carried out in accordance with the accompanying table.

3. All trench stores and bombs will be handed over to the 6th Infantry Brigade and all Programme of work proposed and in hand.

4. The relief of the machine guns will be carried out in accordance with attached table. Arrangements will be made by Battalion Machine Gun Officers. Guides to be at HARLEY STREET at 8.30 a.m.

5. The 62nd Trench Mortar Battery will remain with the 6th Brigade.

6. The 2/1 Field Coy. R.E. will be relieved by the 11th Field Coy. R.E. and will move to the 83rd Infantry Brigade Area.

7. On relief units will march independantly to their destinations which will be detailed later. Movements by companies.

8. Completion of relief and arrival of battalions at their destination will be reported to Brigade Headquarters.

9. The G.O.C. 83rd Brigade will remain in Command until relief is completed.

10. All transport will be prepared to move to new area tomorrow morning. Orders will be issued later.

Issued at 1.15 p.m.

Copy No.1 War Diary
2 2/King's Own
3 2/East Yorks
4 1/K.O.Y.L.I.
5 1/York & Lancas
6 5/King's Own
7 6th Inf. Bde.
8 28th Divn.
9 No.2 Coy. A.S.C.
10 2/1 Field Coy.R.E.
11 84th Field Ambulance
12 62nd Trench M. Batty.
13 Staff Capt. 83rd Bde
14 O.C. Signals83rd Bde

[signature]
Captain
for Brigade Major
83rd Infantry Brigade.

UNIT	LINE	RELIEVED BY	GARRISON IN AREA	GUIDES TO BE IN HARLEY ST.
1/K.O.Y.L.I.	From THE LANE to RIDLEY WALK inclusive	5/King's Liverpool R.	PARK LANE Redoubt STAFFORD REDOUBT	10 a.m.
1/K.O.Y.L.I.	From RIDLEY WALK exclusive to HANOVER ST. exclusive	2/South Staffords R.	BRICKSTACKS KEEP	11 a.m.
2/King's Own R.	From HANOVER ST. inclusive to CANAL	2/South Staffords R.	LOVERS Redoubt CABBAGE PATCH Redoubt.	11 a.m.
1/York & Lanca'r R.	Support Area	1/King's Regt.	CUINCHY S.P. CAMBRIN S.P. PONT FIXE	12 Noon.
2 Platoons 1/York & Lancaster Regt.	BRADDELL POINT	5/King's Liverpool		10 a.m.

MACHINE GUNS WILL BE RELIEVED AS FOLLOWS.

P O S I T I O N	R E L I E V E D B Y
Railway Embankment PORTLAND PLACE B BRICKSTACKS.	South Staffords
GUN STREET WATERLOO PLACE SEYMOUR STREET OXFORD STREET	5/ Liverpools
CABBAGE PATCH IKEY TRENCH LOVERS REDOUBT.	1/King's Regt.
CUINCHY Support Point Machine Gun House STAFFORD REDOUBT BRADDELL REDOUBT	1/Herts Regt.

S E C R E T. Copy No...5.....

AFTER OPERATION ORDER No.80 83rd Brigade.

Reference, BETHUNE combined sheet. 1/40,000 20th October 1915.

1. On relief tomorrow units will march by BEUVRY - BETHUNE - OBLINGHEM to the same billetting areas they occupied when the Brigade were at GONNEHEM. Except that the 2/East Yorkshire Regt. with 1st Line transport will march at 10 a.m. by LE QUESNOY - BETHUNE-& OBLINGHEM to billets in LENGLET V.22.a.
5/King's Own Regt. will await further orders.

2. The 1st Line transport of the Brigade less cookers and less transport of 2/East Yorks & 5/King's Own will march under the Brigade Transport Officer to the billetting area of the Brigade, and proceed to same fields as before, leaving ANNEQUIN at 10.30 a.m.

3. 2/King's Own 1/K.O.Y.L.I. 1/York & Lancs will march to about F.13 West of BEUVRY by Companies and from there by Battalions independantly.

4. 2/1 Northumbrian Field Co.R.E. will march to billets in farm V.18.b.9.3. at 9 a.m.

5. 84th Field Ambulance will occupy same billets as before in GONNEHEM.

Issued at 5.45 P.M.

Copy No.1 War Diary
2 2/King's Own
3 2/East Yorks
4 1/K.O.Y.L.I.
5 1/York & Lancs
6 5/King's Own
7 6th Brigade
8 28th Divn.
9 84th Field Ambulance
10 2/1 Northumbrian Fd.Co.R.E.
11 No.2.Coy.A.S.C.

12 62nd Trench M. Batty
13 O.C. Signals 83rd Bde
14 Staff Capt. 83rd Bde.

[signature]
Captain,
for Brigade Major,
83rd Infantry Brigade.

Copy No 2 Operation Orders No 82 Appx 11

By

Lieut Colonel P.E. Bayley, D.S.O

Commanding 1st Bn York Lancaster Regt

Wednesday, 20th October 1915.

---

1. The 83rd Brigade will be relieved by the 6th Infty Bde on 21st October. The relief will be carried out in accordance with attached Schedule.

2. On relief Cos. will march independently under Coy Commanders to Billets previously occupied in GONNEHEM.

Route - BEUVRY - BETHUNE - VBLINGHEM.

When the Machine Guns of relieving Brigade are in position the Machine Gun Officer will be informed and will collect his Guns and Teams at Battn. Hdqrs where the limbers will be found.

3. Coy QMSgts will proceed independently at 9 am to take over Billets.

4. All officers Kits must be at Battn Hdqrs by 9 am where they will be collected by the Transport Officer.

5. The 1st Line Transport (including pack animals) less cookers and mess cart will march under the Brigade Transport Officer leaving ANNEQUIN at 10.30 am

The Cookers will go with their Cos.

6. All trench stores and bombs will be handed over to the relieving Regiments and all programmes of work proposed and in hand

7. Completion of reliefs will be reported to Bn Hdqrs

8. Officers chargers will be at Bn Hdqrs at the following hours -

C Coy at 10 am

Machine Gun Officers at 11 am

Remainder of Bn at 1 pm

9. Each Coy will detail its own Rear Party.

10. Marching in States will be rendered to the Adjutant on arrival at Billets.

T Knox Shaw Captain,

A/Adjutant, 1st Bn York Lancaster Regt

Copies 1 & 2 War Diary. Copy 3 OC A Coy

Copy 4 OC B Coy 5 C

6 D 7 M Gun Section

8 Quartermaster 9 Transport Officer

10 Hdqrs. Coy.

Schedule of Reliefs

Coy	Position	Relieved by	Guides to be at HARLEY ST. by	Remarks.
A Coy	QUINCHY POINT. HARLEY ST.	1st Kings Regt	12 noon	
B Coy	PONT FIXE	1st Kings Regt	12 noon.	
C Coy	BRADDELL POINT 2 platoons.	5th Kings Regt.	10 a.m.	When BRADDELL POINT is relieved the whole Coy will move to Billets.
	HARLEY ST. 2 platoons.	1st Kings Regt		
D Coy	CAMBRIN SP. TOUBIERES TRAMWAY HARLEY ST.	1st Kings Regt	12 noon.	

SECRET. Copy No.

83RD Brigade Operation Order No 81. App 12

Reference BETHUNE 21st Oct. 1915.
Combined Sheets. 1/40.000.

1. The Brigade will entrain on the 22nd and 23RD at FOUQUEREUIL STATION according to details issued by 28th Division.

2. Units will march in accordance with table of times and train already issued, by the following Route GONNEHEM - CHOCQUES cross roads D.6.B.0.8 - FOUQUEREUIL

3 Bde Headquarters will close at GONNEHEM at 2.30 PM 22nd inst.

Issued at M.

[signature] Captain.
Brigade Major.
21st Oct 1915. 83rd Inf Brigade

App 13

Coy No 1

OPERATION ORDERS No 33

by

Lieut Colonel G. E. Bayley. D.S.O.

Commanding 1st Bn York & Lancaster Regt.

Friday 22nd October 1915

(1) The Battalion will entrain at 9.35 AM on the 23rd inst at FOUQUEREUIL STATION.

(2) The Battalion will march via CHOCQUES to FOUQUEREUIL.
Starting Point – Fork Roads by Adqr Coy. Billet.
C Coy. and the Transport will pass the starting Point at 5 AM.
The remainder of the Battalion:–
Order of March:– Signallers, Pioneers, Orderlies, B Coy.
A Coy, D Coy, Machine Gunners and Stretcher Bearers.
TIME — 7 AM.

(3) O.C. "C" Coy and Transport will arrange to have breakfasts for the men cooked in cookers, ready to be served at the Station.
For the remainder of the men O.C. Coys will arrange to have bacon cooked overnight and make their own arrangements for tea tomorrow morning.

(4) All Officers Kits must be packed ready to be collected by the Transport Officer by 4 AM.

(5) One blanket per man will be drawn at the Station and will not be handed in at Point of detrainment.
Straw for trucks will be available at the entraining Station and will be issued under Battalion arrangements.

(6) Immediately on arrival of the Battalion at the Station parties of 40, including the N.C.O. in charge will be detailed by Coy Commanders.

(7) The first halting place for tea and water is at LONGUEAU.

8 The following arrangements are made for rations for the journey.

Rations for the 23rd inst will be issued today.

For the 24th inst they will be drawn at the Station.

On 25th inst Iron Rations now in possession will be consumed (Iron Rations to replace these will be drawn at the Station.)

Cos will be informed later as to the issue of rations.

9 No NCO or man may leave the train without orders.

10 OC Cos & M Gun Section will render Marching out States to Orderly Room by 10pm tonight.

T Brown Shaw Captain
Adjutant 1st Bn York & Lancaster Regt

Issued at pm

Copies 1 & 2 War Diary
3 OC A Coy
4 B
5 C
6 D
7 Transport
8 M Gun Section
9 Quartermaster
10 Hdqr Coy.

1st Bn York & Lancaster Regt

ENTRAINING STATE

23rd October 1915

Personnel		Horses	Mules	Vehicles		Remarks
Officers	Other ranks			Two wheeled	Four wheeled	
33	409	65	8	4	16	

[illegible signature] Lieut Colonel

Commanding 1st Bn York & Lancaster Regt

www.ingramcontent.com/pod-product-compliance
Lightning Source LLC
Chambersburg PA
CBHW081423300426
44108CB00016BA/2286
* 9 7 8 1 4 7 4 5 1 4 2 5 5 *